palgrave macmillan law masters

land law

palgrave macmillan law masters

land law

joe cursley
former Senior Lecturer in Law, University of East London

mark davys
Senior Teaching Fellow in Law, Keele University

kate green
formerly Principal Lecturer in Law, University of East London

Sixth edition

Series Editor: Marise Cremona
Professor of European Law
European University Institute
Florence
Italy

palgrave
macmillan

This edition first published 2009 by
PALGRAVE MACMILLAN

Palgrave Macmillan in the UK is an imprint of Macmillan Publishers Limited,
registered in England, company number 785998, of Houndmills, Basingstoke,
Hampshire RG21 6XS.

Palgrave Macmillan in the US is a division of St Martin's Press LLC,
175 Fifth Avenue, New York, NY 10010.

Palgrave Macmillan is the global academic imprint of the above companies
and has companies and representatives throughout the world.

Palgrave® and Macmillan® are registered trademarks in the United States,
the United Kingdom, Europe and other countries

ISBN-13: 978-0-230-22239-7   paperback
ISBN-10: 0-230-22239-0   paperback

This book is printed on paper suitable for recycling and made from fully
managed and sustained forest sources. Logging, pulping and manufacturing
processes are expected to conform to the environmental regulations of the
country of origin.

A catalogue record for this book is available from the British Library.

10   9   8   7   6   5   4   3   2
18 17 16 15 14 13 12 11 10 09

Printed and bound in Great Britain by
CPI Antony Rowe, Chippenham and Eastbourne

Contents

Part II   The Estates and Interests

Part III   Resolving Disputes

Part IV   Trusts of Land; Proprietary Estoppel

Part V   Licences in Land

Preface to the Sixth Edition

I can think of no better way to summarize the purposes of this book than to repeat the words that Kate Green used in her preface to the first edition:

> This book is intended to be a clear and straightforward explanation of basic land law rules, a text which both introduces the subject and will be referred to during a land law course. A further aim is that the book should remove the unwarranted reputation of land law as a difficult and abstract subject. I hope to encourage students to consider the role of land law in their own world; I wish all who read it a lasting interest in land law and its concerns.

Perhaps one of the main reasons for land law's reputation amongst students is that almost every part of the subject can only be understood by reference to the whole – and to topics that are traditionally studied as part of other law subjects. So, no matter where we start, we find that there are things that we already need to know. This book is offered both as an introduction to land law and as a companion to be referred to as expertise in the subject grows during the course of study. Regrettably it cannot make the components of land law any less interdependent, but hopefully the section numbers and cross-references will help trail blaze some of the connections.

This is the first edition of this book to be complemented by a website. Electronic learning, like electronic conveyancing, provides opportunities that are beyond the scope of printed text alone. However, also like e-conveyancing, e-learning must be built on the firm foundations of the law itself. Ultimately, learning the law is about handling cases and statutes. This book and its e-resources stand or fall on their ability to help the student make sense of the primary sources and use them effectively.

The law has continued to develop since the last edition. Although the recent rush of land law statutes seems to have abated, the Courts have been active, not least in the areas of estoppel and constructive trusts. The Human Rights Act 1998 continues to make its presence felt, and adverse possession seems strangely reluctant to die. As well as being able to take account of these new developments, this new edition has offered the scope to expand some sections of the text and to restructure others. This book remains, however, an introduction and guide: like my predecessors, I have sometimes had to mention difficult issues only in passing and leave their detailed consideration to others.

My thanks are due to those who have shared their enthusiasm for the study and practice of land law with me; to all my students and colleagues who continue to nurture my excitement for the subject. So far as this book is concerned, I particularly wish to thank Jasmin Naim at Palgrave Macmillan for her invitation to undertake it and her vision for its companion website. I am very grateful to all who have been kind enough to comment on drafts of this text, especially Michael Haley and Charlotte Woodhead: any errors remain, of course, my own. I should also like to thank Andrew Meggy for his help with producing the diagrams. I dedicate this book to Annabelle.

The law is stated as at the end of September 2008.

Mark Davys
Michaelmas, 2008

The Companion Website

www.palgrave.com/law/davys6e

The companion website includes the following resources:

- Interactive quizzes to test your knowledge of each chapter.
- Additional diagrams and other resources, some of which are more interactive than others.
- Podcasts reflecting further on some of the issues raised.
- Suggested answers to the problem questions included in the exercises at the end of almost every chapter.
- Answers to some commonly asked questions

The symbol '@' in the margin indicates particularly relevant material on the companion website. Updates and other materials will be added during the life of the text, so it is worth revisiting the companion website from time to time.

The companion website makes very little use of links to external sites. This is deliberate. Whether or not students plan to practice as lawyers, they need to develop the research skills required to find primary sources of law (and learned comment upon it) for themselves. Such skills are, I think, better honed through use and practice rather than the use of hypertext.

Many of the materials on the companion website are based on originals first used by land law students at Keele University. I am grateful for the comments and suggestions made by both students and colleagues that have helped enhance the existing resources and continue to inspire new ones.

www.palgrave.com/law/davys6e

Table of Cases

Table of Statutes

Table of European Legislation

Table of Statutory Instruments

References

In addition to the Further Reading listed at the end of each chapter, reference may be made to the following texts:

Burn E. H., Cartwright, J., *Modern Law of Real Property*, 17th edn (Oxford: OUP, 2006) (referred to as 'Cheshire')

Cooke, E., *Land Law* (Oxford: OUP, 2006)

Gray K., Gray S. F., *Elements of Land Law*, 5th edn (Oxford: OUP, 2009)

Harpum C., Bridge, S., Dixon, M., *Megarry & Wade: The Law of Real Property*, 7th edn (London: Sweet & Maxwell, 2008) ('Megarry and Wade')

Murphy W. T., Roberts S., *Understanding Property Law*, 3rd edn (London: Sweet & Maxwell, 1998).

Smith R. J., *Property Law*, 6th edn (Harlow: Longman, 2008).

Thompson M. P., *Modern Land Law*, 3rd edn (Oxford: OUP, 2006) ('Thompson')

Part I

Introduction

Chapter 1

Introduction to Land Law

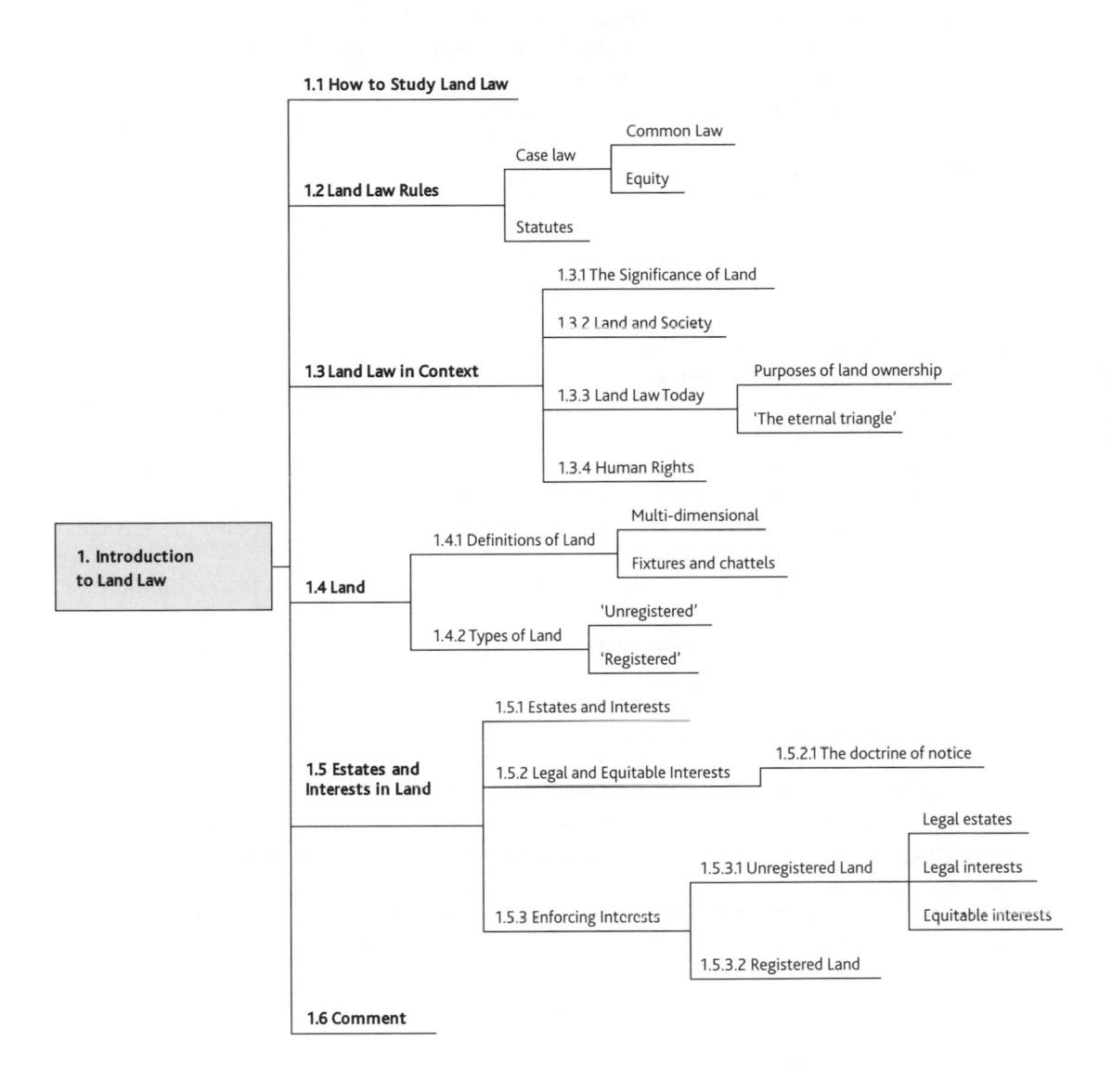

1.1 How to Study Land Law

Land law is an interesting and challenging subject, involving profound questions about the way we choose to live our lives, for land is vital to human life. In any society – even our technological, high-speed one – the use of land is of the utmost importance; where the supply is limited, as in England and Wales, the problems are acute. The dry and legalistic façade created by the artificial language and technical concepts of land law tends to conceal the fundamental issues: land law is really just about the sharing out of our limited island.

Land law has been developing ever since people got ideas about having rights over certain places, probably beginning with the cultivation of crops. Through the long process of development there have been periods of gradual change, and also more dramatic times, such as the Norman conquest of 1066, the property legislation of 1925 and, most recently, the Land Registration Act 2002. By and large, lawyers have, over the centuries, continued to use the words and ideas of their predecessors. However, although land law has kept its feudal roots and language, the substance of today's law is fundamentally changed. The law can certainly seem obscure – cloaked in the fog, rather than the mists, of time – so it is perhaps best at the start to treat it like a foreign language. The vocabulary soon becomes natural, especially through reading about the same topic in different books.

As explained further below, lawyers are concerned with various rights to land, called 'interests in land'. They might talk about someone 'owning land', but really they mean someone owning *an interest in* the land; these interests are not the land itself – the earth and the buildings – but abstract concepts, like the freehold and the lease.

The first thing to do when studying any interest in land is to grasp the definition thoroughly. This helps to avoid two of the most depressing things that can happen to land law students: the first is staring at a problem without having any idea of what it is about, and the second – possibly worse – is recognising what the problem is about, but feeling incapable of writing anything down. If in doubt, start with the interests in the land.

The rules which constitute land law are like a complicated machine: moving one lever, or adjusting one valve, changes the end product. Some authors compare the subject with playing chess: there are various 'pieces' (which correspond to interests in land) and they can be moved about according to strict rules. The owner of an interest in land has limited freedom of action, and one small change in her position can affect the relative value of other interests in the land.

In practical terms, the complicated connections within the machine mean that one part of the subject cannot be fully grasped until all the others have been understood. There is no single starting place: it is necessary to watch the machine, piece by piece, until the connections become clear. It is useful, from the beginning, to ask, 'What would happen if…?'; if one lever is moved, what interests will be affected, and why?

As a consequence of the complex definitions and the interdependent rules, land law may only make sense when the course is nearly complete. However, in the meantime, it is necessary to make mistakes in order to grasp the way the rules relate to one another. It *will* eventually come together, with hard work and faith and hope: the charity, with any luck, will be provided by the teacher.

The language used by land lawyers expresses the way in which they think they see the world. This is a world in which people's relationships to land can only occur within the legal structure of interests in land, so lawyers squeeze the facts of ordinary life into the pre-existing moulds of 'the interests'. A land law student's job is to learn the shapes of the moulds and imitate the squeeze; then she will be able to operate the whole machine. Finally, armed with this knowledge and skill, she may begin to question whether land law really does operate like this in practice.

1.2 Land Law Rules

Land law is made up of rules in statutes and cases; case law rules are further divided into legal and equitable rules. That is, the rules were created, if not by an Act of Parliament, by either a court of 'law' or a court of 'equity'. The development of these two sets of rules is well described by others (for example, Murphy and Roberts, 2004 and Cooke, 2006), and is merely outlined here.

The customs which became known as the 'common law' were enforced with extraordinary rigidity by judges who followed the strict letter of the law. Aggrieved citizens – in the absence of crusading television journalists – wrote begging letters to the King. These received replies from his 'secretary', the Chancellor, who employed the King's power to override the decisions of the King's judges. Appealing to the Chancellor's conscience, to 'equity', grew in popularity, and from about 1535 the Chancellor's court, Chancery, was regularly making decisions overriding the law in the King's court.

However, this new system of justice did not set out to replace the rules of law, but merely to intervene when conscience required it: *equity came not to destroy the law but to fulfil it*. The common law and Chancery courts existed separately, each with its own procedures and remedies, to the great profit of the legal profession. Eventually things became intolerably inefficient and the two courts were merged by the Judicature Acts 1873 and 1875, but even today lawyers keep the legal and equitable rules and remedies separate (see Section 1.5).

Many land law statutes are dated 1925, an emotive date for land lawyers. The law was actually changed by a very large Law of Property Act in 1922, but that Act was not brought into force, being divided into the various 1925 Acts. The main 1925 statutes are:

- Administration of Estates Act (AEA)
- Law of Property Act (LPA)
- Land Charges Act (LCA) (now 1972)
- Land Registration Act (LRA) (replaced by LRA 2002)
- Settled Land Act (SLA) (now see Trusts of Land and Appointment of Trustees Act (TLATA) 1996)
- Trustee Act (TA)

The 1925 statutes contained many radical reforms and also 'wordsaving' provisions, some of which had appeared in earlier statutes. In the old days, lawyers were 'paid by the yard', so the more words they used the better for their bank balances, but Parliament ensured that many common promises in land transactions no longer needed to be spelt out in full, being implied by statute: in effect, the customs of conveyancers (lawyers who manage the transfer of land) became enshrined in statute.

One of the aims of the 1925 legislation was to make conveyancing (the buying, selling, mortgaging and other transfers of land) simpler in order to revive the depressed market in land and to make it easier to deal with commercially. It is impossible to say whether it had this effect. Certainly, the reasons for the great increase in home ownership in the twentieth century were not connected to the reforms, some of which were inappropriate to the modern world of owner-occupation. More recent statutes have introduced further reforms to better reflect modern attitudes to land ownership and to equip land law for the electronic age (including, for example, the Trusts of Land and Appointment of Trustees Act 1996 and the LRA 2002 respectively).

1.3   Land Law in Context

1.3.1   The Significance of Land

At the most basic level, human beings are land animals; they need somewhere to put their bodies, a piece of land on which to 'be'. On the emotional plane, humans must have contact with land, their roots in the earth. Physically, they need air to breathe and space in which to move about, food and shelter; all these are provided by land.

As a resource, land also has other special characteristics. Except in the rare cases of land falling into or being thrown up from the sea, it is geographically fixed and immoveable; it is also ultimately indestructible. Its nature means that the boundaries between one piece of land and another are normally touching, so neighbouring owners are aware of one another's business. Further, to its occupant one piece is never exactly the same as another: each is unique – even in apparently uniform tower blocks, each floor, each flat, has its own particular characteristics.

The permanence and durability of land are matched by its flexibility. It has an infinite number of layers, and is really 'three-dimensional space'. A plot of land can be used by a number of people in different ways simultaneously: one person can invest her money in it, while two or more live there, a fourth tunnels beneath to extract minerals and half a dozen more use a path over it as a short-cut, or graze their cattle on a part of it.

Land can be shared consecutively as well as simultaneously; that is to say, people can enjoy the land one after another. The great landowning families traditionally created complicated 'settlements' of their estates, whereby the land would pass through the succeeding generations as the first owner desired. Each 'owner' only had it for a lifetime, and could not leave it by will because, at death, it had to pass according to the directions in the settlement (see Section 12.2.1). In this way the aristocratic dynasties preserved their land, and consequently their wealth and their political power.

1.3.2   Land and Society

Each society develops its own cultural attitudes to its land. These attitudes are coloured by the kind of land (for example desert or jungle) because this determines the uses to which it can be put. The view taken of land is also influenced by its scarcity or otherwise, and by the economic system. In places where land was plentiful, it was not normally 'owned'. When European colonists arrived in America, the indigenous people believed that:

> ...the earth was created by the assistance of the sun, and it should be left as it was... The country was made without lines of demarcation, and it is no man's business to divide it... The earth and myself are of one mind. The measure of the land and the measure of our bodies are the same... Do not misunderstand me, but understand me fully with reference to my affection for the land. I never said the land was mine to do with as I chose. The one who has the right to dispose of it is the one who created it (McLuhan, T. C., *Touch the Earth* (Abacus, 1972), p. 54).

Similarly, native Australians regarded the land with special awe; as concluded in one of the cases about aboriginal land claims, it was not so much that they owned the land, but that the land owned them (*Milirrpum* v. *Nabalco Pty Ltd and the Commonwealth of Australia* (1971) 17 FLR 141). A traditional African view was that the land was not capable of being owned by one person but belonged to the whole tribe:

> land belongs to a vast family of which many are dead, a few are living and countless numbers still unborn (West African Lands Committee Cd 1048, p. 183).

In early English land law, the fundamental concept was 'seisin'. The person who was seised of land was entitled to recover it in the courts if she were disseised. Originally, 'the person seised of land was simply the person in obvious occupation, the person "sitting" on the land' (Simpson, 1986, p. 40). Seisin thus described the close relationship between a person and the land she worked and lived on. This simplicity was, over centuries, refined and developed, and the concepts of ownership and possession took over. Nevertheless, actual possession or occupation can still be of great importance in land law, for example in adverse possession (see Chapter 3).

1.3.3   Land Law Today

Over the last three or four hundred years, the land law of England and Wales has been developing alongside the growth of capitalism and city living. There has been a huge population increase. In 1603, there were about 4 million people in Britain: by 2001 there were some 59 million on the same area, about 235,000 square kilometres (that is, about 4,000 square metres of surface area per person, although, of course, most people are confined to a comparatively tiny urban space). During the second part of the twentieth century there has also been an enormous increase in the number of ordinary people who own land. The percentage of households which lives in owner-occupied accommodation – a house or a flat – has more than doubled since 1971, and is currently about 70% of all households (source: Census 2001). It is unlikely to grow much more than this, however, as a significant part of the population either does not wish to take on the responsibilities of owner-occupation or is unable to afford it.

For the majority of owner-occupiers, the land they own (although subject to a huge debt in the form of a mortgage) is both a home and an investment. It is an expression of their personality and a retreat from the world; at the same time it represents a status symbol and – they hope – an inflation-proofed savings bank. For other people (for example, those who rent their home on a weekly tenancy), home ownership with its apparent psychological and financial advantages may be only a hope for the future. In the meantime, their relationship with their land may be less secure, subject to the authority of a lessor. However, in a lawyer's view, tenants are also 'landowners', in theory at least (see Section 1.4).

Some authors interpret the modern law as treating land merely as if it were money, but a law which actually dealt with land in this way would not fulfil the needs of today's society. Many of the difficult issues in contemporary land law focus on the informal arrangements of people who – unlike the landowners of previous centuries – do not see the need to transact their family business via a lawyer. Take the following situation as an example. Jane lets Raj share her house and, in exchange, he pays the mortgage. Later she sells the house to Chris. Chris wants to live there by himself, but Raj does not want to leave. This kind of problem, where a transaction between buyer and seller involves a third person's interest in land, appears in various forms throughout this book. It is a kind of eternal triangle, as in Figure 1.1.

It is often said that disputes in land law centre on the conflicting requirements of the market in land. In order to maximise the value of land, ownership must be capable of being

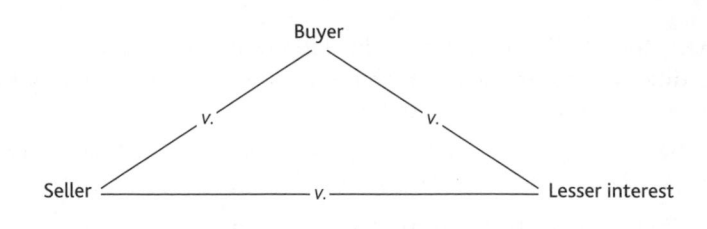

Figure 1.1 The eternal triangle.

freely and safely traded, while people who have lesser interests in the land must also feel secure. The market certainly seems to have an influence on the development of the law. One of the most influential factors in the attitudes of judges to difficult decisions is their view of the state of the market. When there was a slump at the end of the nineteenth century they tried to ensure that liabilities attached to land (that is, the lesser, third-party interests) were minimised so that the land would be attractive to buyers. Periods of booming prices, such as the 1970s, 1980s and the early 2000s tend to stimulate a greater interest in the security of 'non-owners', like Raj. A falling market, such as that of the early 1990s and the end of the first decade of the twenty-first century, produces its own response, significantly influenced by the interests of lenders, such as building societies and banks (see Chapter 7).

1.3.4   Human Rights

The market is not the only influence on land law. The Human Rights Act 1998, which came into force on 2 October 2000, means that the rules and practices of land law are now open to challenge if they offend against rights contained in the European Convention on Human Rights. The Act requires the courts to interpret legislation 'in a way which is compatible with the Convention rights' (s.3), and is directly applicable against public authorities (s.6), which include courts and tribunals, central and local government and any body exercising functions of a public nature. The extent to which the Act has 'horizontal' effect – in other words, how far it is applicable in a dispute between two private individuals – is uncertain. It may be that it has wider horizontal effect than originally intended, since the s.3 requirement applies even if the parties are private individuals, and s.6 prevents the courts (as public bodies) from interpreting common law as well as statute in a way which is incompatible with Convention rights.

In the context of land law, the most important of these Convention rights are:

- Article 1, Protocol 1 – the right to peaceful enjoyment and protection of possessions;
- Article 8 – the right to respect for a person's private and family life and home;
- Article 6 – the right to a fair and public hearing;
- Article 14 – the right to enjoy Convention rights without discrimination.

Article 1, Protocol 1 guarantees a person's right to enjoy her property free from interference from the state, unless this is in the public interest and in accordance with the law. This might well allow the compulsory purchase of a person's land by a local authority, for example, and it has permitted long leaseholders to buy the freehold of their land under the Leasehold Reform Act 1967, since this is in the interests of social justice (see *James* v. *UK* (1986) 8 EHRR 123 and Section 5.5).

Under Article 8, no public authority may interfere with the exercise of the right to respect for a person's private and family life and home, except in accordance with the law and to the extent that it is necessary in a democratic society. In *Harrow LBC* v. *Qazi* [2004] 1 AC 983, the House of Lords held that the Article concerned rights of privacy rather than property, and that it cannot be used to defeat contractual and proprietary rights to possession. Consequently the Article did not affect the powers of a local authority to recover possession from a former tenant. However, in *Connors* v. *United Kingdom* (66746/01) (2005) 40 EHRR 9 the European Court of Human Rights at Strasbourg decided that there were circumstances in which the exercise by a public authority of an unqualified proprietary right under domestic law to repossess its land will constitute an interference with the occupier's right to respect for his home. For repossession in these circumstances to be lawful, it must be shown that the authority had sufficient procedural safeguards in place to ensure that so serious an interference with the occupier's rights was justified and proportionate in the circumstances of the case. The principles in *Connors* have since been applied by the House Lords in *Kay* v. *Lambeth BC* [2006] 2 AC 465 and *Doherty* v. *Birmingham CC* [2008] 3 WLR 636. All three cases concerned the eviction of gypsies from local authority-owned sites.

The effect of the Human Rights Act and the Convention rights it incorporates will be further discussed where relevant during the course of this book.

1.4   'Land'

1.4.1   Definitions of Land

At common law, 'land' means the soil, the rocks beneath and the air above. Section 132(1) of the LRA 2002 provides that:

'Land' includes:
(a)   buildings and other structures,
(b)   land covered with water, and
(c)   mines and minerals, whether or not held with the surface.

Land, therefore, includes things growing on the land, and buildings 'attached' to it. It also includes the airspace above the surface of the land necessary to allow the reasonable enjoyment of the surface of the land and any buildings on it (*Bernstein of Leigh (Baron)* v. *Skyviews and General Ltd* [1978] QB 479). The general rule is that whatever is attached to the land becomes part of it. If Jane sells her land to Chris, she is selling not merely the surface, but also the grass and trees, and the bricks, tiles and chimney-pots of the house. The extent to which things fixed to a building, or cemented into the ground, are 'fixtures', that is, part of the land itself, is a question of fact in every case.

In *Elitestone Ltd* v. *Morris* [1997] 1 WLR 687, Mr Morris lived in a rented chalet on a plot of land which Elitestone Ltd owned and wished to develop. The chalet had no intrinsic foundations, but merely rested on a number of concrete blocks. If Mr Morris could show that the chalet was land, then he would have protection under the Rent Act 1977 and Elitestone Ltd would not be able to throw him off. The House of Lords held that it was necessary to ask the two questions identified by Blackburn J in *Holland* v. *Hodgson* (1871-72) LR 7 CP 328:

- first, to what degree was the item annexed (attached) to the land, and
- second, for what object or purpose had it been annexed?

Normally an object will have to be fixed to the land to some degree if it is to be a fixture. However, the House of Lords said that that was not required in this case because the chalet was heavy enough to rest on the ground by its own weight. The purpose of annexation is an objective question to be determined on the facts: it is not affected by what the parties thought or agreed between themselves about the status of the object. In *Elitestone*, the fact that the chalet could not be removed without destroying it was sufficient to establish sufficient purpose of annexation. If it had been possible to remove the chalet without destroying it, it would probably have been considered a chattel and Mr Morris would have lost his home. The form of the test for purpose of annexation will depend upon the nature of the objects concerned. For example, in *Botham* v. *TSB Bank Plc* (1997) 73 P & CR D1 the main factors determining the purpose of annexation of bathroom and kitchen equipment were whether the items were a lasting improvement, intended to be permanent (fixture) or merely temporary (chattel), and whether they could be removed without damaging the fabric of the building (chattel).

When considering whether a thing is a fixture (other than a building) or a chattel, the law now puts greater emphasis on the purpose of annexation and looks at the degree of attachment as evidence of the intention. *Elitestone* is an example of a modern development in the law which distinguishes between a thing which is a fixture and one which is 'part and parcel of the land' – both count as land, but the terminology makes more sense. The three-fold distinction referred to in *Elitestone* is summarised in Table 1.1. The term 'fixture' is confined to objects that although part of the land, can, in certain circumstances, be detached from it. This is much closer to its common, everyday meaning and there is no longer any need artificially to describe a building as a fixture.

Table 1.1 The threefold categorization of objects after *Elitestone Ltd* v. *Morris*.

Category	Status	Comments
'Part and parcel'	Part of the land	Impossible to remove intact
Fixture	Part of the land	May be removed by the landowner Tenants may remove fixtures falling within the definition of 'tenants fixtures'
Chattel	Not part of the land	May be removed by the owner of the chattel

Land is also defined in s.205(1)(ix) LPA 1925:

'Land' includes land of any tenure, and mines and minerals... buildings or parts of buildings... and other corporeal hereditaments, also... a rent, and other incorporeal hereditaments, and an easement right, privilege, or benefit in, over, or derived from land...

Thus both freeholds and leases are 'land', so a person who buys a lease (that is, becomes a leaseholder or a tenant) is a buyer of land. The term 'corporeal hereditaments' is an ancient way of referring to the land and the fixtures, while 'incorporeal hereditaments' are the invisible interests in land, such as mortgages and easements (rights of way, for example). A person who buys a right of way over her neighbour's land, therefore, is also buying land.

1.4.2   Types of 'Land'

Since 1925 all titles to land in England and Wales are either 'unregistered' or 'registered'. Although people often refer to 'registered land', and the main statute in question is the Land Registration Act 2002 (which replaced the Land Registration Act 1925), technically it is a person's *title* to the land which is registered, not the land itself.

One of the aims of the 1925 legislation was that ultimately every title to land would be registered in a central registry (see Chapter 11), but even now, although most titles have been registered and all land must be registered when it changes hands or is first mortgaged, in 2007 about 10% of titles in England and Wales were not yet registered, amounting to about 40% of the total area of the land. Up-to-date figures can be found in the publications available from the Land Registry's website: http://www.landregistry.gov.uk/.

Registered and unregistered land involve two distinct systems of conveyancing, each with its own set of rules for determining how interests in land are created and transferred and how disputes about those interests will be resolved. These rules will be explained in detail as they become relevant in the chapters that follow. For the moment, however, it will be useful to identify some of the main differences between the two systems. The meaning and significance of these differences should become more apparent as your study of land law progresses. The main differences are set out in Table 1.2.

It is very important to apply the correct set of rules (registered or unregistered) when addressing a land law issue, not least because the two sets of rules occasionally produce different results. Therefore the very first question to ask when faced with any land law issue is:

Question 1
Is the title to the land concerned registered or unregistered?

Table 1.2 A comparison between unregistered and registered title.

	Unregistered	**Registered**
Underlying nature	Private	Public
Basis of title (ownership)	Possession	Entry in Land Register Title is guaranteed by the state
Evidence of title	Title deeds	Official copy of the register
Types of interest	Legal estates Legal charges Other legal interests Equitable interests	Registerable estates Registerable charges Interests completed by registration Interests subject to registration Interests capable of overriding the register
Discovery of interests in the land	Deeds Land Charges Register Notice (including inspection of the land)	Register Inspection of the land for interests capable of overriding the register

1.5   Estates and Interests in Land

1.5.1   Estates and Interests

It has already been mentioned that the land lawyer views every piece of land as potentially fragmented into an infinite number of interests. For historical reasons, she sees people owning an abstract estate or interest in land, not the land itself. The lesser interests are carved out of the major ones, which are called the 'estates'. This word 'estate' has a long lineage; it means 'an interest in land of some particular duration' (Megarry and Wade, 2008, section 3-001), but today this definition is an academic relic of no practical importance. It is only necessary to know that there are now two legal estates:

> Law of Property Act 1925
> S.1(1)   The only estates in land which are capable of subsisting or of being conveyed or created at law are–
> (a)   An estate in fee simple absolute in possession [a freehold];
> (b)   A term of years absolute [a lease].

The term 'interest in land' is significant to land lawyers because it shows that the rights and duties of the people concerned are not merely personal or contractual. These rights and duties are attached to the land itself and they automatically pass to anyone who buys or inherits the land; they can therefore be transferred to other people and bind third parties. In lawyers' vocabulary, interests in land are 'property'.

On reading land law problems, it is crucial to develop an instinct for the various interests so that you can immediately say, for example, 'This looks like an easement'. The second question to ask in problem solving is therefore:

Question 2
What interests may exist here?

1.5.2   Legal and Equitable Interests

The courts of *common law* recognised various estates and interests in land. Because property rights in land automatically affect anyone who subsequently acquires that land, the courts of *common law* restricted the classes of proprietary interests to rights that were relatively certain and easily discoverable. In most cases this required certain formalities to be complied with when the rights were created (although the doctrine of *adverse possession* and the acquisition of easements by *prescription* are significant exceptions to this rule; see Chapters 3 and 8).

However, there are circumstances in which a person with a very strong moral right to a parcel of land might find that her right does not meet the strict requirements of the *common law*. For example, her interest may have been created without complying with the necessary formalities, or the nature of the interest being claimed may be such that it would be unreasonable to expect any formalities to be observed at all. Consequently, the courts of *equity* were prepared to override the legal title in favour of a person with, in their view, a stronger moral right to the land. The owner of the legal interest was deemed by equity to hold it on behalf of (on trust for) the person who had the better right. Today there are many pieces of land where legal title and equitable enjoyment are divided in this way.

This can be illustrated by the well-known case of *Bull* v. *Bull* [1955] 1 QB 234. A son and mother both contributed to buying a house on the outskirts of London, but only the son's name appeared on the conveyance (the deed), so he was the legal owner. He then married and, since his wife and his mother could not get on with each other, tried to evict his mother. The Court of Appeal held that he could not simply turn her out. She had a share of the equitable title because of her contribution to the purchase, so the son held the legal title on behalf of the equitable owners (himself and his mother). Another way to express this is to say that the son is a trustee for himself and his mother; they share the 'beneficial' interest. Equity normally recognises a trust relationship like this when the apparent owner *ought* to hold the land wholly or partly for the benefit of someone else. The trust is a useful, and very common, device by which land can be shared (see Chapters 12 and 13).

As well as allowing land to be shared in this way, the courts of *equity* also recognised some interests in land that are not recognised at law. One of the most important examples is the *restrictive covenant*, which first became enforceable against third parties as a property right in the nineteenth century (see Chapter 9).

There are three main reasons why it is important to label interests as 'legal' or 'equitable'. The first is that equitable interests depend on equitable remedies, and these depend on the court's discretion: the court of equity, being 'a court of conscience', only grants a remedy if the claimant has behaved fairly. Legal remedies on the other hand – damages, for example – are available 'as of right'; a plaintiff is entitled to damages if her strict legal rights have been infringed, whether or not this is fair. Thus the mother in the *Bull* case, who was relying on an equitable interest, could not have succeeded if she had been deceitful (this is expressed in the maxim, 'she who comes to equity must come with clean hands') or had delayed unreasonably, as in *Tse Kwong Lam* v. *Wong Chit Sen* [1983] 1 WLR 1349 (see Section 7.3.1.2).

The second reason to distinguish between legal and equitable interests is that the formalities required when someone wishes to expressly create an interest will vary, depending on whether that interest is to be legal or equitable. Legal interests normally have to be created by a deed, and, in many cases, registered. Writing alone is usually sufficient to create an express equitable interest, although further rules need to be completed if it is to bind a third party.

The final reason to distinguish between legal and equitable interests is that the courts of equity could not bring themselves to enforce equitable rights against a completely innocent and honest legal buyer. Therefore, the rule was established that the owner of an equitable interest in land would lose it if someone paid for the legal estate, in good faith and without notice (whether actual, imputed or constructive) of the equitable interest. This rule about the *bona fide* purchaser is known as the 'doctrine of notice'.

1.5.2.1 The Doctrine of Notice

Before 1925, an equitable interest did not bind the *bona fide* purchaser of the legal estate for value without notice (actual, imputed or constructive).

Proof of any one of the three kinds of notice would mean that the buyer would be bound by the equitable interest. If she actually knew about, for example, the mother's interest in *Bull* v. *Bull* [1955] 1 QB 234, or if her agent knew about it ('imputed notice'), she would step into the son's shoes and would be bound by the mother's rights. Under 'constructive notice' (also known as the rule in *Hunt* v. *Luck* [1902] 1 Ch 428), the buyer would be taken to know – whether or not she actually did – anything a prudent purchaser would have discovered by inspecting the land and the title deeds to the land. Any buyer of the bungalow in the *Bull* case would probably have discovered, had she looked around it carefully, that someone other than the son and his wife lived there; she would have had constructive notice of the mother's right and would have been bound by it.

1.5.3   Enforcing Interests

There are, therefore, a number of legal interests in land and, in a kind of parallel universe, many equitable interests. As a general rule, anyone who buys or inherits land owns it subject to any interests, legal and equitable, which have been created by previous owners of the land. However, this rule has numerous exceptions. The detailed rules depend upon whether title to the land concerned is registered.

1.5.3.1 Unregistered Land

If title to the land is unregistered, the effect of a particular interest depends upon whether it is legal or equitable. Legal rights are effective against anyone in the world, but equitable rights are only 'good' against certain people. As part of the reforms directed at making conveyancing simpler, the number of legal rights to land was strictly limited in 1925; many interests could no longer be legal but could be equitable only.

> Law of Property Act 1925
> S.1(1) The only estates in land which are capable of subsisting or of being conveyed or created at law
>   are–
> (a)   An estate in fee simple absolute in possession [a freehold];
> (b)   A term of years absolute [a lease].
> (2)   The only interests or charges in or over land which are capable of subsisting or of being conveyed or created at law are–
> (a)   An easement, right, or privilege in or over land for an interest equivalent to an estate in fee simple absolute in possession or a term of years absolute [rights of way, for example];
> (b)   A rentcharge in possession issuing out of or charged on land being either perpetual or for a term of years absolute [a periodical payment secured on land, but which does not arise out of a lease or a mortgage];
> (c)   A charge by way of legal mortgage;
> (d)   ... and any other similar charge on land which is not created by an instrument [effectively repealed];
> (e)   Rights of entry exercisable over or in respect of a legal term of years absolute [a lessor's right to end a lease].
> (3)   All other estates, interests, and charges in or over land take effect as equitable interests...

It must be emphasised that s.1 LPA 1925 does not say that the estates and interests listed there *are* legal, merely that they *may* be. Whether or not an interest is legal or equitable is an interesting question: the answer will be clearer after reading the next chapter.

The 1925 legislation also introduced new statutory rules to determine when someone acquiring land will be bound by any equitable interests in that land (found in the Land Charges Act 1972 and ss. 2 and 27 of the LPA 1925 and considered in detail in Chapter 10). Although these rules considerably modify the traditional doctrine of notice, they preserve the significance of the distinction between legal and equitable interests. Legal rights over unregistered land are effective against anyone in the world: they automatically bind anyone who subsequently acquires an estate or any other interest in the land. However, equitable rights are only 'good' against certain people – exactly who will depend upon the detailed rules explored in Chapter 10. The third question that must be asked about a land law problem concerning unregistered land is, therefore:

Question 3 (unregistered title)
Is this interest legal or equitable?

1.5.3.2 Registered Land

The distinction between legal and equitable interests contained in the LPA 1925 is preserved in the regime of registered title, introduced in 1925 and now set out in the LRA 2002. However, when title to land is registered, the question of whether a particular interest will affect someone acquiring the land will be determined by the rules set out in the LRA 2002 rather than by whether the interest is legal or equitable.

The aim of the LRA 2002 is for as many interests as possible to be entered on the register of title to the estates affected. Any interest that appears on the register will normally be binding on whoever acquires the estate concerned (provided that that interest actually exists, of course). The doctrine of notice 'has no application in registered land' (Mummery LJ in *Barclays Bank PLC* v. *Boulter* [1998] 1 WLR 1 and see (2001) Law Com No 271, para. 5.16). However, it would be unjust, and impracticable, to insist that every interest in the land must be registered if it is to be enforceable against the owner of the land. Consequently, the LRA 2002 lists a limited number of interests that are capable of binding the owner of a registered estate even though they do not appear on the register of title. These interests are commonly referred to as interests that are capable of *overriding* the register. Some of these interests are legal, others equitable. The rules are examined in more detail in Chapter 11.

There is some debate amongst academics and judges about whether the LRA 2002 changes land law itself, or whether it merely changes conveyancing practice (that is to say, the way in which the rules of law are used in practice). Whatever the answer to this question, the result is the same: the third question to be asked when answering a problem about land law is different from the question asked when the title to the land is unregistered. If the land is registered, the third question is:

Question 3 (registered title)
Is this interest entered on the register, and, if not, does it override the register?

1.6 Comment

It can be seen, even from this brief introduction, that land law works within a special language, using a set of abstract interests as the basis for the ownership and enjoyment of land. The language, abstractions and interdependent rules can cause difficulties initially, but perseverance overcomes these. The fascinating history of land law can, if there is time to read in depth, provide a more profound understanding of the roles played by the law and by lawyers in relation to people sharing their space.

Summary

1.1 Land law is fundamentally about how people share land.

1.2 In your approach to land law, it is essential to grasp the language and definitions of interests in land as well as the rules about them.

1.3 'Land' means the physical land and fixtures and includes any interest in land.

1.4 Title to land may be either registered or not yet registered (unregistered).

1.5 There are many interests capable of existing in a piece of land. The rules for determining whether a particular interest binds the present owner of the land depend on whether the land is registered or unregistered.

1.6   Historically, legal interests would bind anyone who owned the land; equitable interests would bind everyone except a buyer of a legal estate in good faith for value without notice, actual, imputed or constructive.

1.7   Land law was reformed in 1925:
- the number of estates capable of being legal is now limited to two (freehold and leasehold);
- the number of interests capable of being legal is limited to four;
- the doctrine of notice was modified in so far as it applies to unregistered land; and
- registered land has its own set of rules for determining when an interest binds the land.

1.8   In analysing a land law question, the following three primary questions should be asked:
- is the title registered or not yet registered?
- What interest may exist here?
- Will the interest bind the owner of the land (how to answer this question will depend upon whether the land is registered or not)?

1.9   The provisions of the Human Rights Act 1998 must be considered when considering land law issues.

Exercises

1.1   Is an equitable interest as good as a legal interest?

1.2   Why does it matter whether land is registered or not yet registered?

1.3   Why is s.1 LPA 1925 important?

1.4   How does a lawyer define land?

@ **1.5**   Waheeda has bought Jack's house. When she first viewed the house, she was particularly taken with the garden, which contained an ornamental pond and a statue of a mermaid set on a plinth in its centre. She was also pleased that she would be getting a large garden shed which rested on a concrete base.

When she moved in, she was horrified to discover that Jack had taken away both the statue and the shed. The fitted carpets in the house had also been removed. Waheeda checked the contract for the sale, but found that it made no mention of any of these items.

Advise Waheeda, who also tells you that she cannot understand how Jack managed to remove the shed, since he would have had to dismantle it completely in order to do so.

@ **1.6**   Read *A Tale of Three Students* on the companion website. How are the principles and rules discussed in this chapter relevant for the three friends?

@ **1.7**   An online quiz on the topics covered in this chapter is available on the companion website.

Further Reading

Bright, 'Of Estates and Interests: A Tale of Ownership and Property Rights' in Bright and Dewar (eds), *Land Law Themes and Perspectives* (Oxford: OUP, 1998)

Haley, 'The Law of Fixtures: An Unprincipled Metamorphosis?' [1998] Conv 138

Howell, 'The Human Rights Act 1998: "The Horizontal Effect" on Land Law' in Cooke (ed), *Modern Studies in Property Law*, Volume 1 (Oxford: Hart, 2001)

Rook, 'Property Law and the Human Rights Act 1998: A Review of the First Year' [2002] Conv 316

Simpson, *History of the Land Law* (Oxford: Clarendon Press, 1986)

Chapter 2

Buying and Selling Land

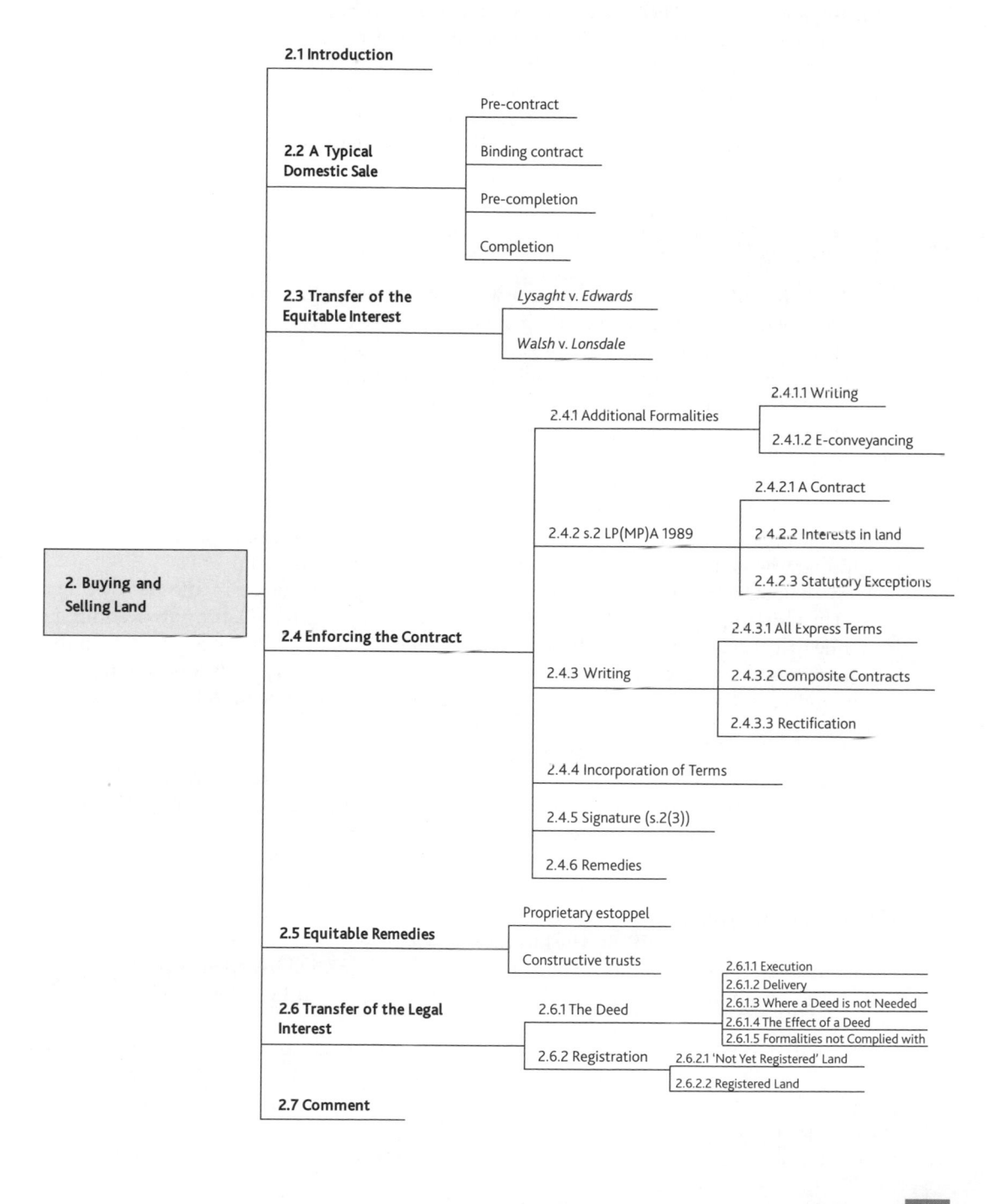

2.1 Introduction

2.2 A Typical Domestic Sale
- Pre-contract
- Binding contract
- Pre-completion
- Completion

2.3 Transfer of the Equitable Interest
- *Lysaght* v. *Edwards*
- *Walsh* v. *Lonsdale*

2. Buying and Selling Land

2.4 Enforcing the Contract
- 2.4.1 Additional Formalities
  - 2.4.1.1 Writing
  - 2.4.1.2 E-conveyancing
- 2.4.2 s.2 LP(MP)A 1989
  - 2.4.2.1 A Contract
  - 2.4.2.2 Interests in land
  - 2.4.2.3 Statutory Exceptions
- 2.4.3 Writing
  - 2.4.3.1 All Express Terms
  - 2.4.3.2 Composite Contracts
  - 2.4.3.3 Rectification
- 2.4.4 Incorporation of Terms
- 2.4.5 Signature (s.2(3))
- 2.4.6 Remedies

2.5 Equitable Remedies
- Proprietary estoppel
- Constructive trusts

2.6 Transfer of the Legal Interest
- 2.6.1 The Deed
  - 2.6.1.1 Execution
  - 2.6.1.2 Delivery
  - 2.6.1.3 Where a Deed is not Needed
  - 2.6.1.4 The Effect of a Deed
  - 2.6.1.5 Formalities not Complied with
- 2.6.2 Registration
  - 2.6.2.1 'Not Yet Registered' Land
  - 2.6.2.2 Registered Land

2.7 Comment

2.1 Introduction

This chapter explains the normal process of buying and selling land and the effects of the sale. It will focus on the rules about the creation and enforcement of contracts for the sale of land, and about deeds. These rules are crucial to land law because unless they are observed there will not be a contract, or the buyer may only obtain an equitable interest which may be insecure, as explained in Section 1.5. Other aspects of the process of buying and selling land will be referred to, but their details belong to courses on conveyancing (the word that describes the process of dealing with interests in land) rather than the study of land law.

First, it is important to remember that 'land' includes all interests in land (see Section 1.4) and that:

'purchaser' means a purchaser in good faith for valuable consideration and includes a lessee, mortgagee or other person who for valuable consideration acquires an interest in property (s.205(1)(xxi) LPA 1925).

Therefore, the rules in this chapter control not only sales of freehold land, but also other *dispositions* of interests in land, including, for example, the creation of leases, mortgages and easements, and the assignment of leases.

The transfer of a form of property which is financially and emotionally so important is bound to be the subject of some ritual and, therefore, of technical rules. These conveyancing rules are also, to a large extent, a recognition of the good practices of conveyancing lawyers. The roles of Parliament and the courts can often be seen as approving retrospectively the accepted practice of the experts. All land in England and Wales must now be registered on sale, transfer or first legal mortgage, and therefore every sale today is subject to at least some of the rules about registration of title. The consequences of the need for registration are considered briefly at the end of this chapter and in more detail in Chapter 11.

As in all areas of land law, the rules on which this chapter focuses are affected by other rules. The most important are those about registered and unregistered land, but, in addition, legal title can also be obtained by long use and equitable title by means of a trust. Given the interdependent parts of the land law machine, it is only possible fully to understand the rules about buying and selling land when the rest of land law is also understood.

2.2 A Typical Domestic Sale

Table 2.1 shows the important steps in a typical conveyance of freehold land. The word *conveyance* is used to describe both the transfer of the property and the document (technically a deed of grant) which brings the transfer about. In a typical domestic transaction, the buyer's aim is to own the legal title to the house. For many purposes, however, the term 'conveyance' includes not only the transfer of freehold land, but also the granting of mortgages and leases (s.205(1)(ii) LPA 1925). The business of dealing with the transfer of interests in land is known as 'conveyancing'. Its detailed rules are usually studied in separate conveyancing courses, although the line between what is conveyancing law and what is land law is rather blurred.

The first step which has any binding effect takes place at exchange of contracts (see Sections 2.3 and 2.4). In many cases the contract will be based on a standard form (either pre-printed or, more usually now, selected from a set of precedents stored on computer or forming part of a conveyancing software package). In some cases most of the terms of the contract will be the result of substantive negotiation, but most residential transactions

Table 2.1 The main stages in the purchase of a house.

Time	Facts	Law	Section
	Compilation Home Information Pack (HIP) Advertising the house for sale Buyer makes an offer	Failure to supply a HIP can result in a warning or a fixed penalty of £200 (See HA 2004)	2.2
About 8 weeks	Negotiation of price, fittings, etc. Survey and finance arranged Draft contract prepared by seller Buyer checks the details of the property and makes additional searches and enquiries not contained in the HIP Contract agreed by buyer and seller	None of these steps has any legal or equitable implications: there is no contract (s.2 1989 Act)	2.4
	Contracts signed by both parties are exchanged and the buyer pays a deposit to the seller	The contract is made Equitable title passes to the buyer	2.4 2.3
Usually between 2 and 4 weeks	Pre-completion searches of title Deeds of conveyance and mortgage are prepared The lender releases the mortgage moneys Completion by execution of the deeds and payment of the balance of the purchase price to the seller		2.6.1
Within 2 months	The transfer and mortgage are sent to the Land Registry for Registration		2.6.2
	The Land Registry completes registration and issues an official copy of the register of title, etc.	Legal title is transferred to the buyer	

incorporate a set of standard conditions published by the Law Society of England and Wales (presently the Standard Conditions of Sale (4th Edition)). However, exchange of contracts is not sufficient in itself to transfer legal title to the buyer. If the land is not yet registered, legal title must initially be transferred by means of a deed and the new owner must then register the title at the Land Registry. If title is already registered, a document of transfer is still required (at present), but legal ownership changes only when the transfer is recorded at the Land Registry.

During the period of pre-contractual enquiries and negotiation, neither side can be sure of completing the sale. The buyers might fail to get their loan, or might decide that the house is too expensive; the sellers might receive a higher offer from another prospective buyer or might decide to withdraw the house from the market. Each side would like the other to be bound as soon as possible, but is wary of committing itself too soon. Historically, it was the buyer's responsibility to carry out all the checks, searches and enquiries that he and his solicitor felt necessary before he could commit himself to buying the property. This is still the case if the land being sold does not comprise a dwelling house. However, since 14 December 2007, anyone selling a residential property has been obliged to provide a Home Information Pack (HIP) for prospective buyers. The HIP must contain certain documents, including evidence of title, the standard searches, and an Energy Performance Certificate, whilst other documents, including a Home Condition Report (a sort of mini survey), are optional. It was originally proposed that every HIP should include a Home Condition Report, but this requirement was dropped when it became apparent that mortgage lenders were likely to insist upon undertaking their own inspection of the property even if the seller had already gone to the expense of providing a Home Condition Report. The detailed rules are contained in regulations made pursuant to Part 5 of the Housing Act (HA) 2004. There is considerable doubt amongst professionals and academics that HIPs will be effective in reducing the delay, cost and uncertainty that had become inherent in the pre-contract stage of buying and selling a home.

2.3 Transfer of the Equitable Interest

The parties to a sale of land can usually feel secure some time before the final transfer of legal ownership. The rules of equity provide that the contract may be specifically enforced before the deed is executed. The remedy is available because 'equity regards as done that which ought to be done'. Since specific performance is an equitable remedy, it is discretionary and will only be ordered if the claimant has behaved properly.

If equity is prepared to grant specific performance of the contract, the sellers become, effectively, trustees for the new equitable right of the buyers to become the legal owners when the contract is completed. As Jessel MR explained in case of *Lysaght* v. *Edwards* (1875-76) LR 2 ChD 499:

> What is the effect of the contract? It appears to me that the effect of a contract for sale has been settled for more than two centuries... What is that doctrine? It is that the moment you have a valid contract for sale the vendor becomes in equity a trustee for the purchaser of the estate sold, and the beneficial ownership passes to the purchaser, the vendor having a right to the purchase-money, a charge or lien on the estate for the security of that purchase-money, and a right to retain possession of the estate until the purchase-money is paid... (at pp. 505–506).

The case of *Walsh* v. *Lonsdale* (1882) LR 21 Ch D 9 (see also Section 5.4.2) is an example of the rule that an equitable interest in land is created as soon as there is a contract. In this famous old case, Lonsdale made a contract to grant a seven-year lease of a mill to Walsh, but the parties never completed the deed necessary for transfer of the lease, the legal estate. Jessel MR said:

> The tenant holds under an agreement for a lease. He holds therefore under the same terms in equity as if a lease had been granted, it being a case in which both parties admit that relief is capable of being given by specific performance (at p. 14).

A written contract for the sale of land is, therefore, an equitable interest in land (called an 'estate contract'). Walsh had a seven-year equitable lease, and one might have expected him to be delighted with this result. Unfortunately for him, it meant that he had to observe all the terms of the lease, including payment of rent in advance: he owed Lonsdale £1005.

The trust relationship that is created between the buyers and the sellers allows the sellers to retain some rights to enjoy the land – they can remain in possession of the land and exclude the buyers. However, the seller must take care to keep the land in the same condition as it was when contracts were exchanged. The passing of the beneficial interest in the land to the buyer means that the buyer must observe any obligations attached to that beneficial interest (which is why Walsh had to pay the rent due to Lonsdale). The burden of the risk of damage to the property is also transferred to the buyer at exchange of contracts. This means that the buyer must pay the whole of the purchase price, even if the house has been completely destroyed between exchange and the completion of the legal transfer of the land. However, this rule can cause significant complications (particularly with respect to the insuring of the property between exchange and completion), so it is usual for the contract to reverse it by expressly providing that the seller will retain the risk until completion.

2.4 Enforcing the Contract

2.4.1 Additional Formalities

2.4.1.1 Writing

It has long been the rule that some form of writing was usually required when entering into a contract to buy and sell land. From the late seventeenth century until 1989 the rule was that a contract for the sale of any interest in land was not enforceable until there was some evidence of it either by writing, or by part performance (see s.40 of the LPA 1925, which restated s.4 of the Statute of Frauds 1677, designed to reduce the 'frauds and Perjuryes' committed by people trying to enforce alleged oral contracts). Over time the legal rules about what would constitute sufficient written evidence and what counted as part performance of the contract became detailed and confusing. As a result a completely new set of rules was introduced in s.2 of the Law of Property (Miscellaneous Provisions) Act 1989. These rules apply to all agreements for the sale of any interest in land made after 26 September 1989.

Section 2(1) of the 1989 Act states:

> A contract for the sale or other disposition of an interest in land can only be made in writing and only by incorporating all the terms which the parties have expressly agreed in one document or, where contracts are exchanged, in each.

Section 2(3) of the 1989 Act requires the document or documents to be signed by or on behalf of each of the parties to the contract.

In brief, under s.2 there is no contract at all until there is a signed document containing all the agreed terms. It is no longer a question of a contract being merely unenforceable (as under the old s.40(1)) without written evidence; now, there *cannot be any contract without writing*. Further, the requirements of s.2 are far stricter than the old law.

Section 2 has, inevitably, produced its own flow of case law, much of which involves the same practical problems as those which faced the courts under s.40. To these were added the difficulty of trying to enforce an agreement which, because of the provisions of s.2 of the 1989 Act, has no contractual effect (see Chadwick LJ in *Bircham & Co Nominees (2) Ltd* v. *Worrell Holdings Ltd* (2001) 82 P & CR 427 at para. 15). Initially, judges appeared reluctant to find that an unwritten agreement was not a 'contract' because of s.2, and sought to hold people to their word. However, a stricter view subsequently emerged, in which the courts were more ready to insist upon compliance with all the formal requirements of s.2. Partly as a result of this, many of the recent cases have been concerned with the non-contractual remedies that may be available when an agreement fails to satisfy s.2 (see Section 2.5).

2.4.1.2 Electronic Conveyancing

The Electronic Communications Act 2000 and Part 8 of the LRA 2002 provide the statutory framework for discarding the printed page in favour of electronic conveyancing, 'the most revolutionary change ever to take place in conveyancing practice' ((1998) Law Com No 254, *Land Registration for the Twenty-first Century*, p. 1). Ultimately all stages of conveyancing will be capable of being completed electronically, and contracts and deeds (see Section 2.6) will have to be created, signed and communicated to the Land Registry by electronic means in order to have any effect. The intention is that paper, and the rules set out in the 1989 Act (see below) will become obsolete. At present the Land Registry hope to introduce electronic land transfers during 2009 and electronic contracts some time later. Up-to-date information can be found on the Land Registry's web gateway at http://www.landregistry.gov.uk/.

2.4.2   Section 2 of the 1989 Act

If an agreement falls within the scope of s.2 there will normally be no contract until there is:

- one document or two identical documents (the latter is more usual);
- containing all the expressly agreed terms;
- that has been signed by (or on behalf of) the both buyer and the seller.

2.4.2.1 'A Contract' (s2.(1))

The requirements of s.2 are additional to the normal common law rules for the existence of a contract. Consequently the normal prerequisites of a valid contract must be present, including offer, acceptance and consideration and the intention to create a legally binding relationship. Negotiations for the sale and purchase of land frequently include agreements that are expressed to be made 'subject to contract'. Such an agreement is not an enforceable contract, but '... a transaction in which each side hopes the other will act like a gentleman and neither intends so to act if it is against his material interests' (per Sachs J in *Godding* v. *Frazer* [1967] 1 WLR 286 at 293). Prior to 1989 Act, it was usual for all pre-contractual negotiations concerning land to be headed 'subject to contract'. This was to prevent an oral agreement accidentally becoming enforceable under the provisions of s.40 of the LPA 1925. Although it is no longer possible to create a valid oral contract, 'subject to contract' remains in common use during negotiations. It has been suggested that its use may have significant consequences for the availability of alternative remedies if s.2 has not been complied with (see Section 2.5).

The contract must include mutual obligations to buy and sell the land. In *Ruddick* v. *Ormston* [2005] EWHC 2547 Ch the claimant wrote what he alleged was a contract for the sale of a flat on two pages in a diary. One page stated that the defendant would sell his flat for £25,000 and the other page stated that the claimant would buy the flat for £25,000. Both parties signed both pages. It was held that there was no contract as neither page contained mutual obligations to buy and sell the flat.

Section 2 only applies to *executory* contracts, that is contracts which have yet to be completed.

If the parties choose to complete an oral land contract or a contract that does not in some respect comply with s.2, they are at liberty to do so. Once they have done so it becomes irrelevant that the contract that they have completed may not have been in accordance with s.2 (per Scott LJ, *Tootal Clothing Ltd* v. *Guinea Properties Ltd* (1992) 64 P & CR 452 at p. 455).

2.4.2.2 'For the sale or other disposition of an interest in land' (s.2(1))

For the purposes of the 1989 Act an 'interest in land' means:

any estate, interest or charge in or over land (s.2(6) (as amended by s.25(2), Trusts of Land and Appointment of Trustees Act 1996 (TLATA))

Consequently s.2 applies not only to the sale and purchase of legal estates, but also to the creation and disposition of other interests in land, including:

- the grant of an option to buy land (*Spiro* v. *Glencrown Properties* [1991] 2 Ch 537).
- A contract to create a mortgage (*United Bank of Kuwait Plc* v. *Sahib* [1997] Ch 107). Equity treats such contracts as though they are mortgages. Prior to the 1989 Act all that was required to create an equitable mortgage was for the landowner to deposit the title deeds to the land with the lender with the intention of creating a mortgage.

However, the following have been held not to be dispositions of an interest in land:

- An agreement by the vendor not to consider any offers for the land from any other parties for a specific period (a 'lock-out agreement'): *Pitt* v. *PHH Property Management Ltd* [1994] 1 WLR 327.
- The grant of a right of first refusal (or 'pre-emption') if the landowner decides to sell a particular piece of land. However, any exercise of the right of pre-emption must satisfy s.2 for it to create a valid contact (see *Bircham & Co Nominees (2) Ltd* v. *Worrell Holdings Ltd* (2001) 82 P & CR 427).
- An agreement about the priority of two mortgages (*Scottish & Newcastle Plc* v. *Lancashire Mortgage Corporation Ltd* [2007] EWCA Civ 684).
- The exercise of an option to buy land. *Spiro* v. *Glencrown Properties* [1991] 2 Ch 537, concerned an option to purchase land and raised the question of whether the letter giving notice that the buyer was going to exercise the option and buy the land had to satisfy the section by containing also the seller's signature. Hoffmann J held:

'Apart from authority, it seems to me plain enough that section 2 was intended to apply to the agreement which created the option and not to the notice by which it was exercised ... The exercise of the option is a unilateral act. It would destroy the very purpose of the option if the purchaser had to obtain the vendor's countersignature to the notice' (at p. 541)

The only document which required both signatures was the contract creating the option and, since both parties had signed this, the buyer was entitled to demand enforcement of the contract.

2.4.2.3 Statutory Exceptions

S.2(5) of the 1989 Act lists a number of types of contract that do not have to satisfy the formalities set out in s.2.

1   contracts to grant leases of three years or less which take effect in possession and are at the market rent (see s.54(2) LPA 1925 and Section 2.6.1.3); and
2   contracts made in a public auction (where the agreement is made in public, with the auctioneer acting for both parties); and
3   contracts regulated under the Financial Services and Markets Act 2000 except for regulated mortgage contracts, regulated home reversion plans and regulated purchase plans. This exception governs investments such as shares, which may include interests in land.

The rule that there is no need for writing for a contract for a short lease tidied up the old law which was anomalous and illogical, since s.40(1) had required written evidence of a contract for a lease which, by s.54(2), was itself legal even if created orally.

In addition, s.2(5) provides that s.2 has no effect 'on the creation or operation of resulting, implied or constructive trusts'. This allows the courts to mitigate the consequences of the strict requirements of s.2 in some cases by recognising a constructive trust (see Chapter 13). Section 2(5) is silent as to any possible role for proprietary estoppel. The availability of equitable remedies when s.2 has not been complied with is considered in Section 2.5.

2.4.3   Writing

2.4.3.1 Incorporating all the Express Terms of the Agreement (s.2(1))

To satisfy s.2, all of the expressly agreed terms of the agreement must be written in a single document (or duplicates for exchange) or incorporated into that document by reference to some other document (s.2(2)). Any variation of the terms must also satisfy s.2, as Lord Morritt explained in *McCausland* v. *Duncan Lawrie Ltd* [1997] 1 WLR 38:

> 'The choice lies between permitting a variation, however fundamental, to be made without any formality at all and requiring it to satisfy section 2. In my view it is evident that Parliament intended the latter. There would be little point in requiring that the original contract comply with section 2 if it might be varied wholly informally' (at p. 40).

Where a formal contract in two parts is drafted all the terms must be recorded identically in each part. This is the most usual way of preparing contracts for the sale of land. The seller signs one copy and the purchaser signs the other. The contract comes into being when the two copies are exchanged and any deposit paid. It seems that if the two parts of the contract are not identical records of the terms, the formalities of s.2 are not satisfied.

Before s.2 came into force it was possible to create a valid contract through the exchange of correspondence. The Law Commission proposed that creation of contracts by correspondence should continue ((1987) Law Com No 164, para. 4.15). However, s.2 as enacted was significantly different from the draft proposed by the Law Commission. In *Hooper* v. *Sherman* [1994] NPC 153, the Court of Appeal held that the exchange of two informal letters between the parties, each containing the terms and signed by the senders' solicitors, could amount to an 'exchange of contracts'. The majority in the Court of Appeal held that the letters could be joined together and thus satisfy s.2: all the terms were in writing and signed by both parties. Morritt LJ dissented, however, on the ground that, although these letters would have been enough for s.40, they were not sufficient for the clear terms of the new law. Shortly afterwards, in *Commission for New Towns* v. *Cooper (GB) Ltd* [1995] Ch 259, a differently constituted Court of Appeal decided that it was not bound by *Hooper* for procedural reasons and then went on to agree with the dissenting judgment of Morritt LJ. In *Cooper* the parties were in dispute as to the terms of payment for building work as part of a complex arrangement of various land agreements. They reached an agreement, subject to the approval of the plaintiff's directors, the terms of which were included in an exchange of faxes. One side claimed that this amounted to an 'exchange of contracts' for s.2, but the Court of Appeal unanimously held that it did not, because 'exchange of contracts' in s2(1) refers to the exchanging of identical documents as part of a formal process indicating the intention to enter a contract:

> In my judgment, when there has been a prior oral agreement, there is only an 'exchange of contracts' within section 2 when documents are exchanged which set out or incorporate all of the terms which have been agreed and when, crucially, those documents are intended, by virtue of their exchange, to bring about a contract to which section 2 applies (per Evans LJ at p. 295).

Thus, it is not sufficient under s.2 for the documentation signed by the parties to confirm a prior oral agreement: the documents must, on proper construction, create the contract itself.

In the case of *Oun* v. *Ahmad* [2008] EWHC 545 Ch Morgan J set out how the principles of s.2(1) should be applied when seeking to determine the validity of a contract.

28. Section 2(1) requires the written document to incorporate all the terms which the parties have expressly agreed.

29. The first matter to be explored is a question of fact: what were all the terms which the parties had expressly agreed?

30. Once one has found all the terms which the parties have expressly agreed, then one can examine the written document to see if it incorporates all those terms or whether it omits any.

31. If, on examination of the written document, it is found that it does not incorporate all the terms which the parties have expressly agreed, then prima facie there is no binding contract at all.... There cannot be a binding contract for only those terms which have been incorporated because they are not the complete set of terms which were expressly agreed.

32. The prima facie position may be displaced in two cases, in particular.

33. The first particular case is where there are two separate contracts and not one composite contract...

34. The second particular case is where the written document, which does not incorporate all of the terms expressly agreed, can be rectified to include in the written document all of the terms expressly agreed...

2.4.3.2 Composite Contracts

The question of composite contracts arises when one of the parties argues that the transaction consists of two agreements and that only one of these is a contract for the sale of land. If the term that is missing belongs to the agreement concerning the land then that agreement must fail as a contract because of s.2. However, if the missing term is part of the other agreement s.2 does not apply, so the agreement can create a binding contract even if all the terms are not set out in writing. The Law Commission Report which preceded the 1989 Act ((1987) Law Com No 164) suggested that unincorporated terms could be valid if they fell within the doctrine of 'collateral contracts' (that is, contracts 'on the side'). Initially the Courts seemed receptive to this approach, as in *Record* v. *Bell* [1991] 1 WLR 853. In this case an additional term was agreed after the two copies of the contract had been signed. The seller promised that there were no unforeseen burdens affecting the title to the land registered at the Land Registry. The buyer subsequently wished to withdraw from the contract and argued that the extra term meant that s.2(2) of the 1989 Act had not been complied with and that the contract was, therefore, void. Judge Paul Baker QC rejected this argument. He held that there were two contracts: (1) the sale of the land and (2) the agreement to complete this sale in consideration of the seller's extra promise. He went on to hold that the second contract was collateral to the first and did not relate to a disposition of an interest in land. Consequently neither agreement failed for non-compliance with s.2. The first contained all of its terms in writing and the second agreement did not need to be in writing as it was not a contract for the disposition of land. However, the courts have subsequently taken a stricter line in respect of collateral contracts. In *Godden* v. *Merthyr Tydfil Housing Association* (1997) 74 P & CR D1, the Court of Appeal stressed that the existence of a collateral contract was a question of fact based on the commercial reality of the agreement. The court cannot artificially divide what is in reality a single agreement.

2.4.3.3 Rectification

The availability of the equitable remedy of rectification is expressly recognised by s.2(4) of the 1989 Act and has been used by the courts on a number of occasions. When applied in these circumstances rectification converts an invalid contract. Section 2(4) gives the court the power to specify the date upon which the contract became legally effective.

In *Wright* v. *Robert Leonard Developments Ltd* [1994] EGCS 69, contracts were exchanged for the sale of a show flat, but the expressly agreed term that the furnishings would be included in the sale was omitted. Although the furnishings were not fixtures and were not, therefore, land within the meaning of s.2(1), the Court of Appeal refused to treat the agreement about the furnishings as separable from the rest of the transaction. Consequently, the exchange of contracts did not satisfy s.2, and therefore, it would appear, there was no contract. However, the Court agreed that the document could be rectified to include the missing term. Once the missing term was inserted, the contract satisfied s.2.

'Rectification is about setting the record straight', (per Morgan J in *Oun* v. *Ahmad* [2008] EWHC 545 Ch, para. 46). It is a discretionary remedy which allows the court to correct a mistake in the way in which the terms of the agreement have been recorded in writing. It is not a vehicle for varying or clarifying the terms of the agreement. Peter Gibson LJ summarised the basic requirements to justify rectification in the case of *Swainland Builders Ltd* v. *Freehold Properties Ltd* [2002] 2 EGLR 71 at para. 33:

(1) the parties had a common continuing intention... in respect of a particular matter in the instrument to be rectified;

(2) there was an outward expression of accord;

(3) the intention continued at the time of the execution of the instrument sought to be rectified;

(4) by mistake, the instrument did not reflect that common intention.

In *Sargeant* v. *Reece* [2008] 1 P & CR D8, Edward Bartley Jones QC, sitting in the High Court, reviewed the Court of Appeal cases on the doctrine of rectification and particularly the burden of proof falling on the claimant. He concluded that the claimant does not need to be able to prove the exact form of words that should have been used in the written document, provided that he can establish the substance of the missing term or terms in sufficient detail. The amount and type of evidence needed to do this will depend upon the quality of the document concerned, but will need to be sufficiently convincing to outweigh the evidence of the written contract itself.

It is not, I think, the standard of proof which is high, so differing from the normal civil standard, but the evidential requirement needed to counteract the inherent probability that the written instrument truly represents the parties' intention because it is a document signed by the parties (per Brightman LJ in *Thomas Bates and Son Limited* v. *Wyndham's (Lingerie) Limited* [1981] 1 WLR 505 at p. 521).

2.4.4 Incorporation of Terms

Section 2(2) allows the terms to be incorporated into a document either by being set out in it or by reference to some other document. In *Courtney* v. *Corp Ltd* [2006] EWCA Civ 518, the finance company's contract letter expressly incorporated its standard terms and conditions, which were contained in a separate document. The claimant did not read these conditions before signing the contract letter, and subsequently claimed that the contract was invalid. The Court of Appeal held that the express incorporation of the standard conditions was sufficient to satisfy s.2, even if Mr Courtney had not seen or read them.

2.4.5   Signature (s.2(3))

Prior to the 1989 Act, the rules about what constitutes a signature were somewhat complex, and would have surprised most non-lawyers. Any occurrence of the name of the party who had written or typed the agreement (or on whose behalf it had been written) could be regarded as the signature, even if the party had not written his name with his own hand on the document. Fortunately, the Court of Appeal has held that these rules do not apply to the 1989 Act. In the case of *Firstpost Homes* v. *Johnson* [1995] 1 WLR 1567, Peter Gibson LJ refused to '...encumber the new Act with so much ancient baggage, particularly when it does not leave the word "signed" with a meaning which the ordinary man would understand it to have' (at p. 362). For the purposes of s.2, signature has its ordinary meaning as recognised in the case of *Goodman* v. *J Eban Ltd [1954]* 1 QB 550:

> In modern English usage, when a document is required to be 'signed' by someone, that means that he must write his name with his own hand on it (per Denning LJ at p. 561).

Section 2 allows a valid contact to be signed by the parties themselves, or by someone else on their behalf. In the unreported case of *Grunhut* v. *Ramdas* (2002) the signature appeared to be that of the relevant party, but was actually a forgery. It was held, however, that even though the party did not sign it herself, the contract was still valid because (on the facts) she had authorised someone else to sign it on her behalf.

Where the contract is to incorporate terms from another document, it is important that both parties sign the primary document. In *Firstpost Homes* v. *Johnson* [1994] 4 All ER 355, Mrs Johnson orally agreed to sell some farmland to the claimant. The buyer drafted a letter which had his name typed on it as addressee and contained the terms of the contract to sell the land 'shown on the enclosed plan'. He signed the plan but not the letter, and sent both documents to Mrs Johnson, who signed and dated them both. She then died. When the buyer sought to enforce the agreement, Mrs Johnson's personal representatives claimed there was no contract because s.2 was not satisfied. On appeal it was held that the two documents could not be joined as one, since the plan – the only document signed by both parties – did not incorporate the letter. Enclosing the letter in the same envelope as the plan was insufficient to combine the two documents. In fact, as it was the letter which expressly incorporated the plan it was the letter that should have been signed by both parties. The buyer's typed name on the letter did not amount to his signature.

2.4.6   Remedies

If there is a valid contract, then the buyer or the seller may be entitled to specific performance if the other party defaults, provided that damages would be an insufficient remedy (which will usually be the case, given the unique nature of land). However, specific performance is an equitable remedy available at the discretion of the Court. It may be denied, for example, because of the claimant's conduct ('he who comes to equity must come with clean hands'). In *Wilkie* v. *Redsell* [2003] EWCA Civ 926, the Court of Appeal declined to grant a rogue specific performance of his contract to buy land, since firstly there was no evidence that he would be able to pay the purchase price and thus complete his side of the bargain, and secondly he had 'abused the facilities of the court in relation to the very matter in respect of which he [sought] relief' (para. 34) and so did not have clean hands.

Even if a person is entitled to specific performance, the court may award damages instead if it would be fairer: for example, where the land has now been sold to a third party. Under the Law Society's Standard Conditions of Sale, if the buyer refuses to complete, the seller may retain the deposit (a powerful incentive for the buyer), subject always to the courts' statutory discretion to order the return of the deposit pursuant to s.49(2) of the LPA 1925.

Other remedies for the buyer include suing for the restitution of a lost deposit, or for misrepresentation. In *McMeekin* v. *Long* (2003) 29 EG 120, buyers of a house were awarded £67,000 damages for fraudulent misrepresentation when the sellers deliberately failed to disclose a dispute with their neighbours.

2.5 Equitable Remedies

The requirements of s.2 of the 1989 Act cause no problems in the vast majority of transactions concerning land. The need to satisfy the provisions of s.2 means that the parties can be certain both as to whether they have entered into a binding contract and the terms of that contract. If s.2 is not satisfied there are no reciprocal contractual obligations between the parties. Consequently, if a party spends money or other resources in reliance upon an agreement that has yet to satisfy s.2 he does so at his own risk. Without a valid contract he cannot force the other party to honour the agreement. As Chadwick LJ observed in *Bircham & Co Nominees (2) Ltd* v. *Worrell Holdings Ltd* (2001) 82 P & CR 427:

> There are obvious difficulties in the way of a claimant who seeks specific performance of an agreement which, by reason of the provisions enacted in s.2 of the 1989 Act, has no contractual effect (at para. 15).

Equity has long recognised that there are circumstances in which it would be unfair not to provide a remedy to a claimant who has acted to his detriment as a result of the other person's actions simply because of the absence of the signed document. Otherwise the provisions of s.2 become a charter for rogues to exploit people prepared to trust and honour informal 'gentleman's agreements'.

Prior to s.2, a contract relating to land was merely unenforceable if the formality requirements had not been complied with. However, evidence that the plaintiff had performed a part of (or had done some other act showing the existence of) the unwritten contract and that the defendant knew of this would render the contract enforceable in equity. This is the doctrine of 'part performance'. Although the 1989 Act does not expressly abolish part performance, it is difficult to see how the doctrine can apply within the provisions of s.2. After some initial doubt, the Court of Appeal has now confirmed on a number of occasions that the doctrine of part performance is not applicable to contracts made after 26 September 1989 (see, for example, *United Bank of Kuwait Plc* v. *Sahib* [1997] Ch 107 and *Yaxley* v. *Gotts* [2000] Ch 162.

The Law Commission expected part performance to be replaced by proprietary estoppel, although it did not anticipate frequent resort to equity:

> In putting forward the present recommendation we rely greatly on the principle, recognised even by equity, that 'certainty is the father of right and the mother of justice ((1987) Law Com No 164, para. 4.13).

The doctrine of proprietary estoppel and the related doctrine of constructive trusts are considered in detail in Chapter 13. Lord Scott set out its basic principles in the recent case of *Yeoman's Row Management Limited* v. *Cobbe* [2008] 1 WLR 1752,

> An 'estoppel' bars the object of it from asserting some fact or facts, or, sometimes, something that is a mixture of fact and law, that stands in the way of some right claimed by the person entitled to the benefit of the estoppel. The estoppel becomes a 'proprietary' estoppel – a sub-species of a

'promissory' estoppel – if the right claimed is a proprietary right, usually a right to or over land but, in principle, equally available in relation to chattels or choses in action (at para. 14).

The circumstances that may give rise to an estoppel can arise were summarised by Mr Edward Nugee QC, sitting as a high court judge, in the case of *Re Basham* [1986] 1 WLR 1498:

> where one person, A, has acted to his detriment on the faith of a belief, which was known to or encouraged by another person, B, that he either has or is going to be given a right over B's property, B cannot insist on his strict legal rights if to do so would be inconsistent with A's belief (at p. 1503).

An agreement labelled 'subject to contract' (see Section 2.4.2.1) will not ordinarily be capable of giving rise to a proprietary estoppel as the label reveals that neither party expects to be bound by it. This is because

> the would-be purchaser's expectation of acquiring an interest in the property in question is subject to a contingency that is entirely under the control of the other party to the negotiations (per Lord Scott, *Yeoman's Row Management Limited* v. *Cobbe* [2008] 1 WLR 1752 at para. 22; see also *James* v. *Evans* (2000) 80 P & CR D39).

There is some doubt, however, whether the doctrine of proprietary estoppel is ever appropriate in the context of an agreement that fails to be a contract because of failure to comply with s.2. A number of judges have expressed concern that using the doctrine in these circumstances contravenes the intention of Parliament underlying the 1989 Act, not least because estoppel is not one of the exceptions listed in s.2(5) (see Section 2.4.2.3). In an *obiter* comment in *Yeoman's Row Management Limited* v. *Cobbe* [2008] 1 WLR 1752, Lord Scott expressed his view that:

> proprietary estoppel cannot be prayed in aid in order to render enforceable an agreement that statute has declared to be void. The proposition that an owner of land can be estopped from asserting that an agreement is void for want of compliance with the requirements of section 2 is, in my opinion, unacceptable. The assertion is no more than the statute provides. Equity can surely not contradict the statute ... statute provides an express exception for constructive trusts (at para 29, see also *Halsbury Laws of England*, 4th edition (Reissue), Volume 16(2), para. 960).

In *Yaxley* v. *Gotts* [2000] Ch 162, Yaxley, a builder, orally agreed with a friend (Gotts senior) that he would take the ground floor of a house that his friend was about to buy, in return for renovating and rebuilding the house as a number of flats. In fact, the friend's son (Gotts junior) bought the house, but Yaxley carried out the work as he had promised. A few years later, Yaxley fell out with the father and son. They barred him from the premises and denied that he had any right to the ground floor of the house. At first instance, Yaxley, having relied on the father's oral promise (which had apparently been adopted by the son), successfully claimed an interest in the house by virtue of proprietary estoppel and was awarded a 99-year lease of the ground floor. On appeal, Robert Walker LJ was reluctant to find an estoppel in Yaxley's favour for the reason identified above, although he was not prepared to rule out the possibility of estoppel never being appropriate in circumstances in which s.2 had not been complied with. Instead, he imposed a constructive trust on Gotts. Typically this type of constructive trust arises where the parties have agreed that A shall have a proprietary interest in property, and A has acted to his detriment in reliance on that agreement. Robert Walker LJ felt able to impose a constructive trust on Gotts because of the provision in s.2(5) that the creation or operation of constructive trusts is not affected by s.2. Beldam and Clarke LJJ, while agreeing with the imposition of a constructive trust, also supported the first instance judge's finding of proprietary estoppel. They were prepared to give much more weight to the views of the Law Commission when interpreting s.2 since the 1989 Act was based on the Commission's Report. According to Bedlam LJ, the underlying policy behind s.2 was not to prohibit informal agreements relating to land, but to make them void for the purposes of contract law if they did not satisfy the formalities contained in the statute. The House of Lords has yet to decide this question, although Lord Scott made his view clear in *Yeoman's Row Management Limited*.

2.6 Transfer of the Legal Interest

2.6.1 The Deed

As mentioned already, a deed is normally necessary to transfer a legal estate or interest. When the land is registered the deed is a Land Transfer form from the Land Registry.

Section 52(1) LPA 1925 states:

> All conveyances of land or of any interest therein are void for the purpose of conveying or creating a legal estate unless made by deed.

Before 31 July 1990, a deed was a document that was 'signed, sealed and delivered'. Now, the ancient requirement for a seal is replaced by the need for a witness. The requirements for a deed are defined in s.1 Law of Property (Miscellaneous Provisions) Act 1989.

A deed is a document which:

- makes clear on its face that it is a deed;
- is validly executed;
- is delivered.

2.6.1.1 Execution

An individual 'executes' the deed (that is, makes the document his deed) by signing it in the presence of one witness who also signs. Alternatively, the deed can be signed 'at his direction and in his presence' by another person, and in this case there must be two witnesses present who also sign the deed. Different rules apply to corporations, including limited companies.

2.6.1.2 Delivery

A deed is 'delivered' when the 'grantor' (the person executing the deed) does or says something to 'adopt the deed as his own'. In practice, solicitors usually treat a deed as delivered at the moment they add a date to a document which has already been signed and witnessed; this is said to show that they adopt it.

2.6.1.3 Where a Deed is not Needed

There are a number of circumstances where a legal estate or legal interest can be obtained without a deed.

1   *Short leases* (defined in s.54(2) LPA 1925): by s.52(2)(d), a lease is legal without any formality (even writing) if it does not exceed three years, the tenant is entitle to occupy the premises from the date of the lease (that is, the lease 'takes effect in possession') and it is at a market rent. There is no need for any special formality, or even writing, for this

kind of short lease, because there is little risk that a buyer of the property will be caught unawares – the tenant will be present on the property and paying rent. In addition, the expense and delay in conforming to the formality requirements of ss. 1 and 2 of the 1989 Act would be bound to inhibit the creation of these commonly found leases or would lead to non-compliance. However, somewhat illogically, a deed is still needed to *assign* any lease (to transfer the whole of the legal interest to another person, as opposed to creating a sublease), as shown in *Crago* v. *Julian* [1992] 1 WLR 372 (see Section 5.4.1).

2   *Long use*: in unregistered land, using someone else's land for a minimum of 12 years can ensure that the user cannot be defeated by anyone; effectively, he becomes a legal owner. This is known as 'adverse possession'. It is also possible to obtain title to registered land by adverse possession, although the rules are somewhat different. Adverse possession is considered in detail in Chapter 3. Long use of an easement or profit (for example a right of way or a right to fish) can create a legal right by 'prescription' (see Section 8.5.1.3).

3   *Personal representatives' assent* (s.36(1) AEA 1925): if a landowner dies, his land automatically goes to ('vests in') his legal representatives. When they have completed their administration of the estate, they transfer the land to the heir(s). Writing, but no deed, is necessary to do this; it is called an 'assent'.

4   *Trustee in bankruptcy's disclaimer*: where a landowner becomes bankrupt, the land automatically vests in his trustee in bankruptcy. If the land is more trouble than it is worth (for example a lease with a high rent) the trustee can disclaim it in writing; a deed is not necessary.

5   *Court order*: a court can order land to be transferred.

2.6.1.4 The Effect of a Deed

The deed not only transfers the interest but also any advantages which belong to the land, unless the parties show that they intend otherwise; s.62 LPA 1925 states:

> A conveyance of land shall be deemed to include and shall by virtue of this Act operate to convey, with the land, all buildings, erections, fixtures, commons, hedges, ditches, fences, ways, waters, water-courses, liberties, privileges, easements, rights, and advantages whatsoever, appertaining or reputed to appertain to the land, or any part thereof, or, at the time of conveyance, demised, occupied, or enjoyed with, or reputed or known as part or parcel of, or appurtenant to, the land or any part thereof.

Thus, a buyer of land may, by s.62, get the right enjoyed by his predecessor to park his car in his neighbour's drive (see Section 8.5.1.2.3). Sections 78 and 79 respectively ensure that he will automatically have the right to enforce, and will be bound by, any valid restrictive covenant over the land (see Section 9.2). (These three sections are some of the 'wordsaving provisions' mentioned in Section 1.2.)

2.6.1.5 Where the Formalities of the Deed Have not Been Complied With

The formalities described above are necessary for the valid execution of a deed. However, in the case of *Shah* v. *Shah* [2002] QB 35, a person was induced to rely on what appeared on the face of it to be a deed. A later representation by the executor of the deed that it was invalid since it had not been properly witnessed was unsuccessful, and the executor was estopped from relying on his strict legal rights.

2.6.2   Registration

Almost every sale, transfer, lease or first legal mortgage of land in England and Wales must now be registered at the Land Registry. The main exception relates to leases with less than seven years to run, although it is anticipated that this period will eventually be reduced to three years. The consequences of failing to register the disposition will depend upon whether the land was already registered at the time of the transfer.

2.6.2.1 'Not Yet Registered' Land

Section 4(1) of the LRA 2002 requires all transfers of freehold and the grant and transfer of leases for a term exceeding seven years to be registered. The grant of a first mortgage will also trigger compulsory first registration. In these circumstances, the legal title to the land is transferred to the buyer on the date set out in the deed of transfer. The buyer has two months within which to apply for registration (s.6), otherwise the legal title will revert to the seller, who will then hold the land on trust for the buyer (s.7). It is the responsibility of the buyer to ensure that the legal title is retransferred to him and properly registered (s.8). In the meanwhile the buyer will only have title to the land in equity and he will not enjoy all the protection afforded to a legal owner. The implications of this are explored more fully in Chapter 11.

2.6.2.2 Registered Land

Different rules apply to the transfer of legal title to land that is already registered at the date of the transfer. In this case there is no two-month window. Section 27 of the LRA 2002 provides that the transfer of registered estates (and the creation of several types of interest over them) will not operate at law until the registration requirements are met. In the gap between completing the transfer deed and completion of its registration (the so-called 'registration gap') the buyer will have only an equitable interest in the land. Again, the detailed implications of this are considered in Chapter 11.

2.7   Comment

The rules relating to the buying and selling of interests in land are, in general, formalistic and detailed, but, in an area where the law is seeking to achieve a simple and certain resolution of complicated and dynamic human relationships, this is hardly surprising. Cases on s.2 suggest that the law does not successfully address all of the tensions between certainty and justice inherent in any system of formalities and that it may add a few problems of its own.

In the compromise between the need for a clear rule, and the need to make sure that people do not unfairly take advantage of one another, the 1989 Act tends towards a more ruthless simplicity, but the extent to which this is reflected in the decisions of the courts may change according to the state of the property market, and according to the attitude adopted by the courts towards proprietary estoppel and constructive trusts. In any event, despite the nature of the rules, many hundreds of thousands of interests in land are successfully conveyed each year; the state of the property market is far more important to most non-lawyers than the technical rules.

In the future, the law will increasingly have to come to terms with developments in new technology. The Electronic Communications Act 2000 and Part 8 of the LRA 2002 provide the statutory framework for electronic conveyancing, and it is envisaged that contracts and deeds will soon have to be created, signed and communicated to the Land Registry by electronic means. Completion of the transfer and its registration will be simultaneous, thereby closing the registration gap. The intention is that paper will become obsolete in the convey-ancer's office of the future, as will the 1989 Act and its rules on land contracts and deeds. Whether this means that there will be no longer be room for the 'do-it-yourself' conveyancer remains uncertain. There are also significant technical difficulties in developing and imple-menting sufficiently reliable and secure technology and procedures, although the Land Registry hopes to introduce electronic land transfers during 2009. The Land Registry has a dedicated section on its website with information about the progress being made with elec-tronic conveyancing (at http://www.landregistry.gov.uk/).

Summary

2.1 The normal procedure for buying and selling interests in land is governed by rules relating to the need for formality in land contracts, by writing and by deeds, and is supplemented by equity.

2.2 As soon as there is a contract for the sale of an interest in land, the buyer effectively becomes the equitable owner of the land, provided the discretionary remedy of specific performance is available.

2.3 In order for there to be a contract for the sale of an interest in land, normally all the terms must be in writing and signed by both sides.

2.4 If there is no contract, equity may nevertheless enforce the 'agreement' by finding a constructive trust or under the doctrine of proprietary estoppel if it would be unconscionable for the defendant to deny that he made a promise to transfer the interest, provided that the plaintiff acted to his detriment in reliance on the promise.

2.5 A deed, signed, witnessed and delivered, is normally necessary to create or transfer a legal interest in land. It also transfers benefits attached to the land.

2.6 Some legal leases not exceeding three years (or a contract to grant one) may be created, but not assigned, without any formality.

Exercises

2.1 At what stage in the conveyancing process is the equitable interest in land transferred?

2.2 What is are the requirements set out in s.2 of the 1989 Act? Why do they matter?

2.3 What are constructive trusts and the doctrine of proprietary estoppel? How are they relevant to the rules for buying land?

2.4 What is a deed? Why is the definition significant?

@ 2.5 William owned the freehold of a rather dilapidated house. He agreed to sell it to Ajay for £150,000 and, once contracts were exchanged, Ajay began work on the repairs. Due to a change in his circumstances, William has decided he no longer wishes to sell the house to Ajay. William's solicitor has told him that, since no deed has yet been executed, William can withdraw from the arrangement. It also turns out that Ajay never signed his copy of the contract.

Advise Ajay.

@ 2.6 Read *Three Students: a Further Tale* on the companion website. Is there a valid contract for the sale and purchase of the house?

@ 2.7 An online quiz on the topics covered in this chapter is available on the companion website.

Further Reading

Capps, 'Conveyancing in the Twenty-first Century: An Outline of Electronic Conveyancing, and Electronic Signatures' [2002] Conv 443

Critchley, 'Taking Formalities Seriously' in Bright and Dewar (eds), *Land Law Themes and Perspectives* (Oxford: OUP, 1998)

McFarlane, 'Proprietary Estoppel and Failed Contractual Negotiations' [2005] Conv 501

Thompson, 'Oral Agreements for the Sale of Land' [2000] Conv 245

Chapter 3

Adverse Possession

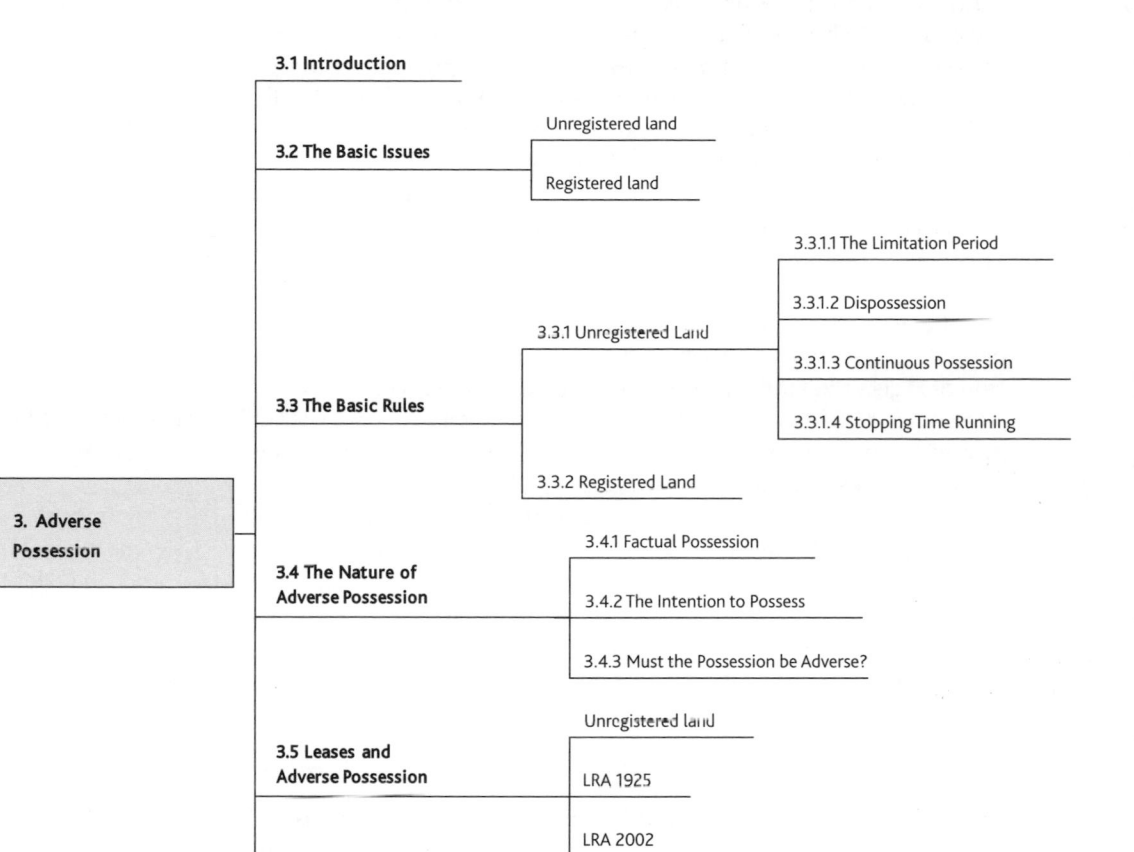

3. Adverse Possession

- **3.1 Introduction**
- **3.2 The Basic Issues**
  - Unregistered land
  - Registered land
- **3.3 The Basic Rules**
  - 3.3.1 Unregistered Land
    - 3.3.1.1 The Limitation Period
    - 3.3.1.2 Dispossession
    - 3.3.1.3 Continuous Possession
    - 3.3.1.4 Stopping Time Running
  - 3.3.2 Registered Land
- **3.4 The Nature of Adverse Possession**
  - 3.4.1 Factual Possession
  - 3.4.2 The Intention to Possess
  - 3.4.3 Must the Possession be Adverse?
- **3.5 Leases and Adverse Possession**
  - Unregistered land
  - LRA 1925
  - LRA 2002
- **3.6 Human Rights**
- **3.7 Comment**

3.1　Introduction

The last chapter explored the rules governing the formal transfer of interests in land, and was concerned with land which clearly belonged to a particular person. This chapter investigates the issues which arise when the owner's title is challenged because someone else has been in possession of her land for many years. Such a dispute might concern a narrow strip of land between two houses, perhaps where one householder has failed to take care of her boundaries and the other has encroached or a large area of land with valuable potential for development.

Historically, adverse possession is part of the general law of limitation of actions, now contained in the Limitation Act 1980. The basic principle is straightforward and quickly grasped: through adverse possession, a person can effectively become the legal owner of land solely because of her occupation of it. After a certain length of time, a person using land may have a better title to it than anyone else, including the real or 'paper' owner, simply because the law will not permit anyone to remove her. Since 13 October 2003 adverse possession of registered land has been governed by a new set of rules contained in the Land Registration Act 2002. Anyone claiming adverse possession of a registered title must now apply to be registered as its owner with the existing registered proprietor having the right to object in all but a few circumstances.

The statutes provide the structure of the rules, but the cases are of great importance because the substantive question of whether a person is in 'adverse possession' is a question of fact: it is necessary to examine carefully all the details of each individual story in order to decide whether a person has adversely possessed the land for the period required by the relevant statute. The cases also help in grasping the way the judges see the issues: they are concerned to do justice in disputes between neighbours and at the same time to satisfy the various demands of public policy.

3.2　The Basic Issues

Many of the justifications offered for the doctrine of adverse possession arise out of the limitations of the traditional method of conveyancing (unregistered land), where there may be considerable uncertainty about who owns a particular parcel of land. The interests of certainty and the market in land require a rule that actions to recover possession may not be brought after a certain length of time (they become 'time-barred'), otherwise 'stale claims' will haunt landowners and their purchasers indefinitely. In addition, deeds can get lost and people can forget what they own, but the land itself remains. If the law did not provide for cases where there is no formal proof of title, areas of land would be 'outside the law' and unmarketable. Adverse possession thus provides a way of curing defective titles in unregistered land, since, after the required period of possession, the paper owner cannot evict the squatter.

In registered land, the justifications for retaining rules on adverse possession are different but no less compelling. Here, title is not based on possession, as it is in the unregistered system, but on the fact that ownership has been recorded at the Land Registry, which guarantees the title (see Chapter 11). Although the Land Registration Act 1925 incorporated the rules that applied to unregistered land with little significant amendment, it is now generally recognised that adverse possession has a much more limited role within the registered title scheme. In their consultation prior to the LRA 2002 ((1998) Law Com No 254, para. 10.98) the Law Commission stated that:

the title that registration confers should be capable of being overridden by adverse possession only where it is essential to ensure the marketability of land or to prevent unfairness... namely –
(1) where the registered proprietor cannot be traced;
(2) where there have been dealings 'off the register';
(3) in some cases where the register is not conclusive; and
(4) where an adverse possessor has entered into possession under a reasonable mistake as to his or her rights.

If it were not for adverse possession, many pieces of land would be waste, forgotten and unutilised by the paper owner. However, the law of adverse possession inevitably causes problems for people who think that legal title to land – private property, for which the owner has probably 'paid good money' – ought to be protected by the law, come what may. The idea that people can be deprived of their land in such a way certainly raises issues under the Human Rights Act 1998, which are considered in detail in Section 3.6. In real life, few unregistered titles are perfect and innumerable difficulties arise when a title needs to be traced to its origin. In most cases, however, it is normally sufficient to prove a good title (the 'root of title') going back only 15 years to satisfy a purchaser of land that has not yet been registered (s.23 Law of Property Act 1969).

In addition to these practical justifications for adverse possession, there is also an ethical issue, at least in cases where an industrious and careful squatter is making better use of the land than a neglectful paper. Land is, after all, a national, and not completely unlimited, resource. It may be argued that the public interest lies in encouraging the efficient use of land resources (see *Hounslow LBC* v. *Minchinton* (1997) 74 P & CR 221). Clearly, protecting private ownership is only one of the policy considerations.

The case of *Williams* v. *Usherwood* (1982) 43 P & CR 235 illustrates the interplay of the various policies behind the law. Here, neighbouring suburban houses (numbers 31 and 33 Rosedale Road), which were built in 1934, shared a drive; the legal arrangement was that each owner had title to the half running alongside her house and an easement over (a right to use) the other's half of the drive (such rights are considered in more detail in Chapter 8). For convenience, the fence between the houses was built close to Number 33, and it therefore looked as if the drive belonged to Number 31. As it happened, the owner of Number 33 never did use the drive and, from 1952, never even had access to the strip. The people who bought Number 31 in 1962 paved it and used it for parking their cars.

In 1977, the Williams family moved into Number 33 and decided to pursue their apparent legal right, as the 'paper owners', to half the width of the drive. They lost. The owners of Number 31 successfully argued adverse possession (by earlier owners of the house) so that the Williams family could not enforce any remedy against them. In this case, the land was registered and therefore, under the old rules for adverse possession in registered land, it was necessary for the judge also to order that the Land Register should be corrected to show the owners of Number 31 as owners of the whole drive (see Section 11.10).

The argument in favour of the Williams family was that they were the legal owners of the strip of land – the original title deeds stated it clearly – and they ought therefore to have been entitled to legal protection against trespassers. From their point of view, the law of limitation of actions was a 'cheat's charter' (McCormick [1986] Conv 434). On the other hand, the earlier owners of their house had 'slept on their rights', even later acknowledging that they did not think they owned the strip of land, whereas the owners of Number 31 had used it and repaved it 'at some expense, which went beyond any normal maintenance requirements'. The Court of Appeal was not prepared to allow the Williams family years later to resurrect a stale claim.

3.3 The Basic Rules

Before discussing the meaning of adverse possession, it is helpful to consider how the rules operate. Before 13 October 2003, they were in many respects similar in both registered and unregistered land. In its 1998 Consultation Paper, the Law Commission recognised that many of the traditional justifications for adverse possession discussed above hold no relevance in a regime where title to land is registered and proposed fundamental changes to the operation of the principles of adverse possession which were enacted in the LRA 2002 (see (1998) Law Com No 254, Part X). Consequently, although the kind of conduct which will amount to adverse possession is the same whether title to the land is registered or unregistered (LRA 2002, Schedule 6, para. 11(1)), the rules that determine the consequences of such possession are very different.

3.3.1 Unregistered Land

3.3.1.1 The Limitation Period

Section 15(1) Limitation Act 1980 provides:

> No action shall be brought by any person to recover any land after the expiration of twelve years from the date on which the right of action accrued to him or, if it first accrued to some other person through whom he claims, to that person.

The section states clearly that the paper owner cannot bring an action if 12 years have passed since the right to do so arose: that is, since the squatter – by definition, a trespasser – moved onto the land with the necessary intention to occupy it (see Section 3.4). The statute does not operate to transfer the paper owner's title to the adverse possessor, but, by refusing any remedy, merely ensures that no one can remove her.

Not only can the paper owner not bring an action to recover possession after 12 years, her title to the land is extinguished after that period (s.17 Limitation Act). It is important to remember that, as the squatter herself is not a 'purchaser' of land, she is, like someone who simply inherits land, bound by all earlier interests in the land, whether they are legal or equitable, and whether or not they were protected by registration or she had notice of them.

By s.38 Limitation Act, 'land' means more than just the legal freehold; it includes, for example, equitable freeholds and legal and equitable leases. Consequently, it is possible to obtain title to a long lease by adverse possession as well as title to freehold land (see Section 3.5). There are special rules for adversely possessing Crown land (the limitation period is 30 years) and for special classes, such as between trustees and their beneficiaries (see Megarry and Wade, 2008, sections 35-037 to 35-041 for more details).

3.3.1.2 Dispossession of the Paper Owner

In order for time to start running in the squatter's favour, the paper owner must either have been dispossessed of the land or have discontinued possession (Limitation Act 1980, Schedule 1, para. 1). It is now clear, following the leading case of *JA Pye (Oxford) Ltd* v. *Graham* [2003] 1 AC 419, that all that is required is for the squatter to take possession of the land without the permission of the owner.

If a tenancy is an oral periodic tenancy (see Section 5.3.2.1), time can begin to run in favour of the tenant from the time she stops paying rent, since the tenancy is then deemed to have ended (Limitation Act 1980, Schedule 1, para. 5(2)). In *Hayward* v. *Chaloner* [1968] 1 QB 107, a quarter of an acre of land was let as a garden on such a tenancy to whomever was the rector of a small village, but for some 25 years from 1942 no rent was paid and there was no acknowledgement of the paper owners' title. The then rector decided to sell the land as his own and the paper owners decided to fight him; they had failed to collect the rent, not because they forgot, but because of 'their loyalty and generosity to the church'. The rector won by a majority decision in the Court of Appeal, although all the judges regretted it:

> The generous indulgence of the plaintiffs and their predecessors in title, loyal churchmen all, having resulted in a free accretion at their expense to the lands of their church, their reward may be in the next world. But in this jurisdiction we can only qualify them for that reward by allowing the [Rector's] appeal (Russell LJ, pp. 123–4).

3.3.1.3 Continuous Possession

The squatter must prove that she has been in continuous possession throughout the required period. Any interruption to her possession means that the period must begin again. However, the adverse possession need not have been by one squatter. In *Williams* v. *Usherwood* (1982) 43 P & CR 235 (see Section 3.2), there were several different owners of Number 31 who, in succession, adversely possessed the land continuously for the period.

3.3.1.4 Stopping the Time Running

A paper owner can bring an action for possession within the limitation period. Of itself, this does not 'stop time running' but simply means that the paper owner is not time-barred. She must, therefore, pursue the action and bring it to a successful conclusion (*Markfield Investments Ltd* v. *Evans* [2001] 1 WLR 1321).

The Limitation Act 1980 provides that the adverse possession will cease if the squatter acknowledges in writing the title of the paper owner (ss. 29–31). In *Edginton* v. *Clark* [1967] 1 QB 367, the claimant had occupied bombed land in the East End of London for about seven years and then offered to buy it from the owner. No sale followed and, after a further ten years, he claimed adverse possession. It was held that the offer to buy was an acknowledgment of the owner's title and that therefore the squatter's possession was interrupted.

Under s.32 of the Limitation Act, the adverse possessor must prove that she did not deliberately conceal her activities or keep her possession through fraud. If there is any deception, time starts to run from the date when the paper owner 'could with reasonable diligence have discovered it'. In *Beaulane Properties Ltd* v. *Palmer* [2006] Ch 79 Palmer had originally occupied the disputed land under the terms of a licence granted by Beaulane's predecessor in title, but continued in occupation when this was terminated in 1986. In 1991, Palmer told a representative of the then paper owner of the land that he had an arrangement to use the land without making it clear that it had been terminated in 1986. Nicholas Strauss QC, sitting as a deputy judge in the Chancery Division held that this informal and unexpected conversation was sufficient to amount to concealment, and that the period of adverse possession only started to run in 1991.

3.3.2 Registered Land

Prior to 13 October 2003, where the title to the land was registered, the rules again prevented the registered owner from bringing an action to evict the squatter after 12 years. Unlike the position in unregistered land, however, her title was not extinguished; instead, she held it on trust for the squatter (s.75(1) LRA 1925). The squatter could also, if she wished, apply to the Land Registry to become the registered proprietor after 12 years (s.75(2) LRA 1925).

In accordance with the view that the role of adverse possession in registered land should be more restricted, the new rules, in force from 13 October 2003, have made it much more difficult for a squatter to obtain title. Section 96 of the Land Registration Act 2002 provides that the rules set out by the Limitation Act 1980 do not apply to registered land. Registered proprietors will no longer, therefore, be statute barred from pursuing claims against trespassers. Instead, an adverse possessor must make good their claim to the land by applying to the Registrar to be registered as the proprietor of the land. The procedure is set out in Schedule 6 of the 2002 Act.

Paragraph 1, states that, in most cases, a squatter may apply to the Land Registry to be registered as owner of the land after *ten* years' adverse possession (60 years in the case of the foreshore owned by the Crown – para. 13). When such an application is made, the Land Registry informs the registered proprietor, any owner of a registered charge on the land (such as a mortgage lender) and, if the land is leasehold, the proprietor of the freehold (para. 2). If the Registrar has received no response within three months, the adverse possessor becomes the new registered proprietor.

However, if there is an objection within the three-month period, the application will automatically be rejected unless one of the three conditions set out in para. 5 applies. These are:

(i)   The paper owner has acted unconscionably and is estopped from denying title. This would not include a situation where the applicant is on the land with the permission of the owner, since such occupation could not amount to adverse possession (see Section 3.4.3), but it could arise where a person has developed land thinking it belonged to her, and the paper owner, aware of the true position, has allowed this to happen. It could also happen where a buyer of land has paid the purchase price but there has been no valid contract and thus no transfer of the equitable title.

(ii)   The adverse possessor is entitled to be registered as the owner for some reason other than her adverse possession of the land. This might arise, for example, where the possessor is entitle to a conveyance of the land under the terms of a will, perhaps, or because, despite having purchased and paid for the land, the registered title has not yet been transferred to her (see Section 2.6.2). In the latter case, the possessor would, of course, also be entitled to specific performance of the contract.

(iii) The disputed land is next to land already owned by the adverse possessor, the boundary between the two plots is unclear and she has occupied the land for ten years, thinking it belonged to her.

If the squatter's application is rejected and none of the conditions in para. 5 applies, she may make a further application to have title to the land transferred into her name if she has not been thrown off the land after a period of two years from the date of the original rejection (unless possession proceedings are in the process of being taken against her, or unless judgment has already been given against her (para. 6)). Following this second application, she is entitled to be registered as the new proprietor with the same class of title as that of the paper owner she has dispossessed (see Section 11.5.1).

These reforms in registered land mean that the paper owner cannot automatically lose her right to evict a trespasser after 12 years' adverse possession, as formerly, but will be warned by the Registry that a squatter is attempting to gain title to her land. However, if she does nothing to regain possession of the land, she will lose it. Other differences between the two schemes include:

- Neither written acknowledgement of title nor concealment or fraud by the squatter have any specific consequences under Schedule 6 (compare ss.29–31 and 32 of the Limitation Act 1980; see Section 3.3.1.4). In many cases, however, such factors will be sufficient to demonstrate that the squatter did not meet the requirements for being in adverse possession (see Section 3.4.2). They are only likely to be relevant if the registered proprietor fails to object in time to the squatter's application to be registered as proprietor of the land.
- Paragraph 11 of Schedule 6 limits the circumstances in which a occupation by a previous squatter can count towards the ten year period to:
  - where the applicant is the successor in title of the first squatter, having bought the land from her or having inherited it, and then moved into possession; and
  - where the applicant was the original squatter, was dispossessed by another squatter but then was able to regain possession.

3.4 What is the Nature of Adverse Possession?

The most difficult issues in this area of law arise when the courts have to consider what the squatter must do if she is to show that she actually was in adverse possession of another person's land. In *JA Pye (Oxford) Ltd* v. *Graham* [2003] 1 AC 419, the House of Lords reviewed the law of adverse possession, and identified two fundamental elements.

The requirements of adverse possession:

- The possession must be real (or 'factual') – the squatter must act as owner, showing an 'appropriate degree of physical control'.
- The trespasser must have an intention to possess the land (*animus possidendi*).

3.4.1   Factual Possession

The case of *Buckinghamshire CC* v. *Moran* [1990] Ch 623, illustrates the sort of behaviour required from the trespasser if she is to be able successfully to claim adverse possession. From 1971, Moran had used as an extension to his garden a patch of land owned by the council which they intended to use for a future bypass; his predecessor had probably done the same since 1967. Moran built a new fence, enclosing the land, and added a new gate and a lock. The council finally noticed him in 1985 and sued for possession. In its analysis of the sort of acts required to constitute factual possession, the Court of Appeal quoted with approval from the first instance judgment by Slade J in *Powell* v. *McFarlane* (1979) 38 P & CR 452:

> Factual possession signifies an appropriate degree of physical control ... The question of what acts constitute a sufficient degree of exclusive physical control must depend on the circumstances, in particular the nature of the land and the manner in which land of that nature is commonly used or enjoyed (at p. 470).

Physical control can be shown if the squatter encloses the land or improves it in some way, but trivial acts performed on the land will generally be insufficient to establish factual possession. In *Pye*, Mr Graham was a farmer who had occupied some 25 hectares of Pye's land under a grazing licence. Pye refused to renew the licence because it wanted vacant possession of the land in order to get planning permission to develop it. The Grahams continued to occupy the land, keeping animals on it all year round, maintaining and improving it, and excluding everyone from it. An occupying owner could not have done more, and the House of Lords found that Mr Graham had clearly been in factual possession of the land.

What acts are required to show 'an appropriate degree of physical control' of residential property such as a house or flat? In *Lambeth LBC* v. *Copercini*, unreported, 1 March 2000, a housing co-operative had squatted in a council-owned property for many years. The judge found clear evidence of factual possession, since the co-operative had decided who should live there, had arranged lettings, funded repairs and maintenance and 'without doubt ... treated the property as their own'. In *Ofulue* v. *Bossert* [2008] 3 WLR 1253 Bossert and his daughter were let into a flat by a former tenant in 1981 and took up residence. At that time the flat was in so bad a state of repair that the local authority had condemned it as uninhabitable. Bossert spent a considerable amount of time and money repairing the flat and by 1989 estimated its value to be between £150,000 and £200,000. Unsurprisingly, the Court of Appeal found that Bossert's acts were sufficient to amount to factual possession.

3.4.2   The Intention to Possess (*animus possidendi*)

Exactly what constitutes the necessary intention to possess the land has been a contentious issue until recently. It might be thought that a trespasser must show that she intends to become the owner of the land, but, although this may have been the case in the past, it clearly no longer is. The leading case is now *JA Pye (Oxford) Ltd* v. *Graham* [2003] 1 AC 419, in which Lord Browne-Wilkinson expressly approved the attempts of two earlier judges to explain *animus possidendi*. At first instance in *Buckinghamshire CC* v. *Moran* (1988) 56 P & CR 372, Hoffman J had observed that what is required is:

> not an intention to own or even an intention to acquire ownership but an intention to possess (Hoffmann J, at p. 378),

and in *Powell* v. *McFarlane* (1979) 38 P & CR 452, Slade J explained:

> *animus possidendi* involves the intention, in one's own name and on one's own behalf, to exclude the world at large, including the owner with the paper title ... so far as is reasonably practicable and so far as the process of the law will allow (at pp. 471–472).

It is rare that the court will have direct evidence of an intention to possess the land and exclude the world, but the intention can be inferred from the acts of the trespasser, such as the enclosure of the land by the squatter in *Moran*, or through otherwise controlling access. Lord Browne-Wilkinson, who gave the leading speech in *Pye*, stated that 'intention may be, and frequently is, deduced from the physical acts themselves' (para. 40).

Depending on the facts, a person may be deemed to have sufficient intention to possess the land even if she were prepared to accept a licence or a lease from the paper owner, so her claim to adverse possession could still succeed if the licence was not in the end forthcoming. In *Pye*, Mr Graham had admitted that he would have accepted a licence from the paper owners if one had been offered. This was an admission that Lord Diplock thought 'any candid squatter hoping in due course to acquire a possessory title would be almost bound to make' (*Ocean Estates Ltd* v. *Pinder* [1969] 2 AC 17, at p. 24) and did not prevent him from being in possession.

There is a clear difference, though, between a squatter's willingness to recognise the title of the paper owner if asked to do so, and the squatter's written acknowledgment of that title, perhaps through asking for a lease or a licence, or in court pleadings (see *Ofulue* v. *Bossert* [2008] 3 WLR 1253). Such an acknowledgment of title is enough to stop time running in the squatter's favour under ss.29–31 of the Limitation Act 1980. In cases decided under the LRA 2002 it will be a question of whether the acknowledgement precludes *animus possidendi* on the part of the squatter

Must the Possession be Adverse to the Paper Owner?

Possession clearly cannot be adverse if it is enjoyed with the paper owner's permission. In the words of Romer LJ,

> if one looks to the position of the occupier and finds that his occupation, his right to occupation, is derived from the owner in the form of permission or agreement or grant, it is not adverse... (*Moses* v. *Lovegrove* [1952] 2 Q.B. 533, at 544).

However, a difficulty has arisen in cases where the paper owner intends to use the land in the future for some particular purpose, but has no present use for it. The uncertainty can be traced back to the judgment of Bramwell LJ in *Leigh* v. *Jack* (1879-80) 5 Ex D 264, where he said:

> in order to defeat a title by dispossessing the former owner, acts must be done which are inconsistent with his enjoyment of the soil for the purposes for which he intended to use it (at p. 273).

Subsequently, the courts developed the doctrine of the implied licence to show that the possession is not adverse. In *Wallis's Cayton Holiday Camp Ltd* v. *Shell-Mex and BP Ltd* [1975] QB 94, a petrol company bought a garage by a proposed new road with the intention of extending the garage if the new road were to be built. Wallis's farmed this land and then used it to enlarge their holiday camp business. Their use of the land totalled just over the necessary 12 years and they claimed adverse possession of it. They lost by a majority decision in the Court of Appeal. Lord Denning stated:

> When the true owner of land intends to use it for a particular purpose in the future, but has no immediate use for it, and so leaves it unoccupied, he does not lose his title to it simply because some other person enters on it and uses it for some temporary purpose ... his user is to be ascribed to the licence or permission of the true owner (at p. 103)

This heresy, had it been allowed to stand, could have spelled the end of adverse possession in cases where the paper owner had in mind a future use for the land, or at least severely limited its effect. The doctrine of the implied licence was expressly abolished by Limitation Act 1980, Schedule 1, para. 8(4). In *JA Pye (Oxford) Ltd* v. *Graham* [2003] 1 AC 419, Lord Brown-Wilkinson made it clear that the 'heresy' had not survived the 1980 Act.

> The suggestion that the sufficiency of the possession can depend on the intention not of the squatter but of the true owner is heretical and wrong. ... The highest it can be put is that, if the squatter is aware of a special purpose for which the paper owner uses or intends to use the land and the use made by the squatter does not conflict with that use, that may provide some support for a finding as a question of fact that the squatter had no intention to possess the land in the ordinary sense but only an intention to occupy it until needed by the paper owner ... (at para. 45).

The spectre of the *Leigh* v. *Jack* heresy briefly returned in *Beaulane Properties Ltd* v. *Palmer* [2006] Ch 79, when Nicholas Strauss QC held that the only way in which the law of adverse possession (under s. 75 of the LRA 1925) could be consistent with the European Convention on Human Rights was to require the squatter's use of the land to be inconsistent with the use of the paper owner. This judgment was rejected by the Court of Appeal in *Ofulue* v. *Bossert* [2008] 3 WLR 1253 as inconsistent with the subsequent decision of the European Court of Human Rights in *JA Pye (Oxford) Ltd* v. *UK* (2008) 46 EHRR 45.

An interesting question arises if the paper owner writes to the squatter, granting her a licence to use the land. On the face of it, since the squatter now occupies the land with permission, the possession can no longer be adverse. Indeed, in *BP Properties* v. *Buckler* (1987) 55 P & CR 337, a case which has been subject to some criticism (see Wallace [1994] Conv 196), the paper owner wrote to the squatter, giving her permission to remain on the land for the rest of her life. The result was that:

> So far as Mrs. Buckler was concerned, even though she did not 'accept' the terms of the letters, B.P. Properties Ltd. would, in the absence of any repudiation by her of the two letters, have been bound to treat her as in possession as licensee on the terms of the letters (per Dillon LJ, at p.346).

Although the squatter did not respond to the letter (indeed, probably because she failed to respond), the paper owner was deemed to have ended the adverse possession.

3.5 Leases and Adverse Possession

The rules about leases and adverse possession can be complex and, again, the results may differ depending on whether title to the land is registered or unregistered.

If a squatter takes possession of land subject to a lease, the possession is adverse to the tenant; that is, it is the tenant who is liable to lose her interest in the land, not the lessor. This is because it is the tenant who is entitled to possession; the lessor is entitled only to the rent. The lessor has no right to possession until the lease ends, and it is also at that time that the squatter's period of adverse possession against the lessor begins.

An interesting situation arises if the tenant (of an unregistered 99-year lease, let us say), against whom a squatter has been in adverse possession for 12 years and who therefore could now look forward to many more years of possession, surrenders her lease to her lessor (see Section 5.5: surrender requires the agreement of the lessor to accept the early termination of the lease). There is little point in the tenant continuing with the lease, since she now has no cause of action against the squatter. Rather surprisingly, perhaps, following the tenant's surrender of the lease, the lessor can bring an action for possession against the squatter (*Fairweather* v. *St Marylebone Property Co Ltd* [1963] AC 510). Having evicted the squatter, there is then nothing to prevent the lessor from granting a new lease to her former tenant.

Under the old rules for registered land, the position was different. In *Central London Commercial Estates Ltd* v. *Kato Kagku Ltd* [1998] 4 All ER 948, a squatter had adversely possessed registered land against the tenant for more than 12 years, but had not made an application under s.75(2) LRA 1925 to be registered as proprietor (Section 3.3.2) when the tenant surrendered the lease to the landlord. Applying s.75(1) LRA 1925, Sedley J held that the tenant was trustee for the squatter, who was now entitled to remain on the land for the remaining term of the lease. This decision effectively prevented a tenant of registered land from surrendering her lease once the 12 year period of adverse possession had been completed.

It is unlikely that this situation will arise under the new rules contained in Schedule 6 of the LRA 2002, as adverse possession now gives rise to a right to apply to become the registered proprietor of the estate, rather than to a trust. The tenant will have no need to surrender the lease to the landlord, since either she will object to the squatter's application and subsequently gain possession, or the squatter will succeed in her application, with the result that the squatter's name will be registered at the Land Registry with the title of the former tenant (Section 3.3.2). This means that she will now be subject to the covenants in the lease and failure to comply with them may result in forfeiture of the lease by the lessor (see Section 6.5).

3.6 Adverse Possession and Human Rights

In *JA Pye (Oxford) Ltd* v. *Graham* [2003] 1 AC 419 the Court of Appeal was asked whether the use of the Limitation Act to deny a landowner the right to bring an action to recover her land amounted to a breach of Article 1, Protocol 1 of the European Convention on Human Rights (depriving a person of her property without compensation). Although the action was between private individuals, the deprivation of the property resulted from statutory authority (s. 75 LRA 1925), thus allowing the Convention to be invoked. By the time the case had reached the House of Lords, it had become clear that the Human Rights Act had no retrospective effect and so did not apply in *Pye*. However, Pye was able to refer the matter to the European Court of Human Rights at Strasbourg. The period between the decisions of the House of Lords and the Court of Human Rights provides the context for the first instance judgment in *Beaulane Properties Ltd* v. *Palmer* [2006] Ch 79 (see Sections 3.3.1.4 and 3.4.3). Like *Pye* this case concerned s. 75 LRA 1925, but unlike *Pye* the Human Rights Act 1998 applied. The judge held that s. 75 LRA 1925 could only be interpreted as being consistent with the Human Rights Act 1998 if the doctrine of adverse possession was limited to those cases where the squatter's use was inconsistent with the paper owner's purpose for the land and that, for that reason, the House of Lord's decision in *Pye* was not binding on him.

The Grand Chamber of the European Court of Human Rights finally settled the *Pye* case in 2007 (see *JA Pye (Oxford) Ltd* v. *UK* (2008) 46 EHRR 45). A majority of the court concluded that the pre-LRA 2002 law of adverse possession was compatible with the principles of the European Convention on Human Rights, since:

- it was already accepted that periods of limitation were compatible with the Convention;
- the period required in this case was not excessively short;
- the paper owner should have been aware of the limitation period; and
- relatively limited action was required by the paper owner to stop the period from running.

The decision in *Pye* v. *UK* means that s. 75 LRA 1925 is generally compliant with the convention and that compliance does not need to be determined on a case by case basis: *Ofulue* v. *Bossert* [2008] 3 WLR 1253, applying *Harrow LBC* v. *Qazi* [2004] 1 AC 983. It also means that the decision in *Beaulane Properties Ltd* is wrong.

There is little doubt that the provisions in the LRA 2002, Schedule 6, are compliant with the Human Rights Act: indeed, this was expressly recognised by the dissenting minority of the Grand Chamber in *Pye* v. *UK*.

3.7 Comment

The traditional justifications for retaining adverse possession in a private system of unregistered title to land remain as convincing as ever. In unregistered land, titles to land are relative and an English court will assist the party with the better claim to possession. However, in a public system of registered land, where most titles are absolute and guaranteed by the state, some of the traditional justifications are not so persuasive. The law on adverse possession in cases where title to the land is already registered is intended to allow adverse possession of registered land only in order to ensure that the land remains marketable and in order to prevent injustice.

It is evident that the LRA 2002 scheme in registered land will make it much more difficult for a squatter to gain title to the land and, as a result, may well also provide an incentive for the owners of unregistered titles to apply for voluntary registration in order to protect themselves from being dispossessed by a squatter of whose presence they may be unaware. Despite the high number of important cases during the first decade of the twenty-first century, not least those that explore the interface between land law and human rights, it seems likely that the doctrine of adverse possession will become less and less significant as rules of the LRA 2002 become increasing dominant.

Summary

3.1 In *unregistered* land:
    (a) adverse possession allows a weak title to be cured as time passes and prevents ancient claims being revived; and
    (b) twelve years' unconcealed adverse possession, without interruptions, prevents the paper owner repossessing the land.

3.3 In *registered* land, the registered proprietor is given warning of the threat to her land and has two years to evict the squatter.

3.4 The squatter's possession must be real, with intent, and without the permission of the paper owner.

Exercises

3.1 What can a landowner do to prevent a squatter acquiring title by adverse possession?

3.2 In unregistered land, when does the trespasser become the owner of the land?

3.3 How easy is it for a registered proprietor to lose her land to a trespasser?

3.4 What intention is required by an adverse possessor?

3.5 In what ways is the nature of the piece of land relevant to an adverse possession dispute?

3.6 When may an apparently successful adverse possessor lose the land?

@ 3.7 Olwen owns a 300 year lease in Animal Farm, the freehold owner of which is a pension company called Trusties. Neither the leasehold nor the freehold titles are registered. At one corner of the farm lies a small triangle of woodland of about one-third of an acre. Here Kate, an eccentric old woman, lives in a barrel with her tame goat, Peter, who finds his food in the wood. She moved into the barrel when Gordon Brown became Prime Minister, just after the death of her friend Mumtaz, who had lived in the barrel, so he had claimed, since well before 1970. Mumtaz had originally been a weekly tenant but had never paid rent after the first week.

Olwen has just been offered an excellent price for her lease, if she can deliver vacant possession. She wishes to sell but Kate refuses to leave. Olwen claims that, although she never gave permission for anyone to live there, she did not really mind as it was so far from the house. She had no particular use for the woodland, although, if she could have got a grant, she would have cut down the trees and erected battery hen units. Kate says that it is her woodland now and points out that her boundary was marked out by large boulders and electric cable (hung between the trees) by Mumtaz. She claims that Olwen has not been allowed in the woodland for years and years.

In an action for possession, who will win? Who should win? Would your answers be different if Olwen's leasehold title were registered?

@ 3.8 An online quiz on the topics covered in this chapter is available on the companion website.

Further Reading

Davis, 'Informal Acquisition and Loss of Rights in Land: What Justifies the Doctrines?' (2000) 20 Legal Studies 198

Dixon, 'Human Rights and Adverse Possession – The Final Word' [2008] 72 Conv 160

Dockray, 'Why Do We Need Adverse Possession?' [1985] Conv 272

McCormick, 'Adverse Possession and Future Enjoyment' [1986] Conv 434

Tee, 'A Harsh Twilight' [2003] CLJ 36

Wallace, 'Limitation, Prescription and Unsolicited Permission' [1994] Conv 196

Part II

The Estates and Interests

Chapter 4

Freehold Land

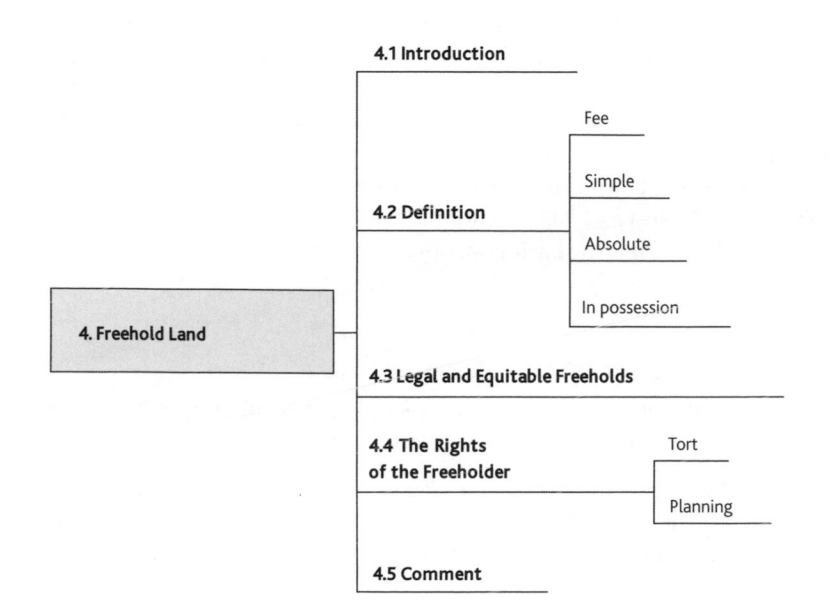

4.1 Introduction

In English land law, the predominant method of owning land is to hold the 'freehold estate'. At this point, the ancient historical roots of modern English land law show through the ground: the origins of freehold land can take lawyers straight back to the conquest of England by William of Normandy in 1066. In theory, all the land in England and Wales is still owned by the Crown, with individuals holding interests in the Queen's land.

There used to be many different legal estates, with different rules about inheritance and transfer, but only two of these remain: *freehold* is a holding for an indefinite period (providing there is someone able to inherit the land under a will or through the rules of intestacy on the freeholder's death) and *leasehold* is a holding for a fixed time. Because of the reforms of 1925, the legal freehold estate is the basic concept of landownership in both registered and unregistered land.

4.2 Definition of the Freehold Estate

The fee simple is the only surviving legal freehold estate; its proper name is *fee simple absolute in possession*. Each of these words has a particular significance.

- *Fee*: This word comes from 'fief' (*feudum* in Latin), the basic concept of the feudal system. By the sixteenth century a fee had come to be recognised as an estate which could be inherited because it did not automatically return to the feudal landlord when the tenant died.
- *Fee simple*: The fee is 'simple' because it does not suffer from the complications of the other fee, the fee tail or 'entail', which has to go to a particular kind of heir when the owner dies. The fee simple can be inherited by anyone the owner wishes, but the fee tail has to pass to a direct descendant (child, grandchild and so on), and it could be restricted to, for example, a male child (a 'tail male'). In modern times, the use of the fee tail has fallen into obsolescence and it has not been possible to create new entails since 1997 (Trusts of Land and Appointment of Trustees Act 1996, Schedule 1, para. 5). Entails created before 1997 remain valid.
- *Fee simple absolute*: The word 'absolute' is used to distinguish this fee simple from others which are limited in some way. For instance, there is a 'fee simple upon condition'; an example is where a mother gives land to her son *but if* he marries a solicitor, the land will go to his cousin. This must be distinguished from the 'determinable fee simple', which is created by words such as '*until* he marries a solicitor': a very subtle difference. It is important because, although in 1925 only the fee simple absolute could be a legal estate (s.1(1) LPA 1925; see Section 1.5.1), a special exception was made in 1926 for conditional fees simple (s.7(1) LPA 1925, as amended): these can now be legal, but the other limited fees simple (including determinable fees) must be equitable.
- *Fee simple absolute in possession*: All interests in land can be 'in possession', 'in remainder' or 'in reversion'. In possession means that the owner is entitled to enjoy the interest *now* (occupy the land or collect the rent and so on); the other two mean that the owner will have the right to enjoy the interest after another interest (for example an interest for life) has ended. In the example above, therefore, the son has a conditional fee simple in possession, and the cousin has a fee simple absolute in *remainder*. However, if the mother gives land to her son on the condition that it will return to her if he marries a solicitor, the mother would have a fee simple absolute in *reversion*.

4.3 Legal and Equitable Freeholds

Out of all the possibilities raised in the sections above, only the fee simple absolute in possession can be a legal estate (subject to the exception for conditional fees), because of s.1 LPA 1925 (see Section 1.5). The fee tail, therefore, can only be equitable, held behind a trust.

4.4 The Rights of the Freeholder

In theory, at common law the owner can do whatever he likes with his land. In 1885, Challis wrote that ownership of the fee simple 'confers ... the lawful right to exercise over, upon, and in respect of the land, every act of ownership which can enter into the imagination' (see Challis H. W., *The Law of Real Property, Chiefly in Relation to Conveyancing* (3rd edn by C. Sweet; London: Butterworth & Co., 1911), page 218).

However, even then this was not true because, for example, the law of tort could be used to prevent a landowner unreasonably interfering with this neighbour's enjoyment of his land (the doctrine of nuisance). Today, legislation has imposed great limitations on the owner of land, so that, for instance, he cannot prevent aeroplanes from flying above his land, may not mine coal, demolish a listed building, kill protected species or pollute water; he must also observe building regulations and licensing laws.

The Town and Country Planning Acts impose probably the best known limitation on landowners. When the first was passed, in 1947, it was suggested by some that the fee simple had been destroyed by the powers taken by the government to control land use. Few people would say so now, since most landowners appreciate the fact that the value of their land is maintained for them by the local authority, which can forbid or permit their neighbours to open an amusement arcade or a garage, for example.

4.5 Comment

This chapter has given a glimpse of the ancient law hidden within the modern rules; even the basic concept of today's law, the fee simple, can only be explained by reference to events which took place nearly 1,000 years ago. However, although we may use the same words as lawyers in the eleventh or fifteenth centuries, the meaning and context are quite different: our forebears might recognise the terms but they would not understand our law.

Part of the fascination of the history of land law is the tracing of threads which link us to very different worlds. Many people find the history interesting for its own sake, but the methods of historians can also be used to illuminate our own world. Historians explain changes in land law by reference to the political, economic and social events of the time. Modern cases and statutes, which appear as merely technical rules, should be viewed in the same light (see for example Anderson [1984] CLP 63).

Summary

4.1 The basic unit of ownership in modern land law is the legal fee simple absolute in possession which originates in the feudal system imposed after 1066.

4.2 'Fee simple absolute in possession' means an interest in land which can be inherited by anyone, is not restricted by some future event and which is enjoyed at the moment.

4.3 Although it has been asserted that the owner in fee simple absolute in possession has unlimited powers over his land, both common law and statute have greatly restricted his freedom of action.

Exercises

4.1 Does the history of land law matter?

4.2 Which is more important, planning law or the doctrine of estates?

4.3 What is special about a fee simple upon condition?

4.4 What is an entail? Can it be legal?

@ **4.5** An online quiz on the topics covered in this chapter is available on the companion website.

Further Reading

Anderson, 'Land Law Texts and the Explanation of 1925' [1984] CLP 63
Simpson, *History of the Land Law* (Oxford: Clarendon Press, 1986)

The Leasehold Estate

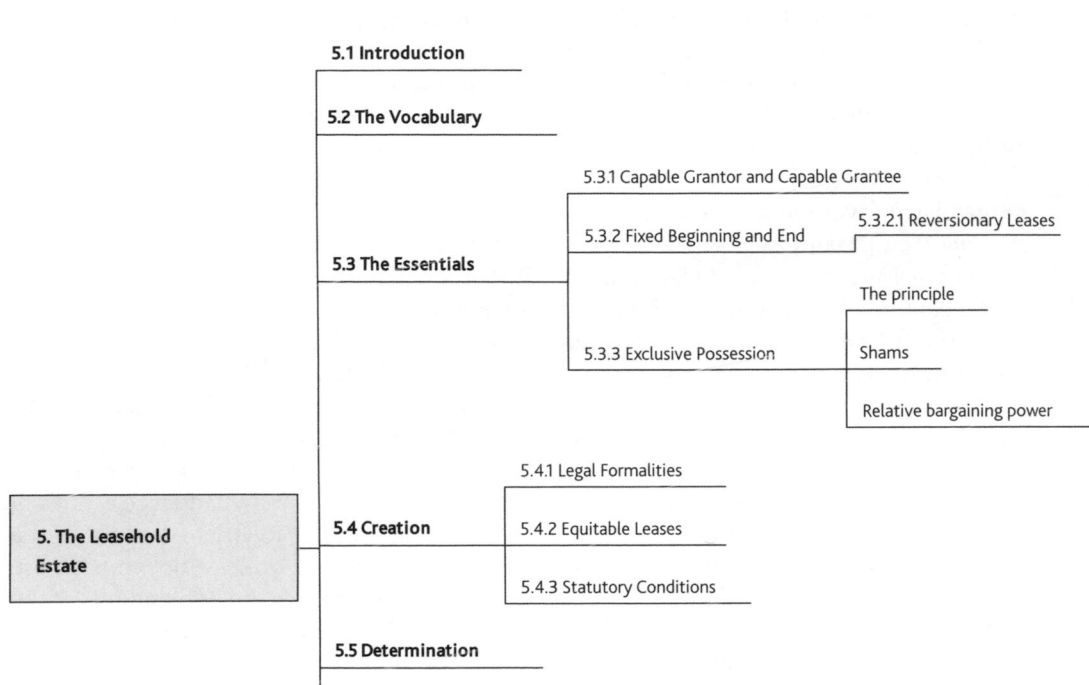

5.1 Introduction

5.2 The Vocabulary

5.3 The Essentials
- 5.3.1 Capable Grantor and Capable Grantee
- 5.3.2 Fixed Beginning and End
  - 5.3.2.1 Reversionary Leases
- 5.3.3 Exclusive Possession
  - The principle
  - Shams
  - Relative bargaining power

5. The Leasehold Estate

5.4 Creation
- 5.4.1 Legal Formalities
- 5.4.2 Equitable Leases
- 5.4.3 Statutory Conditions

5.5 Determination

5.6 Some Odd Kinds of Lease
- 5.6.1 Leases for life
- 5.6.2 Tenancy at will
- 5.6.3 Tenancy at sufferance
- 5.6.4 Lease of the reversion
- 5.6.5 Tenancy by estoppel

5.7 Comment

5.1 Introduction

By s.1 LPA 1925 (see Section 1.5), the freehold (the fee simple absolute in possession) and leasehold are the only estates in land which can be legal. A lease was originally a contract for the occupation of land, and it was only in the sixteenth century that leases were recognised as interests in land, so that the rights and duties of the parties were no longer merely contractual, but became attached to the land. However, much of the law of leases is still based on contract law, albeit with overarching statutory provisions controlling residential, business and agricultural tenancies. At times the courts have tended to emphasise the proprietary nature of leases (as in *Street* v. *Mountford* [1985] AC 809; see Section 5.3.3). More recently, judges have favoured a more contractual approach (as in *Bruton* v. *London and Quadrant Housing Trust* [2000] 1 AC 406 (see Section 5.3.1) and *National Car Parks Ltd* v. *The Trinity Development Company (Banbury) Ltd* [2002] 2 P & CR 18 (see Section 5.3.3).

The commercial advantages of the lease are obvious. A landowner can let other people use her land for a certain period of time – to farm, mine for gravel, or live there – in exchange for a regular income. She can make rules about the kinds of things that are – or are not – to be done on the land and, at the end of the period, she will get the land back. The wealth of the powerful land-owning families came, to a large extent, from rental income. Great cities like London were developed in the eighteenth and nineteenth centuries through building leases. The ancestors of the Duke of Westminster owned large estates in London and granted long leases to speculative builders, subject to strict rules about the density and type of housing. The builders made their profit, the Dukes enjoyed the rent, and at the end of the period the valuable housing estates reverted to the descendants of the first Duke. Thus London and other cities grew through the carefully planned, high quality developments of far-sighted landowners – and also, of course, through get-rich-quick rented slums.

Today, leasehold arrangements are still very important. In financial terms, the most significant use of leases is in the business world, for office blocks and factory units, for example. In addition, most flats are bought on long (often 99-year) leases. One of the problems with long leases is that they are a diminishing asset, so Parliament has intervened – not particularly successfully so far – to allow the owners of long residential leases either to extend the period of their leases or to buy the freehold (the Leasehold Reform Act 1967). The introduction of the commonhold scheme designed to avoid some of the difficulties associated with leases is considered in Section 6.6.

There are also many other tenants, those who are unable to or do not wish to climb on to the so-called 'property ladder', with much shorter leases. Short leases for housing have been greatly affected by Acts of Parliament since 1915 because of the social and economic importance of decent housing for the community as a whole. Statutes on rent control, security and repairs were intended to protect poor tenants with little bargaining power against more powerful lessors. However, much of this protection, latterly found in the Rent Act 1977, has been removed in recent years (especially by the Housing Act 1988) in order to provide realistic commercial opportunities for those willing to let land for residential use. These changes, together with a healthy economy, helped stimulate the so-called 'buy-to-let' market, with lenders eager to provide mortgages to support it, in the early twenty-first century. The detail of this area of the law is usually outside the scope of land law courses and is referred to only occasionally in this chapter.

5.2 The Vocabulary of Leases

There are several words to describe a lease, including tenancy, letting, demise and term of years absolute (see Section 5.3). All these words have the same meaning, but lawyers tend to use 'tenancy' and 'letting' for a short period and 'lease' or 'demise' for a long one.

The following story is typical of leases: Louise let the basement flat in her house to Teresa, for three years at £500 per month. Teresa decided to live elsewhere and sold ('assigned') her lease to Ahmed, who then rented the flat to Sam for six months. Then Louise decided to move, and sold her whole house (including the freehold, the 'reversion', of the flat) to Robert.

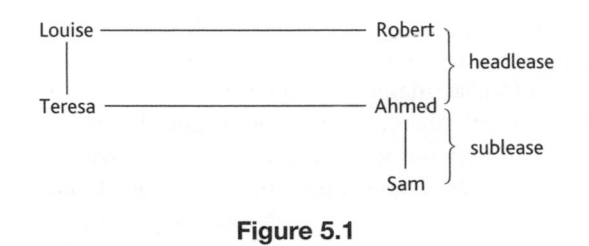

Figure 5.1

This story could be continued indefinitely, but thus far it illustrates the possibilities of leases, and is shown diagrammatically in Figure 5.1. These diagrams are very useful for sorting out the characters in a problem on leases. In this book leases (including subleases) are always shown as vertical lines and assignments as horizontal lines. Louise owned the freehold; she is the original lessor (landlord, owner of the freehold, owner of the leasehold reversion). Robert is the new lessor (assignee of the reversion). Teresa is the original tenant (lessee, owner of the lease). Ahmed is the current tenant (lessee, owner of the headlease, tenant's assignee, assignee of the headlease). He is also the lessor in the middle, the *mesne* (pronounced 'mean') landlord. Sam is the subtenant (sublessee, owner of the sublease).

The difference between an assignment and a sublease is important. Teresa assigned her lease when she sold the whole of her remaining interest to Ahmed (shown by a horizontal line in Figure 5.1). Ahmed created a sublease when he sold Sam a lesser period than he himself owned (shown by a vertical line in the diagram). Setting out the chain of events in a diagram, even in a fairly simple case or problem question, can help avoid confusing such events.

5.3 The Essentials of a Lease

It will often be of significant importance to the parties whether the relationship between them is a lease or mere contract (or licence) to use the land. Normally, only a lease will be attached to the land so as to automatically bind any third party who acquires the freehold reversion. A lease will often give the occupier of the land greater rights (many of them under statute) than those enjoyed by a mere licensee. Licences are considered in more detail in Chapter 14.

The full title of a lease (leasehold estate) in the 1925 legislation is a *'term of years absolute'*. This phrase is defined at great length in s.205(1)(xxvii) LPA 1925, but most of the rules about what does and does not constitute a lease are to be found in the case law. Essentially:

A term of years absolute requires:

- A capable grantor and a capable grantee (see Section 5.3.1),
- a fixed beginning and a fixed end (see Section 5.3.2), and
- *exclusive possession* to be given to the tenant (see Section 5.3.3).

Although it is usual for a rent and/or a premium (a premium is an upfront capital payment to the lessor) to be paid by the tenant, there is no requirement for consideration if the lease is created by a deed. Section 205(1)(xxvii) LPA 1925 defines a term of years absolute as existing 'whether or not at a rent' (see also, *Ashburn Anstalt* v. *WJ Arnold & Co* [1989] Ch. 1).

5.3.1 Capable Grantor and Capable Grantee

The requirement for a capable grantor and capable grantee is not usually a problem. A minor (person under the age of 18) may not hold a legal estate in land (s.1(6) LPA 1925). The law also restricts the rights of those unable to deal with their own affairs because of mental illness or deterioration to create or transfer legal estates in land. The power of corporate bodies to grant and accept leases will depend upon whether they are given the necessary powers by their memorandum and articles of association (in the case of a limited company) or by statute (in the case of local authorities, and government created agencies).

Prior to the case of *Bruton* v. *London and Quadrant Housing Trust* [2000] 1 AC 406, it was generally thought that a lessor could only grant a lease if that lease was capable of existing as a legal estate. This required the lessor to own an estate in the land greater than the lease being granted (based on the principle of *nemo dat quod non habet* – no-one can give something which they do not have). However, in *Bruton*, the House of Lord's held that it was possible to create a purely contractual (or 'non-estate') lease. As Blackburne J (sitting in the Court of Appeal) explained in the case of *Islington LBC* v. *Green* [2005] EWCA Civ 56:

> The relationship of landlord and tenant is not dependent on whether the lease or tenancy creates an estate or other proprietary interest which may be binding on third parties. Whether a lease creates a proprietary interest in turn will depend upon whether the landlord has an interest out of which he has granted it (at para. 10).

In *Bruton*, the Lambeth Borough Council had entered into an agreement with the Trust allowing them to use a block of flats that was due to be redeveloped to provide temporary housing accommodation. It was agreed that this agreement did not give the Trust any legal estate in the land. The Trust allowed Mr Bruton to occupy one of the flats on a weekly 'licence'. The flats were in a relatively poor state of repair, and Mr Bruton brought an action against the Trust to enforce the covenants for repair implied into residential tenancies by s.11 Landlord and Tenant Act 1985. As s.11 only applies to leases, the House of Lords had to determine whether or not the agreement with Mr Bruton was a tenancy or a contractual licence. Having decided that the agreement satisfied all of the other requirements for a lease (the main issue was whether exclusive possession had been granted – see Section 5.3.3), the House of Lords concluded that there was a tenancy, even though Mr Bruton held no legal estate in the land. Whilst non-estate tenancies like Mr Bruton's may have significant implications for the original parties, their impact on third parties is much more limited since they do not constitute proprietary interests (see *Kay* v. *Lambeth LBC* [2006] AC 465 considered in Section 5.6.5).

5.3.2 A Fixed Beginning and a Fixed End

The period of a lease (its term) can be anything from a few hours to thousands of years. It must, however, be certain. The beginning and the end of the term must be ascertainable at the outset (but the lease may end ('determine') earlier; see Section 5.5). Many leases will state a fixed beginning and a fixed end, but even where this is not the case the facts may be fitted into the definition of a 'term of years absolute'. As Lord Greene explained in *Lace* v. *Chantler* [1944] KB 368,

> A term created by a leasehold tenancy agreement must be expressed either with certainty and specifically or by reference to something which can, at the time when the lease takes effect, be looked at as a certain ascertainment of what the term was meant to be. In the present case, when this tenancy agreement took effect the term was completely uncertain (at pp. 370–371).

In *Prudential Assurance Co Ltd* v. *London Residuary Body* [1992] AC 386 a London council in 1930 let some land until it was 'required by the council for the purposes of the widening of Walworth Road and the street paving works rendered necessary thereby'. Confirming previous authorities, including *Lace* v. *Chantler* [1944] KB 368, the House of Lords held that there was insufficient certainty about the date of the end of the lease and therefore it could not be a valid term of years absolute. However, they agreed instead that this was a lease 'from year to year' (a periodic legal tenancy: see Section 5.3.2.1) which the council's successor in title could end by giving six months' notice (as is usual under a yearly tenancy).

This rule on the need for there to be certainty in the duration of a lease may be due for some reconsideration: indeed, the Court of Appeal had departed from it in a number of cases prior to the decision in *Prudential Assurance Co Ltd* v. *London Residuary Body* [1992] AC 386. Although these cases were overruled by the House of Lords in that case, not all of their Lordships were satisfied with the result. Lord Browne-Wilkinson said:

> This bizarre outcome results from the application of an ancient and technical rule of law which requires the maximum duration of a term of years to be ascertainable from the outset. No one has produced any satisfactory rationale for the genesis of this rule. No one has been able to point to any useful purpose that it serves at the present day (at p. 395).

However, the House of Lord's was not prepared to alter the law, and no statutory change has yet been proposed.

5.3.2.1 Reversionary Leases and Periodic Tenancies

Within the definition of a lease as providing a fixed period and exclusive possession, there is a great range of types of leases. The start can be set for a date in the future, but it must start within 21 years of the date of the document creating it (s.149(3) LPA 1925); this is called a reversionary lease.

A lease for a specific period, such as a week, which can be continually repeated until one side gives notice, is called a periodic tenancy. A weekly or monthly period is common for furnished accommodation and a yearly period for agricultural tenancies. If a person uses land and regularly pays money to the owner, then – providing the tenant has exclusive possession (see Section 5.3.3) – the common law implies a periodic tenancy unless the parties intended something else. The period of the tenancy is decided by the period by which rent is assessed, not necessarily by the period of payment (*Richardson* v. *Langridge* (1811) 128 ER 277 at 278). Thus, if the rent is '£1000 per year, payable monthly', there is an implied legal yearly tenancy. For a more detailed consideration of periodic tenancies, see Cheshire, 2006, pp. 214–217.

The perpetually renewable lease differs from the periodic tenancy because the lease continues as long as the tenant chooses, with the lessor unable to give notice. This kind of arrangement was formerly common in agricultural lettings with absentee lessors, but is anomalous within the 1925 structure of landownership. Since 1925 all new leases of this type are automatically converted into a lease for 2,000 years, with special rules for giving notice. The courts now lean against interpreting a renewal clause as being perpetual (see, for example, *Marjorie Burnett Ltd* v. *Barclay* (1980) 258 EG 642, where Nourse J held that a right to renew with a further right of renewal gave the tenant the right to renew twice, rather than perpetually).

5.3.3   Exclusive Possession

Normally, if a person occupying another's land does not have exclusive possession (the right to keep the owner out), she is not a tenant under a lease but only a lodger, or a licensee. The word 'licensee' describes anyone who has a permission to be on land, such as readers in a library; these 'non-interests-in-land' are discussed in more detail in Chapter 14. A licence can be created by contract, with a regular payment of what looks like rent, and then it may closely resemble a lease. However, leases are interests in land, while licences are merely personal rights: they cannot usually be transferred and will probably not bind a buyer of the land.

  The difference between a lease and a licence is 'notoriously difficult' (Bridge [1986] Conv 344); there are hundreds of pages of judgments devoted to explaining the difference. Historically, the distinction was very important because many residential tenants had, through the Rent Act 1977 or its equivalent, statutory protection of their occupation and could claim a fair rent, while 'mere licensees' enjoyed neither of these statutory protections (but see also Section 14.4 for terms implied into licences). However, this difference is no longer of such importance. Lessors are unlikely now to try to create a licence rather than a lease, since, with effect from 15 January 1989, the Housing Act 1988 created the form of short-term residential tenancy known as the 'assured shorthold' tenancy, which allows lessors to receive a market rent and considerably limits a tenant's security. The case law nevertheless remains relevant to commercial agreements, to any occupation agreements made before that date and in cases where an occupier must hold a lease in order to gain the benefit of a statute (as, for example, in *Bruton* v. *London and Quadrant Housing Trust* [2000] 1 AC 406, above).

  The decision of the House of Lords in *Street* v. *Mountford* [1985] AC 809 was a milestone in the case law on the lease/licence distinction. Mr Street (a solicitor) let Mrs Mountford live in his house in return for a weekly payment. In a written agreement, headed 'Licence', she accepted rules about visitors and heating, and eviction if the 'licence fee' was more than a week late. Mr Street reserved the right to enter the house to inspect it. Such agreements had formerly been assumed to be licences, since this seemed, on paper, to be the clear intention of the parties. However, the House of Lords held that this was a weekly tenancy, thus allowing Mrs Mountford to claim the protection of the Rent Act.

  Lord Templeman was clear that an occupier of residential land must be either a tenant or a licensee, and that:

> A tenant armed with exclusive possession can keep out strangers and keep out the landlord (at p. 816).

The normal test of a tenancy is the factual question of 'exclusive possession' rather than the expressed intention of the parties:

> The occupier is a lodger [licensee] if the landlord provides attendance or services which require the landlord or his servants to exercise unrestricted access to and use of the premises ... If on the other hand residential accommodation is granted for a term at a rent with exclusive possession, the

landlord providing neither attendance nor services, the grant is a tenancy ... The manufacture of a five-pronged implement for digging results in a fork even if the manufacturer, unfamiliar with the English language, insists he intended to make, and has made, a spade (per Lord Templeman at pp. 817–18, 819).

The case was held to apply to all occupation agreements, including shops and agricultural land. It soon became clear, however, that multiple occupation, as is common in rented flats, posed different problems. In *A.G. Securities* v. *Vaughan*; *Antoniades* v. *Villiers* [1990] 1 AC 417 the House of Lords held, in the first of this pair of cases heard together, that a group of four people who shared a flat could not be tenants because they did not fulfil the requirements of a 'joint tenancy', the only way in which people can co-own a legal estate (see Section 12.5). They did not all arrive at the same time, so they did not share 'unity of title': they were merely licensees. In the second case, however, a 'Licence Agreement', which seemed to give the owner the right to sleep in the tiny flat with a cohabiting couple, was held to be a tenancy; the term looked as if it denied exclusive possession to the couple but it was held to be a sham, inserted into the agreement merely in order to avoid giving Rent Act protection to the occupants, and it therefore had no effect.

These cases, and the many subsequent decisions, cannot provide all the answers. Essentially, the question is whether the agreement itself gave exclusive possession to the tenant (or the tenants jointly) so that they had the right to keep the owner out. However, it is often impossible to decide what the agreement means or whether a term in it is a sham without looking at the facts of the whole case. Thus, the House of Lords decided in *Westminster CC* v. *Clarke* [1992] 2 AC 228 that a person given temporary accommodation by a local council did not have a tenancy but only a licence. Lord Templeman held that this was 'a very special case' (at p. 703), quite different from private lettings. He held that there was no exclusive possession here because of the purpose of this agreement: a term that the occupant could be moved at any time to another room was not a sham because the council needed it in order to fulfil its statutory duty to vulnerable people.

The decision in *Clarke* may be compared with *Bruton* v. *London and Quadrant Housing Trust* [2000] 1 AC 406 (see Section 5.3.1). Despite the very clear wording of the licence agreement (and the fact that the Trust did not hold a legal estate in the land), the House of Lords found that Mr Bruton had exclusive possession of his flat. He was, therefore, a tenant and not a mere licensee. Lord Hoffmann stated:

> There is nothing to suggest that he was to share possession with the trust, the council or anyone else. The trust did not retain such control over the premises as was inconsistent with Mr Bruton having exclusive possession, as was the case in *Westminster City Council* v. *Clarke*. The only rights which it reserved were for itself and the council to enter at certain times and for limited purposes. As Lord Templeman said in *Street* v. *Mountford* ... such an express reservation 'only serves to emphasise the fact that the grantee is entitled to exclusive possession and is a tenant' (at 413, 414).

The principle in *Street* v. *Mountford* [1985] AC 809, that the status of an agreement depends upon the substantive rights granted by it and not the labels used within it, does not mean that the wording of the agreement is irrelevant, especially in cases where both parties have equal expertise and bargaining power. In *National Car Parks Ltd* v. *The Trinity Development Company (Banbury) Ltd* [2002] 2 P & CR 18 Arden LJ observed:

> ...the court must look to the substance and not to the form. But it may help, in determining what the substance was, to consider whether the parties expressed themselves in a particular way .... It would in my judgment be a strong thing for the law to disregard totally the parties' choice of wording and to

do so would be inconsistent with the general principle of freedom of contract and the principle that documents should be interpreted as a whole (at para. 28).

In *Clear Channel UK Ltd* v. *Manchester CC* [2005] EWCA Civ 1304, Clear Channel was given the right to erect large advertising signs within various plots of land owned by the council. In each case the agreement identified the general site of the signs, without defining the specific land on which the signs were to be erected. The Court of Appeal held that for exclusive possession to exist, the extent of the land concerned must be capable of precise definition. Although this was sufficient to decide the issue, Jonathan Parker LJ went on to say:

> ...the fact remains that this was a contract negotiated between two substantial parties of equal bargaining power and with the benefit of full legal advice. Where the contract so negotiated contains not merely a label but a clause which sets out in unequivocal terms the parties' intention as to its legal effect, I would in any event have taken some persuading that its true effect was directly contrary to that expressed intention (at para. 29).

Both Arden LJ and Jonathan Parker LJ emphasised that they had no intention of undermining the principles of *Street* v. *Mountford*. However, at least in the case of a commercial agreement, an examination of the agreement as a whole would now seem to include considering what the parties had indicated about their intentions, even if this is subsequently negated by the reality of the transaction.

5.4　The Creation of Leases

5.4.1　Legal Formalities

The rules for the creation of legal interests in land were set out in Chapter 2. Briefly, a deed is necessary to *create* a legal lease, unless it is within the exception in s.54(2) LPA 1925 for short leases (see Section 2.6.1.3). A deed is always required to *assign* a legal lease (even a lease falling within s.54(2): see *Crago* v. *Julian* [1992] 1 WLR 372, in Section 2.6.1.3). If the lease is for a period of over seven years then it must be registered in order to operate at law (see Sections 2.6.2 and 11.5). If there is no deed where one is needed (or the registered land procedure is not followed), then only an equitable interest will be created or transferred.

5.4.2　Equitable Leases

Between the original parties, an equitable lease is probably as good as a legal lease. It will be recalled that in *Walsh* v. *Lonsdale* (1882) 21 Ch D 9 (see Section 2.3), there was an equitable seven-year lease of a mill. Since the tenant had moved in and was paying a yearly rent, there was also an implied legal periodic yearly tenancy. The Judicature Acts of 1873 and 1875 (now see s.49(1) Supreme Court Act 1981) required that where the rules of equity and the common law conflicted on the same matter, the equitable rules should prevail. The landlord of the mill was therefore able to enforce the 'rent-in-advance' term in the equitable seven-year lease against the tenant.

An equitable lease can be converted into a legal lease through the equitable remedy of specific performance (Section 2.4 – it must, of course, comply with the requirements of s.2 of the Law of Property (Miscellaneous Provisions) Act 1989) but it should be remembered that, while the behaviour of a claimant is not relevant if she is seeking a legal remedy, equitable remedies are discretionary and are unlikely to be available if she has behaved badly and does not come to equity 'with clean hands'. It follows, therefore, that if the remedy of specific performance is not available, no equitable interest will have been created.

Walsh v. *Lonsdale* was followed in the *R* v. *Tower Hamlets LBC, ex parte von Goetz* [1999] QB 1019. Miss von Goetz had a ten-year assured shorthold tenancy of a house. Although a written contract had been agreed (so the requirements of s.2 Law of Property (Miscellaneous Provisions) Act 1989 were satisfied), no deed had ever been executed. The council argued that this equitable lease could not attract a renovation grant under the Local Government and Housing Act 1989, since, in its view, such leases had to be legal. In rejecting the council's appeal, Mummery LJ stated that Miss Goetz had:

> for all practical purposes an interest as good as a legal interest ... [and that] if she asked the grantors for a deed to perfect the legal title, there is no ground on which that could be refused (at pp. 1023 and 1025)

As indicated above, the terms in the equitable lease will normally prevail as between the original parties. However, this may not be the case if either the lease or the freehold is assigned. The most important rule here is that legal interests bind the world, but equitable interests are subject to the doctrine of notice and its statutory replacements (see the rules in Chapters 10 and 11 on the protection of estate contracts). In addition, depending on the date of its creation, the rights and duties in an equitable lease may not pass with the land (see Section 6.4). Whether an equitable lease is as good as a legal lease is an ancient essay question; a useful discussion on this issue is provided in Cheshire, 2006, pp. 225 –7.

5.4.3 Statutory Conditions

Generally the parties to a lease are free to agree what terms they wish, although the common law will imply certain terms deemed characteristic of the relationship between lessor and lessee. Certain types of lease are also subject to terms implied by statute, such as the repairing obligations imposed on lessors or residential accommodation by s. 11 Landlord and Tenant Act 1985 (see, for example, *Bruton* v. *London and Quadrant Housing Trust* [2000] 1 AC 406, and Section 6.2.2).

When choosing a tenant, the owners of property may not discriminate on the grounds of sex, race or disability (s.30 Sex Discrimination Act 1975; s.21 Race Relations Act 1976; ss. 22, 23 Disability Discrimination Act 1995). The only common exceptions concern small houses or flats where the lessor lives on the premises. Such discrimination is a tort and the victim can take action for damages, an injunction and/or a declaration.

5.5 Determination of Leases

Since all leases must be only for a limited period, sooner or later they must end ('determine'). This happens through:

1 *Forfeiture* (where the lessor repossesses the land following the tenant's breach of covenant – see Section 6.5).
2 *Expiry* (when the period ends).
3 *Notice* (for example, a month's notice for monthly period tenancies, half a year's notice for yearly tenants, or as specified in the lease).
4 *Surrender* (where the tenant gives up the lease with the agreement of the lessor – there can be no unilateral surrender).

5   *Frustration* (very rarely: for example where there is some physical catastrophe). For discussion of the principles involved, see *National Carriers Ltd* v. *Panalpina (Northern) Ltd* [1981] AC 675.

6   *Repudiatory breach* (rarely, but where the lessor is in fundamental breach of her obligations under the lease, it may be possible for the tenant to accept this breach and walk away from the lease – see *Hussein* v. *Mehlman* [1992] 2 EGLR 87 and Section 6.5).

7   *Merger* (where the tenant obtains the freehold). Certain tenants have the right under statute to extend their long lease or to buy their freehold – the main example being tenants of houses held on long leases at a low rent. When a number of his tenants exercised their rights under the Leasehold Reform Act 1967 to claim the freehold of their leases, the Duke of Westminster in *James* v. *UK* (1986) 8 EHRR 123 (see Section 1.3.4) argued unsuccessfully that his rights to his property under ECHR, Article 1, Protocol 1, had been violated. The European Court of Human Rights found that the provisions of the 1967 Act, intended to provide a measure of protection for certain tenants against the diminishing value of their leases (see Section 5.1), were not disproportionate.

5.6   Some Odd Kinds of Lease

5.6.1   Leases for Life

Before 1926 there were two types of lease: the term of years absolute and the lease for life (or until marriage), and both could exist as legal estates. By s.1 LPA 1925, only the first of these can now be legal, but because some people with legal leases for life or marriage would have suddenly found themselves to be merely equitable lessees on 1 January 1926, s.149(6) LPA 1925 converts their interests into legal leases for 90 years, providing rent is payable. Such a lease can be determined by one month's notice following the death or marriage.

5.6.2   Tenancy at Will

This is, in some respects, similar to a licence; the 'tenant' has exclusive possession of the land but either side can end the arrangement at any time. It is not an estate in land. Tenancies at will can be created expressly or by implication, typically where the tenant has moved into possession, or is holding over at the end of the lease whilst the terms of a new lease are being negotiated.

The circumstances giving rise to an implied tenancy at will can be very similar to those creating an implied periodic tenancy (see Section 5.3.2.1). The distinction is important, because whereas periodic tenants have the protection of various statutory schemes, tenants at will do not. In many cases the question of rent will be decisive. In *Banjo* v. *Brent LBC* [2005] 1 WLR 2520, Mr Banjo originally occupied his house under a long lease, and continued in occupation after the lease had expired. The Court of Appeal held that this was a tenancy at will and not an implied periodic tenancy because, as Chadwick LJ observed,

> Mr Banjo paid no rent after the end of the contractual term of the long lease; and, so far as appears from the evidence, the Borough did not demand (or take any steps to enforce) payment of rent (at para. 18).

However, payment of rent is not conclusive:

The law will imply, from what was agreed and all the surrounding circumstances, the terms the parties are to be taken to have intended to apply (per Nicholls LF, *Javad* v. *Mohammed Aqil* [1991] 1 WLR 1007, at 1012).

London Baggage Company (Charing Cross) Ltd v. *Railtrack Plc (No 1)* (2000) 80 P & CR D38, concerned Unit 26,the left luggage facility, at Charing Cross Station in London. The lease had expired and the claimant had remained in occupation whilst unsuccessfully trying to negotiate a new tenancy. Pumfrey J held that the intention of the parties and all the surrounding circumstances pointed to a tenancy at will, despite rent having been paid and accepted. Not only was holding over during negotiations for a new tenancy a classic example of the circumstances in which a tenancy at will is implied, but the claimant had known from the outset that Unit 26 would not survive as a left luggage facility for much longer due to plans to redevelop the station.

5.6.3 Tenancy at Sufferance

This arises if a tenant remains in occupation ('holds over') after the lease has expired, without the lessor's agreement. The lessor can evict the tenant at any time, but if she accepts rent, the tenant becomes a tenant at will or even a periodic tenant.

5.6.4 Lease of the Reversion

Where a lessor creates a lease of her remaining interest, she is leasing the reversion; it is also called a concurrent lease. The tenant of the reversion has the right to collect rent and enforce other covenants against the tenant of the lease. (Compare the reversionary lease explained in Section 5.3.2.1.)

5.6.5 Tenancy by Estoppel

If a person attempts to grant a lease which she could not grant because she had no title, she is estopped from subsequently denying her tenant's rights against her. This is part of the ordinary principle of estoppel. Such a tenancy is personal and does not create an estate in land. However, if the lessor subsequently gains the legal title, then the tenant is automatically 'clothed' with the legal lease (this is known as 'feeding the estoppel'). For recent judicial comment on tenancies by estoppel, see Lord Hoffmann's judgment in *Bruton* v. *London and Quadrant Housing Trust* [2000] 1 AC 406.

In the *Bruton* case, the Trust expressly granted a licence rather than a tenancy; however, because its terms included all the ingredients characteristic of a tenancy, Mr Bruton was held to have a non-estate lease (see Section 5.3.2.1). In *Kay* v. *Lambeth LBC* [2006] AC 465 the House of Lords had to consider whether Mr Bruton's non-estate lease was binding on the council as the owner of the freehold in the block of flats. The tenancy could not have been binding on the council when it was originally created as the council did not grant it, and neither was it carved out of any estate granted by the council to the Trust. However, in 1995, after the grant of the tenancy to Mr Bruton, the council had granted the Trust a legal lease of the block of flats. This legal leasehold estate in the land was enough to 'feed the estoppel' implicit in the non-estate lease to Mr Bruton, converting Mr. Bruton's tenancy into a legal estate. Unfortunately for Mr Bruton, however, his estate was subject to the terms of the 1995 lease (the Trust could not give Mr Bruton a greater estate than they themselves owned). In 1999 the council terminated the lease to the Trust, automatically determining any lesser estates dependent upon it – including those held by Mr Bruton and the other tenants of the flats. Consequently, the occupiers of the flats had no estate that they could enforce against the council, although they might have an action in damages against the Trust if they could demonstrate that it was in breach of its obligations under the tenancies.

5.7 Comment

Despite all its faults, the lease is an instrument of enormous flexibility. Leases can control housing development, providing both long- and short-term housing; they provide for the changing needs of businesses and are a common means of holding agricultural land; and they allow land to be used to provide an income and raise capital.

The post-war consensus about the need to protect the security of private residential tenants ended in the 1980s: their statutory protection was reduced, partly in order to revitalise the private rented sector. Public authorities became less able to provide adequate housing for those excluded from home-ownership, and the responsibility in this area was transferred mainly to housing associations.

In its 2006 the Law Commission published its proposals, including a draft bill, to abolish the present complicated statutory regime of residential tenancies in favour of a much simpler system of occupation contracts based on a consumer protection approach, as in much of the rest of Europe (2006 Law Com 297). The statutory provisions would apply to any agreement conferring the right to occupy premises as a home (clause 1(2)(a) of the draft bill), effectively removing the distinction between the lease and the licence in the residential sector: both would become *occupation contracts*. Issues such as those discussed in *Bruton* would be irrelevant.

Summary

5.1 A lease must have a fixed beginning and a fixed end and the tenant must have exclusive possession.

5.2 In deciding whether an arrangement is a lease or a licence, the court looks to the substance of the agreement, not the name given to it.

5.3 No formalities are required to create a lease not exceeding three years, providing it is at a market rent and takes effect in possession.

5.4 An equitable lease may be as good as a legal lease between the original parties but, once the lease or reversion is sold, an equitable lease may be less secure.

Exercises

5.1 How certain must a 'term of years absolute' be?

5.2 What is the difference between a lease and a licence?

@ **5.3** Pilbeam owns a house in London which he converted into three one-bedroomed flats some years ago. He granted Yasmin a lease of Flat 1 until she got married. The tenant of Flat 2 is Javed, who was told by Pilbeam that he could have a lease until his parents come over from Pakistan. Six months ago, Pilbeam rented Flat 3 to Brenda on a one year 'licence agreement' in which Brenda agreed that Pilbeam could sleep there whenever he stayed in London. The three occupants all pay their rent monthly.

Advise Pilbeam whether Yasmin, Javed and Brenda have leases of their flats and, if so, what kind of leases.

@ **5.4** Read *Three Students Revisited* on the companion website. Does Charlie have a lease or a licence?

5.5 An online quiz on the topics covered in this chapter is available on the companion website.

Further Reading

Bright, 'Uncertainty in Leases – Is it a Vice?' (1993) 13 Legal Studies 38

Bright, 'Article 8 Again in the House of Lords' [2006] Conv 294.

Hinojosa, 'O Property, Leases, Licences, Horses and Carts: Revisiting *Bruton* v. *London & Quadrant Housing Trust* [2005] Conv 114

Morgan, 'Exclusive Possession and the Tenancy by Estoppel: a Familiar Problem in an Unusual Setting' [1999] Conv 493

Pawlowski, 'Occupational Rights in Leasehold Law: Time for Rationalisation' [2002] Conv 550

Pawlowski, 'The Bruton Tenancy – Clarity or More Confusion' [2005] Conv 262

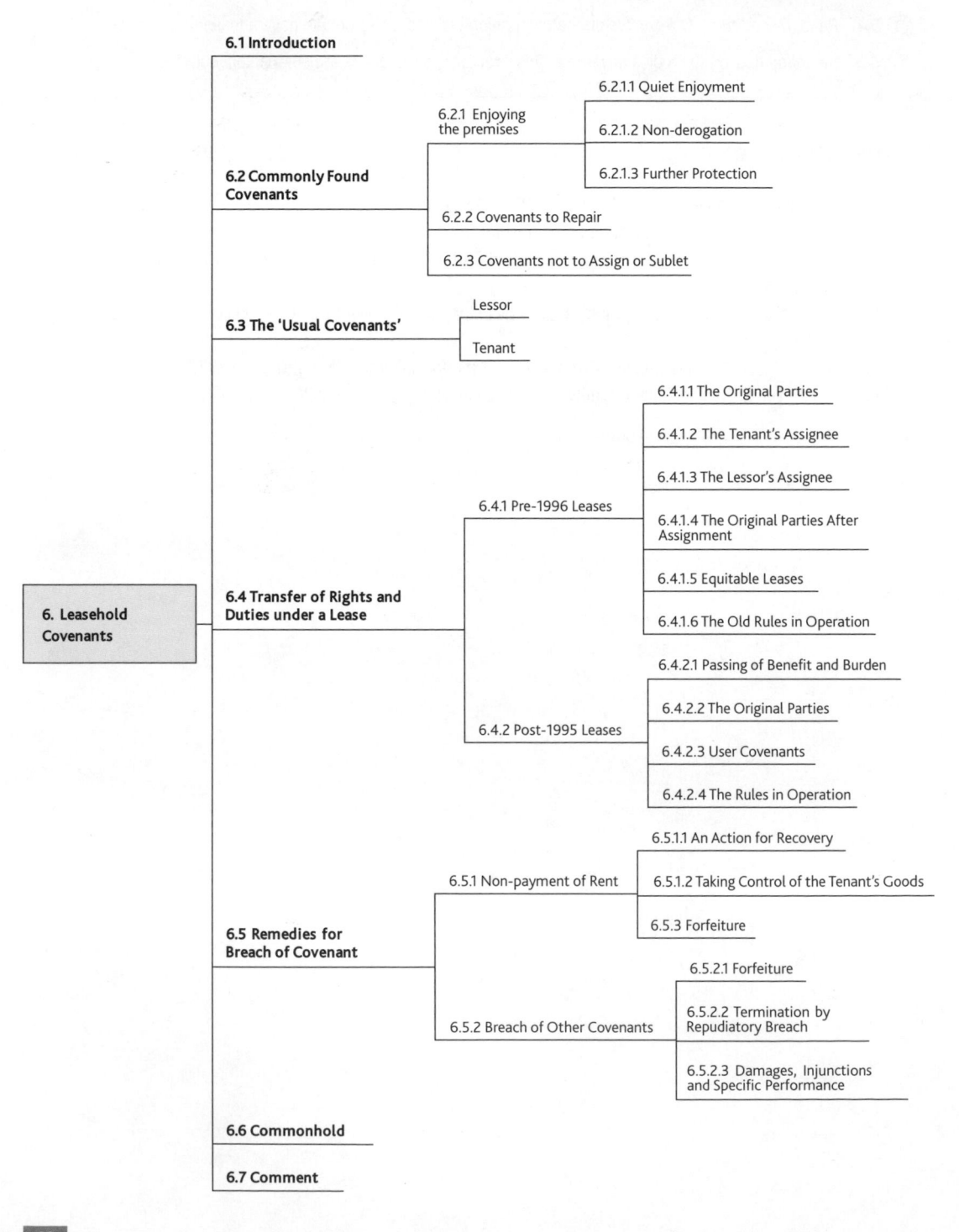

Chapter 6

Leasehold Covenants

- **6.1 Introduction**
- **6.2 Commonly Found Covenants**
  - 6.2.1 Enjoying the premises
    - 6.2.1.1 Quiet Enjoyment
    - 6.2.1.2 Non-derogation
    - 6.2.1.3 Further Protection
  - 6.2.2 Covenants to Repair
  - 6.2.3 Covenants not to Assign or Sublet
- **6.3 The 'Usual Covenants'**
  - Lessor
  - Tenant
- **6.4 Transfer of Rights and Duties under a Lease**
  - 6.4.1 Pre-1996 Leases
    - 6.4.1.1 The Original Parties
    - 6.4.1.2 The Tenant's Assignee
    - 6.4.1.3 The Lessor's Assignee
    - 6.4.1.4 The Original Parties After Assignment
    - 6.4.1.5 Equitable Leases
    - 6.4.1.6 The Old Rules in Operation
  - 6.4.2 Post-1995 Leases
    - 6.4.2.1 Passing of Benefit and Burden
    - 6.4.2.2 The Original Parties
    - 6.4.2.3 User Covenants
    - 6.4.2.4 The Rules in Operation
- **6.5 Remedies for Breach of Covenant**
  - 6.5.1 Non-payment of Rent
    - 6.5.1.1 An Action for Recovery
    - 6.5.1.2 Taking Control of the Tenant's Goods
    - 6.5.3 Forfeiture
  - 6.5.2 Breach of Other Covenants
    - 6.5.2.1 Forfeiture
    - 6.5.2.2 Termination by Repudiatory Breach
    - 6.5.2.3 Damages, Injunctions and Specific Performance
- **6.6 Commonhold**
- **6.7 Comment**

6. Leasehold Covenants

6.1 Introduction

The last chapter examined the characteristics of different kinds of lease and how they may be created and ended. This chapter considers the contents of a lease – more specifically, the obligations of the landlord and the tenant. A properly drafted business lease or long residential lease will be lengthy and detailed, and probably devoted mostly to the obligations of the tenant. On the other hand, some short leases, especially of residential tenancies, may not even be in writing and any express agreement may have gone no further than to stipulate the amount of rent payable and the frequency with which the tenant should pay it. Even the simplest of leases, however, will contain many more terms than this, and it is fundamental that the parties should understand their obligations under the lease, whether assignees are bound by or can enforce these obligations, and the remedies which are available for either party in case of the other's breach.

6.2 Commonly Found Covenants

'Covenant' is the general name given to promises made in a deed (see Section 2.6.1). In this chapter it is also used to the obligations entered into by the parties to an oral lease (see Sections 2.6.1.3 and 5.4.1). Covenants may be express (written or spoken) or implied (either by common law or by statute). The following covenants are commonly found in leases:

Common leasehold covenants

By the lessor
- not to derogate from her grant
- to allow the lessee quiet enjoyment
- to repair

By the lessee
- to pay rent (sometimes also land taxes and/or a service charge)
- to repair
- to permit the lessor to enter to inspect (or repair)
- to insure
- not to alter the structure
- not to assign or sublet without permission
- to use the premises only for a specific purpose (such as a dwelling)
- not to deny the landlord's title

The most important are explained here.

6.2.1 Covenants for Quiet Enjoyment and Non-derogation

These are the essence of the lease: if they are not expressed in the lease, they are implied by common law. The two promises are very closely connected and whether or not the covenants have been breached is a question of fact.

6.2.1.1 Quiet Enjoyment

First, the landlord promises not to interfere with the tenant's enjoyment of the land: this does not mean keeping quiet, but refers to the tenant's right to take possession as promised and to be able to enjoy all aspects of her possession without interference. It is the counterpart of the tenant's right to exclusive possession.

In *Browne* v. *Flower* [1911] 1 Ch 219, the tenants of a ground-floor flat complained that a new outside staircase, which ran alongside their bedroom windows, invaded their privacy and breached the covenants. As regards the covenant for quiet enjoyment, Parker J said:

> there must be some physical interference with the enjoyment of the demised premises and ... a mere interference with the comfort of a person using the demised premises by the creation of a personal annoyance such as might arise from noise, invasion of privacy, or otherwise is not enough (at p. 228).

The nature of the covenant for quiet enjoyment was considered by the House of Lords in *Southwark LBC* v. *Mills* [2001] AC 1. The tenants in a local authority block of flats complained that, due to inadequate sound insulation, they could hear all the sounds made by their neighbours and that this was causing them tension and distress. Lord Hoffman said:

> The flat is not quiet and the tenant is not enjoying it. But the words cannot be read literally ... The covenant for quiet enjoyment is ... a covenant that the tenant's lawful possession of the land will not be substantially interfered with by the acts of the lessor or those lawfully claiming under him (at p. 10).

When the flats were built in 1919 there had been no statutory requirement that they should be soundproofed; the tenant had accepted the flat in the physical condition she had found it, and subject to the rest of the building being used as flats. There had been no substantial interference with the tenant's possession – her ability to use the flat in an ordinary lawful way – and thus no breach of the landlord's covenant to allow her quiet enjoyment. In addition, the resource implications on the local authority would have been unsustainable had the House of Lords found in favour of the tenants, since it would have cost over a billion pounds to bring all their premises up to modern building standards.

6.2.1.2 Non-derogation

Second, the landlord promises not to take back what she has given. In *Browne* v. *Flower* [1911] 1 Ch 219, Parker J held that derogation from grant only occurs if property is

> rendered unfit or materially less fit to be used for the purpose for which [it was] demised, (at p. 226).

As the rooms could still be used as bedrooms if they drew the curtains, the tenants failed to establish a breach of in regard to either quiet enjoyment or non-derogation of grant.

In *Aldin* v. *Latimer Clark, Muirhead & Co* [1894] 2 Ch 437, land was let for use as a timber yard and included a shed used for drying timber and therefore requiring a free flow of air through it. The landlord built on neighbouring land he owned in such a way as to obstruct the free flow of air, and thus prevented the timber merchant from using the land for the purpose for which he had leased it. The landlord's activities amounted to breach of his covenant not to derogate from his grant. Similarly, in *Harmer* v. *Jumbil (Nigeria) Tin Areas Ltd* [1921] 1 Ch 200 land was leased expressly for the storage of explosives and then the landlord decided to build on his neighbouring land, which would have made the storage illegal. The tenant was able to prevent the building.

6.2.1.3 Further Protection

These common covenants are reinforced by s.1 Protection from Eviction Act 1977, amended by s.29 Housing Act 1988. The section allows a local authority to prosecute a lessor for the crime of harassment where she 'does acts likely to interfere with the peace or comfort of the residential occupier' or refuses any facilities (such as the electricity supply) knowing or believing that this will discourage the occupier from enforcing her rights. (This section protects residential licensees as well as tenants.)

An example is *Cardiff CC* v. *Destrick*, unreported, 14 April 1994. A landlord cut off the gas and electricity of a flat rented by a couple with a young baby. He was charged with the offence of doing an act with intent to cause the occupier to leave (s.1(3)), and also with doing an act which was likely to make the occupier leave (s.1(3A)), but was acquitted of both charges. He had argued that he had no intent to force them out (it was summer, not winter), and, further, that it was reasonable (under s.1(3B)) to act as he did because the tenants were behind with their payments. The magistrates agreed with him. On appeal, the court recognised that Parliament's intent was to protect residential tenants by ensuring that if a lessor wants an eviction, she must go to court and may not rely on self-help or 'indulge in harassment'. However, the court found that the magistrate's decision had not been so irrational that it should be overruled. This case may have opened a useful escape route for lessors, but it will be a question on the evidence of the reasonableness of the lessor's conduct in every case.

Section 27 Housing Act 1988 also creates a tort of unlawful eviction with the potential for substantial damages to be awarded against the landlord. *Tagro* v. *Cafane* [1991] 2 All ER 235 is 'a cautionary tale for landlords who are minded unlawfully to evict their tenants by harassment or other means' (Lord Donaldson MR at p. 236). The landlord here harassed the tenant and eventually 'totally wrecked' her room and possessions. The tenant won £31,000 damages, assessed on the difference between the value of the premises with the tenant in occupation and their value with vacant possession (s.28). The recent trend is towards the award of much lower damages, perhaps reflecting the landlord's ability more easily to end the tenants' possession lawfully under the assured shorthold regime.

6.2.2 Covenants to Repair

At common law, a furnished dwelling must be fit for habitation at the start of the lease (although no such covenant is implied into leases of other kinds of property). A well known breach of this implied covenant occurred in *Smith* v. *Marrable* (1843) 11 M & W 5, where a house was leased and found to be full of bugs.

The only statutory provision which requires the lessor of a dwelling to keep it fit for human habitation at the start and throughout the lease is s.8 Landlord and Tenant Act 1985. However, the section applies only to tenancies let at a very low rent and, since there are probably very few of these tenancies left, it is nowadays very much a dead letter.

The covenant to repair the property is fundamental to the lease of a building or part of a building. Whether the burden of this covenant falls on the landlord or the tenant will depend on the kind of property and the length of the lease. If there is nothing expressed in the lease, under common law a periodic tenant with a year's term or less will normally be required to use the premises in a 'tenant-like manner'. This is a vague expression, but Lord Denning MR has given some examples. A weekly tenant must, for example, clean windows and unblock sinks:

> In short, he must do the little jobs about the place which a reasonable tenant would do. In addition, he must, of course, not damage the house ... But ... if the house falls into disrepair through fair wear and tear or lapse of time, or for any reason not caused by him, then the tenant is not liable to repair it (*Warren* v. *Keen* [1954] 1 QB 15, at p. 20).

Sections 11–14 Landlord and Tenant Act 1985 impose a duty on the lessor of any dwelling (for a term granted for less than seven years) to keep the external structure in repair, and certain items in proper working order, including installations for the supply of water, gas and electricity and for sanitation and space and water heating. This is a complex area of law, but the courts have tended to interpret these requirements as not putting an obligation on the landlord to correct some design defect in the building's structure so long as the structure was not itself in a state of disrepair. An example might be a design fault that caused excessive condensation and thus made the premises unfit for human habitation. However, if the various installations do not perform as they should, they are not in proper working order and the landlord is liable. In *O'Connor* v. *Old Etonian Housing Association Ltd* [2002] Ch 295, water pipes which had been working properly failed to provide a proper supply when the water pressure dropped. The Court of Appeal held that the Housing Association would be in breach if the drop in pressure had been foreseeable, unless the reason for it was temporary and external, such as a drought.

The lessor's liability under ss.11–14 is subject to her being given notice that remedial work is needed and having a reasonable opportunity to carry it out (*O'Brien* v. *Robinson* [1973] AC 912).

6.2.3   Covenant not to Assign or Sublet

Theoretically, tenants have an unlimited right to assign or sublet. In practice, a tenant often covenants not to assign or sublet, since the lessor needs to be able to protect her reversionary interest against unsuitable assignees or subtenants. This covenant may be 'absolute', in which case the lessor can prevent the tenant from assigning or subletting, however unreasonable this may be. If the covenant is 'qualified' – in other words the tenant may not assign or sublet without the landlord's consent – s.19(1) Landlord and Tenant Act 1927 provides that the consent cannot be unreasonably withheld, 'notwithstanding any provision to the contrary'. The Landlord and Tenant Act 1988, s.1, places the burden of proof on the lessor to show that her refusal of consent was reasonable.

The Landlord and Tenant (Covenants) Act 1995, s.22 amended these rules for new commercial leases. It inserted a new s.19(1A) into the 1927 Act, which provides that, in the case of non-residential leases made after 1 January 1996, lessors and lessees may agree the circumstances under which consent to assignment may be given or refused, and in such cases the courts may not inquire into the reasonableness of a refusal. This provision is likely significantly to alter commercial negotiations for future leases, but has not affected non-business or pre-1996 leases.

If the consent is withheld, the tenant is placed in a difficult position. She can take a chance that the refusal is unreasonable and assign or sublet regardless, but if she wrongly assigns or sublets, she may lose her lease (see Section 6.5.2). If she is not sure whether the lessor is being reasonable, she can go to court for a declaration, but the delay may lose her the prospective assignee or subtenant.

By statute, it is unreasonable to refuse consent on the grounds of a person's sex, race or disability unless the lessor lives on the premises (s.31 Sex Discrimination Act 1975; s.24 Race Relations Act 1976; ss.22(4), 23 Disability Discrimination Act 1995). Otherwise, whether a refusal is reasonable is a question of fact in every case. As Lord Denning MR remarked:

> No one decision will be a binding precedent as a strict rule of law. The reasons given by the judges are to be treated as propositions of good sense – in relation to the particular case – rather than propositions of law applicable to all cases (*Bickel* v. *Duke of Westminster* [1977] QB 517 at p. 524).

A useful test can be found in *International Drilling Fluids Ltd* v. *Louisville Investments (Uxbridge) Ltd* [1986] Ch 513, where it was said to be a question of whether the lessor's decision was one 'which might be reached by a reasonable man in the circumstances', providing the refusal was connected to the lessor/lessee relationship. Reasonable refusals include the unsatisfactory references of the proposed tenant and the fact that the subletting would create a tenancy protected by statute.

The Court of Appeal was faced with an interesting issue in *Olympia and York Canary Wharf Ltd* v. *Oil Property Investments Ltd* [1994] 29 EG 121, where the lessor refused leave to an assignee of the lease who wanted to sell it to the original tenant. The reason for refusal was that the original tenant had the personal right to end the lease (and this would reduce the value of the lessor's interest by £6 million). The Court held that this was a reasonable ground to refuse consent to assignment.

In *Jaison Property Development Co Ltd* v. *Roux Restaurants* (1997) 74 P & CR 357, Aldous LJ quoted with approval from the judgment of Warrington LJ in *Houlder Bros & Co Ltd* v. *Gibbs* [1925] Ch 575:

> When you look at the authorities ... this, at any rate, is plain, that in the cases to which an objection to an assignment has been upheld as reasonable it has always had some reference either to the personality of the [proposed] tenant or to his proposed user of the property (at p. 585).

In *Ashworth Fraser* v. *Gloucester CC* [2001] 1 WLR 2180, the House of Lords considered the status of a landlord's refusal to consent to an assignment where the landlord thought that the proposed assignee would probably be in breach of a user covenant in the lease. Approving the approach in *International Drilling Fluids Ltd*, the Court held that reasonable lessors:

> need not confine their consideration to what will necessarily happen ... they may have regard to what will probably happen (per Lord Roger at para. 70).

6.3 The 'Usual Covenants'

The phrase 'usual covenants' is a technical expression, quite different from the list of common covenants above. This set of covenants is implied into a lease if the lease states that the parties will be bound by the 'usual covenants', or if the lease is silent as to most matters (as is common in short periodic tenancies). These usual covenants are also implied in a contract for a lease, unless the parties intend otherwise.

The usual covenants

By the lessor

- quiet enjoyment and non-derogation from grant
- right of re-entry for non-payment of rent

By the tenant

- to pay rent
- to pay land taxes
- to repair (or to allow access to the lessor to repair)

Other covenants may be 'usual' in the circumstances, for example, because of local or trade customs.

6.4 The Transfer of Rights and Duties under a Lease

It is the automatic transfer of both parties' rights and duties under the lease (the fact that covenants 'run with the land') which makes leases so useful; anyone who buys either the lease or the reversion takes the benefits and burdens of covenants in the lease. ('Benefit' means a right to sue and 'burden' a liability to be sued.) Thus, a person who buys the freehold and becomes the new landlord can sue for the rent; one who buys the lease can sue for repairs. This is also the main reason why almost all flats in England and Wales are sold by means of leases, rather than freehold. Only certain negative freehold covenants are enforceable against successors in title of the original covenantor (see Chapter 9). Mortgage lenders would be unlikely to lend money to buy a flat or a maisonette if it were not possible to force the owners of the neighbouring flats to maintain their premises, thus ensuring the continuing value of the lender's security.

The Landlord and Tenant (Covenants) Act 1995 has revolutionised this area of the law for leases granted after 1995, but the old rules still apply to the thousands of leases (and contracts for leases) made before that date.

6.4.1 The Law for Pre-1996 Leases

6.4.1.1 The Original Parties

Under the old law, the original parties to the lease are bound by their contract and, with some exceptions in the case of the lessor, remain liable for the whole period of the lease, no matter how long.

6.4.1.2 The Tenant's Assignee

When the lease is assigned the benefit and the burden of the leasehold covenants will pass to the new tenant providing there is 'privity of estate' and the covenant 'touches and concerns' the land (*Spencer's Case* (1583) 5 Co Rep 16a).

Privity of estate means that there is a current legal relationship of landlord and tenant between the parties. A sign of privity of estate is that one person pays rent to the other, so there is therefore no privity of estate between a head lessor and a subtenant (see Figure 6.1).

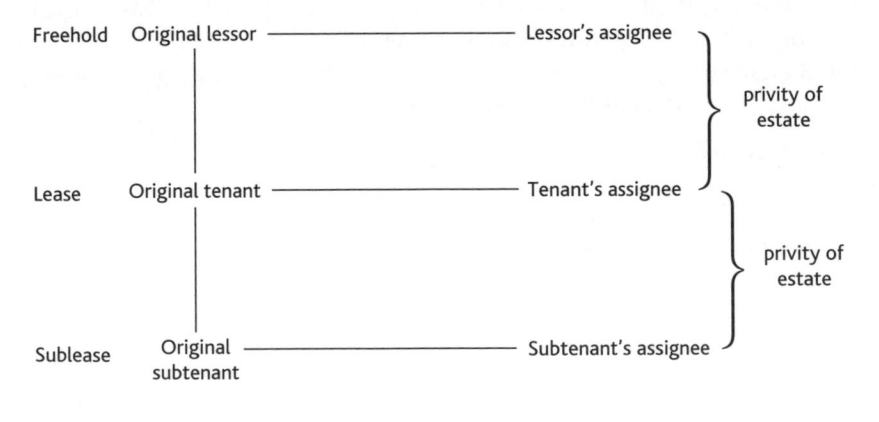

No privity of estate between Headlessor and Subtenant

Figure 6.1 Privity of estate.

The phrase 'touches and concerns' originates from the sixteenth century and is used by the courts to decide whether promises ought, as a matter of public policy, to be attached to the land. The test is easy to explain but harder to apply; the basic question is whether the promise really affects the parties in their roles as lessor and tenant, or whether it affects them in their personal capacity. In Cheshire's terms, the promise must be 'reasonably incidental to the relation of landlord and tenant' (Cheshire, 2006, p. 295). In *P & A Swift Investments* v. *Combined English Stores Group Plc* [1989] AC 632, the test was explained in the following terms: whether the covenant benefits the lessor for the time being but would cease to do so if it were separated from her ownership of the land; whether it affects the nature, quality or value of the land, or the way the land is used; or whether it is expressed to be a personal covenant (in which case it could not touch and concern the land, of course). All the commonly found covenants in Section 6.2 do touch and concern the land. In Cheshire, 2006, pp. 296–7, there are long lists of covenants which do, and do not, touch and concern the land.

6.4.1.3 The Lessor's Assignee

Where the freehold reversion (or headlease) is sold, by s.141 LPA 1925 the lessor's assignee will be able to enforce the benefit of all the covenants which 'have reference to the subject matter of the lease' (which means exactly the same thing as 'touch and concern the land'). By s.142 LPA 1925, any assignee of the lessor will be bound by the burden of all covenants which 'have reference to the subject matter of the lease'.

6.4.1.4 The Original Parties After Assignment

As already indicated, the original lessor and lessee have promised to obey the covenants for the whole lease and through the doctrine of privity of contract they may be liable – for the whole term of the lease. The liability to be sued for unpaid rent and service charges can be a continuing worry for the original tenant of an expensive commercial lease. Although the original tenant and the original lessor can still be sued after they have assigned their interest, they cannot generally sue. This rule is based on the common law principle that a person cannot be sued by two parties for the same breach of covenant (see *Re King* [1963] Ch 459).

Liability of original parties after assignment

> *On assignment by the original tenant*, the original tenant remains liable on the tenant's covenants, and can be sued by the original landlord if her assignee (or any subsequent assignee) breaches those covenants. However, the original tenant can no longer sue for breach of the lessor's covenants.

> *On assignment by the original lessor*, the original lessor remains liable to the original tenant for breaches of covenant committed by any assignee of the reversion. However, the original lessor can no longer sue.

It is sometimes argued that the right to sue the original tenant passes automatically to the assignee of the lessor under s.141 LPA 1925, without the need for express assignment. This would amount to imposing a statutory privity of contract between lessor and the original tenant, so that any owner of the reversion can choose to sue the original tenant of a lease for a breach of leasehold covenant by the present tenant. Although the editors of Megarry and Wade seem to favour this interpretation of s.141 (see 2008, Section 20-011), there is no specific authority to support it.

The question may arise as to whether the original tenant is liable for subsequent variations or extensions of the lease. In *City of London Corporation* v. *Fell* [1994] 1 AC 458 the House of Lords offered 'a meagre crumb of comfort to the unfortunate original tenant' (Bridge [1994] CLJ 28), in this case a firm of solicitors. It held that the original tenant was not liable for rent unpaid by a later assignee of the lease in the case of a tenancy which was extended after the end of the term under the provisions of Part II of the Landlord and Tenant Act 1954. The

Court of Appeal in *Friends' Provident Life Office* v. *British Railways Board* [1996] 1 All ER 336 found that an original tenant was not bound by later variations of the lease between the lessor and an assignee of the lease unless the variation had been envisaged in the terms of the original lease (such as a rent review clause).

The potential difficulties faced by the original tenant in leases created before 1 January 1996 have been addressed to some extent by the Landlord and Tenant (Covenants) Act 1995. The decision in *Friends' Provident* is now translated into a statutory provision (s.18) which applies to all leases. By s.17 of the Act, the lessor of any lease (again, whenever created) must give a 'problem notice' to the original tenant if she is planning to sue her for money unpaid by the current tenant. If no s.17 notice was given, the original tenant escapes all liability for that debt. If the original tenant pays the sums due, she is now entitled by s.19 to an 'overriding lease'. This places her between the lessor and the current tenant, thus gaining some potential relief in exchange for her liability. She may, for example, take steps to terminate the lease and either occupy the premises, or assign the overriding lease with vacant possession.

If the original tenant is sued, the common law provides that she can claim an indemnity from the current tenant (*Moule* v. *Garrett* (1871-72) LR 7 Ex 101). If the present tenant is not worth suing (as is likely in such circumstances), under s.77 LPA 1925 (implied into all leases since 1925) the original tenant can choose to sue the person to whom she assigned her interest, provided that the assignment was made for valuable consideration. A well-advised tenant will normally seek an express indemnity from her assignee, rather than rely on s.77. As a further protection, when a business lease is assigned, the landlord will probably insist that the proposed new tenant obtain a guarantor (a 'surety'). If the new tenant fails to pay the rent, the guarantor may also be sued for it.

6.4.1.5 Equitable Leases

There are different rules for equitable leases because in such cases there is no privity of estate, since this depends on a *legal* relationship. Due to the wording of ss.141 and 142, the benefits and burdens of all covenants which touch and concern the land pass to any lessor, whether legal or equitable. As far as the equitable tenant is concerned, the benefit of covenants which touch and concern may pass, but it seems that the burden may not (but see Section 6.4.2 for equitable leases made after 1995).

6.4.1.6 The Operation of the Old Rules for Pre-1996 Leases

Take the following leasehold story: Alpha Co granted a 99-year lease of the top floor flat in a large block to Bella in 1928. Alpha covenanted to keep the roof in repair and Bella covenanted to pay £500 per year rent and to use the premises as a private dwelling house only. There was a provision for forfeiture for breach of any covenant. Alpha went into liquidation and the reversion was conveyed to Bravo Co and then to Charlie Ltd. Bella sold the lease to Gerald who then sold it to Dino. The roof is now leaking badly. Dino is running an umbrella repairing service from the flat, and is in arrears of rent. The lease and all assignments were made by deed (see above for equitable leases).

The rights and duties of the various people in this tale obviously change as time passes. The present situation is as shown in diagram form in Figure 6.2.

1   As regards the leaking roof, there is privity of estate between Dino and Charlie and the covenant to repair touches and concerns the land: Dino can sue Charlie because the covenant was breached as soon as the roof leaked.

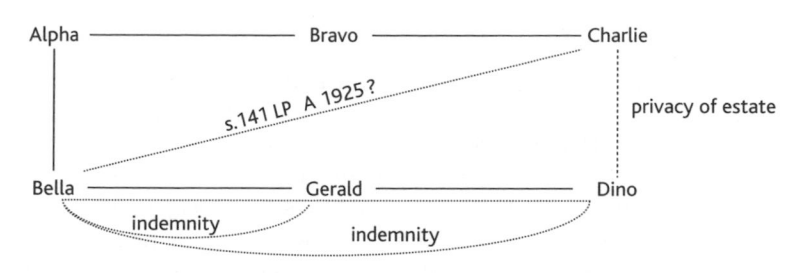

Figure 6.2 Applying the rules for pre-1996 leases.

2 As regards the arrears of rent and the umbrella business, there is privity of estate and the covenants touch and concern the land: Charlie can sue Dino. If s.141 LPA 1925 transfers the lessor's rights in privity of contract (but see Section 6.4.1.4), Charlie may sue Bella as the original tenant. Charlie would need to give Bella notice of her liability pursuant to s.17 of the 1995 Act. Bella, if liable, could sue either Gerald (s.77 LPA 1925, or express covenant if present) or Dino (common law). The original tenant's liability is only likely to arise in practice when money is a suitable remedy; an injunction against the business use of the flat would not be granted against the original tenant because she is no longer in control of the flat.

Once Alpha and Bravo have assigned the lease they cannot be sued by anyone. If there were a subtenant, in theory she could neither sue Charlie Ltd (the head lessor) nor be sued by them because there would be no privity of estate between them. However, a head lessor may be able to sue a subtenant for breach of a restrictive (negative) covenant under the rule in *Tulk* v. *Moxhay* (1848) 2 Ph. 774 (see Chapter 9). Thus, in *Hemingway Securities Ltd* v. *Dunraven Ltd* (1996) 71 P & CR 30 a landlord company was able to prevent a subtenant from taking a sublease in breach of a covenant between the company and its tenant. In addition, by s.1 Contracts (Rights of Third Parties) Act 1999, a third party can enforce a term in a contract if there is express provision for her to do so, or if the term purports to confer a benefit on her and nothing in the contract rebuts this presumption, as long as she is named in the contract or can be identified from it. If Dino had a subtenant who breached a covenant in the sublease, and this covenant was made for the benefit of Charlie or whomever was for the time being the owner of the freehold reversion, Charlie or Charlie's assignee could enforce the covenant against the subtenant (see *Amsprop Trading Ltd* v. *Harris Distribution Ltd* [1997] 1 WLR 1025 and Section 9.2).

6.4.2 The Law for Leases Granted After 1995

On 1 January 1996, the Landlord and Tenant (Covenants) Act 1995 came into force. Described as 'a statute without precedent ... [which] will have an untold impact on ... commercial leases in this country' (Bridge [1996] CLJ 313), the Act was passed as a result of a Law Commission Report ((1988) No 174), the commitment of a single MP, and the lessor and lessee lobbies (see Davey (1996) 59 MLR 78). The Act contains a number of highly detailed and complex provisions for the new regime which will no doubt keep lawyers busy for many years to come. The negotiations around the new law resulted in a series of hurriedly drafted provisions to effect compromises between the lessor and lessee lobbies. In the application of the rules for leases granted after 1995, there is no distinction made between legal and equitable leases (s.28).

6.4.2.1 The Passing of the Benefit and Burden

The 1995 Act sets out new rules that regulate the transmission of the burden and benefit of covenants contained in leases granted after 2005. Sections 2 and 3 effectively abolish the test of 'touch and concern', so that all landlord covenants and tenant covenants (the obligations of whomever is the landlord and the tenant at the time) automatically pass when the lease or freehold is assigned, unless they are specifically expressed to be 'personal'. In *BHP Petroleum* v. *Chesterfield Properties* [2002] Ch 194 the question arose as to whether the original landlord or its assignee should be liable for carrying out remedial work on defects on the premises. Since the covenant was, on the facts, a personal obligation on the part of the original landlord, the liability did not pass to the assignee, and the original landlord was held liable for the duration of the lease.

6.4.2.2 The Original Parties

Section 5(2) provides that any tenant who assigns the whole of her lease:

(a) is released from the tenant covenants of the tenancy, and
(b) ceases to be entitled to the benefit of the landlord covenants of the tenancy, as from the assignment.

However, in leases where the landlord's consent to an assignment of the lease is required, the landlord can insist that assigning tenant guarantees that her assignee will perform the tenant covenants – an *authorised guarantee agreement* (s.16). In this case, therefore, the assigning tenant will not escape liability if and when her assignee transfers the lease to a further assignee with the consent of the landlord. The *BHP Petroleum* case, however, serves as a reminder that a personal covenant will continue to be binding throughout the term of the lease, and this applies to tenants as well as landladies.

When a lessor assigns her leasehold reversion, under s.6 of the Act she must still perform her covenants under the lease. However, in order to avoid this liability she may obtain from the current tenant a release under s.8 from her obligations (unless, of course, they are personal) and, if the lessee refuses her consent, the former lessor may apply to the court. It is important that the tenant should have some say in this, since an insolvent or reluctant lessor would be less likely to be able to perform her covenants, and in such circumstances the tenant would probably want the existing lessor to continue to be bound.

However, despite anti-avoidance provisions within the 1995 Act, it is possible for a lessor to effectively sidestep ss.6–8 of the Act, with potentially serious consequences for the tenant. In *London Diocesan Fund* v. *Avonridge Property Company Ltd* [2005] 1 WLR 3956 Avonridge had acquired the headlease of seven shop units (LDF was the head landlord) before subletting six of them for substantial premiums, but nominal rents. Avonridge covenanted with its subtenant that it would pay the rent due under the headlease, 'but not, in the case of Avonridge Property Co Ltd only, so as to be liable after the landlord has disposed of its interest in the Property...'. Avonridge had then assigned the headlease to a Mr Phithwa, who promptly disappeared, leaving unpaid the rent due under the headlease. The subtenants were granted relief from the forfeiture of the headlease on condition that they paid the rent arrears and take new leases of their individual units at market rents. The subtenants brought proceedings against Avonridge on the grounds that Avonridge had not complied with ss.6–8 of the 1995 Act. The majority of the House of Lords held that s.6 was not relevant and that Avonridge was not, therefore, liable for the non-payment of rent by its assignee. Lord Nicholls explained:

> Whatever its form, an agreed limitation of liability does not impinge upon the operation of the statutory provisions because... the statutory provisions are intended to operate to relieve tenants and

landlords from a liability which would otherwise exist. They are not intended to impose a liability which otherwise would be absent. They are not intended to enlarge the liability either of a tenant or landlord (at para. 19).

This reasoning could be applied to almost all covenants made by landlords. Consequently, a careful draftsperson should be able to minimise the future exposure of an original lessor. Whether tenants will accept such limitations will depend upon their relative bargaining power (and the quality of their legal team).

6.4.2.3 User Covenants

Section 3(5) of the 1995 Act allows head-lessors to enforce restrictive covenants directly against any person 'who is the owner or occupier of any demised premises demised to which the lease relates. Thus, a head-lessor can enforce a user covenant against a subtenant without the need to resort to the rule in *Tulk* v. *Moxhay*, or the Contracts (Rights of Third Parties) Act.

6.4.2.4 The Operation of the Rules for Post-1995 Leases

Using the rules contained in the 1995 Act to establish the rights and duties of the parties to a post-1995 lease requires a similar approach to that taken to pre-1996 leases (see Section 6.4.1.6), except that greater attention needs to be paid to the circumstances of each assignment and the negotiations between the parties. If the lease between Alpha and Bella (had been made in 1996, the position of the parties would, to a large degree, be similar to that of the parties under the pre-1996 lease – except, of course, that their position must be established using the rules in the 1995 Act (see Figure 6.3).

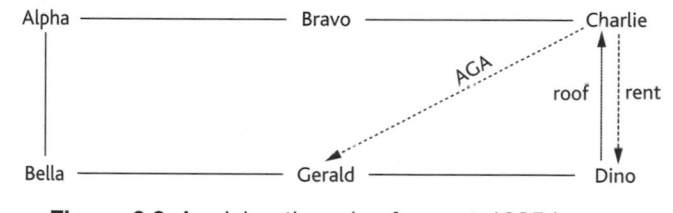

Figure 6.3 Applying the rules for post-1995 leases.

1   As regards the leaking roof, the covenant to repair is a landlord covenant to which the Act applies (s.2). The burden of this covenant passed to Charlie by virtue of s. 3(3) and benefit to Dino by s.3(2). Therefore, Dino can sue Charlie for the breach of this covenant. Whether Dino can sue Alpha or Bravo will depend upon whether steps were taken to release the respective the companies from their covenants when they assigned the reversion (ss.6–8). This may be important to Dino, especially if Charlie has insufficient resources to repair the roof.

2   As regards the arrears of rent and the umbrella business, again the covenants fall within s.2 of the 1995 Act and the benefit and burden have passed by virtue of s.3. Charlie can sue Dino. However, he will only be able to sue Gerald if Gerald entered into an authorised guarantee agreement (s.16) and a problem notice is served in respect of the unpaid rent (s.17). Bella is no longer liable. She was released from liability when she assigned the lease to Gerald (s.5). Any authorised guarantee that she may have provided at the time of that assignment expired when Gerald assigned the lease to Dino.

The practical effect of many of the 1995 Act rules will depend on the relative negotiating strengths of the parties, especially after *London Diocesan Fund* v. *Avonridge Property Company Ltd* [2005] 1 WLR 3956, which will, in turn, be influenced by the state of the property market.

6.5　Remedies for Breach of Covenant

The important question for a practical lawyer is always, 'What remedy is available?' A lease is a contract and, in general, contractual remedies are available. There are also remedies particular to leases. The rules are complicated and only the briefest details of the main remedies are given here. For historical reasons there are differences between the lessor's remedies for the tenant's breach of the covenant to pay rent and her remedies for the tenant's breach of other covenants. First, however, it is necessary to distinguish between covenants and conditions.

If a promise in a lease is called a 'condition', or is clearly intended to be a condition of the lease, then the lessor can automatically take possession of the land if the condition is broken. This is called repossession (or re-entry, or forfeiture). If the promise is not a condition, but merely a covenant, there is no such automatic right and the lessor can forfeit the lease (re-enter) or give notice to quit only if there is a clause to that effect.

If the usual covenants (see Section 6.3) are implied, then there will be a provision for forfeiture for non-payment of rent but not for breach of any other covenant.

It is important to be aware of the doctrine of waiver. If a lessor accepts rent knowing of a breach of covenant or condition, she will be taken to have waived her right to take action for the breach. Any lessor wishing to enforce a forfeiture must avoid any action by which she indicates to the tenant that the lease will continue, but there is no waiver if the lessor did not know of a breach when she indicated the continuance of the lease.

6.5.1　Non-payment of Rent

The possible remedies are an action for recovery of rent, distress and forfeiture. The lessor can only choose one of these at a time.

6.5.1.1 An Action for Recovery

An action can be brought for recovery of arrears of rent. Only the last six years of rent can be recovered (s.19 Limitation Act 1980).

6.5.1.2 Taking Control of the Tenant's Goods

Since 1066 a lessor has been able to enter the premises between sunrise and sunset and 'levy distress': she, or a certified bailiff, could take the tenant's belongings and sell them if the rent is not paid within five days.

In its Report No 194 (1991), the Law Commission concluded that distress for non-payment of rent is 'wrong in principle', and recommended its abolition. There are also concerns that levying distress may be in breach of the rights to the peaceful enjoyment of their possessions, to a fair trial and to respect for private and family life and the home protected by the Human Rights Act 1998 (see ECHR, Articles 1, Protocol 1 and Articles 6 and 8). Consequently, the common law right to levy distress for rent is due to be abolished, by s.71 Tribunals Courts and Enforcement Act 2007 (TCEA). Part 3 of the TCEA provides a new statutory remedy of Commercial Rent Arrears Recovery (CRAR) for lessors of commercial premises, provided that the lease is evidenced in writing (s.74). CRAR allows a lessor to recover rent arrears (but not arrears in respect of service charges or other payments (s.76(2)) by taking control of her tenants' goods. To ensure that the remedy is proportionate, the amount of rent in arrears must exceed a prescribed minimum amount (s.77(3),(4)).

6.5.1.3 Forfeiture (the Right of Re-entry)

The right to re-enter makes it sound as if the lessor can just barge in, but, although she may physically re-enter commercial property, such re-entry must be peaceable and without the use of force, or she will commit an offence under s.6 Criminal Law Act 1977, as amended. The House of Lords in *Billson* v. *Residential Apartments Ltd (No 1)* [1992] 1 AC 494 criticised the use of this self-help remedy, and it is usually safer for the lessor to go to court for an order for possession, particularly in the light of potential claims under the Human Rights Act. Where the premises are residential and the tenant is in occupation, under s.2 Protection from Eviction Act 1977 the lessor *must* apply to the court for a possession order before re-entering.

However, before the lessor may proceed to forfeit the lease for non-payment of rent, she must issue a formal demand for payment, although most carefully drafted leases will contain a term permitting the lessor to forfeit the lease for non-payment of rent 'whether formally demanded or not'. If the lease contains such a term, or if the rent is six months or more in arrears, no formal demand is necessary before seeking to forfeit the lease.

Once the lessor has gone to court, the tenant might be able to claim 'relief' against forfeiture for non-payment of rent under s.212 Common Law Procedure Act 1852 (in the High Court) or s.138 County Courts Act 1984 (in the County Court). This is exactly what it sounds like: very simply, if the tenant pays the arrears and costs, she may be reinstated. (The rules here are intricate and somewhat illogical because of the interplay of equity, common law and statute.)

6.5.2 Breach of Other Covenants

General remedies for breach of a tenant's covenant are forfeiture (available only to the lessor) or damages or an injunction. Although a tenant cannot forfeit the lease when the lessor is in breach, it is possible that a tenant might be able to use contract law to repudiate a tenancy where the lessor is in fundamental or repudiatory breach of a significant covenant (see Section 6.5.2.2).

6.5.2.1 Forfeiture

This remedy is only available to the lessor if it is included in the lease. If there is a forfeiture clause, the lessor must give notice to the tenant by s.146 LPA 1925.

The s.146 notice must specify:
- the specific breach complained of; and
- the remedy (if the breach is capable of remedy); and
- the compensation (if appropriate or required).

(Section 146 notices do not apply in respect of non-payment of rent.)

The purpose of the s.146 procedure is to give tenants an opportunity to remedy their breach, if this is possible, so that they do not lose their lease through forfeiture. It is, therefore, important to know which breaches can be remedied and which cannot.

The traditional view had been that the breach of a positive covenant could be remedied by the tenant simply performing whatever it was the lease required her to do, and some negative covenants could be remedied by ending the activity which was causing the breach and promising to comply with the lease thereafter. The issue of remediability was examined in *Expert Clothing Service and Sales Ltd* v. *Hillgate House Ltd* [1986] Ch 340. In this case it had been agreed that the tenant should convert the premises but, because of lack of money, the tenant had not even begun the work by the date by which it should have been completed. Expert Clothing issued a s.146 notice, claiming that the breach was irremediable. The Court of Appeal stated that the purpose of s.146 was to give the tenant 'one last chance', and that whether a breach was capable of remedy depended, not on the nature of the breach but rather on the nature of the harm caused to the lessor and whether financial compensation would be sufficient.

In *Savva* v. *Hussein* (1997) 73 P & CR 150, the tenants were in minor breach of covenants not to put up signs or to alter the premises. On the question of whether such breaches were capable of remedy, Staughton LJ stated:

> When something has been done without consent, it is not possible to restore the matter wholly to the situation which it was in before the breach. The moving finger writes and cannot be recalled. That is not to my mind what is meant by a remedy; it is a remedy if the mischief caused by the breach can be removed. In the case of a covenant not to make alterations without consent or not to display signs without consent, if there is a breach of that, the mischief can be removed by removing the signs or restoring the property to the state it was in before the alterations (at p. 154).

Akici v. *L R Butlin Ltd* [2006] 1 WLR 202 concerned an alleged breach of covenant by the tenant by sharing possession of the premises. Neuberger LJ felt that there were very few breaches not capable of remedy:

> In principle I would have thought that the great majority of breaches of covenant should be capable of remedy, in the same way as repairing or most user covenant breaches. Even where stopping, or putting right, the breach may leave the lessors out of pocket for some reason, it does not seem to me that there is any problem in concluding that the breach is remediable (at para. 65).

The lessor is not disadvantaged in such circumstances because the lessor is entitled to 'compensation in money ... for the breach' under s.146(1).

A wrongful subletting is irremediable, and using the premises for immoral purposes in breach of covenant may well be, since this activity might cast a stigma on the premises which could only disappear with the removal of the tenant (*Rugby School (Governors)* v. *Tannahill* [1935] 1 KB 87). In *Glass* v. *Kencakes Ltd* [1966] 1 QB 611 the tenant's breach was remediable, since he himself had committed no immoral act on the premises and had taken the appropriate action against his immoral subtenant by evicting her.

If the tenant does not, or cannot, remedy the breach within a reasonable time, the lessor can go to court for a possession order. Again, the tenant (or subtenant) can apply for relief under s.146(2) LPA 1925, even if the breach is considered irremediable. The House of Lords held in *Billson* v. *Residential Apartments* [1992] 2 WLR 15 (see Section 6.5.1.3) that a tenant can apply for relief whether or not the lessor has actually re-entered the land, providing there is no final court order granting possession. Here the tenant was carrying out building work in breach of covenant so the landlord served a s.146 notice and then re-entered by changing the locks. Since there was no court order granting possession at this stage (these were not residential premises, so there had been no breach of the criminal law – see Section 6.5.1.3), the House of Lords sent the case back to the trial court for a decision as to whether relief was to be granted.

If the lease is forfeit, any sublease will also disappear since its existence depends on the headlease. Therefore, s.146(4) LPA 1925 allows the subtenant to apply for relief and, if she is successful, she steps into the shoes of the tenant but cannot gain a term longer than her original sublease. Mortgagees of the leasehold interest can also apply for relief, remedy the breach and add the cost of doing so to the mortgage debt.

In an attempt to prevent abuse of the s.146 procedure by lessors, especially when attempting to forfeit the lease against leaseholders who are unable or unwilling to pay unreasonable service charges, ss.168, 169 Commonhold and Leasehold Reform Act 2002 prevent most lessors of residential leases over 21 years from issuing a s.146 notice unless either the leaseholder has admitted the breach of covenant or the lessor has established the breach to the satisfaction of a leasehold valuation tribunal. If the breach consists of arrears of service charges, the lessor must also show that the charges are not excessive. Even if the tribunal is satisfied as to the breach, the leaseholder may not be served with the s.146 notice for a further 14 days.

6.5.2.2 Termination by Repudiatory Breach

It is a general rule of contract law that a contract may be terminated if one of the parties breaches its terms in such a way as to make it clear that they no longer intend to be bound by the contract. Some older cases cast doubt on whether this remedy applies to leases, but since the county court decision in *Hussein* v. *Mehlman* [1992] 2 EGLR 87 the list of circumstances in which it has been granted has been growing steadily. *Hussein* v. *Mehlman* a rented house was uninhabitable due to the lack of repair; the tenant not only won damages but also was entitled to end the lease because of the fundamental nature of the landlord's breach of covenant. Since *Hussein* the Court of Appeal has, on a number of occasions, accepted that repudiation by a tenant can be appropriate, although in none of the cases is the Court of Appeal's decision dependent upon this. For example, in *Chartered Trust Plc* v. *Davies* (1998) 76 P & CR 396, the lessor allowed the occupier of a neighbouring unit to obstruct access to the defendant's unit. The Court of Appeal dealt with this as a case of derogation from grant, but Henry LJ concluded his judgement by noting:

> The trial judge found this to be a repudiation of the lease – a substantial interference with the tenant's business driving her to bankruptcy. That was a judgment he was entitled to come to on the evidence he heard (at 409).

This is a welcome extension of contractual principles but, although appearing similar to the lessor's remedy of forfeiture, it is, by its very nature, clearly limited to cases where the lessor has breached a fundamental term of the lease. It is not clear whether the remedy is also available for the lessor in the case of a tenant's repudiatory breach. It seems unlikely, since that would mean that an uncompromising lessor could avoid the statutory and common law protection available to tenants (see Section 6.5.2.1). Without deciding this question, the Court of Appeal in *Reichman* v. *Beveridge* [2007] 1 P & CR 20 held that there was no obligation on a lessor to minimise the tenant's liability under the lease by accepting the tenant's repudiatory breach of contract.

6.5.2.3 Damages, Injunctions and Specific Performance

Damages and/or an injunction may be appropriate remedies for some breaches, and are available to both lessor and lessee. Specific performance was thought, until recently, to be available only to the tenant in cases of the lessor's breach of her repairing covenant. *Rainbow Estates* v. *Tokenhold* [1999] Ch 64 has extended this remedy to the lessor 'in appropriate circumstances', although these will be rare – in this case the lease had no provision for the landlord to forfeit the lease for the tenant's breach or even to enter the premises to carry out the repairs himself. Specific performance will not usually be available if damages are an appropriate remedy, but here the property was a listed building in serious disrepair and the condition of the premises was continuing to deteriorate; an award of damages would not have helped the landlord. The traditional reason for the courts' reluctance to order specific performance in these circumstances, that the order would need continuing supervision by the court, was not seen as presenting a difficulty if there was a clear definition of the work to be done.

The House of Lords took the orthodox approach to specific performance in *Co-operative Insurance Society Ltd* v. *Argyll Stores (Holdings) Ltd* [1998] AC 1, in which it refused to make an order preventing Safeway from closing one of its stores, despite the company having contracted with its landlord, the owner of a shopping mall, to keep it open. Lord Hoffmann distinguished the performance of repairing obligations in a lease from the obligation to continue in a business relationship.

At present, tenants often have very serious problems in persuading their lessors to carry out repairs; one rationale for the introduction of 'commonhold' has been the need to address the problems faced by tenants in rundown blocks of flats (see Section 6.6). Although tenants can seek the remedies discussed above, if they hold a comparatively insecure assured shorthold tenancy, they may often be reluctant to bring an action against their lessor knowing that renewal or extension of their tenancy would probably be unlikely. An alternative remedy could be to pay for the repairs themselves and deduct the cost from the rent without becoming liable for non-payment (a 'right of set-off' – see *Lee Parker* v. *Izzet (No 1)* [1971] 1 WLR 1688).

Instead of relying on contractual provisions within the lease (whether set out in the lease or implied by statute), sometimes the residential tenant's best solution is to get the local authority to take action. Part 1 of the Housing Act 2004 gives local authorities the power to take steps against the lessor to ensure that residential accommodation is brought up to a reasonable standard.

6.6 Commonhold

If someone wants to buy a flat rather than merely rent one on a short-term basis, the only way to do so, until recently, has been through buying a long lease on it, frequently by means of a mortgage. As will become evident (see Chapter 9), in freehold land it is frequently not possible to enforce covenants against successors of the original covenantor. However, this is precisely what the owner of a flat in a block of flats, for example, might wish to do. In order to protect the structural integrity of her own property, the owner of a flat, or her lessor, might have occasion to seek to enforce a repairing covenant against her neighbour. The only answer has been for all the flats in the block to be held on long leases, since, as we have seen, leasehold covenants are enforceable against successors in title.

However, there are difficulties with the use of the lease in such situations. The most obvious is that a lease is a diminishing asset and, eventually, will disappear (see Section 5.1). Even before that happens the lease will become unmarketable, since mortgage lenders are unwilling to lend on leases with less than 60 years to run. A further difficulty may be the inability of the tenants to get the lessor to manage the building and carry out her obligations to repair and maintain the common parts while keeping the tenants' financial contributions at a reasonable level. These problems have been addressed at various times by Parliament, but no entirely satisfactory solution has been found. The latest statute, the Commonhold and

Leasehold Reform Act 2002, Part 2, contains further provisions for allowing qualifying tenants of long residential leaseholds the right to take over management of the property from the lessor, even if the latter is not at fault.

For about twenty years, there have been discussions on proposals to introduce a new form of land holding called 'commonhold', based to some extent on strata title in Australia and condominium title in the USA. After a good deal of uncertainty and procrastination, these proposals have been enacted in the Commonhold and Leasehold Reform Act 2002, Part 1, which came into force on 27 September 2004. Commonhold is intended to avoid the problems with long leaseholds mentioned above.

A property to be owned on a commonhold basis (for example, a block of flats or an industrial estate) is registered at the Land Registry by the freehold owner as a 'freehold estate in commonhold land'. The property is divided into 'units', each held by the unit owner on a freehold basis. The owner of each unit becomes a member of the Commonhold Association, a private company limited by guarantee, which owns and has responsibility for the upkeep of the common parts of the building. Under the regulations in the Commonhold Community Statement (CCS), each unit owner has obligations (for example to maintain her unit in good repair and to contribute to the commonhold expenditure), binding on her successors and enforceable by the Association – a kind of private local community law. The enforcement of the rules in the CCS takes place initially through an internal complaints procedure, then, depending on Regulations introduced through secondary legislation, through some form of mediation or arbitration or through an Ombudsman, before finally moving towards formal legal proceedings.

The advantage of the commonhold scheme is that all the obligations in the CCS are binding on all unit holders at all times, so that there is no longer any need to use the unsatisfactory device of a long lease in order to buy an interest in a shared building. The scheme should also remove the associated problems of 'unreasonable and oppressive behaviour by unscrupulous landlords' (Commonhold and Leasehold Reform Consultation Paper, Cm 4843, 2000, p. 107) and the difficulties of getting mortgage finance in the later years of a lease. Of course, as the Law Commission has remarked, the scheme will not by itself solve the problems: neighbours will not always cooperate, and buildings cannot be repaired for ever. Nevertheless, commonhold gives land developers a new flexibility when building new blocks of flats or developing industrial areas.

However, the new Act does little to help those tenants who currently hold long leases on residential flats and who may wish to convert to commonhold, since the consent of all the long leaseholders (those with leases over 21 years) must be obtained, and it is thought unlikely that this will be feasible in practice. Most commonholds, therefore, will be the result of new property developments. Thus far, developers seem to have been slow to adopt commonhold, with fewer than 20 commonholds being registered by the middle of 2008. For commentary on and detailed criticism of the implementation of commonhold, see Clarke [2002] Conv 349.

6.7 Comment

The law on leasehold covenants is complex and extensive, with many detailed rules, areas of uncertainty and a lack of proportionality in the remedies available to landladies and tenants. To some degree, the history of the law demonstrates the failure of legislators and judges to resolve political, social and economic problems in this field. It has never been easy to balance the varying interests of landladies, tenants and society in general – the passage of the Landlord and Tenant (Covenants) Bill 1995 is an example of the operation of the powerful interests and lobbies which influence the making of new laws.

The Law Commission has recognised the need for reform, particularly in regard to forfeiture which remains extremely complex (see, for example *Termination of Tenancies for Tenant Default* (2006) Law Com No 303), and formal proposals are awaited. The last chapter referred to residential leases having the status of consumer contracts (see Section 5.8) and this would result in residential tenants receiving the benefit of consumer remedies against their lessors, considerably strengthening their position.

Much is expected of the commonhold regime, but its effectiveness may well depend on the willingness of property developers to engage with this novel form of land holding.

Summary

6.1 Commonly found leasehold covenants include: the lessor's covenants for quiet enjoyment and non-derogation from grant; covenants to repair; the tenant's covenant not to assign or sublet without consent.

6.2 In leases made before 1996, a covenant automatically runs with the land if there is privity of estate and the covenant touches and concerns the land; the original tenant remains liable on all the covenants but may claim an indemnity from her assignee or the current tenant; the original tenant is entitled to an overriding lease when she has paid money due by the current tenant.

6.3 In leases made after 1995, all covenants run with land unless expressed to be personal; the original tenant ceases automatically to be liable for any breach after assigning the lease (but can be liable under an authorised guarantee agreement), but the original lessor may remain liable, unless she obtains a release from the current tenant or from the court.

6.4 Remedies for non-payment of rent are normally forfeiture, distress or an action for recovery.

6.5 Remedies for breaches of other covenants include forfeiture, damages and injunction; a tenant's may also have the right to repudiate the lease in certain circumstances. A tenant of residential property may be able to involve the local authority if the lessor is in breach of her repairing covenant.

6.6 The procedures for forfeiture for breach of the covenant to pay rent and forfeiture for other breaches are different.

6.7 A new form of landownership – commonhold (a special type of freehold estate) – was introduced in 2004.

Exercises

6.1 What is the difference between 'common covenants' and 'usual covenants'?

6.2 When is a lessor liable for repairs under a lease?

6.3 Under what circumstances may a lessor repossess her land?

6.4 Will the introduction of commonhold be an improvement on the use of the lease for long-term occupation of shared buildings?

@ 6.5 Four years ago, Ronald granted a six-year lease of a house to Alan. Alan covenanted that he would pay the rent on time, would paint the exterior every three years and would not use the premises for illegal or immoral purposes. Ronald reserved the right to re-enter the premises for breach of any covenant.

The following year, Ronald sold his freehold reversion to Keegan. Two years ago Alan assigned his lease to Jane.

Keegan has found out that Jane has been smoking cannabis in her house, that she has allowed her friend Sally to use it for prostitution (much to the annoyance of the next door neighbour), and that she has not painted the house at all. She is five months in arrears with her rent. Four months ago, the roof began to leak badly whenever it rained and the bedroom ceiling has collapsed as a result. Keegan has steadfastly refused to carry out any repairs, and Jane is obliged to live on the ground floor.

Jane wants to know what she can do about the state of the house and whether Keegan can evict her. Advise her.

@ 6.6 An online quiz on the topics covered in this chapter is available on the companion website.

Further Reading

Bridge, 'Former Tenants, Future Liabilities and the Privity of Contract Principle: The Landlord and Tenant (Covenants) Act 1995' [1996] CLJ 313

Clarke, 'The Enactment of Commonhold – Problems, Principles and Perspectives' [2002] Conv 349

Davey, 'Privity of Contract and Leases – Reform at Last' (1996) 59 MLR 78

Dixon, 'A failure of Statutory Purpose or a Failure of Professional Advice?' [2006] Conv 79

Pawlowski, 'Acceptance of Repudiatory Breach in Leases' [1995] Conv 379

Walter, 'Landlord and Tenant (Covenants) Act 1995: a Legislative Folly' [1996] Conv 432

Chapter 7

Mortgages

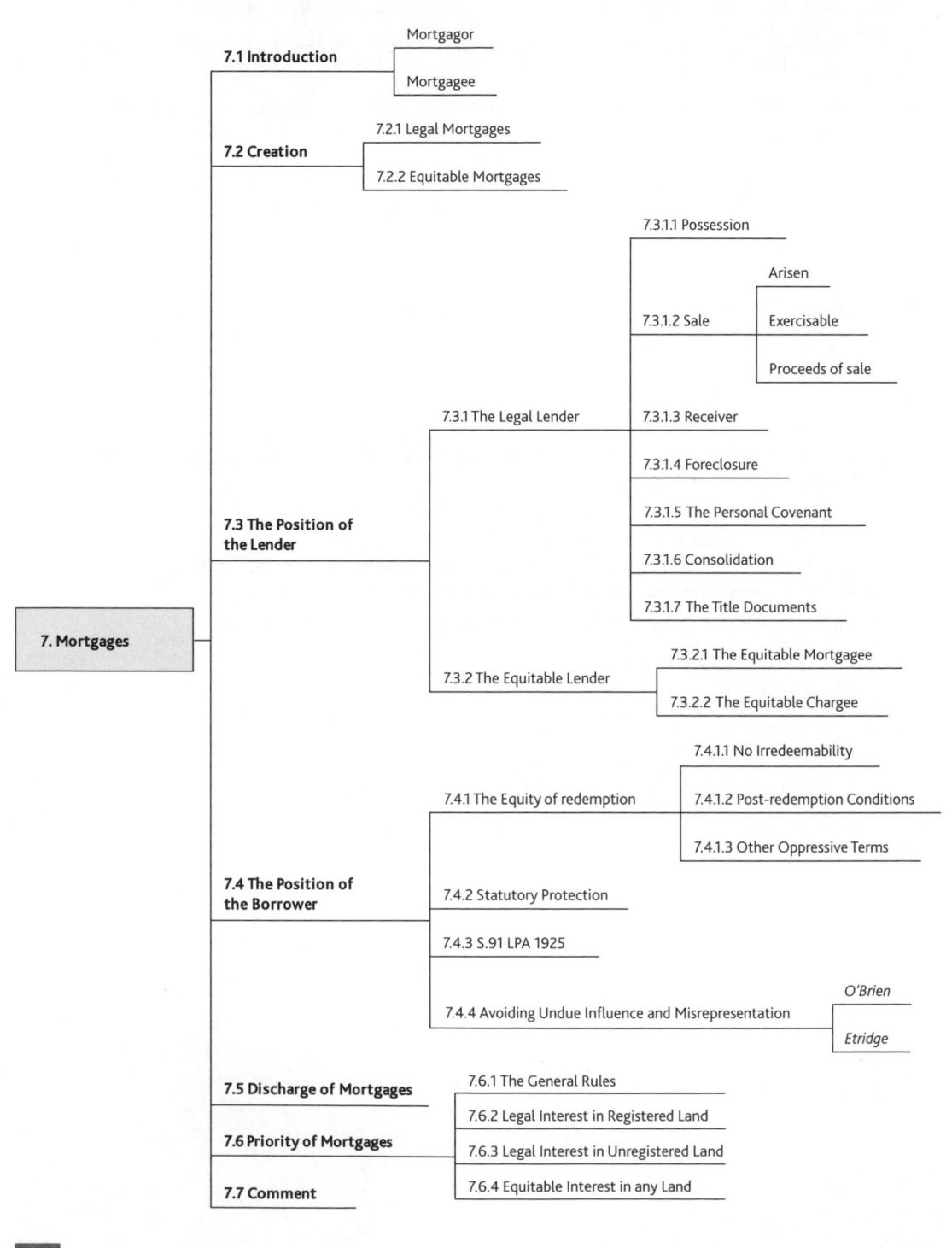

7.1 Introduction

Many of the rules in the law of mortgages are relatively straightforward and conform with common sense. However, the language and the concepts are not quite as they might appear at first sight. It used to be said that a mortgage deed was 'a suppression of truth and a suggestion of falsehood'. This mismatch of expectation and theory can at first be disconcerting, and it is essential to keep hold of the rules while exploring the theory. As far as the language is concerned, perhaps the easiest way to assimilate the technical terms is to try to explain them to your most tolerant friend.

Lawyers use the word 'mortgage' in two senses:

1   It is a relationship between a landowner and a money-lender. The landowner creates a charge over the land in favour of the lender (see Section 7.2).
2   As a way of referring to the interest – the charge – granted as security.

Contrary to the way most people talk, the mortgage is the interest in the land exchanged for the money: a mortgage is not borrowed money. When the letter arrives to say that a bank or a building society will lend the money to buy a house, the pedantic borrower should not say, 'They're giving me a mortgage!', but rather, 'They're letting me grant them a mortgage'. Thus, the mortgagor (the borrower) grants a mortgage to the mortgagee (the lender): see Figure 7.1.

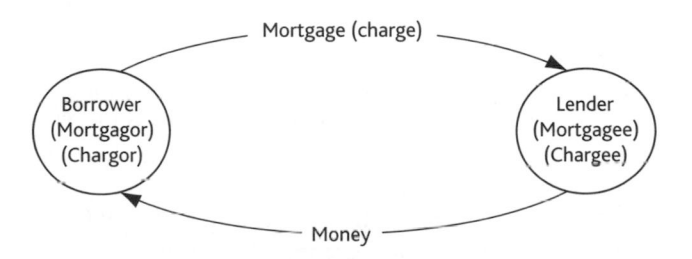

Figure 7.1 A mortgage arrangement.

Mortgage relationships have existed since Anglo-Saxon times, but their form has changed a good deal since then. Since the seventeenth century, the harsh common law approach has been softened by equity which intervened in contracts between borrowers (typified as the poverty-stricken sons of the aristocracy) and money-lenders. The basic principle behind equity's intervention in mortgages is that one party (the lender) should not take an unconscionable advantage of the other (the borrower). In more recent times, Parliament has intervened to offer some measure of statutory protection to borrowers, and the courts now generally recognise the commercial and contractual reality of mortgage agreements, while at the same time attempting to preserve equity's protection for the vulnerable.

This area of land law illustrates very clearly the way in which land simultaneously fulfils several functions. With the development of capitalism, land was seen as an asset to be mortgaged in order to raise finance for commercial enterprise. This is very much the case today – for example, many small businesses are financed by means of a mortgage on the home of the owner of the business. The mortgage is also the device by which many people become landowners – the bank or the building society lends money to buy land which itself provides the security for the loan. Such mortgages are known as 'acquisition mortgages'. The land is used as a home by the borrowers. Most homeowners hope that their land is also an investment, an appreciating asset. The assumption that land would always increase in value was shaken by the slump in property values in the early 1990s, with many borrowers finding themselves in negative equity – having a debt larger than the value of their home. A similar slump is now being experienced during the closing years of the first decade of the twenty-first century.

Because of the many functions which land fulfils – shelter, security, direct or indirect investment – it can be difficult to untangle the financial interests when there is a dispute. Some cases, for example, concern the lender coming into conflict with an owner of a beneficial interest in land subject to a trust where the trustee has mortgaged it without declaring the beneficial interest. Where the court decides against a commercial lender, the burden is spread across the lender's portfolio; the lender may also have insured against bad debts. Should the court decide against the beneficiary, he alone bears the cost.

There may be several mortgages created over one interest in land. Also, mortgages may be granted on any interest in land; thus, mortgages are frequently granted on leases, although a lender would tend to consider that only a long lease provides sufficient security (see Section 6.6). Mortgages of other property, such as company shares, can be created and the same general rules apply. Some of the commercial cases in this chapter concern such mortgages.

7.2 The Creation of Mortgages

7.2.1 Legal Mortgages

The legal charge (s.87 LPA 1925) is nowadays the customary means of creating a legal mortgage and is now the only way of mortgaging registered land (s.23(1)(a) LRA 2002). Charges by way of legal mortgage are simply created by the execution of a deed and can be used for mortgages of either freehold or leasehold land.

Under s.85 LPA 1925, it is still possible to create a mortgage of freehold land that has not yet been registered *by demise, the borrower* granting the lender a long lease (perhaps 3000 years) containing terms setting the date for the money to be repaid (the contractual date of redemption) and for the lease to be surrendered to the borrower when the mortgage is redeemed (the mortgage money is repaid). In a similar way, by s.86 a long lease of land which has yet to be registered can be mortgaged by *subdemise* (the creation of a sublease). These two methods of creating a mortgage are more or less obsolete: they are more complex than using the charge and can only be used where the land concerned is unregistered. The grant of a first legal mortgage over an unregistered freehold, or over a lease with more than seven years left to run, will trigger compulsory first registration of the land (s.4(1)(g) LRA 2002 (see Section 11.2.2), regardless of what method is used to create it.

Before 1925, legal mortgages were created by transferring the estate to the lender subject to his promise to reassign it to the lender when the debt was paid. Any attempt to create a mortgage in this way by the owner of an unregistered legal estate will now create a 3,000-year lease (or a sublease) instead (ss. 85(2), 86(2) LPA 1925). A registered proprietor cannot create a legal mortgage in this way (s.23(1)(a) LRA 2002).

7.2.2 Equitable Mortgages

It is important to know whether a mortgage is legal or equitable because, as well as the lesser security of equitable interests if the land is sold, the remedies of the lender may be different.

An equitable *mortgage* may arise:

▷ Where the borrower has only an equitable interest in the land, such as a beneficial interest under a trust (see Chapter 12). This equitable interest is mortgaged by assigning it in writing to the lender who will promise to reassign it when the debt is repaid. Before 1925, this was also the means by which legal estates were mortgaged (see Section 7.2.1).

▷ Where, in unregistered land, there has been an attempt at creating a legal mortgage by means of a forgery the mortgage will only be effective against the equitable interest of the forger and not against the interests of any innocent co-owner – see *First National Securities Ltd* v. *Hegerty* [1985] QB 850.

▷ Where there is a contract for a legal mortgage under s.2 Law of Property (Miscellaneous Provisions) Act 1989, or by estoppel. An equitable mortgage, therefore, will come into existence before its conversion into a legal mortgage through the execution of a deed (see Chapter 2). Before the 1989 Act an equitable mortgage could be created by depositing the title deeds or land certificate with the lender in exchange for the loan, since this was seen as part performance of an oral contract. Now that part performance has been abolished, this method of creating a mortgage is obsolete, as confirmed by *United Bank of Kuwait Plc* v. *Sahib* [1997] Ch 107.

7.3   The Position of the Lender

7.3.1   The Legal Lender

The lender (mortgagee) has remedies to enforce the payment of the money due to him and certain other rights. The legal mortgagee may:

1   take possession of the property;
2   sell the property;
3   appoint a receiver;
4   foreclose;
5   sue on the personal covenant;
6   consolidate;
7   hold the title deeds if the land is still unregistered;
8   exercise rights in connection with a series of mortgages ('tacking' – see Section 7.6).

The lender does not have to choose between the remedies: it is possible to pursue several at the same time. They were developed when mortgages were not so commonly used for home buying and have been adjusted by statute to protect the security of home buyers, just as tenants' security has been protected to some extent by modern legislation.

7.3.1.1 Taking Possession

In theory, because he either has a lease or, if the mortgage has been created by a charge, he is treated as though he has a lease (s.87(1) LPA 1925), a lender has the right to:

> go into possession before the ink is dry on the mortgage unless there is something in the contract, express or by implication, whereby he has contracted himself out of that right (per Harman J in *Four-Maids Ltd* v. *Dudley Marshall Properties Ltd* [1957] Ch 317, at p. 320).

Usually, of course, the lender will not wish to take possession unless the borrower fails to pay. It might seem extraordinary that the lender has the right to move in as soon as the mortgage deed is signed but, although it was common in the past, in practice this now only happens if the borrower defaults. The lender will then probably want to sell the property with vacant possession (but see below for other remedies) and will generally obtain a court order before taking possession. A court order is not always necessary, but, unless the lender is sure that the premises are unoccupied, it is the safest way of ensuring that there is no breach of s.6 Criminal Law Act 1977, which makes it an offence to use or threaten violence to gain entry into premises.

Where the property is (or includes) a home, s.36 Administration of Justice Act 1970 (as amended by s.8 Administration of Justice Act 1973) gives the court the discretion to postpone an order giving the lender possession if the borrower is likely to be able to pay his arrears 'within a reasonable period'. In the harsh economic climate of the late 1980s and early 1990s, repossessions increased in frequency – doubling between 1989 and 1991 – and affected the whole market in land. A number of cases have therefore focused on the issue of when the court might exercise its s.36 discretion; some have concerned the defaulting borrower's likelihood of finding employment and repaying arrears, and others on the chances of his being able to sell the land within a reasonable period.

The Court of Appeal stated in *Cheltenham and Gloucester Building Society* v. *Norgan* [1996] 1 WLR 343 that, although a 'normal' period of two years had become fairly established in judgments, 'a reasonable period' was not limited to any particular length of time. In *Norgan*, the mortgage term was to end 13 years from the time of the claim for a possession order, and the Court held that this could be a reasonable period within 'the logic and spirit of the Act'; they effectively asked the lower court to decide whether it could reschedule the debt over the whole repayment period. In future cases, such a rescheduling from the outset of the mortgagor's difficulties might avoid the continuing struggle and repeated orders and delays in repossession proceedings.

A borrower is only entitled to apply for relief under s.36 if an action for possession has been brought. *Ropaigealach* v. *Barclays Bank Plc* [2000] 1 QB 263 was a relatively rare example of a case where the lender did not obtain a court order for possession. In this case the borrowers had moved elsewhere and the house subject to the mortgage was standing empty. The Court of Appeal concluded, albeit reluctantly, that the borrowers were not entitled to s.36 relief in such circumstances. To allow relief in these circumstances would effectively prevent a mortgagee from taking possession without first obtaining a court order, which went beyond what Parliament had enacted in s.36. It has been suggested that this result contravenes the borrower's rights under Articles 6 and 8 and Article 1, Protocol 1 of the European Convention on Human Rights (see Rook, 2001, p. 199), although this line of argument was rejected by Briggs J in the recent case of *Horsham Properties Group Ltd* v. *Clark* [2008] EWHC 2327 Ch.

7.3.1.2 Sale

Although the mortgagee has no power of sale at common law, there is a statutory power of sale provided by the LPA 1925. All mortgages that satisfy the conditions set out in s.101 LPA 1925 benefit from the statutory power of sale, except in so far as it is modified or excluded by the terms of the mortgage (as, for example, in *Ropaigealach* v. *Barclays Bank Plc* [2000] 1 QB 263, where different conditions were substituted for those set out in s.103 LPA 1925 (see below)).

The power of sale *arises* if:

- the mortgage is made by deed s.101(1);
- the deed contains no provision excluding the statutory power (s.101(4)); and

▷ the contractual date for redeeming the mortgage has passed (that is, the mortgage money has become due, s.101(1)(i)).

On most domestic mortgages, the contractual date of redemption is usually set six months after the creation of the mortgage in order to allow the lender to realise its security if this becomes necessary.

However, the lender cannot exercise a power of sale that has *arisen* by virtue of s.101 LPA 1925 unless one of the conditions listed in s.103 LPA 1925 is satisfied:

The power of sale becomes *exercisable* if:
▷ the default continues three months after a notice requiring payment is served; or
▷ interest is two months in default; or
▷ the borrower has broken another term of the mortgage.

Although the lender only has a charge (or a long lease or sublease), he may sell the borrower's whole interest as soon as one of these conditions has been fulfilled (ss.88–9 LPA 1925). The lender does not need a court order to sell the land, but in most cases he will obtain an order granting possession before proceeding with the sale. The exercise of the power of sale against the family home can have distressing effects on the family, but any attempt to invoke ECHR Article 8 (the right to respect for a person's private and family life and home) will not succeed, since the Article cannot be used 'to diminish the contractual and proprietary rights of the mortgagee under the mortgage' (*Harrow LBC* v. *Qazi* [2004] 1 AC 983, per Lord Scott at para. 135).

Although the lender may choose when to sell and does not have to wait for an upturn in the market, when he does sell he is under a duty to the borrower to take reasonable care to get the best price reasonably obtainable 'on the day'.

In a Privy Council case from Hong Kong, *China and South Seas Bank* v. *Tan* [1990] 1 AC 536, there was a mortgage loan of $HK30m on the security of shares. Mr Tan, as surety for the mortgage, undertook to repay all the moneys owed by the debtor. When the repayment became due, the shares were worth enough to repay the debt, but by the time the mortgagee decided to exercise his power of sale the shares were worthless. Mr Tan argued that the mortgagee owed him a duty of care to sell as soon as possible, but this was rejected:

> If the creditor chose to exercise his power of sale over the mortgaged security he must sell for the current market value but the creditor must decide in his own interest if and when he should sell. The creditor does not become a trustee of the mortgaged securities (Lord Templeman, at p. 545).

In another case from Hong Kong, *Tse Kwong Lam* v. *Wong Chit Sen* [1983] 1 WLR 1349, Tse had granted a mortgage to Wong in 1963 on a large development in Hong Kong. Three years later he was in arrears and the land was sold at auction to the only bidder, a company owned by the lender and his wife and children. This in itself would not necessarily have been relevant, but the lender could not show that:

> he protected the interests of the borrower by taking expert advice as to the method of sale, as to the steps which ought reasonably to be taken to make the sale a success and as to the amount of the reserve [minimum price] (Lord Templeman, at p. 1359).

The normal remedy in such a case is for the sale to be set aside, but here the Privy Council did not do so because the borrower had been 'guilty of inexcusable delay'; he had not pursued the matter for many years. He won the alternative remedy of damages, the difference between the price which was obtained and the price which should have been obtained.

An example of where the lender was negligent in exercising its power of sale is *Cuckmere Brick Ltd* v. *Mutual Finance Ltd* [1971] Ch 949. In this case, the lender had failed to advertise to prospective purchasers the full extent of the planning permission which attached to the property. The Court of Appeal held that the mortgagee had failed to meet the duty that it owed to the mortgagor to take reasonable care to obtain a proper price. As a result the lender was liable to the mortgagor for any shortfall between the price obtained by the lender and the true value of the land.

Once the land is sold, the lender is under a duty to account to the borrower. He must also take care to protect the interests of others. He must apply the proceeds in the order set out in s.105 LPA 1925.

Application of the proceeds of sale

- any prior mortgages, unless the property was sold subject to them;
- the expenses of the sale;
- the capital and interest due under the mortgage;
- any second or subsequent mortgages; and
- the borrower.

Although the lender is not a trustee of his power of sale, he is, by virtue of s.105, a trustee of the proceeds of sale and must act in good faith.

A buyer from a mortgagee must check that a power of sale exists, but need not make sure that it has actually become exercisable (s.104(2) LPA 1925). However, if he knows of, or suspects, any 'impropriety' he might not get a good title and for this reason he would be wise to ensure that the mortgagee has taken reasonable care, otherwise he might lose the land and have to try to get the purchase price back from the mortgagee (see Megarry and Wade, 2008, section 25-016).

In addition to the power given mortgagees by s.101 LPA 1925, courts have the general power to order sale at the instance of any 'person interested' by virtue of s.91 LPA 1925. The court's general power to order sale may be employed as an alternative to foreclosure (see Section 7.3.1.4) and can be also be used at the request of the borrower (for example, when the mortgagee will not agree to a sale; see Section 7.4.3).

Occasionally, as in *Target Home Loans Ltd* v. *Clothier* [1994] 1 All ER 439, the courts will postpone a possession order to allow the borrower, rather than the lender, to sell the property, since the borrower is much more likely to get a higher price. However, following the Court of Appeal decision in *Cheltenham & Gloucester Plc* v. *Krausz* [1997] 1 WLR 558, it is unlikely that the courts will take this line in cases where there the value of the property is less than the balance owed (negative equity).

7.3.1.3 Appointing a Receiver

A lender can appoint a receiver – who manages the land – in the same circumstances in which he has the power of sale (s.101 LPA 1925). This can be very convenient in a commercial mortgage, for example, if the land is let to tenants and the mortgagee wants the rents to pay off interest which is due. The advantage of appointing a receiver rather than going into possession is that a mortgagee in possession is personally liable to the borrower for any loss but, if he appoints a receiver, the receiver must pay for his own mistakes. This is because, by s.109 LPA 1925, the receiver is deemed to be the agent of the mortgagor (the borrower). In *Medforth* v. *Blake* [2000] Ch 86, the Court of Appeal considered that the duties owed by a receiver to a borrower and others interested in the equity of redemption (see Section 7.4.1) are not confined to a duty of good faith but extend to managing the property with due diligence, subject to trying to create a situation whereby the debt can be paid off. In *Silven Properties* v. *Royal Bank of Scotland Plc* [2004] 1 WLR 997, the Court of Appeal confirmed that the receiver's duty to manage the property does not require him to go so far as to undertake its improvement in order to increase its value. The receiver's primary duty is to effect the repayment of the secured debt.

7.3.1.4 Foreclosure

Once the legal date of redemption has passed, a foreclosure order is theoretically available from the court, but these equitable orders are rarely, if ever, sought today. A foreclosure order transfers legal and equitable title in the land to the lender, free from all the borrower's rights in the land (including the right to redeem the mortgage). An order is only granted if the court is clear that the borrower will never be able to repay, but even when an order has been granted the court has the power to reopen the foreclosure (see *Campbell* v. *Holyland* (1877-78) LR 7 Ch D 166). Any application for a foreclosure order will now almost certainly result in the court making an order for sale pursuant to its powers under s.91 LPA 1925 (see Section 7.4.3).

7.3.1.5 Suing on the Personal Covenant

If the amount realised on the sale of the mortgaged land is insufficient to cover the amount owed to the lender, the borrower remains personally liable to the lender for the shortfall, and the lender may sue him for the outstanding sum.

The right to sue on the personal covenant to repay the mortgage debt must be exercised within 'twelve years from the date on which the right to receive the money accrued' (s.20 Limitation Act 1980). Initially, this date is the contractual date of redemption set by the mortgage (see Section 7.3.1.2), but the twelve year period recommences each time any payment of capital or interest is made and if written acknowledgement of liability is given by the mortgagor (ss.29,30 Limitation Act 1980). The limitation period for interest due under the mortgage (as opposed to the capital debt) is six years from the date that the interest fell due (s.20(5) Limitation Act 1980).

In *West Bromwich Building Society* v. *Wilkinson* [2005] 1 WLR 2303 the lender obtained an order for possession of the borrowers' home in 1989, selling it a year later leaving a shortfall of nearly £24,000. In 2002 the lender began proceedings for nearly £47,000 (the initial shortfall and the interest on it since 1990). The lender argued that s.20 did not apply, and that even if it did the limitation period did not start running until after the land hand been sold, when the total shortfall would be known. The House of Lords rejected both arguments. Section 20 applied to all actions derived from a mortgage, even if the lender had sold the land concerned. The affect of the wording of this particular mortgage and ss.101 and 103 LPA 1925 was that the whole of the mortgage advance fell due as soon as the borrowers had defaulted and the lender made demand for payment. Consequently, the twelve years began to run in 1989, with the result that the action was statute-barred.

The borrower's liability on his personal covenant can have very serious consequences for himself, and for others. In *Alliance and Leicester Plc* v. *Slayford* (2000) 33 HLR 743, a lender had been unable to get an order for possession against a borrower due to the wife of the borrower having a very small equitable interest in the house that was not subject to the mortgage. The lender decided to sue on the borrower's personal covenant to repay, which would have had the eventual effect of making the borrower bankrupt. The trustee in bankruptcy could then apply for sale of the house under s.14 Trusts of Land and Appointment of Trustees Act 1996 and would almost certainly succeed (see 12.7). Although the lender would lose its priority over the bankrupt borrower's unsecured creditors, at least by these means it would get some of its money back. The wife, however, would lose her home, despite the mortgage having earlier been declared void against her. In somewhat forthright language the trial judge stated that the mortgagee's tactic amounted to an abuse of the process of the court. However, the Court of Appeal had little difficulty in finding for the mortgagee: it was not an abuse for it to employ any or all of the legal remedies available to it.

7.3.1.6 Consolidation

In rare cases, where the mortgagee has lent money on mortgages granted by the same borrower over different pieces of land, he has a right to consolidate them. This means that he may join the various mortgages together; he can refuse to allow the borrower to redeem one of the mortgages without redeeming any others. Consolidation can be useful if one piece of land is not sufficient security for the debt. The right arises when the power is contained in the mortgage itself, and is exercisable only when the contractual date for redemption has passed. There are a number of technical rules, very clearly explained in Megarry and Wade, 2008, sections 25-055 to 25-070.

7.3.1.7 Holding the Title Documents

The first legal mortgagee of unregistered land is entitled to hold the deeds which are returned to the borrower on redemption. However, all first legal mortgages created after March 1998 will trigger the first registration of the land (see Section 11.2), and the deeds sent to the Land Registry in order to complete the registration of the title.

If the title is registered, any charge is protected by entry on the register (see Chapter 11). Prior to 13 October 2002, the Land Registry issued a charge certificate to the mortgagee each time a new mortgage was registered. Charge certificates have not been issued since the LRA 2002 came into force, although the registration of a new legal charge will prompt the issue of a new 'title information document' (see Section 11.2.1).

7.3.2 The Equitable Lender

Both equitable mortgagees and equitable chargees can sue on the borrower's personal promise to pay, but, apart from this, their rights differ.

7.3.2.1 The Equitable Mortgagee

Unless an equitable mortgage has been made by deed, there is no automatic power to sell or appoint a receiver (s.101 LPA 1925). However, the mortgagee can obtain a court order for sale using s.91 LPA 1925). If there is a deed, the equitable lender generally has the same remedies as a legal lender, but he must be careful to draft the document to give him the right to sell the legal estate. It is not clear whether he has an automatic right to go into possession.

7.3.2.2 The Equitable Chargee

The rights of 'a mere equitable chargee' are fewer than those of other lenders. This kind of lender only has the remedy of sale or appointment of a receiver, both by order of the court.

7.4 The Position of the Borrower

As well as the rights which arise directly out of the lender's duties – for example to take precautions against undue influence and to obtain a good price on sale – the borrower has special rights to protection against oppression by a mortgagee, especially in relation to the terms of the contract. Many of these rights are creations of equity created to protect borrowers against exploitative money-lenders, whilst others have been introduced by statute.

7.4.1 The Equity of Redemption

As mentioned in Section 7.3.1.2, mortgage agreements normally specify a contractual date for the repayment of the loan. This is the legal date of redemption (usually six months from the date of the loan in modern mortgage deeds). Where it is fair to do so, equity refuses to enforce this contractual date. Instead, the lender is required to accept the money even though the legal date of redemption has passed, thereby creating an equitable right to redeem.

Historically, equity looks at the substance of an agreement and not at the name given to it. If the effect of an agreement is to create a loan on the security of land, equity will recognise the transaction as a mortgage and protect the borrower, following the maxim 'once a mortgage always a mortgage'. The rules are summarised in the expression that there must be 'no clogs or fetters on the equity of redemption' and are explained below. However, it must be noted that some of the older cases reflect a different financial world, and, furthermore, one in which the House of Lords was bound to follow its own earlier decisions. It is becoming evident that modern judges will attempt to find a way around inconvenient precedents by, for example, applying general contractual doctrines such as duress and restraint of trade, rather than considering whether a term amounts, in mortgage law theory, to a 'clog'.

7.4.1.1 No Irredeemability

Equity will not allow a vendor to enforce a promise that prevents a borrower from ever redeeming the mortgage. For example, *Samuel* v. *Jarrah Timber and Wood Paving Co Ltd* [1904] AC 323 concerned a mortgage of company stock (a debenture). In the mortgage deed the borrower gave the lender an option to purchase; the lender could therefore choose to buy the stock from the borrower, thus preventing the borrower from redeeming the mortgage. The House of Lords declared the option void because it made the equitable right to redeem 'illusory'. The decision was made very reluctantly (in 1904 the House could not reverse its own judgments) as their Lordships felt that this arrangement, made by two large companies, was quite different from the kind of case for which the rule had been established:

> The directors of a trading company in search of financial assistance are certainly in a very different position from that of an impecunious landowner in the toils of a crafty money-lender (Lord Macnaghten, at p. 327).

In *Jones* v. *Morgan* [2002] 1 EGLR 125, the Court of Appeal struck out a term in a mortgage agreement that purported to give the lender a right to buy a half share in the mortgaged land. In an ordinary contract, the term would have been valid, but since the term was contained within a mortgage agreement, the doctrine of clogs and fetters applied since, again, the Court found itself bound by precedent. However, the doctrine received considerable criticism in the case:

the doctrine of a clog on the equity of redemption is, so it seems to me, an appendix to our law which no longer serves a useful purpose and would be better excised (Lord Phillips MR, at para. 86).

If the option to purchase is seen as a separate agreement from the mortgage agreement, it will be enforced. In *Reeve* v. *Lisle* [1902] AC 461, a mortgage of a ship was created and, some 12 days later, the mortgagor granted the lender an option to purchase it. The court did not see this as a clog, since the later agreement could be separated from the mortgage, and the option was held to be enforceable. Whether or not there is a separate agreement is not always easy to determine. For example, in *Jones* v. *Morgan*, Pill L.J. dissented from the majority judgement, holding that the right to buy the half share was a separate agreement and that it was not, therefore, a clog on the equity of redemption.

In *Warnborough Ltd* v. *Garmite Ltd* [2003] EWCA Civ 1544, the Court of Appeal had the opportunity of reviewing the law on the extent to which an option to purchase amounts to a clog on the equity of redemption. Jonathan Parker LJ stated:

that the mere fact that, contemporaneously with the grant of a mortgage over his property, the mortgagor grants the mortgagee an option to purchase the property does no more than raise the question whether the rule against 'clogs' applies: it does not begin to answer that question ... the court has to look at the 'substance' of the transaction in question: in other words, to inquire as to the true nature of the bargain which the parties have made (at para. 73).

He went on to state that where the original seller of the property was also both mortgagee and the grantee of the option, as in *Warnborough*, there would be a strong likelihood that the transaction would be held to be one of sale and purchase rather than one of mortgage, and so the doctrine of clogs would not apply.

An agreement which postpones the equitable right to redeem so that it effectively becomes meaningless is likely to be void. This happened in *Fairclough* v. *Swan Brewery Co Ltd* [1912] AC 565, where Mr Fairclough held a 17-year lease of a hotel. His lessor was the Swan Brewery, which lent him money on the security of his lease. The contractual date of redemption was fixed for a few weeks before the lease was due to expire. As the equitable right to redeem does not arise until the contractual date has passed, the mortgage was effectively irredeemable and the promise was therefore held void. However, in *Knightsbridge Estate's Trust Ltd* v. *Byrne* [1939] Ch 441, a case between two large companies, the contractual date for redemption of the mortgage (for £310,000) was set 40 years in the future. Given the reluctance of the courts to intervene when the parties are of equal bargaining power, and also the fact that the land was freehold, the Court of Appeal held that the term was enforceable. This was:

a commercial agreement between two important corporations, experienced in such matters, and has none of the features of an oppressive bargain (per Greene MR, at p. 455).

7.4.1.2 Post-redemption Conditions

Another of equity's concerns was the unfair advantage taken by a lender who sought to restrict the borrower's commercial activities, such as requiring a shopkeeper mortgagor to buy wholesale goods only from the mortgagee. These kinds of agreement are known as *solus* agreements and are common between oil companies and filling stations, and breweries and publicans. Equity had declared void any terms in a mortgage agreement which would prevent the borrower from freely enjoying his land after he has repaid all the money. An example of this is *Noakes & Co Ltd* v. *Rice* [1902] AC 24, where the owner of a 26-year lease of a pub mortgaged it to a brewery, promising he would buy liquor only from the lender for the whole term of the lease. The House of Lords held that the promise was ineffective: the lender could not prevent him regaining his property free of ties when he repaid the loan. In *Kreglinger* v. *New Patagonia Meat & Cold Storage Co Ltd* [1914] AC 25, however, the House decided that a collateral promise that the borrower would sell his sheepskins to no-one but the lender for five years, regardless of when the loan was repaid, was valid. This was not a clog on the equitable right to redeem. The mortgage agreement was a commercial arrangement on reasonable terms between two companies at arm's length and, after redemption, the mortgagor would be able to enjoy the land in the same state as it had been before the mortgage. Nowadays, the courts tend to apply the contractual doctrine of restraint of trade to this kind of issue – see *Esso Petroleum Co Ltd* v. *Harpers Garage (Stourport) Ltd* [1968] AC 269.

7.4.1.3 Other Oppressive Terms

Equity developed rules against other clogs on the equity of redemption, and declared void any other 'unconscionable or oppressive terms' in the mortgage. In *Multiservice Bookbinding Ltd* v. *Marden* [1979] Ch 84, the bookbinding company granted a mortgage as security for a loan of £36,000. The interest rate was linked to the Swiss franc, because the pound was very unstable. The fluctuation in the money markets meant that the borrower would have to pay £45,000 in interest. Browne-Wilkinson J held that this may have been unreasonable, but it was not oppressive or unconscionable. For a promise to be struck out, it must be shown that the objectionable terms were imposed 'in a morally reprehensible manner ... which affects [the mortgagee's] conscience'. Again, the court showed its reluctance to intervene in a commercial agreement between equals.

Many mortgage agreements permit the lender at its discretion to vary the interest rate payable by the borrower. The Court of Appeal in *Paragon Finance Plc* v. *Nash* [2002] 1 WLR 685 protected the borrower against the arbitrary exercise of this discretion by holding that such agreements contain an implied term that the interest rates 'would not be set dishonestly, for an improper purpose, capriciously or arbitrarily' (Dyson LJ, at para. 36). In a later case concerning the same lender (*Paragon Finance Plc* v. *Pender* [2005] 1 WLR 3412) a differently constituted Court of Appeal decided that there was nothing in this implied term that prevents a lender from increasing the interest rate above that of most of its competitors, provided that the decision to do so is a genuinely commercial one.

7.4.2 Statutory Protection from Unfair Agreements

The vast majority of first mortgages of residential property will fall within the provisions of the Financial Services and Markets Act 2000, which came into force on 31 October 2004. This Act imposes a code of practice on mortgage lenders designed to promote transparency and preclude extortionate charges being imposed.

Until April 2008 most other mortgages granted by individuals fell within ss.137–140 of the Consumer Credit Act 1974 regulating extortionate credit bargains. Mortgagors could ask the courts to reopen a credit bargain if the payments were 'grossly exorbitant' or 'grossly contravene ordinary principles of fair dealing'. Sections 137–140 have now been repealed and replaced by a new scheme allowing the court to intervene if it finds that the relationship between the creditor and the debtor arising out of a credit agreement is unfair to the debtor (ss.19–22 Consumer Credit Act 2006).

Like ss.137–140, the new scheme applies to agreements between an individual borrower (including an individual in the course of business) and anyone who lends money. It does not apply to first legal charges over residential land regulated under the Financial Services and

Markets Act 2000 (see above), but will apply to many second mortgages. Many second mortgages are arranged for purposes such as home improvements or securing a business loan, but sometimes they are an act of desperation by a defaulting borrower and it is particularly here that the borrower needs protection.

The court may decide that the relationship is unfair to the debtor because of one or more of:

(a) any of the terms of the agreement or of any related agreement;
(b) the way in which the creditor has exercised or enforced any of his rights under the agreement or any related agreement;
(c) any other thing done (or not done) by, or on behalf of, the creditor (either before or after the making of the agreement or any related agreement.

(s.140A Consumer Credit Act 1974, as amended).

If satisfied that an agreement is unfair, the court has considerable powers to intervene on behalf of the borrower and may, for example, alter the terms of the agreement, or order repayment or the return of property (s.140B). It has yet to be seen how willing the courts will be to intervene in credit agreements. There are relatively few examples of the courts using their earlier powers under ss.137–140, possibly because the more needy (and therefore weak) the borrower, the more justified is the lender in imposing a high interest rate because of the risk he is taking. The counter-argument, that if the borrower defaults the lender can realise the security of the land, appears to hold little attraction.

7.4.3   Section 91 LPA 1925

There may be circumstances, especially when the value of land has been falling, when the mortgagee might seek to prevent a sale of the mortgaged land, despite the borrower being unable to repay the loan. Where there is negative equity, the borrower may be keen sell the land to repay as much of the debt as possible in order to prevent the interest due on the loan from spiralling upwards. The lender may be equally keen to prevent a sale, leasing out the land in the meantime in the hope that it might increase in value at some point in the future. This situation arose in *Palk* v. *Mortgage Services Funding Plc* [1993] Ch 330, where the borrower had found a buyer for the land, but the price was about £50,000 less than the then mortgage debt. The interest on the debt was accumulating at a rate of £43,000 a year and an annual rent would not be more than about £13,000. The mortgagee argued that it could prevent a sale if the price was less than the amount needed to repay the debt in full. Mrs Palk claimed, however, that under s.91 LPA 1925 (originally intended to facilitate sales in foreclosure proceedings) the court has a discretion to order a sale of mortgaged property. Here the Court of Appeal held for Mrs Palk: any borrower, even one suffering with a negative equity, can ask the court to order a sale because the court has an 'unfettered discretion' under s.91 to prevent 'manifest unfairness'.

7.4.4   Avoiding Undue Influence and Misrepresentation

The question of mortgages entered into because of undue influence and misrepresentation has been raised in a large number of cases since the increase in family home repossessions which occurred in the early 1990s when interest rates were high and the value of property was falling. In a typical undue influence case, a lender seeks to repossess a home because of arrears, and one of the joint borrowers then claims to have signed the mortgage deed or stood surety for the loan under the undue influence of the other, claiming that she (generally) was unaware of the implications of her actions. Misrepresentation occurs when one joint borrower induces the other to sign the mortgage by lying about the extent of the loan facility which it is securing. In both situations, the question for the court is not whether one party acted towards the other unconscionably or in breach of trust; it is whether the lending institution had notice of the undue influence or was in some other way responsible for it. If the lender did not take steps to ensure that the signature was properly obtained without any undue influence or misrepresentation, the mortgage will be void as far as the injured party is concerned.

The facts of two House of Lords cases are typical of the kind of situations where a lender might be fixed with notice of the undue influence of the borrower. In the first of the cases, *Barclays Bank Plc* v. *O'Brien* [1994] 1 AC 180, Mr O'Brien was the sole legal owner of the matrimonial home, but his wife had an equitable share in it. He told her he was borrowing £60,000 on a mortgage for three weeks to save his business, so she signed all the surety forms at the bank without reading any of them and without any independent advice. In fact, the loan was for £135,000. Within six months the repayments were seriously in arrears and the bank sought possession. Mrs O'Brien successfully argued that her agreement to the mortgage was the result of her husband's misrepresentation about the size of the loan being secured on the house, and that the bank had constructive notice of this, giving rise to her right to set the mortgage aside.

In the second case, *CIBC Mortgages* v. *Pitt* [1994] 1 AC 200, the facts were fairly similar, but here Mrs Pitt, the wife, was a joint legal owner of the home. As joint legal owner she could be presumed, on the facts, to be benefiting financially from the mortgage loan (its purpose was expressed to be to pay off an outstanding mortgage and to buy a second home, but the husband really wanted the money in order to play the stock market) and therefore the bank was not put on notice to take steps to protect her position.

After a series of undue influence cases in the lower courts the House of Lords, reviewed this area of the law in what is now the leading case on undue influence: *Royal Bank of Scotland Plc* v. *Etridge (No. 2)* [2002] 2 AC 773. The issues were these:

- what are the requirements that need to be met in order to prove that undue influence has occurred;
- under what circumstances is a lender put on notice that there may have been undue influence; and
- if the lender is on notice, what steps must it take to avoid any subsequent claim by the innocent joint borrower or surety?

For transactions that pre-date the House of Lords' decision in *Etridge*, a lender is placed on inquiry in situations where the surety trusted the debtor to deal with her financial affairs or where both were living together in a close emotional relationship. Lord Nicholls said that in such circumstances:

> the bank will ordinarily be regarded as having discharged its obligations if a solicitor who was acting for the wife in the transaction gave the bank confirmation to the effect that he had brought home to the wife the risks she was running by standing as surety (at para. 80).

There will be circumstances, however, where such confirmation may be insufficient to protect a bank. In the case of *National Westminster Bank Plc* v. *Amin* [2002] UKHL 9, Mr and Mrs Amin had granted a mortgage of their home to the Bank in 1988 to secure the business debts of one of their sons. The son experienced financial difficulties and the Bank sought possession of the house. At a preliminary stage of proceedings the Bank argued that Mrs Amin had no reasonable defence to their claim, and that possession should be granted without the matter having to go to full trial. The House of Lords reached no conclusions as to the actual facts of the case (it was remitted back to the lower court for trial), but Lord Scott expressed a number of concerns that needed to be addressed, including:

- whether the bank knew that Mr and Mrs Amin's circumstances made them specially vulnerable to exploitation;
- the apparent failure of the bank to impress upon the solicitor the importance that the Amins should receive proper and sufficient advice about the legal implications and effect of the transaction being proposed; and
- the fact that the solicitor's subsequent letter to the bank '... simply said that the author had 'explained' the terms and conditions. It said nothing about their apparent understanding of the explanation' (at para. 24).

For transactions entered into after the House of Lords' decision in *Etridge*, the lender will be on inquiry in all cases where the relationship between the debtor and the surety is non-commercial.

In such circumstances:

> The furthest a bank can be expected to go is to take reasonable steps to satisfy itself that the wife has had brought home to her, in a meaningful way, the practical implications of the proposed transaction. This does not wholly eliminate the risk of undue influence or misrepresentation. But it does mean that a wife enters into a transaction with her eyes open so far as the basic elements of the transaction are concerned (Lord Nicholls, *Royal Bank of Scotland Plc* v. *Etridge (No. 2)* [2002] 2 AC 773 at para. 54).

The bank will be considered to have taken these reasonable steps if:

- it tells the wife or other person in a non-commercial relationship to the debtor that it requires her to consult a solicitor of her choice (who may be the family solicitor, but who must be acting for her);
- it provides the necessary financial information to allow the solicitor properly to advise the borrower (if the debtor will not allow such confidential information to be passed on the transaction will not be able to proceed); and
- it obtains written confirmation from the solicitor that the documents and the practical implications of the arrangement (that is, that she risks losing her home if the mortgage payments are not met) have been explained to the borrower.

If the bank has reason to believe that the wife is not acting of her own free will, it must inform the solicitor of this.

This complex area of mortgage law indicates the sort of policy tensions which can arise in land law and how the courts deal with them; it is important that lenders are able to lend money on the security of property without being concerned that their security will be lost, and at the same time it is just as important that the rights of more vulnerable owners are protected (see also, for example, *Williams & Glyn's Bank Ltd* v. *Boland* [1981] AC 487, *City of London Building Society* v. *Flegg* [1988] AC 54, and Section 11.7.2.1).

7.5   Discharge of Mortgages

A mortgage is ended when the lease, sublease or charge is removed from the title to the property. Normally, in unregistered land, the borrower obtains a signed receipt on the mortgage document. In registered land a form is sent to the Land Registry. In the case of a mortgage by a long lease, repayment of the loan means that the lease becomes a satisfied term.

7.6 Priority of Mortgages

7.6.1 The General Rules

The rules about priority in mortgages come into play when there are several mortgages of one piece of land. If the borrower defaults and the land is not worth enough to pay back all the debts, then one or more of the lenders may lose money. The priority rules determine which of the lenders is to be unlucky. There have been few cases in the last hundred years on priorities, but some land lawyers greatly enjoy creating and solving priority puzzles, especially those concerning three or more mortgages. The basic rules are stated very briefly in the next sections; for further details see, for example, Megarry and Wade, 2008, Ch. 26.

There are also special rules about the situation where several mortgages exist on one piece of land and a mortgagee owns two or more of them. In these circumstances, the mortgagee may be allowed to 'tack'. This means that where (1) Oliver has borrowed money on a mortgage of his flat from Andy, and then (2) borrowed on a (second) mortgage from Belinda, if (3) Andy lends more money (by a third mortgage) on the security of the flat, Andy may be able to jump over Belinda's second mortgage and tack (or attach) his first and third mortgages (compare consolidation of mortgages, Section 7.3.1.6).

7.6.2 Mortgages of a Legal Interest in Registered Land

In registered land the general rule is that, once a mortgage or charge has been protected on the Register, it will defeat all later mortgages as well as earlier mortgages which have not been so protected. Thus the first mortgage entered on the Register ranks first and the remainder rank according to the date of their registration (s.48 LRA 2002).

7.6.3 Priority of Mortgages of a Legal Interest in Unregistered Land

The rules relating to the priority of mortgages in unregistered land are now mainly of historic interest: all new first mortgages of freeholds and long leases since 1998 will have triggered first registration of the land (see Section 11.1). Mortgages in unregistered land must be protected either by the deposit of title deeds or by registration as a land charge (Chapter 10). Where a mortgage has to be registered as a C(i) land charge (legal mortgage) or a C(iii) land charge (equitable mortgage of a legal estate) its priority is ranked according to the date of registration, not the date of its creation. Briefly, subject to fraud or negligence, any legal mortgage with deposit of title deeds takes priority over all mortgages except any earlier mortgage which was properly registered. Any mortgage without deposit of title deeds is subject to (a) any earlier mortgage with deposit of deeds, and (b) any other mortgage which was properly registered.

7.6.4 Mortgages of an Equitable Interest in any Land

In the rare case where the interest mortgaged is an equitable interest under a trust, the mortgages rank according to the order in which notice of the mortgage was received by the trustees, whether the title is registered or unregistered (s.137 LPA 1925).

7.7 Comment

The law of mortgages illustrates very clearly the difference between legal rules and what really happens: in every part of this area of law, theory and practice diverge. In 1991 the Law Commission (No. 204) recommended that the complex theoretical foundations and the miscellaneous protections offered by a random combination of common law, equitable and statutory rules should be completely replaced by new interests in land, called 'formal' and 'informal land mortgages'. The only function of these new interests would be to provide security for the loan, and some of the terms would be laid down in legislation. At the same time, the jurisdiction to set aside unfair terms would be codified.

The existing law, however, shows how, behind the facade of unchanging concepts and rules, it is possible to provide a flexible response to social and economic change. Although the courts may occasionally be finding difficulty with the traditional equitable doctrine of clogs and fetters, cases such as *Palk* indicate how judges can generally readjust the balance between borrowers and lenders according to changes in lending practice and in the marketplace.

The case of *Etridge* is an example of how the courts have decided where to draw the line between commercial expediency and the need to protect the vulnerable. Institutional lenders will be alerted more frequently than before to the possibility that undue influence may have taken place, but it will not be difficult for them to discharge their obligations. The use of the mortgage of family property remains such an important source of capital for small businesses that any shift in the balance towards the further protection of the wife would tend to limit that source of financial provision. Equally, if the restrictions on lenders are eased too much, the consequences will be unacceptable for vulnerable and emotionally involved occupiers who have been persuaded by their partners in financial difficulties to agree to a risky mortgage loan. This real tension in land law will be addressed again, in a slightly different context, in Chapter 11.

Summary

7.1 Legal mortgages are made by deed; in unregistered land they may be created by demise (or subdemise) or legal charge, but in registered land by legal charge only.

7.2 Equitable mortgages may be of a legal or equitable interest. Legal interests may be mortgaged equitably by a contract to grant a legal mortgage or by equitable charge. Equitable interests can also be mortgaged by conveyance and reconveyance.

7.3 The lender must take care to avoid being fixed with the undue influence of a mortgagee over a surety where there is a non-commercial relationship between the two.

7.4 The legal lender has the right to take possession of property, but usually only does so when the borrower defaults; mortgagors of residential premises are given limited protection by statute.

7.5 In a legal mortgage, the power of sale (or to appoint a receiver) normally arises once the legal date of redemption has passed, and becomes exercisable if s.103 is satisfied: the lender is then a trustee of the proceeds, not the power, of sale.

7.6 Equitable mortgagees and chargees may have fewer rights than legal lenders.

7.7 The borrower's rights include:
  ● the equitable right not to have the equitable right to redeem restricted; and

- equitable rights (reinforced by statute) not to have to suffer unconscionable or oppressive terms. Cases now often depend on whether the lender has taken an unfair advantage.

7.8 Where there is a succession of mortgages, priority rules decide in what order the lenders should have their money repaid.

Exercises

7.1 What is the difference between the legal and equitable rights to redeem a mortgage?

7.2 When does a mortgagee have a power of sale?

7.3 How may a legal lease be mortgaged?

7.4 Can there be a term in a mortgage which continues after the mortgage has been redeemed?

7.5 To what extent is a mortgagee a trustee?

7.6 What protection does a wife have when her husband is pressuring her to agree to mortgage the family home in order to support his ailing business?

@ **7.7** Clayton owns a freehold shop with a flat above, where he lives with Emily who has an equitable share in the land. For some years he has run a business selling computer games from the shop. In 2006, a rival company set up nearby and took away most of Clayton's trade. In 2007, in order to clear his previous mortgage and his other debts and to provide a financial restructuring of the business, he borrowed £150,000 on mortgage from Sharks Ltd who gave him documents for Emily to sign; she did so without reading them when he told her that they were 'just something about my will'. The interest rate was set at 5 per cent above the bank rate.

The restructuring has not worked out, and in the last six months Clayton has been unable to make any repayment. There is little or no equity in the property. Advise Emily.

@ **7.8** There is an online quiz on the topics covered in this chapter available on the companion website.

Further Reading

Andrews, 'Undue Influence – Where's the Disadvantage' [2002] Conv 456

Brown, 'The Consumer Credit Act 2006; real additional mortgagor protection?' [2007] Conv 316

Dixon, 'Combating the Mortgagee's Right to possession: New Hope for the Mortgagor in Chains?' (1998) 18 Legal Studies 279

Haley, 'Mortgage Default: Possession, Relief and Judicial Discretion' (1997) 17 Legal Studies 483

Rook, *Property Law and Human Rights* (London: Blackstone, 2001)

Thompson, 'The Cumulative Range of a Mortgagee's Remedies' [2002] Conv 53

Chapter 8

Easements and Profits

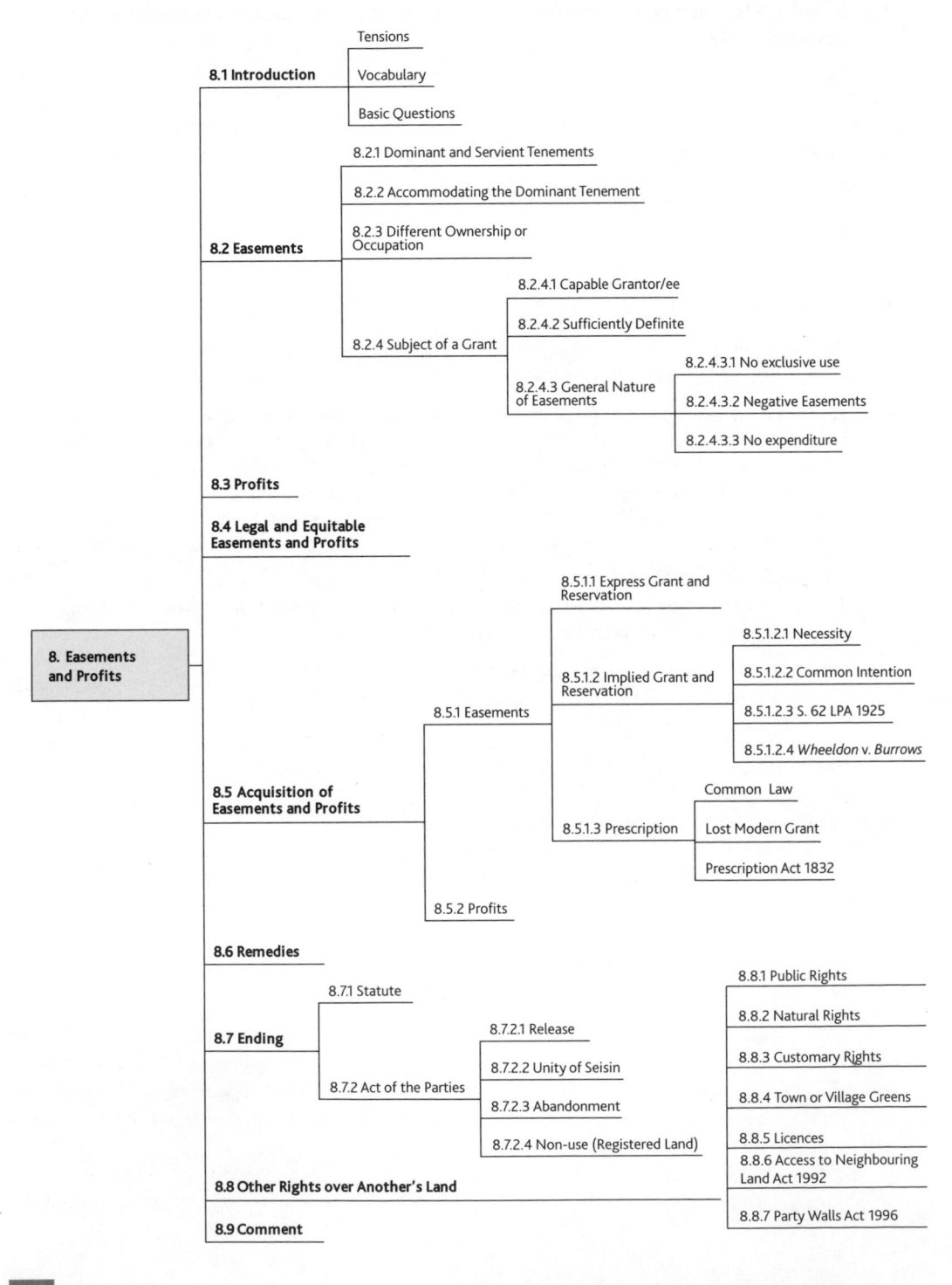

8. Easements and Profits

- **8.1 Introduction**
  - Tensions
  - Vocabulary
  - Basic Questions
- **8.2 Easements**
  - 8.2.1 Dominant and Servient Tenements
  - 8.2.2 Accommodating the Dominant Tenement
  - 8.2.3 Different Ownership or Occupation
  - 8.2.4 Subject of a Grant
    - 8.2.4.1 Capable Grantor/ee
    - 8.2.4.2 Sufficiently Definite
    - 8.2.4.3 General Nature of Easements
      - 8.2.4.3.1 No exclusive use
      - 8.2.4.3.2 Negative Easements
      - 8.2.4.3.3 No expenditure
- **8.3 Profits**
- **8.4 Legal and Equitable Easements and Profits**
- **8.5 Acquisition of Easements and Profits**
  - 8.5.1 Easements
    - 8.5.1.1 Express Grant and Reservation
    - 8.5.1.2 Implied Grant and Reservation
      - 8.5.1.2.1 Necessity
      - 8.5.1.2.2 Common Intention
      - 8.5.1.2.3 S. 62 LPA 1925
      - 8.5.1.2.4 *Wheeldon* v. *Burrows*
    - 8.5.1.3 Prescription
      - Common Law
      - Lost Modern Grant
      - Prescription Act 1832
  - 8.5.2 Profits
- **8.6 Remedies**
- **8.7 Ending**
  - 8.7.1 Statute
  - 8.7.2 Act of the Parties
    - 8.7.2.1 Release
    - 8.7.2.2 Unity of Seisin
    - 8.7.2.3 Abandonment
    - 8.7.2.4 Non-use (Registered Land)
- **8.8 Other Rights over Another's Land**
  - 8.8.1 Public Rights
  - 8.8.2 Natural Rights
  - 8.8.3 Customary Rights
  - 8.8.4 Town or Village Greens
  - 8.8.5 Licences
  - 8.8.6 Access to Neighbouring Land Act 1992
  - 8.8.7 Party Walls Act 1996
- **8.9 Comment**

8.1 Introduction

Easements and profits (*profits à prendre*) are property interests over someone else's land. Easements are rights to do something on land belonging to someone else (for example, to use it to gain access to your land). A profit is a right to take something from another's land (such as firewood or gravel). In medieval times, profits were very nearly as important as the fee simple; the rules concerning them were settled centuries ago and have changed little. Easements are also ancient, but they only achieved their present form within the last hundred years or so, after the enclosures of commonly held rural land and the rapid growth of towns and cities. Easements are now much more important than profits. New profits are rarely created these days, having largely been replaced by contractual licences. Both profits and easements are generally liable to be affected by decisions in the law of tort, and this chapter illustrates some of the interrelationships of contract, tort and land law.

The nature of land means that its value can often be increased if it benefits from a right over neighbouring land. An extreme example is the right to drive across a neighbour's field in order to reach land which is otherwise accessible only by helicopter. More common instances are the running of gas and water pipes, drains and electric cables from one house or flat to the next.

The essential problem for the judges in this area of land law – which is hardly touched by the 1925 legislation – is that they have to balance at least two conflicting demands. They would like to increase the value of land, for example by allowing a right to walk through a neighbour's garden as a short cut to a garage, because this will make that land 'a better and more convenient property'. This will, however, decrease the value of the other land by reducing privacy and restricting what may be done there, including its future development. As in the old rules about the running of leasehold covenants, the judges seek to ensure that the market in land is not depressed, either by making agreed rights unduly insecure, or by unduly burdening land and preventing the exercise of other valuable rights. As well as these tensions between the interests of private landowners, and between them and the general public interest in the market in land, there is also the tension between private landownership and public access to land. Most public rights of access to land are not easements, but creations of statute (most recently the Countryside and Rights of Way Act 2000), and largely fall outside the scope of this chapter.

The general rule is that (unlike contractual licences) landowners cannot simply create easements as they will:

> [i]ncidents of a novel kind cannot be devised and attached to property at the fancy or caprice of any owner (Lord Brougham LC, *Keppell* v. *Bailey* (1834) 2 My. & K. 517; 39 ER 1042, at p. 1049).

At the same time:

> [t]he category of ... easements must alter and expand with the changes that take place in the circumstances of mankind (Lord St Leonards LC, *Dyce* v. *Hay* (1852) 1 Macq 305).

If a new right is, in the judges' view, not capable of being an easement, it will be only a licence. The significance of this is that, while an easement is a property right, attached to the land and passing automatically with it on assignment, a licence is seen as a personal right rarely binding third parties and thus probably neither passing to a new owner of the land nor burdening a successor of the licensor (see Chapter 14).

Easements and profits have the vocabulary appropriate to their great age: 'dominant tenement' and 'servient tenement' are most important. In the law of easements (and sometimes in profits):

▷ the claimed right to use the land of another must benefit (*accommodate*) one piece of land, known as the *dominant tenement*;
▷ the land which provides the benefit and is therefore *burdened* by the easement or profit is known as the *servient tenement*.

In problem questions, there are usually just two issues:

1 Is the right claimed capable of being an easement or profit (see Sections 8.2 and 8.3)?
2 If so, has an easement or profit actually been created in this case (see Sections 8.4 and 8.5)?

These problems are usually straightforward to answer, providing the two issues are tackled separately and in order, although in many decided cases the two issues merge.

8.2 Easements

It is easy to give examples of easements, but more difficult to find an adequate generic definition. In order for a right to be classified as an easement, it must comply with the four traditional requirements listed by Dr Cheshire in his *Modern Real Property* in 1925, and reviewed by Lord Evershed MR in one of the leading cases on easements, *Re Ellenborough Park* [1956] Ch 131:

1 There must be a dominant and a servient tenement.
2 The easement must accommodate the dominant tenement.
3 The dominant and servient tenements must be owned or occupied by different people.
4 The easement must be capable of being the subject of a grant.

In *Ellenborough Park*, owners of houses near the park (in a square near the sea at Weston-Super-Mare) had been granted the right to use it 'as a leisure garden', but during the Second World War it had been taken over by the government. By statute, individual land-owners were entitled to compensation if they had been deprived of a legal right, and the only possible such right was an easement. They were eventually successful in persuading the Court of Appeal that the right to enjoy the park could amount to an easement.

8.2.1 Dominant and Servient Tenements

Clearly in *Ellenborough Park*, there was a servient tenement (the park) and there were dominant tenements (the houses). Sometimes, however, this is not so obvious. In *Miller* v. *Emcer Products Ltd* [1956] Ch 304, a tenant had an easement to use the landlord's lavatory, and here the dominant and servient tenements were not two plots of land, but two estates in land, the freehold and the leasehold; the tenant had the dominant tenement and the landlord the servient.

In *London and Blenheim Estates Ltd* v. *Ladbroke Retail Parks Ltd* [1994] 1 WLR 31, the Court of Appeal held that there can be no easement if, at the time the easement is purported to have been created, the dominant land is not in the possession of the grantee and if the grantor does not at the same time own the servient land. In this case, an option was claimed for an easement to park cars on land owned by the grantor. At the time the option was granted, the plaintiff did not own the land which was to benefit from it. When he eventually acquired this land and attempted to exercise the option, the land to be burdened had been sold by the grantor to someone, else who was able to argue that the claim to an easement could not succeed.

An easement cannot, therefore, exist in gross, but must be appurtenant to a dominant tenement. This requirement seems to have been adopted during the nineteenth century under the influence of Roman law, and reflects judicial concern to preserve certainty with respect to rights over land.

> If one asks why the law should require that there should be a dominant tenement before there can be a grant, or a contract for the grant, of an easement sufficient to create an interest in land binding successors in title to the servient land, the answer would appear to lie in the policy against encumbering land with burdens of uncertain extent (per Peter Gibson LJ, *London and Blenheim Estates Ltd* v. *Ladbroke Retail Parks Ltd* [1994] 1 WLR 31 at 37).

M. F. Sturley argues that the authority for requiring a dominant tenement is very weak ((1980) 96 LQR 557). He claims that allowing easements to exist in gross (that is, easements which are not attached to benefiting land), such as the right to land a helicopter on distant land, would not now unduly burden titles but could encourage maximum utilisation of land. The arguments put forward by Sturley are considered by the Law Commission in its recent consultation paper on Easements, Covenants and Profits à Prendre (Law Com. CP No 186 (2008)). At present, the Law Commission believes '... that the current requirement that an easement be attached to a dominant estate in the land serves an important purpose and should be retained' (see Law Com., CP. 186, para. 3.3-18).

8.2.2 Accommodating the Dominant Tenement

Just as in the pre-1996 law of leases, where the covenant must 'touch and concern' the land (see Section 6.4.1.2), the test is whether the claimed easement benefits the land itself and not merely the landowner. In *Ellenborough Park*, the Court of Appeal found it difficult to decide whether the easement touched and concerned (or 'accommodated' or benefited) the dominant tenement. Earlier cases had been divided on whether the right to use a garden could accommodate land, but Lord Evershed MR concluded that it is 'primarily a question of fact'. In this case, the dominant tenements did benefit from the garden use; it might have been different if they had not been family homes. In the recent case of *Mulvancy* v. *Gough* [2003] 1 WLR 360, the right to tend a communal garden was held 'clearly' to benefit the dominant tenement.

In *Hill* v. *Tupper* (1863) 2 H & C 121, the claim to an easement failed because it did not accommodate the dominant tenement. The owners of the Basingstoke Canal leased part of the canal bank to Hill and granted him the sole right to hire out pleasure boats. A local publican then also rented out boats and Hill tried to stop him, arguing that the publican was interfering with his easement. The court found that the exclusive right to hire out boats benefited Hill's business rather than his land, was thus a personal right only and therefore could not be an easement. By contrast, in *Moody* v. *Steggles* (1879) 12 Ch D 261, the right to hang a pub sign on neighbouring land was held to be an easement. Fry J refused to accept that it was possible to distinguish between the tenement and the business of the occupant of the tenement:

> It appears to me that that argument is of too refined a nature to prevail, and for this reason, that the house can only be used by an occupant, and that the occupant only uses the house for the business which he pursues, and therefore in some manner (direct or indirect) an easement is more or less connected with the mode in which the occupant of the house uses it (at p. 266).

Although the right to erect the sign benefited the business, it also benefited the land; given the way in which the land was used and had been used for many years.

8.2.3 Different Ownership or Occupation

People cannot have rights against themselves. If both tenements come into the hands of one person, the easement is ended ('extinguished by unity of seisin'). If what was formerly an easement continues to be used by the owner of both tenements, for example to cross one field to get into the next, this still looks like an easement (but is not because of unity of seisin); it is known as a quasi-easement and might one day come back to life (see Section 8.5.1.2.4).

8.2.4 Capable of Being the Subject of a Grant

The requirement that the easement must be capable of being the subject of a grant is not altogether clear. In theory it means that the right claimed must be capable of being conveyed in a deed, and this in turn means that a number of rules need to be satisfied if the right is to be an easement.

8.2.4.1 Capable Grantor and Grantee

There must be a capable grantor and a capable grantee. Both parties must be the owners of the land which are to become the dominant and servient tenements (see *London and Blenheim Estates Ltd* v. *Ladbroke Retail Parks Ltd* at Section 8.2.1) and both must be legal persons.

The principle of *nemo dat quod non habet* (no-one can give something which they do not have – see Section 5.3.1) applies to easements. Consequently an easement granted by a tenant will not normally be binding on the title to reversion. However, in the rather unusual circumstances of *Wall* v. *Collins* [2007] Ch 390, the Court of Appeal decided that such easements are not 'attached' to the leasehold interest out of which they are created and may, therefore, continue to exist for the remainder of the original term of the lease if the lease is brought to a premature end. There are significant problems with this reasoning, not least the failure to explain how the easement can continue when the servient tenement over which it was granted (the leasehold estate) no longer exists. The Court of Appeal seems to have failed to distinguish between the servient tenement and the land comprised within it.

8.2.4.2 Sufficiently Definite

The nature and extent of the right must be capable of sufficiently accurate definition. For example, *Aldred's Case* (1610) 9 Co Rep 57b, 77 ER 816 confirms that the right to a good view cannot amount to an easement since such a thing is too imprecise to describe. It may now be possible to achieve the desired result by using a freehold covenant (see Chapter 9).

8.2.4.3 Within the General Nature of Rights Recognized as Easements

To be capable of being an easement, the right concerned must fall within the general nature of the rights that are already recognized as easements. Many categories of easement are well established. A right of way over a neighbour's land is an obvious and well-known easement. Another is the right to light, normally restricted to enough light coming through a specific window for the 'comfortable' use of the premises. There are also easements for the use of naturally running water and for the support of a building (for example, terraced and semi-detached houses have mutual easements of support). A more detailed list of easements can be found in Chapter 30 of Megarry and Wade, 2008. The list is not closed, but neither is it capable of infinite extension. Determining whether a new right should be added to the list is a question of balancing the need for certainty with the need for flexibility (see the remarks of the two Lord Chancellors, Lord Brougham and Lord St Leonards quoted at Section 8.1). Generally speaking an easement must not give the dominant tenement holder too much control of the servient tenement and must not impose a positive obligation on the owner of servient tenement. However, these rules have not always been applied strictly, particularly in the older cases, and a number of recognised easements do not easily fall comfortably within them.

8.2.4.3.1 No Exclusive Use   The right claimed as an easement must not amount to a claim to rights which 'would amount to rights of joint occupation or would substantially deprive the park owners of proprietorship or legal possession' (Lord Evershed MR, *Re Ellenborough Park* [1956] Ch 131 at 164). This rule should cause relatively little difficulty where the effect of the right being claimed would be to completely exclude the owner of the servient tenement from her land. In such cases an argument based on adverse possession is more appropriate, although a claim to adverse possession where title to the land is registered is now much less likely to succeed than formerly (see Chapter 3).

In many cases, however, the right being claimed will fall short of exclusive use of the servient land, but will nevertheless significantly limit the ability of its owner to enjoy that land. It is not easy to discern a coherent or consistent approach from the decided cases. The right to store goods can be an easement, as in *Wright v. Macadam* [1949] 2 KB 744, providing the servient owner is not excluded and the right is clearly defined. Similarly, the tenant in *Miller v. Emcer Products Ltd* [1956] Ch 304 (see Section 8.2.1) succeeded because he would only have been using the lavatory some of the time. However, in *Copeland v. Greenhalf* [1952] Ch 488, a wheelwright who for many years had used a strip of the plaintiff's land alongside a road for storing and mending vehicles, failed to establish that he had acquired an easement by long use. The absence of any reference in the judgement of Upjohn J (as he then was) to the earlier and binding authority in *Wright v. Macadam* has spawned various judicial and academic attempts to reconcile the two decisions. In reality, however, Upjohn J's decision in *Copeland* rests at least as much on the vague character of the right being claimed (see Section 8.2.4.2) as upon the ouster of the land owner by the rights claimed (see Haley and McMurtry (2007)).

In recent years the question of whether a right is too extensive to be an easement has repeatedly arisen in the context of car parking. It has now been established that the right to park a car can amount to an easement provided that the right is sufficiently certain whilst also allowing the servient owner sufficient use of her land. Such a claim succeeded in *Hair v. Gillman* (2000) 48 EG 117, where the defendant had been given permission to park her car anywhere 'on a forecourt that was capable of taking two or three other cars' (see, also, *Moncrieff v. Jamieson* [2007] 1 WLR 2620).

The issue of what amounts to reasonable use of the servient land came before the Court of Appeal in *Batchelor v. Marlow* [2003] 1 WLR 764. As part of their business activities Mr and Mrs Marlow had parked vehicles on land owned by Mr Batchelor. At first instance, Nicholas Warren QC declared that the Marlows had acquired an exclusive right to park up to six cars on the land on Mondays to Fridays between 8:30 a.m. and 6:00 p.m. It was common ground in the Court of Appeal that the relevant test was that distilled by Judge Paul Baker QC in *London and Blenheim Estates Ltd v. Ladbroke Retail Parks Ltd* [1992] 1 WLR 1278:

> The essential question is one of degree. If the right granted in relation to the area over which it is to be exercisable is such that it would leave the servient owner without any reasonable use of his land,

whether for parking or anything else, it could not be an easement though it might be some larger or different grant (at p. 1288).

The Court of Appeal held that the effect of the rights claimed by the Marlows would seriously curtail Mr Batchelor's ability to use his land for significant periods of each week. The fact that Mr Batchelor could sell the land (subject to the Marlow's rights), or park on the land himself or charge others for doing so outside business hours did not amount to 'reasonable use' of his land. Such ownership would, in the words of Tuckey LJ, be merely 'illusory'. There are indications, however, that this test leans too far in favour of the landowner, and Lord Scott took advantage of the recent Scottish case of *Moncrieff* v. *Jamieson* [2007] 1 WLR 2620 to criticise it:

> I would, for my part, reject the test that asks whether the servient owner is left with any reasonable use of his land, and substitute for it a test which asks whether the servient owner retains possession and, subject to the reasonable exercise of the right in question, control of the servient land (at para. 59).

In Lord Scott's opinion, this would mean that there was no reason why an easement to park nine cars could not be granted over land just large enough to accommodate nine cars (compare *Hair* v. *Gillman* (2000) 48 EG 117).

8.2.4.3.2 Negative Easements   The courts are 'very chary' of creating new kinds of negative easements. In *Phipps* v. *Pears* [1965] 1 QB 76, a neighbour demolished a house which was built very close to that of the plaintiff, who claimed he had an easement of 'protection from the weather' with which the neighbour had interfered. This would have been a negative easement, preventing the neighbour from developing his land. In this case, Lord Denning MR defined the difference between positive and negative easements:

> positive easements, such as a right of way, which give the owner of land a right himself to do something on or to his neighbour's land: and negative easements, such as a right of light, which gives him a right to stop his neighbour doing something on his (his neighbour's) own land (at p. 82).

Of course, a positive easement will, by definition, prevent servient owners doing things on their land which interfere with the exercise of that easement. It is understandable, however, that entirely negative rights should not be capable of being easements, not just because of the policy reasons discussed above, but also because a servient owner might not know that the easement was being acquired (for example by use over a long period of time – see Section 8.5). The right claimed as an easement in *Phipps* was held not to be an easement of support and, indeed, was not an easement at all because it would 'unduly restrict the enjoyment' of the servient land and prevent its development. Despite this, a small number of negative easements, including rights to light and support, are recognised, but the list is unlikely to be extended.

Restrictive covenants may offer more appropriate solutions in situations like this, but the answer might also be found in the law of tort. In *Bradburn* v. *Lindsay* [1983] 2 All ER 408, Mr Bradburn, owner of one of a pair of semi-detached houses, was concerned that the dry rot in his neighbour's derelict house would spread to his own property. The house had to be demolished by the council and Mr Bradburn claimed damages from his neighbour for loss of support and exposure of the side of his house to dry rot and decay. There was clearly an easement of support, but Mrs Lindsay was under no obligation to maintain it by keeping the wall in repair. Mr Bradburn therefore successfully relied on the torts of negligence and nuisance.

8.2.4.3.3 No Expenditure by the Servient Owner   All the easements referred to thus far have been capable of being enjoyed without the owner of the servient tenement having to take any positive action or spend money, and in general this will be the case. There is, however, an exception to this: the 'spurious easement' (see *Lawrence* v. *Jenkins* (1872-73) LR 8 QB 274) of fencing which requires the servient owner to keep in repair her boundary fence if it is used as part of an enclosure to contain livestock on the dominant land.

In *Liverpool CC* v. *Irwin* [1977] AC 239, the House of Lords dealt with the issue of whether a landlord had to maintain easements of access to the flats in a tower block. The tenants had stopped paying rent because the common parts of the block were in such a bad condition. They had no written tenancy agreement, only a list of rules. Easements to use the passages, lifts and rubbish chutes were implied into the tenancies by the judges, along with an obligation to maintain and repair them:

> there appears to be no technical difficulty in making an express grant of an easement coupled with an undertaking by the servient owner to maintain it. That being so, there seems to be no reason why the easement arising in the present case should not by implication carry with it a similar burden on the grantor (Lord Edmund-Davies, at p. 268).

This, though, is probably exceptional, since in attempting to achieve a balance between the competing demands of landowners and aware of the need to maintain a healthy property market (see Section 8.1), the courts do not want to see servient land further burdened.

8.3 Profits

The rules on profits are fairly similar to those on easements, but profits can be either 'appurtenant' (benefiting a dominant tenement) or exist 'in gross' (without a dominant tenement). Thus, a person can own a profit to graze a goat on someone else's meadow, even though she owns no land which can benefit.

Where a profit is attached to land, it must accommodate the dominant tenement, just like an easement. In *Bailey* v. *Stephens* (1862) 12 CB (NS) 91, the owner of a field claimed a profit appurtenant to take wood from a neighbouring copse. It was held that this was not valid because it did not benefit the field. It might have been different if the alleged dominant tenement were a house and the wood used as firewood.

A profit may be 'sole' where only one person can take the thing and the owner of the servient tenement is excluded from it. Alternatively, it can be shared with the servient owner and is then known as a profit 'in common'.

There are profits of piscary (fish), turbary (turf), estovers (wood for firewood or other purposes) and pasture (the right to graze as many animals as can be supported through the winter months); some of them are still economically very important to their owners.

8.4 Legal and Equitable Easements and Profits

Easements and profits can be both legal and equitable.

A legal easement or profit must be:
- for the proper length of time, and
- created by deed or by implication or by long use, and
- registered if it falls within the scope of s.27(2)(d) LRA 2002.

An easement or profit can only be legal provided it is to last forever, like a fee simple, or for a period of time with a fixed beginning and end, like a lease (s.1(2)(a) LPA 1925). If the easement is for an indefinite but limited time, such as 'until I sell my house' or 'for your life', it cannot be legal (see Section 5.3.2). However, even if the easement or profit is 'for ever', or 'for two years, starting next Monday', it may still be equitable if it has not been created with the proper formalities (except for those easements or profits created by implication or by long use – see Section 8.5), or if the grantor owns only an equitable estate in the land.

As usual, it is important to know whether an easement or profit is legal or equitable, since this has a fundamental bearing on whether a successor of the owner of the dominant tenement will be able to enforce it and, equally, whether it will be binding on a successor of the servient owner. In unregistered land, a legal interest binds the world. The rules in registered land are more complicated, not least because of the transition between the LRA 1925 and the LRA 2002 (see Section 11.7.3). It should be noted, however, that easements or profits created expressly since 13 October 2003 will only take effect at law once they have been entered on the title register (s.27(2)(d) LRA 2002). All equitable easements should be protected by registration (for unregistered land; see Section 10.3.3.2; for registered land, see Section 11.6).

8.5 Acquisition of Easements and Profits

There are a number of ways of acquiring a legal easement or profit. The obvious way is to create one in a deed, but other methods of creation are based on behaving as if such a right already existed, together with a – usually mythical – deed. Legal easements and profits can also be directly created by long usage (compare adverse possession in Section 3.1).

8.5.1 Easements

Figure 8.1 shows the various ways in which an easement can be acquired. A *grant* of an easement is where the seller gives a right over a part of her land to a person buying another part of

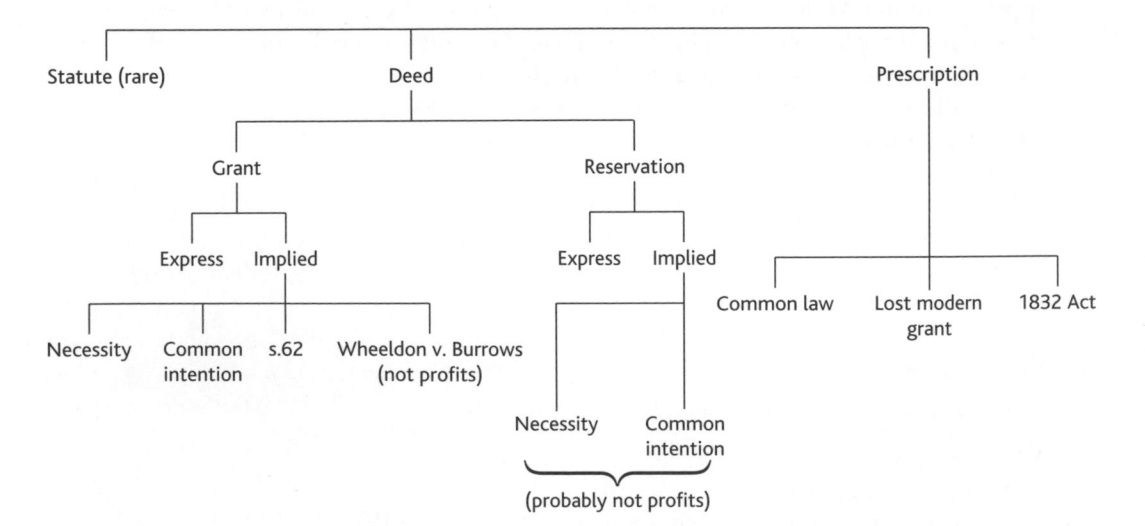

Figure 8.1 Acquisition of easements and profits.

it. *Reservation* is where she reserves for herself a right over a part of her land which she is selling. The distinction between the two is important, especially when considering easements which have been acquired by implication.

There is a considerable body of law on the acquisition of easements. Judges tend not to use categories consistently, so in practice they overlap (especially easements of necessity and intended easements). Much of the law on easements created by implication is based on the old principle of non-derogation from grant (see Section 6.2.1). *Wong* v. *Beaumont Property Trust Ltd* [1965] 1 QB 173 is a good example of this. A basement was let subject to the condition that it was to be used as a restaurant, but the basement could not be used for this purpose without a ventilation duct over the land retained by the lessor. Consequently, it must have been the common intention of the parties that the lease should include such an easement.

Only the bare outlines of the rules are given here. The main thing is to understand the variety of ways in which these interests can be created and acquired, so that you can recognise the circumstances in which one might arise, either to take advantage of it or to avoid it.

8.5.1.1 Express Grant and Reservation

If Imran, the owner of a block of flats, sells a fourth-floor flat to Paula, he will probably expressly grant her an easement over the hall and staircase in the deed transferring the land. If Josh sells part of his garden to Tash he should expressly reserve any rights that he needs in order to continue to use his house; for example, to use the drains running under the land being sold to Tash, and to use the driveway that runs over it.

8.5.1.2 Implied Grant and Reservation

8.5.1.2.1 Necessity
(a) Grant
Where land is (at the time of the sale) completely unusable without an easement, the courts may imply one into the deed transferring the land (or granting a lease of it). However, they will not do so if the wording of the deed expressly excludes the grant of such an easement (see *Nickerson* v. *Barraclough* [1981] Ch 426).

(b) Reservation
It is possible, but very difficult, to reserve an easement of necessity by implication. In *Adealon International Corp Proprietary Ltd* v. *Merton LBC* [2007] 1 WLR 1898 the Court of Appeal refused to infer an easement of necessity because at the time of the transfer, the transferor expected to have access to the retained land from the land of a third party. In *Manjang* v. *Drammeh* (1991) 61 P & CR 194, a person owned land situated between a river and a road. He sold that part of his land by the road but failed to reserve for himself an easement to cross it in order to reach the rest of his land on the bank of the river. The Privy Council refused to imply an easement across the land he had sold, since it was possible for him to get to his retained land by boat, and occasionally in the past he had done so.

In the examples given above, Paula's lease would be useless without a right also to use the stairs so, if no such easement had been expressly created, then one would be implied, by necessity, into the lease, just as in *Liverpool CC* v. *Irwin* [1977] AC 239.

8.5.1.2.2 Common Intention

(a) Grant

If the buyer and seller of land share an intention that the land should be used in a particular way, the courts may find an implied easement, provided that this is necessary for the intention to be fulfilled. In *Cory* v. *Davies* [1923] 2 Ch 95, terraced houses had been built along a private drive which gave out on to public roads at either end. There had been an intention that all the houses should have easements along all parts of the drive and on to the public roads, but such easements had never been expressly granted. The owner of the house at one end of the terrace obstructed his end of the drive, forcing everyone to go the other way. Given the common intention of the parties, the court found little difficulty in implying the necessary easements and requiring the blocked drive to be reopened.

Both easements of common intention and easements of necessity are based upon implication and the doctrine of non-derogation from grant (see *Wong* v. *Beaumont Property Trust Ltd* [1965] 1 QB 173, above). However, whilst easements derived from the parties' intended use of the land may be quite extensive, easements of necessity are normally restricted to the minimum rights needed to gain access to the land.

(b) Reservation

It is possible to reserve an easement of common intention by implication, but the courts will not readily infer such easements.

8.5.1.2.3 Section 62 LPA 1925

Section 62 LPA 1925 is a word saving provision which, on conveyance, transfers with the land all benefits which are attached to it (see Section 2.6.1.4). It can be (and frequently is) expressly excluded by the parties. Section 62 operates on the grant of land only, and cannot, therefore, be used as the basis of an implied reservation.

Wright v. *Macadam* [1949] 2 KB 744 (see Section 8.2.4.3.1) illustrates the potential of s.62. Here, with her landlord's permission, a tenant was storing coal in a shed; then, when a new lease was granted to her (the 'conveyance'), her licence was converted into an easement: it was an 'advantage ... appertaining to the land' and, when s.62 implied it into the deed, it grew into a legal easement and could not be revoked by the landlord. In any problem about a person who lives on land owned by another and has permission to do something extra, and who then receives a grant, the answer will probably involve s.62.

Wright v. *Macadam* was recently followed in *Hair* v. *Gillman* (2000) 48 EG 117 (see Section 8.2.4.3.1), a case in which a licence to park a car was given to the tenant of land used as a nursery school and later 'crystallised' into an easement under s.62 when she was granted the freehold. Chadwick LJ felt it to be a matter of regret that a property right binding the servient land could be created unintentionally. He repeated the comments of Tucker LJ in *Wright*, that such decisions 'may tend to discourage landlords from acts of kindness to their tenants. But there it is: that is the law' (at p. 755).

It has been argued that the section should only operate where the dominant and servient tenements are already in separate ownership or occupation. This was stated by a minority in the House of Lords in *Sovmots Investments Ltd* v. *Secretary of State for the Environment* [1979] AC 144, a case concerning a controversial compulsory purchase order made by a London borough. The order would have been invalid unless s.62 applied to create an easement of way along hallways in the building. It was held that s.62 did not apply to a compulsory purchase order and, further, the section could not be invoked because the building was wholly owned and occupied by Sovmots at the time of the 'conveyance'. The order was therefore invalid. This decision has been subject to criticism (see, for example, Smith [1978] Conv 449). It is possible that s.62 may operate where there is common ownership, provided that the use of the right being claimed has been continuous and apparent. In *P & S Platt Ltd* v. *Crouch* [2004] 1 P & CR 18, the owner of a hotel by a river also owned an island in the river on which he had moorings which could be used by the hotel guests. The hotel was sold. The sale did not include the moorings, but the new owners argued that they had an easement to use them. Peter Gibson LJ stated, without making any reference to the weighty dicta in *Sovmots*, that:

> the rights in question did appertain to ... and were enjoyed with the hotel, being part of the hotel business and advertised as such and enjoyed by the hotel guests. The rights were continuous and apparent, and so it matters not that prior to the sale of the hotel there was no prior diversity of occupation of the dominant and servient tenancies (at para. 42).

8.5.1.2.4 The Rule in *Wheeldon* v. *Burrows*   The rule in *Wheeldon* v. *Burrows* (1878) LR 12 Ch D 31 determines what easements are implied when a landowner sells part of her land. Thesiger LJ stated the rule in this case twice, but unfortunately not consistently. The basic principle is this: where a person sells part of her land which has the benefit of a *quasi-easement* (rights that would be easements but for the fact that the land is in common ownership), the buyer will gain the benefit of the quasi-easement if, at the time of the grant:

1   the seller was using the quasi-easement for the benefit of the land she was selling;
2   the use of the quasi-easement was 'continuous and apparent' (such as an obvious track, or a drain which could have been discovered on inspection); and/or
3   was necessary for the reasonable enjoyment of the land sold.

It is not known whether Thesiger LJ meant conditions 2 and 3 to be alternatives; in many cases, of course, if the quasi-easement (for example a right of way) satisfies one test, it will also satisfy the other. The third condition does not mean 'essential' (as in easements implied by necessity), but that there can be no reasonable enjoyment of the land without the easement.

In *Millman* v. *Ellis* [1996] 71 P & CR 158, the Court of Appeal held that Millman had successfully proved an easement under the rule. He had bought a large house from Ellis and also part of Ellis' remaining land; he claimed the right to use the driveway which Ellis had always used to get to the house and which was safer than using the main road. In *Wheeler* v. *JJ Saunders Ltd* [1995] 2 All ER 697, however, Wheeler had bought part of a farm and claimed an easement to allow him to pass through a gap in a wall southwards to get to a road. It was held that this access was not necessary for the reasonable enjoyment of the house because there was another equally suitable access in the east.

For the rule in *Wheeldon* v. *Burrows* to apply, the land must have been in common occupation immediately prior to the transfer: common ownership (for example, by a common landlord) is not sufficient (see *Kent* v. *Kavanagh* [2007] Ch 1). The rule applies only to the implied grant of an easement and cannot be used to infer a reservation for the benefit of retained land. This was confirmed by the Court of Appeal in *Chaffe* v. *Kingsley* (2000) 79 P & CR 404.

8.5.1.3 Prescription

The use for many years of a right which is capable of being an easement can create a legal easement by 'prescription'. The rules are extraordinarily obscure.

Prescription may arise if an easement has been used openly, as of right, without permission and continuously, by one fee simple owner against another provided that the right could have legitimately been granted by the landowner (see *Bakewell Management Ltd* v. *Brandwood* [2004] 2 AC 519). There are three forms, common law, 'lost modern grant' and statutory, under the Prescription Act 1832. The requirements for each form of prescription are summarised below (for a much more detailed consideration see Megarry and Wade, 2008, sections 28-032 to 28-080).

The three types of prescription:
1   **at common law**:
the claim: the right has been enjoyed since time immemorial (1189)
the proof: 20 years continuous user shown, provided that the right could have been exercised in 1189.

2   **by lost modern grant**:
the claim: the right was granted in a deed, but that deed has now been lost
the proof: user for any 20 years (there is no requirement that the right is still being enjoyed at the date of the commencement of proceedings) provided that the fictitious grant was not impossible.

3   **Prescription Act 1832**:
the proof: user as of right (except easements of light) for statutory period of 20 or 40 years immediately prior to proceedings.

In 1966, the Law Reform Committee recommended the simplification of prescription law (14th Report, Cmnd 3100), but no new statute was ever forthcoming. The Law Commission and the Land Registry proposed (in their 1998 Consultation Paper 'Land Registration for the Twenty-First Century', Law Com No 254, paras 10.79 *et seq*.) that the sole method of acquiring an easement by prescription in registered land should be by the Prescription Act 1832. The methods of creating easements were part of the Law Commissions consultation paper on Easements, Covenants and Profits à Prendre (Law Com. CP No 186 (2008)).

8.5.2   Profits

Profits can be acquired in most of the same ways as easements. However, because a profit cannot be 'continuous and apparent', *Wheeldon* v. *Burrows* (1879) LR 12 Ch D 31 probably cannot apply. In addition, under the Prescription Act the periods are longer for profits than for easements.

8.6   Remedies for Infringement of Easements and Profits

The remedies available to the aggrieved owner of an easement or profit are through the self-help remedy of abatement and by means of an action in the courts.

Abatement means that the owner of the easement or profit can go on to the servient tenement and, for example, break a padlock on a gate if this is necessary. However, the courts are wary of abatement and the dominant owner must choose the least mischievous method and refrain from causing unnecessary damage.

The owner of the easement or profit may claim an injunction and/or damages and/or a declaration against the owner of the servient land. She can also take action against third parties who interfere with her right, so the owner of a profit of piscary could win damages from a factory upstream which polluted the river and killed the fish.

8.7 The Ending of Easements and Profits

Easements and profits may be ended by statute or through an act of the parties, either by release, through abandonment or through unity of seisin.

8.7.1 Statute

There is no statutory provision equivalent to s.84 LPA 1925 (which allows the Lands Tribunal to discharge or modify a restrictive covenant; see Section 9.6.2). However, there are a number of statutes that allow easements and profits to be terminated. For example, under the Town and Country Planning Act 1990, local authorities may, in the course of development, end easements and profits. They can also be ended under the Commons Registration Act 1965.

In certain circumstances the provisions of the LRA 2002 will effectively extinguish easements over registered titles (see Sections 8.7.2.4 and 11.7.3.2).

8.7.2 Act of the Parties

8.7.2.1 Release

An easement or profit can be released explicitly by deed. An agreement to release – without a deed – may be enforceable in equity.

8.7.2.2 Unity of Seisin

As stated in Section 8.2.1.3, a person cannot have an easement or profit against herself, so an easement ends if one person owns both tenements; of course, as indicated earlier, it might be resuscitated under s.62 LPA 1925 or under the rule in *Wheeldon* v. *Burrows*.

One situation that is worthy of special mention is where a leasehold interest is merged with the reversionary freehold title. This may occur when a tenant purchases the freehold to the land that she occupies. Many residential tenants with long leases of residential properties have a statutory right to purchase the freehold title to their homes under the Leasehold Reform Act 1967. One would expect that any easements granted by the tenant would be extinguished by merger of the lease with the freehold estate. However, in *Wall* v. *Collins* [2007] Ch 390, the Court of Appeal held that such easements were not 'attached to' the leasehold estate and would continue to bind the land (including the freeholder) for the full term of the lease. There are considerable problems with this reasoning (see Section 8.2.1.4), especially as it does not seem to be essential to the result that the Court of Appeal wished to achieve.

8.7.2.3 Abandonment

If the owner of the easement or profit abandons the right, she cannot later resurrect it. However, the benefit of an easement cannot be lost simply by non-use, even where the period of non-use is substantial (it was 175 years in the case of *Benn* v. *Hardinge* (1993) 66 P & CR 246). For *abandonment* there must also be a manifest intention to abandon, and this is very difficult for the servient owner to establish. The owner of the dominant tenement:

> must make it clear that his intention is that neither he nor his successors in title should thereafter make any use of the right. ... abandonment is not to be lightly inferred because owners of property do not normally wish to divest themselves of property unless to do so is to their advantage, even if they have no present use for the property in question (Lloyd LJ, *CDC2020 Plc* v. *George Ferreira* [2005] EWCA Civ 611, at para. 24).

Intention to abandon an easement can be implied from the circumstances, but rarely is. In *CDC2020* the Court of Appeal refused to infer an intention to abandon a right of way, even when the garages to which it related had been demolished. Similarly, in the much earlier case of *Moore* v. *Rawson* (1824) 3 B & C 332 the Court held that, even where the windows which benefit from an easement of light are blocked up for many years, this only amounts to abandonment if there is no intention to open them up again.

Swan v. *Sinclair* [1925] AC 227 provides an example of circumstances in which abandonment will be inferred. A number of adjoining houses and their gardens had been sold in 1871. Each garden included part of a strip of land to the rear of the houses that had been designated as the route of a right of way to give access to the back gardens. By the date of the action in 1923, several householders had built fences across the strip of land and one had changed the level of the strip adjacent to his land by some six feet. The House of Lords was satisfied that any right of way over a strip of land had been abandoned by common consent of the various owners: the right had never been exercised, and no action had been taken to enforce it for over fifty years.

8.7.2.4 Non-use of Easements over Registered Land

Unless protected by registration, a legal easement over registered land may be unenforceable against the new registered proprietor of the servient tenement (s.29 and Schedule 3, para. 3 LRA 2002). This statutory provision is entirely independent of the doctrine of abandonment, and its rules are considered in more detail at Section 11.7.3.2. The Law Commission has recommended that, in registered land, an easement created by implication or prescription should be deemed to have been abandoned if the dominant owner cannot show it has been used within the previous 20 years ((1998) Law Com No 254, para. 5.24).

8.8 Other Rights over Another's Land

Listed below are a number of other interests in land which appear similar to easements or profits, but which are classified differently by lawyers.

8.8.1 Public Rights

These are rights which can be used by anyone, such as the right to fish between high- and low-water marks. The most familiar are rights of way, which include roads as well as footpaths, but the 'right' to use a road is now more like a licence, since it can be denied at the discretion of a police officer (see Public Order Act 1986).

The Countryside and Rights of Way Act 2000 provides a limited statutory right of public access to open countryside (the 'right to roam') and is intended to bring about the modernisation of the public rights of way network.

8.8.2 Natural Rights

These rights exist automatically and arise out of the nature of land. There is a right to water flowing naturally in a definite channel, but not to water which percolates through the land. All land has a natural right of support from neighbouring land, so you may not dig a large hole in your garden if your neighbour's land consequently collapses. The question has recently arisen as to whether an action lies against a landowner for failing to prevent the natural subsidence of her neighbour's land. In *Holbeck Hall Hotel* v. *Scarborough BC* [2000] QB

836, the council owned land between the sea cliffs and the hotel. Coastal erosion caused part of the hotel to disappear into the sea and the rest of it had to be demolished. Its owners sued the council in the tort of nuisance. The Court of Appeal stated that a landowner could be liable for not acting to prevent the hazard, but only if she could reasonably be expected to know about it. In this case, the danger could not reasonably have been foreseen by the council and it was therefore not just and reasonable to impose a liability on it. Even where the damage is reasonably foreseeable, if the cost of remedial work would be disproportionate, as here, the duty might be limited to sharing the information with the neighbour.

There are no automatic rights to light and air, so if such rights are to exist they must amount to easements, unless the tort of nuisance can provide a remedy. The quick-growing bush *Cupressus leylandii* has deprived many landowners of natural light for their gardens and homes and has frequently given rise to heated and even violent disputes. The Anti-social Behaviour Act 2003, Part 8 (most of which came into force on 1 June 2005) is designed to provide local authorities with powers to intervene in such neighbourly disputes and to issue remedial notices if they are satisfied that a hedge over 2 metres high is adversely affecting a neighbour's reasonable enjoyment of her property.

8.8.3   Customary Rights

Sometimes a group of people – for example, the residents of a particular village – have a right which looks like an easement, but it is not because 'the inhabitants of a village' are not a legal person.

8.8.4   Town or Village Greens

Since 1970, it has been necessary to protect town or village greens by registration under the Commons Registration Act 1965. However, it is possible for land to become a new town village green if it has been used as such by local inhabitants for a period of not less than 20 years. The Commons Act 2006, when fully implemented, will repeal the 1965 Act, but preserves the requirement for registration and the acquisition of town or village green status by long user. Town or village green status is not restricted to land of the type traditionally associated with the description. For example, the application before the House of Lords in *Oxfordshire CC* v. *Oxford CC* [2006] 2 AC 674 concerned some nine acres of undeveloped land in North Oxford. About one third of the site was permanently under water, and much of the rest (comprising scrub land and builder rubble) was impenetrable even by the hardiest walker.

8.8.5   Licences

See Chapter 14.

8.8.6   Access to Neighbouring Land Act 1992

A particular difficulty can arise for a landowner whose premises are built right up to the boundary with the neighbouring land. In the past, if she did not have an easement to go onto her neighbour's land to repair or maintain her own property and the neighbour refused to give her permission to do so, there was little she could do except watch her wall crumble away. Now, however, under the Access to Neighbouring Land Act 1992, in cases where it is reasonably necessary to carry out work to preserve her land and this work can really only be carried out from her neighbour's land to which she cannot otherwise gain access, a land-owner may apply to the court for an order to allow her access to carry out the work. The court will not automatically make the order and may impose conditions on the applicant.

8.8.7 Party Walls Act 1996

Extensive rights are given under the Party Walls Act to landowners who wish to go onto the neighbouring property in order to carry out repairs to the party wall, so landowners should use this Act rather than the more restrictive Access to Neighbouring Land Act if it is appropriate to do so. The adjoining owner must first be served with a notice in prescribed form; the person carrying out the works has the right to enter any land (and may break open doors to do so, if necessary, so long as a police officer is present); weatherproofing may need to be provided to protect the neighbouring property and there may be a requirement to pay compensation for loss or damage caused to the adjoining owner. This Act would have been very helpful to Mr Bradburn in *Bradburn* v. *Lindsay* (Section 8.2.4.3.2) and exists to prevent exactly that kind of mischief.

8.9 Comment

This chapter has indicated the wide variety of interests which can exist within the categories of easements and profits, and has attempted to show how land law attempts to adapt to changing land use, such as the development of tower blocks of flats and the increasing need for car parking facilities. Although there have been two statutory reforms in recent years, the Access to Neighbouring Land Act 1992 and the Party Walls Act 1996, modern requirements need further reform of the law of easements. As long ago as 1971, the Law Commission in its Working Paper No. 36, 'Transfer of Land: Appurtenant Rights', recommended that certain important easements, such as the right to support, should automatically be statutory rights, and the need to reform the law on the acquisition of easements by prescription has already been discussed.

The laws of contract (in relation to profits) and tort (especially nuisance), together with statute law, have to provide for other situations where the law of easements cannot satisfactorily resolve conflicts between neighbours.

Summary

8.1 To be an easement, a claim over another person's land must fulfil the four requirements: there must be dominant and servient tenements, accommodation of the dominant tenement, different ownership or occupation, and it must be capable of being the subject of a grant.

8.2 Easements include a wide variety of rights, but, in order for a new one to be recognised, it must fit the general character of easements.

8.3 Profits are rights to take something from another person's land; they may or may not be appurtenant, and may be in common or sole.

8.4 A legal profit or easement must be equivalent to an interest in fee simple or to a lease, and must be created expressly by deed or impliedly or by long use; all other profits and easements are equitable.

8.5 Easements and profits may be acquired expressly or impliedly, by grant or reservation or by court order. They may also be acquired by prescription.

8.6 Remedies for infringement of an easement or profit are abatement or action.

8.7 Easements and profits may be ended by statute, release, abandonment or unity of seisin.

8.8 Easements and profits must be distinguished from other claims, such as natural, customary or public rights, from statutory rights and from licences.

Exercises

8.1 What is an easement? In what ways is it different from a profit? How does it differ from a licence?

8.2 What is the importance of dominant and servient tenements in the law of easements and profits?

8.3 Is there an easement to provide protection against the weather? Should there be?

8.4 What is necessary in order for an easement or a profit to be held to have been abandoned?

@ 8.5 In 1985 Megan sold half her farm to Jeff, but she continued to keep her tractors in a barn on the land she sold to him. In 1995 she leased one of her remaining fields to Jeff, by deed, for 20 years, giving him permission to use a short cut to the field across her land 'for as long as he needs to'; he had in fact already been using the field and short cut for several weeks. Last year Jeff agreed in writing with Megan that the children attending her nursery school could play on his smallest field.

Megan has just died and her heir, Sam, wants to know if any of these arrangements will affect him.

@ 8.6 An online quiz on the topics covered in this chapter is available on the companion website.

Further Reading

Davis, 'Abandonment of an Easement: Is it a Question of Intention Only?' [1995] Conv 291.

Harpum, 'The Acquisition of Easements' [1992] CLJ 220

Haley, '*Moncrieff* v. *Jamieson* Easements, exclusionary use and elusive principles: The right to park' [2008] Conv 244

Haley and McMurtry, 'Identifying an Easement: Exclusive Use, *De Facto* Control and Judicial Constraints' (2007) 58 NILQ 163

Law Com. CP No. 186, Easements, Covenants and Profits à Prendre (2008)

Smith, 'Centre Point: Faulty Towers with Shaky Foundations' [1978] Conv 449

Tee, 'Metamorphoses and s.62 of the Law of Property Act 1925' [1998] Conv 115

Chapter 9

Covenants in Freehold Land

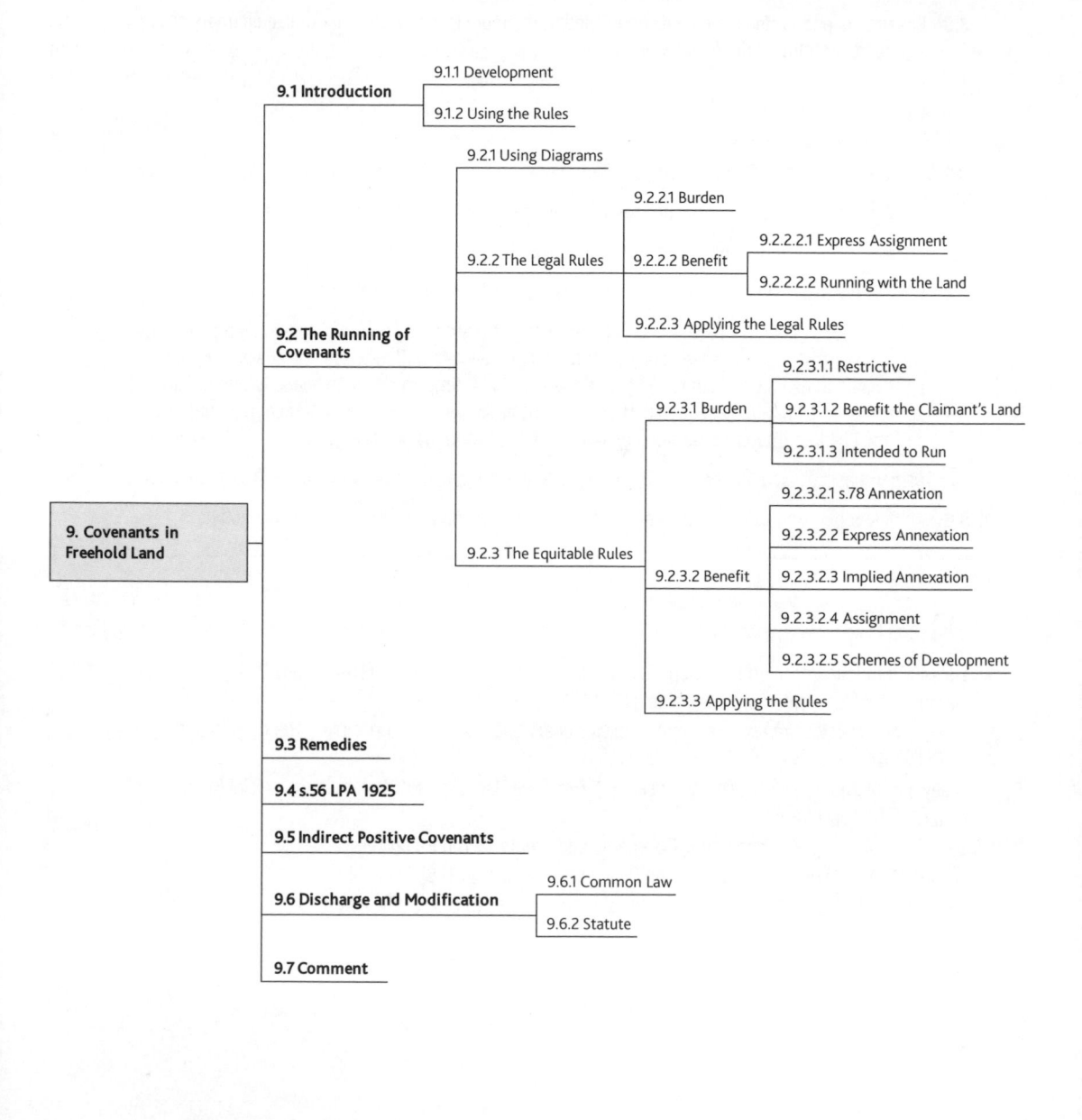

9.1 Introduction

This chapter is about formal promises made between freeholders in relation to the use of their land and the rules that determine whether such a promise can be enforced by and against their successors in title. These rules are different from those for leasehold covenants (see Chapter 6) and those for easements (see Chapter 8). It is important, therefore, to be able to distinguish freehold covenants from these other types of right over land.

- Freehold covenants enable landowner A to directly control what landowner B does on B's land. Easements, in contrast, allow landowner A to use the land belonging to B.
- Like leasehold covenants, freehold covenants arise out of a contract. However, whilst the effect of freehold covenants can also extend well beyond the original parties, this is not dependent upon there being privity of estate between the parties.

Freehold covenants are not the only controls over a landowner's use of his land. He must also, for example, also comply with planning requirements and ensure that his use of the land does not constitute the tort of nuisance.

9.1.1 The Development of the Rules

It has long been possible for the *benefit* of a freehold covenant to be transferred with the land. For example, if Tony sold part of his land to Ray and Ray covenanted to construct and maintain a road on the land, Tony could pass the benefit of the covenant on to his successors in title. So, if Tony subsequently sold the remainder of his land to Giselle, she would be able to enforce the promise made by Ray. However, the *burden* of a covenant cannot run at law. If Ray sold his land to Liz, neither Tony nor Giselle could enforce the covenant against her. This is known as the rule in *Austerberry* v. *Oldham Corporation* (see Section 9.2.2.1).

Although well established at common law, this rule has a number of disadvantages which the courts of equity began to address in the mid-nineteenth century. By the end of that century it was accepted that the *burden* of a freehold covenant could be attached to land (affecting anyone who owned the land) provided that the terms of the covenant were 'restrictive': that is, they prevented the owner from doing something. Even today, restrictive covenants can only be equitable interests. They must be protected by registration and any remedies for breach are discretionary. The courts were concerned with finding a balance between protecting third-party interests in land and encouraging land development, themes which also run through the law of leases and easements. Perhaps inevitably, therefore, the courts adopted the established policy test of whether the covenant 'touches and concerns' or 'accommodates' the land concerned.

Tulk v. *Moxhay* (1848) 2 Ph. 774 is the first major case in which a court enforced a covenant on freehold land against a successor to the original covenantor. Tulk sold freehold land in Leicester Square in London and the buyer promised, on behalf of himself and his successors in title, to:

> keep and maintain the said parcel of ground and square garden, and the iron railing around the same in its [present] form and in sufficient and proper repair, as a square garden and pleasure ground, in an open state, uncovered with any buildings, in a neat and ornamental order.

The land changed hands several times and a later owner decided to build on the garden, although he had known about the covenant before he had bought the land and had paid less because of it. In a dramatic decision by the Court of Chancery, Tulk, the original covenantee (the person to whom the promise had been made) successfully enforced the covenant against the later owner. The decision was based on the doctrine of notice and the inequitable consequences that would follow if:

> the original purchaser should be able to sell the property the next day for a greater price, in consideration of the assignee being allowed to escape from the liability which he had himself undertaken (Lord Cottenham at p. 778).

In succeeding decisions, equity came to provide a cheap and effective planning law nearly a hundred years before the State seriously took on the control of land use. Many urban areas have their present shape and character because of covenants imposed by careful developers. Nowadays the public restrictions on the use of land (for example, planning law and building regulations) are normally of greater significance, but covenants are still imposed and enforced because they allow for a more detailed and individual control than public planning law is able to provide.

Under certain circumstances, statute permits covenants to be discharged or modified. For example, public policy requires that a covenant rendered obsolete because of a change in the character of a neighbourhood should no longer be enforceable. This jurisdiction is briefly reviewed at the end of this chapter. However, first it is necessary to explain the rules about covenants 'running with the land'.

9.1.2 Using the Rules

There are several tasks that need to be addressed when approaching a problem in this area of land law. Examination questions may focus on the first of these tasks, but the others are no less important in practice.

- Identifying who might have the benefit of a covenant and who might have the burden – that is, who might be able to enforce it and who might be bound by it. The easiest way to do this is by using diagrams and the technique explained in Section 9.2.1.
- Determining whether the covenant is enforceable: if relying on the equitable rules, has the covenant been protected by registration?
- Deciding what remedy, if any, is appropriate to deal with the injury to the claimant. In many cases this will be an injunction, prohibiting any breach of the covenant, but the courts may award damages in lieu if satisfied that this will be sufficient.

9.2 The Running of Covenants

9.2.1 The Use of Diagrams

The basic pattern for determining whether a covenant can be enforced is simple.

- There are two sets of rules: *legal* and *equitable*.
- Each set of rules is divided into subsets of rules for the passing of the benefit and the burden respectively.
- The legal and equitable rules in regard to the benefit are similar, but not identical.
- The sets of rules for the burden are quite different.

The sets of rules are the result of case law and are therefore open to argument – and they tend to be expressed differently in each textbook. The present statement seeks to be as simple and accurate as possible. The rules are summarised in Table 9.1 at the end of this chapter.

To take a typical story in this area of land law. Eve was the fee simple owner of Paradise House and in 2000 she sold a part of her garden to Adosh who promised her that he would not build on the land. Eve moved to the seaside for her health and sold her remaining land to Mike. Adosh took early retirement and sold his land to Claire who has obtained planning permission for a block of flats on the land. Mike wishes to know whether he can prevent Claire building the flats.

In order to find an answer, it is necessary to establish the relationships of the plaintiff and the defendant to the promise which has been, or may be, broken. The promise is usually represented by a vertical line, with the benefiting person (the covenantee, Eve in this case) at the top and the burdened person (covenantor, Adosh) at the bottom. As with leases, sales of the land are usually shown by horizontal lines as in Figure 9.1.

Figure 9.1

In most cases it will be easy to identify the original parties to the covenant, as they will be named in the documentation. In this case Adosh is the covenantor (he made the promise) and Eve the covenantee. However, s. 56 LPA 1925 makes it possible for a person to have the benefit of a covenant (that is, to be a covenantee) without being expressly named in the original document. This is considered in more detail in Section 9.4.

Claire is clearly planning to breach the promise made by Adosh, her predecessor. Whether Mike can use the promise made by Adosh to prevent Claire building the flats depends upon the answers to two questions.

- Has the burden of the covenant passed to Claire?
- Has the benefit of the covenant passed to Mike?

In order to find the answers, the rules of law and equity must be applied in turn.

9.2.2 The Legal Rules

9.2.2.1 The Running of the Burden at Law

As indicated earlier, the common law did not (and still does not) allow the burden of a freehold covenant to be attached to land so as to bind buyers. In *Austerberry* v. *Oldham Corporation* (1885) LR 29 Ch D 750, the Court of Appeal applied the contractual doctrine that only a party to an agreement can be burdened by it. The decision in *Austerberry* was confirmed by the House of Lords in *Rhone* v. *Stephens* [1994] 2 AC 310 (discussed in more detail in Section 9.2.3.1.1). There are, however, several ways in which the strictness of the rule can be avoided at law – see Section 9.5.

9.2.2.2 The Running of the Benefit at Law

In answering the question, 'Can the plaintiff sue at law?' ('Has the benefit passed to the plaintiff at law?'), two separate rules must be examined: the first provides for the express transfer of the benefit of a contract, and the second for the automatic running (implied transfer) of a benefit when the land is sold.

9.2.2.2.1 Express Assignment   Anyone can expressly transfer the benefit of any contract to which he is a party provided that the covenant is not a purely personal one. Under s.136 LPA 1925, the benefit of a promise relating to the use of land can be sold and will be enforceable at law by the buyer, provided that the assignment is in writing and express notice in writing has been given to the covenantor.

9.2.2.2.2 Running with the Land   If there has been no express assignment of the benefit of a covenant, the law allows the benefit to pass automatically with the benefited land if:

(a)   the covenant benefits the land; and
(b)   the covenantee had a legal estate in the land when the promise was made; and
(c)   the plaintiff now has a legal estate in that land; and
(d)   the benefit was intended to pass.

For the covenant to benefit the land, it must be shown that the promise affects the land itself rather than its owner: that is to say it must 'touch and concern' the land (see *P & A Swift Investments* v. *Combined English Stores Group Plc* [1989] AC 632 (Section 6.4.1.2)). There is some question about whether it is essential for the original parties to the covenant to have intended that its benefit should pass as it is not included in the requirements set out by the House of Lords in *P & A Swift Investments*. Practically, however, the question is unlikely to be significant because of s.78 LPA 1925. This section provides that the benefit of a promise which 'relates to' (that is, touches and concerns) land is deemed to be made not only with the covenantee but also with all his successors in title. Section 78 means that anyone who owns a legal estate in land automatically has the benefit of any covenant made after 1925 which touches and concerns that land. The section is discussed in more detail in Section 9.2.3.2.1.

The importance of s.78 can be seen in the case of *Smith and Snipes Hall Farm* v. *River Douglas Catchment Board* [1949] 2 KB 500. In 1938 the Board promised Ellen Smith that it would maintain the banks of the Eller Brook adjoining her land in Lancashire. She sold the land to John Smith (the first plaintiff) and he leased it to Snipes Hall Farm. When the river flooded the land because of the Board's failure to carry out proper maintenance, John Smith and the Farm tried to recover their losses from the Board on the ground that the benefit of the covenant had automatically passed to them when they bought the land. It was held that (1) the covenant did benefit their land; (2) it had been made with a legal owner of the land; (3) the present plaintiffs were both legal owners; and (4) the benefit of the covenant had been intended to run by virtue of s.78 LPA 1925. Both plaintiffs could therefore claim damages for the Board's breach of covenant. The Farm, as tenant, succeeded because s.78 enables any legal owner – freeholder or leaseholder – to enjoy the benefit of a covenant relating to the land.

9.2.2.3 Applying the Legal Rules

To enforce the covenant at law, Mike must demonstrate that he has the benefit of the covenant and that Claire is subject to the burden. There is little doubt that Mike has the benefit of covenant, as the promise made by Adosh satisfies the requirements set out in *Smith and Snipes Hall Farm* v. *River Douglas Catchment Board* [1949] 2 KB 500. However, Claire cannot be subject to the burden of the covenant at law because of the rule in *Austerberry* v. *Oldham Corporation* preventing the burden being transferred at law. It will be necessary, therefore, to consider whether Mike can enforce the covenant in equity.

The Equitable Rules

9.2.3.1 The Running of the Burden in Equity

In *Tulk* v. *Moxhay* (1848) 2 Ph. 774 (see Section 9.1.1), Cottenham LC granted the claimant an injunction allowing him to enforce a covenant against the successor in title of the original covenantor. This appeared to be a straightforward decision. Lord Cottenham believed that if the court had failed to enforce the promise, 'it would [have been] impossible for an owner of land to sell part of it without incurring the risk of rendering what he retains worthless'. This is true, although it was, and still is, possible for a landowner to maintain control over the land being sold by granting a long lease (with the appropriate covenants) instead of parting with the freehold. The leasehold covenants would be enforceable against subsequent assignees of the lease.

The decision in *Tulk* v. *Moxhay* turned on the question of notice (see Section 9.1.1). If the purchaser of the affected land was found to have had notice of the burden of the covenant then equity required that he be bound by it. This potentially opened the way to allow the burden of all sorts of covenants, as well as other kinds of non-property obligations, to bind successors in title. However, later in the nineteenth century, the judges seem to have thought that the now depressed land market required restrictions on land use to be kept to a minimum in order to encourage purchasers. They therefore introduced increasingly complex and technical requirements limiting the effect of *Tulk* v. *Moxhay*. Today the burden of a covenant runs in equity if:

(a) it is restrictive, and
(b) it benefits land once owned by the covenantee and now owned by the claimant (or is part of a building scheme – see below), and
(c) it was intended to run with the land

Further, because this is merely an equitable interest:

(d) the notice or registration rules must be complied with (these rules are set out in Chapters 10 and 11), and
(e) the claimant must have 'clean hands'.

9.2.3.1.1 The covenant must be restrictive   Whether a covenant is 'restrictive', or negative, is a question of its substance, not its form. What matters is the real meaning of the covenant rather than what it appears to mean. For example, a covenant to maintain the land uncovered with buildings, although positive in form, is negative in substance because the covenantor can comply by doing nothing (that is, without spending money). In reality, it simply requires the covenantor not to build on it.

The rule that equity will enforce the burden of only those covenants that are restrictive was restated by the House of Lords in *Rhone* v. *Stephens* [1994] 2 AC 310. The case concerned a promise to maintain a roof in good condition – the whole roof belonged to the main house, but part of it protected an adjoining cottage owned by the claimant. The original owners of the house had promised the original buyers of the cottage that they would maintain the roof, but a subsequent owner of the cottage found that the covenant could not be enforced against a new owner of the house. As it was positive, the burden could not pass.

Lord Templeman reviewed all the authorities and concluded that the rule of restrictive covenants is a rule of property: an owner of land cannot exercise a right which has never been transferred to him. Equity follows the law, and:

> Equity cannot compel an owner to comply with a positive covenant entered into by his predecessors in title without flatly contradicting the common law rule that a person cannot be made liable upon a contract unless he was a party to it. Enforcement of a positive covenant lies in contract; a positive covenant compels an owner to exercise his rights. Enforcement of a negative covenant lies in property; a negative covenant deprives the owner of a right over property (at p. 69).

Further, he stated that any judicial alteration of the rule now would cause chaos for landowners.

9.2.3.1.2 The covenant must benefit the claimant's land   The claimant's land (the land once owned by the covenantee) must be identifiable and either benefitted ('accommodated') by the covenant or be part of a scheme of development (see Section 9.2.3.2.5). The point here is that equity will enforce a restrictive covenant if its purpose is to protect the value and amenity of the covenantee's neighbouring land. The person trying to enforce the covenant need not own a legal estate and need not have bought the whole of the covenantee's land, so long as the part he owns is capable of benefiting from the promise. In *London CC* v. *Allen* [1914] 3 KB 642, Mr Allen promised the council that he would not build on a strip of land needed for the continuation of a road. The burdened land was conveyed to Mrs Allen and she proceeded to build on it. It was held, with great regret, that the claimant authority could not enforce the covenant because it had sold the benefiting land. (Statutes now provide that local authorities and certain other bodies, such as the National Trust, are exempt from this rule.)

In *Dano Ltd* v. *Earl Cadogan* [2003] All ER (D) 240, the sixth Earl Cadogan had conveyed some land in 1929 to a local authority which covenanted with him on behalf of itself and its successors that the land would be used for no other purpose than the housing of the working classes 'so long as such adjoining or neighbouring property or any part thereof forms part of the Cadogan Settled Estate in Chelsea but not further or otherwise'. In the 1960s the Cadogan family rearranged its affairs and the Settled Estate was ended. Later, Dano Ltd acquired the land from the local authority, received planning permission to build private houses on some of the land and sought a declaration that the covenant was unenforceable. Although the neighbouring land was still in the Cadogan family, it no longer formed part of the 'Cadogan Settled Estate in Chelsea', and on that basis the Court of Appeal held that there was no longer any land capable of benefiting from the covenant, which was therefore unenforceable, despite its philanthropic objectives.

9.2.3.1.3 The parties must intend the covenant to run   This intention will usually be expressed in the document containing the covenant, but if not (and if the covenant was made after 1925), it may be implied by s.79 LPA 1925. The operation of s.79 can be excluded by demonstrating contrary intention. Usually, such intention will be clearly stated in the wording of the covenant, but the courts can construe the document as a whole in order to determine the intention of the original parties (see, for example, *Morrells of Oxford Ltd* v. *Oxford United FC Ltd* [2001] Ch 459).

9.2.3.2 The Running of the Benefit in Equity

Equity also developed its own rules about the running of the benefit of a covenant, based on the legal rules.

(a) The covenant must touch and concern the land of the covenantee, and

(b) the benefit of the covenant must have passed to the claimant.

There are three ways in which the benefit of the covenant may pass to the claimant:

- by annexation (statutory, express or implied); or
- by assignment; or
- under a scheme of development.

9.2.3.2.1 Section 78 Annexation   For the benefit of a covenant to be annexed to the land it is necessary to establish that this was the intention of the original parties. Traditionally this was dependent upon how the court construed the document containing the covenant. However, the decision of the Court of Appeal in *Federated Homes Ltd* v. *Mill Lodge Properties Ltd* [1980] 1 WLR 594 means that almost all covenants made since 1925 are deemed to be annexed to the land by virtue of s.78 of the LPA 1925.

The facts of the *Federated Homes* case were relatively simple and are shown diagrammatically in Figure 9.2. M Ltd owned a large estate which was divided into three plots, blue, green and red. They sold the blue land to Mill Lodge Properties, who promised, for the benefit of the green and red land, that they would not build more than 300 houses on it. Both the green and the red land then came into the hands of Federated Homes. There was an unbroken chain of express assignments of the benefit of Mill Lodge's promise with the green land, but not with the red (the assignment of benefit is discussed in Section 9.2.3.2.4).

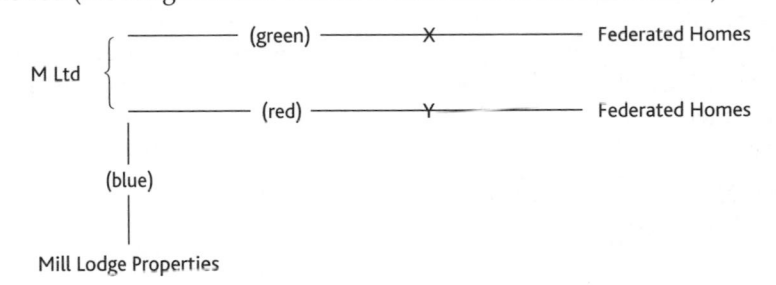

Figure 9.2 *Federated Homes Ltd* v. *Mill Lodge Properties Ltd*

Federated Homes successfully claimed an injunction for breach of the covenant when Mill Lodge began building 32 houses more than was permitted under the covenant. The defendant's arguments centred on technical details of the planning permission, but this was decided in the claimant's favour. It then became clear that, as owners of the *green* land with an unbroken chain of express assignments, Federated Homes had the benefit of the covenant and could enforce it against Mill Lodge. However, the judge at first instance went further and said that, under s.62 LPA 1925 (by which a conveyance of land transfers all rights which benefit it, see Sections 2.6.1.4 and 8.5.1.2.3), Federated Homes could also enforce the covenant as owners of the *red* land.

The Court of Appeal agreed with the judge on the planning issue and the green land, but took a different view on the red land. Rather than s.62 they chose to use s.78 LPA 1925 to pass the benefit of the covenant to the plaintiff. Until then, it had been thought that s.78 was merely a 'wordsaving' provision, but Brightman LJ rejected this interpretation as it seemed to him to 'fly in the face of the wording'.

The widest interpretation of *Federated Homes* is that the benefit of any covenant made since 1925 automatically runs in equity if it touches and concerns the land. This represents the radical obliteration of a century of case law about the annexation or assignment of freehold covenants. Annexation and assignment cases (briefly outlined below) had been lovingly analysed by generations of academics and the Court of Appeal's decision surprised many commentators. Although the decision has not been challenged, the courts have had to address two questions not answered in *Federated Homes*. The first question relates to the need to identify the land benefiting from the covenant. The second to whether the parties can displace the effect of s.78 by expressing a contrary intention. Both of these questions were addressed by the Court of Appeal in *Crest Nicholson Residential (South) Ltd* v. *McAllister* [2004] 1 WLR 2409.

Chadwick LJ answered the first question by confirming that the requirement for express annexation (set out in *Marquess of Zetland* v. *Driver* [1939] Ch 1) also applied to s.78 cases: that is, the land which is intended to be benefited by the covenant must be sufficiently defined so as to be easily ascertainable. In the earlier case of *Stocks* v. *Whitgift Homes* [2001] EWCA Civ 1732 (not referred to by Chadwick LJ in *Crest*), the Court of Appeal stated that it is not necessary for the covenant to exactly identify the land to be benefited, providing that there is sufficient extrinsic identification evidence to determine the extent of the land concerned.

The second question had already been answered at first instance by Judge Paul Baker QC in *Roake* v. *Chadha* [1984] 1 WLR 40. In that case there was a 50-year-old covenant not to build more than one house per plot on land in a London suburb, and a further clause in the conveyance that the benefit of the covenant would not pass unless it was expressly assigned. All the land changed hands, without an express assignment of the benefit of the covenant, and a later owner of the burdened land wanted to build another house in his garden. Judge Paul Baker QC held that there was nothing in the *Federated Homes* decision that prevented the parties to the covenant preventing it being annexed to the land by s.78 if that was their intention:

> The true position as I see it is that even where a covenant is deemed to be made with successors in title as s.78 requires, one still has to construe the covenant as a whole to see whether the benefit of the covenant is annexed (p. 46).

The effect of expressing contrary intention was contentious because, unlike s.62 and s.79 LPA 1925, there is no provision in s.78 allowing the parties to negate its effect by expressing their wish to do so. In *Crest Nicholson Residential (South) Ltd* v. *McAllister* [2004] 1 WLR 2409 Chadwick LJ confirmed the decision in *Roake* v. *Chadha*, explaining that the wording of s. 78 means there is no need for it to include the words 'unless a contrary intention is expressed':

> The qualification 'subject to contrary intention' is implicit in the definition of 'successors in title' which appears in section 78(1); that is the effect of the words 'the land of the covenantee intended to be benefited'. If the terms in which the covenant is imposed show... [that the parties did not intend the benefit of the covenant to be annexed to the land] then the owners and occupiers of the land sold off in those circumstances are not 'owners and occupiers for the time being of the land of the covenantee intended to be benefited'; and so are not 'successors in title' of the original covenantee for the purposes of section 78(1) ... (para. 43).

The same argument does not apply to s.79, because of the specific meaning given to 'successors in title' in s.79(2).

Thus, the effect of *Federated Homes* is to annex the benefit of the covenant to the land (and each and every part of the land) unless the parties have expressed their intention that this should not be the case. There remain, however, a number of additional complications with *Federated Homes'* simplification of the law. For example, the operation of s.78 is almost certainly limited to covenants made since 1925. In addition, because of the wording of the section, it may only apply to the running of the benefit of restrictive covenants.

In cases where the statute may not apply it will be necessary to fall back on the old concepts of annexation and assignment created in nineteenth-century cases.

9.2.3.2.2 Express Annexation   When considering whether the benefit of a covenant made before 1926 has been annexed to the land the situation is the reverse of that when s.78 LPA 1925 applies. For the benefit of a pre-1926 covenant to be annexed it must be possible to establish from the original document that this was the positive intention of the parties. The best evidence for this is the use of express words to this effect, similar to those used in *Rogers* v. *Hosegood* [1900] 2 Ch 388. In 1869, the Duke of Bedford bought a plot of land in Kensington and had promised not to build more than one house on it. The deed stated that this was:

> with intent that the covenants might so far as possible bind the premises ... and might enure to the benefit of the [sellers] ... their heirs and assigns and others claiming under them to all or any of their land adjoining or near to the said premises.

The Duke's land passed to Hosegood who decided to build a large block of flats on it. Rogers, an owner of adjoining land, wanted to prevent the development. The burden of the covenant had clearly passed to Hosegood, so the question was whether the benefit had passed to Rogers. It was held that the benefit had been annexed to his land by the words of the deed, so anyone who subsequently owned that land could enforce the covenant.

9.2.3.2.3 Implied Annexation   If the original document lacks the kind of wording used in the covenant in *Rogers* v. *Hosegood*, it may be possible for the successor to the covenantee to show that annexation can be implied by considering the wording of the original document in the context of all the surrounding circumstances – see *Marten* v. *Flight Refuelling Ltd (No 1)* [1962] Ch 115.

9.2.3.2.4 Assignment   If there is no annexation, the benefit may still have been passed by a chain of assignments such as existed for the benefit of the green land in *Federated Homes*. If there is no complete express chain, it may be that there could yet be an implied assignment of the benefit. For this to happen, the covenant must have been intended to benefit the land of the original covenantee, and the successor who is attempting to enforce the covenant must have had the benefit expressly assigned to him. In *Newton Abbot Cooperative Society* v. *Williamson and Treadgold Ltd* [1952] Ch 286, a covenant preventing the use of a shop as an ironmongery was not expressed to be for the benefit of the land belonging to the covenantee. The judge, however, was able to look at the surrounding circumstances, and found that the covenantee (who herself ran an ironmongery and understandably did not want competition):

> took the covenant restrictive of the user of the defendants' premises for the benefit of her own business of ironmonger and of her property ... where at all material times she was carrying on that business ... (p. 297).

When the covenantee died, her heir received the land and the benefit of the covenant, which he could then assign expressly to his successor who could enforce it.

9.2.3.2.5 Schemes of Development   A final method by which successors in title of the original covenantee might enforce covenants is through what is known as a scheme of development. A scheme of development (or 'building scheme') is another creation of equity and provides a useful method for the modern developer to create and preserve new estates. If the conditions for a scheme are fulfilled, then the burdens (provided the covenants have been protected by registration) and the benefits of restrictive covenants which touch and concern the land run automatically to all owners covered by the scheme, thus greatly simplifying the question of whether one owner can stop another breaching a covenant.

The first known scheme was created in 1767 and upheld in 1866. A large number were created in the nineteenth century and upheld by the courts but, after 1889, the number of successful schemes began to fall. Strict rules were laid down in the judgment in *Elliston* v. *Reacher* [1908] 2 Ch 374, and later judges treated them as if they were part of a statute. According to *Elliston* v. *Reacher*:

1   there had to be one seller, and
2   the plots must have been laid out in advance, and
3   mutual restrictions must have been established for the mutual benefit of the plots, and
4   the purchasers of the plots must have known about the intended mutual enforceability.

Between 1908 and the 1960s only two schemes were successfully enforced in reported cases, but then the climate appears to have changed again and the rules in *Elliston* v. *Reacher* relaxed. In *Re Dolphin's Conveyance* [1970] Ch 654 there was neither a common vendor nor were the plots laid out in advance, but the local authority in Birmingham was nevertheless prevented from developing the site because it was held that a building scheme had been created and that the development would have been in breach of covenant. The judge said that the rules set out in *Elliston* v. *Reacher* were only part of a wider rule, and that a scheme arose because of the existence of 'the common interest and the common intention actually expressed in the conveyances themselves'. According to Stamp J in *Re Dolphin's Conveyance* the requirements for a building scheme are, therefore:

(a) mutually binding covenants
(b) applying within a clearly defined and commonly understood area.

The question of whether the covenants are sufficiently mutual is concerned with both the content of the covenant (are they all in broadly the same terms) and the awareness of the original covenantors that they were part of a building scheme. The recent case of *Small* v. *Oliver & Saunders (Developments) Ltd* [2006] 3 EGLR 141 provides a useful illustration of the application of these rules.

There are often problems in the older cases in finding sufficient numbers of the original documents, and often the original owners are beyond recall as well. In cases where common interest and intention cannot be shown from the covenants (as in *Emile Elias & Co Ltd* v. *Pine Groves Ltd* [1993] 1 WLR 305), the courts will apply the rules in *Elliston* v. *Reacher*. In *Emile Elias & Co Ltd* the Privy Council emphasised the necessity for a 'common code of covenants'.

In *Stocks* v. *Whitgift Homes* [2001] EWCA Civ 1732, a large residential estate of some 440 acres had been developed in the 1920s and 1930s. Some of the estate was clearly intended to be within a building scheme, but there was a good deal of uncertainty about the rest. In finding that no building scheme existed, even between owners of the properties situated within the area originally intended to be part of the scheme, the Court of Appeal stated that:

the authorities show that [a] number of characteristics must be established. Among them is certainty: otherwise, in relation to each plot of land said to fall within the scheme, the question will continually arise: does it or does it not so fall? More precisely, is it, or is it not subject to mutually enforceable benefits and obligations, and, if enforceable, by and against the owners of which plots? This essential requirement of certainty makes obvious practical sense (Judge LJ, at para. 110).

9.2.3.3 Applying the Rules

A return to the story of Claire and Mike told earlier in this chapter (Section 9.2.1) might help make the application of all these rules clearer. The question was whether Mike had the benefit and Claire the burden of the promise made by Adosh to Eve that there should be no building on the land. There is no building scheme here, of course.

A glance at the summary of the rules relating to the benefit and the burden (Table 9.1 in the Summary) shows that the strictest requirement relates to the running of the burden. This is therefore always the place to start in a problem of this kind, since otherwise you may go to all the trouble of tracing the benefit and then find that the burden does not run anyway.

To decide whether the burden has passed with the land from Adosh to Claire, it is necessary to apply the equitable rules in *Tulk* v. *Moxhay* since the burden cannot run at law. In this case: (a) the covenant is negative in substance, (b) it does benefit the land of the original convenantee (Eve) now owned by Mike, and (c) by s.79, it is deemed to have been intended to run (there is no evidence of a contrary intention). The final answer regarding the burden depends on whether the covenant was properly protected by registration (see Sections 10.3 and 11.6).

The next stage is to test whether the benefit has passed with the land from Eve to Mike. Here a fundamental principle emerges. It is not permitted to mix legal and equitable rules: *burden and benefit must run in the 'same medium'*. (In practice this means that if the burdened land has changed hands, and thus equitable principles must be applied, then the equitable rules must also be used for the benefit.) The covenant here does touch and concern the land, so by *Federated Homes* the benefit probably passes in equity. Therefore – subject to registration – Mike will probably be able to enforce the covenant against Claire.

9.3 Remedies for Breach of Covenant

It has already been noted that the equitable nature of restrictive covenants means that the burden of the covenant will need to be registered if it is to be enforced against a successor in title of the original covenantor. The detailed rules are examined in Sections 10.3 and 11.6. Another implication of the rule that the burden of a restrictive covenant runs only in equity is that only equitable remedies are available to the courts when remedying any breach. In principle, therefore, a remedy will only be available if the wrong committed can be solved by an injunction. Further, all equitable remedies are given at the discretion of the court and can be refused if, for example, the claimant has unnecessarily delayed bringing his action or has otherwise acted improperly.

Although the usual remedy for the breach of a restrictive covenant will be a permanent injunction, the court has the power to award damages instead (but not in circumstances where an injunction could not be granted). The circumstances in which damages may properly be awarded in lieu of an injunction were summarised by AL Smith LJ in *Shelfer* v. *City of London Electric Lighting Co. (No 1)* [1895] 1 Ch 287. Damages may be given in substitution for an injunction:

(1) If the injury to the plaintiff's legal right is small,
(2) And is one which is capable of being estimated in money,
(3) And is one which can be adequately compensated by a small money payment,
(4) And the case is one in which it would be oppressive to the defendant to grant an injunction ...
(*Shelfer* v. *City of London Electric Lighting Co. (No 1)* [1895] 1 Ch 287 at 322-323).

The original covenantor will always be liable in contract law (unless a contrary intention is expressed in the contract), but the remedy against him can only be damages once he has parted with ownership of the burdened land.

9.4 The Use of s.56 LPA 1925

Section 56 LPA 1925 may be relevant whenever the person claiming the benefit (or his predecessor in title) owned land nearby at the time the covenant was made. In a sense, it is a legal extension of privity of contract and provides that:

A person may take ... the benefit of any ... covenant ... over or respecting land ... although he may not be named as a party to the conveyance or other instrument.

It is a way of giving the benefit of a covenant to someone other than those who are named in the deed, providing the covenant purports to be made with him. The section applies if the person alleged to have the benefit of the covenant was identifiable in the covenant agreement, and existed at the date of the covenant. The reason for these rules is that it would be unfair if the covenantor were effectively making his promise to everyone in the neighbourhood; he needs to be able to identify, on the day he made the promise, the landowners who might be able to take action against him.

The rules were established in *Re Ecclesiastical Commissioners for England's Conveyance* [1936] Ch 430. In that case, the court had to whether a large house near to Hampstead Heath in London was subject to a restrictive covenant. The issue was whether neighbouring landowners had the right to enforce it, and this depended on whether the original landowners who had owned the neighbouring land at the time of the covenant could enforce it through s.56. A clause in the conveyance stated that the original covenantor made the promise, 'also as a separate covenant with ... owners for the time being of land adjoining or adjacent to the said land hereby conveyed'. This was held to be enough to satisfy for s.56 to apply. The neighbours were identifiable from the agreement and were in existence at its date. Their successors in title were able to claim the benefit from them by the usual rules for the running of the benefit, and thus were able to enforce the covenant.

For covenants made after 11 May 2000, the Contracts (Rights of Third Parties) Act 1999 can also be used in this situation. Under s.1 of the Act, a person who is not a party to the contract may enforce it if it purports to confer or expressly confers a benefit on him, so long as the contract identifies him by name, as a member of a class or as answering a particular description, even though he was not in existence when the contract was entered into. From its wording, it seems that operation of the Act is wider than s.56, since it will allow a landowner to enforce the benefit of a covenant even though it is not purported to be made with him and even though he might not have been identifiable when the covenant was created. However, there are unlikely to be a significant number of cases involving covenants using the 1999 Act as the provisions of s. 56 LPA 1925 will usually be sufficient.

9.5 Indirect Methods of Enforcing Positive Covenants

There are many circumstances where a covenantee may wish the burden of a positive covenants to bind the successor in title of the original covenantor, and where the court's refusal to permit this (as in *Rhone* v. *Stephens* [1994] 2 AC 310) will cause significant inconvenience. It is not surprising, therefore, that lawyers have devised a number of methods of effectively enforcing positive covenants, although each has its own limitations.

- If the original covenantor, and each of his successors in title, obtains an indemnity covenant from the next purchaser, the continuing liability of the original covenantor can be offset by a claim against the landowner in breach of the covenant. It is essential, however, that the 'chain' of indemnity covenants is complete.
- The burden of a positive covenant may bind a successor who wishes to assert the benefit of a covenanted obligation provided that there is reciprocity between the benefit and burden. For example, in *Halsall* v. *Brizell* [1957] Ch 169 Upjohn J held that the purchaser of a house on a residential estate could not enjoy the benefit of use of a private road without performing a freehold covenant to maintain it.
- The performance of a positive covenant can be attached to a right of re-entry that becomes exercisable if the covenant is breached. The right or re-entry, but not the covenant itself, would, if annexed to a rent charge, run with the burdened land.
- Since there is no prohibition on the transfer of a positive leasehold covenant, the landowner may prefer to grant a lease of the relevant part of his land (with appropriate covenants) rather than sell the freehold.

9.6 Discharge and Modification

Covenants are automatically ended ('discharged') in two ways: by the common law, and under statute. Statute also allows covenants to be modified.

9.6.1 Common Law

First, if the burdened and benefiting lands are owned by the same person, the covenant cannot be enforced: a person does not have rights against himself. However, if the covenant is part of a building scheme, life after death is possible: the covenants revive if the plots come into separate ownership again later.

Second, if the covenant has been abandoned the courts will not enforce it. This was argued in *Chatsworth Estates* v. *Fewell* [1931] 1 Ch 224. In this case, there was a covenant on a house in a seaside resort restricting its use to that of a private dwelling only. Thirty years later, the then owner started taking paying guests. The claimants warned him of the breach and asked whether he wished to apply to have the covenant modified or discharged under s.84 LPA 1925 (see Section 9.6.2), but he did nothing. When taken to court for the breach, he argued that the claimants had waived breaches by others in the neighbourhood and had therefore abandoned the benefit. The claimants won their injunction to end the breach. Abandonment is a question of fact in every case; here the essential residential character of the area still remained, and the claimants could not be expected to have to conduct inquisitorial examinations into their neighbours' lives in order to see how they were using the land.

In *Shaw* v. *Applegate* [1977] 1 WLR 970 a café owner in another resort was allowed to keep his amusement arcade, contrary to the covenant, because of the claimant's delay in enforcing it. On the facts, the delay had not meant that the claimants had acquiesced in the breach, which would have made the covenant unenforceable, but an injunction – an equitable remedy – was refused on the grounds that the café owner had been lulled into a false sense of security because of the delay, and damages were awarded instead.

9.6.2   Statute

Several statutes authorise the discharge of a covenant; a well-known example is s.237 Town and Country Planning Act 1971 which allows a local authority to carry out a development against a covenant, providing it pays compensation. The most important provision, however, is s.84 LPA 1925, as amended by s.28 LPA 1969. The power to discharge or modify covenants is important because the very existence of the power encourages people to agree to waive covenants. In many cases which do not go to litigation, it is merely a question of the developer 'buying off' the covenants.

A statutory power to end freehold covenants was deemed necessary in 1925 because restrictions on land use could 'enclose individual premises and often whole streets and neighbourhoods in a legal straitjacket' (Polden (1986) 49 MLR 195). There was no discussion of s.84 in Parliament, although it allows the state to destroy private property (the right to enforce the covenant), sometimes without compensation. The question is now whether s.84 is in breach of Article 1, Protocol 1 of the European Convention on Human Rights. This issue has been tested before the European Commission of Human Rights in *S* v. *UK* (1984) (Application No. 10741/84). The applicant lost her case there, on the particular facts, but it seems unlikely that any other application, even on different facts, would succeed because of the doctrine of proportionality and the public interest element: 'ensuring the most efficient use of the land for the benefit of the community' (see Dawson [1986] Conv 124 at p. 126).

Applications under the section are made to the Lands Tribunal, a body which spends much of its time determining land valuations for the purposes of rating and compulsory purchase. Appeal on a point of law can be made to the Court of Appeal. Under s.84 the Tribunal has power to modify or discharge any restrictive covenant and some covenants in long leases. There is provision for compensation to be paid in certain cases.

Under s.84, a covenant may be discharged or modified if:

- it should be deemed obsolete due to changes in the character of the property or neighbourhood; or
- it impedes some reasonable use of the land, provided money is sufficient compensation and either (a) 'it provides no practical benefits of substantial value or advantage' or (b) it is contrary to the public interest; or
- the parties agree, expressly or impliedly 'by their acts or omissions'; or
- it will not injure anyone entitled to the benefit.

The Tribunal must have regard to any planning permissions or local plans but these are not decisive. There are innumerable cases on s.84 and each turns on its own facts; two examples are briefly considered here.

Re Bass Ltd's Application (1973) 26 P & CR 156 concerned an application to use land, restricted to housing, as a lorry park; the owner of the burdened land already had planning permission, and the objectors to the covenant's discharge (the owners of the benefit) already suffered from serious traffic noise. The adjudicator found, from a visit to the site, that, although living close to heavy lorries was far from pleasant, the restrictive covenant still conferred a substantial advantage on the objectors in preventing any increase in the number of lorries, and the application therefore failed. (This case is useful in that it lists the questions which must be asked in an application under s.84.)

In *Re University of Westminster* [1998] 3 All ER 1014, the University applied to have discharged or modified covenants restricting the use of one of its properties to particular educational purposes. The Court of Appeal upheld the Lands Tribunal's determination that the covenants could be modified to permit the use of the property for the wider educational purposes the University proposed, but that the covenants could not be discharged entirely. The parties who had the benefit of the covenants had not objected to the proposal for discharge. However, the Lands Tribunal was not satisfied that they realised the possible effect of discharging them: the University, and any subsequent owner, would be able to use the property for any purpose. On this basis the Lands Tribunal found that they had not therefore agreed to the discharge of the covenants, as required by s.84(1)(b). Neither was the Lands Tribunal convinced that some reasonable use of the property would be impeded by a failure to allow discharge.

It can be seen, even from this brief review, that the Lands Tribunal has a challenging role. Many different interests are involved in these cases: developers, nearby landowners intent on preserving the status quo, 'expert' planners, the general policy that contracts be respected, the wider public interest in land use, and the views of particular political parties (such as the Conservative government's policy of reducing planning restrictions during the 1980s and 1990s). These difficult issues are part of the background of all planning law, private and public.

9.7 Comment

Restrictive covenants are part of the private law of planning, but are just one of several legal strategies to control use of land by others. Alternative ways are: long leases, which may be enlarged to a freehold with the covenants remaining enforceable; conditional fees simple subject to a right of re-entry (see 4.2); and the 'pure principle of benefit and burden' as in *Hulsall* v. *Brizell* [1957] Ch 169: a person will not be allowed to escape from positive obligations under a covenant if he wishes to enjoy a related benefit. All these methods can also provide the means to avoid the rule that the burden of positive covenants cannot pass, as will a commonhold scheme (see Section 6.6). However, such arrangements require careful planning: *Rhone* v. *Stephens* [1994] 2 AC 310 illustrates the problems which may arise if the buyer of land fails to consider fully the implications of the non-enforceability of a positive covenant.

Reform of covenants in freehold land has been considered several times in the past. The Law Commission Report No 127 (1984) proposed a new and simple law to govern the running of benefit and burden at law of both restrictive and positive covenants through the creation of new legal interests in land, 'Neighbour Obligations', and a new kind of building scheme in 'Development Obligations'. This proposal was supplemented by a Report in 1991 (Law Com No 201) which recommended that a restrictive covenant should cease to be enforceable after 80 years unless the owner of the benefit could show it was not obsolete. In 2008 the Law Commission began a fresh consultation on the reform of the law relating to easements, covenants and *profits à prendre* (Law Com Consultation Paper 186), which included provisional proposals for a single scheme of 'Land Obligations' to replace covenants. It has yet to be seen whether these proposals will fare any better than their predecessors. However, even if the current rules, with all their complexities and uncertainties, are replaced by a more coherent scheme, the difficult decisions about land use will remain, decisions which reveal the usually concealed political and economic forces affecting land law.

Summary

9.1 There are separate sets of rules to pass the benefit of a covenant at law, and to pass both the benefit and the burden of a covenant in equity. Equity also provides for building schemes which create a mutually enforceable local law (see Table 9.1).

Table 9.1 Summary of the rules relating to the running of freehold covenants.

	Benefit runs if...	Burden runs if...
At Law	(1) Expressly assigned (s.136 LPA 1925); or (2) (a) it benefits the land; and (b) the covenantee had a legal estate in the benefiting land; and (c) the claimant has a legal estate in the benefiting land; and (d) it was intended to run	Generally not possible
In Equity	(1) It benefits the land; and (2) (a) s. 78 LPA 1925 applies; or (b) it was expressly or impliedly annexed to the benefiting land; or (c) it was assigned to the claimant	Under the rule in *Tulk* v. *Moxhay* if: (1) it is restrictive; and (2) it benefited land owned by the covenantee and now owned by the claimant; and (3) it was intended to run (s. 79 LPA 1925); and (4) it is protected by registration; and (5) there is no reason to dent the claimant an equitable remedy.

9.2 Only the equitable remedies are available for breach of a restrictive covenant. The usual remedy will be an injunction, but the court has the power to award damages in lieu of an injunction or to decline to give any remedy where it feels this would be justified on the facts of the case.

9.3 Section 56 LPA 1925 allows a person not named in a deed to be a party to it if he was referred to in the deed and identifiable at that time. The Contracts (Rights of Third Parties) Act 1999 is wider and potentially more helpful.

9.4 Covenants (except those in building schemes) may be ended at common law if the benefiting and burdened land come into the same hands or if the benefit is abandoned.

9.5 Section 84 LPA 1925 provides machinery for the discharge or modification of restrictive covenants which have outlived their useful life; each case is decided on its own facts.

Exercises

9.1 To what extent does equity supplement the legal rules about covenants in freehold land?

9.2 Did the decision *Federated Homes* improve the law?

9.3 What are the advantages of proving a building scheme in an action for enforcing a restrictive covenant?

9.4 What are the limitations of s.56 LPA? What is the effect of the Contracts (Rights of Third Parties) Act 1999?

@ **9.5** In 1950 Karen sold part of her large garden in the Chequers Estate to Barry who built 'The Palace' on it. In 1965 she sold another part of her garden to Phil who promised her that he would not build more than one house on the land and that he would erect and maintain a fence around the land. The promise was stated to be made 'also with owners for the time being of adjoining land, formerly part of the Chequers Estate'.

In 1990 a council estate was built in the fields neighbouring the estate. Karen died and her executors sold her remaining land to Yehudi. Rita has bought Phil's land and plans to build a block of flats with an open, unfenced garden.

Who can enforce the covenants, and who is bound by them? What remedies are available to the parties?

@ **9.6** An online quiz on the topics covered in this chapter is available on the companion website.

Further Reading

Dawson, 'Restrictive Covenants and Human Rights' [1986] Conv 124
Gravells, 'Enforcement of Positive Covenants Affecting Freehold Land' (1994) 110 LQR 346
Howell, 'The Annexation of the Benefit of Covenants to Land' [2004] Conv 507
Martin, 'Remedies for Breach of Restrictive Covenants' [1996] Conv 329
Polden, 'Private Estate Planning and the Public Interest' (1986) 49 MLR 195
Todd, 'Annexation After *Federated Homes*' [1985] Conv 177

Resolving Disputes

Chapter 10

Unregistered Land

10.1 Introduction to Part III

10.2 General Framework

10.3.1 Introduction

10.3.2 The Registerable Charges

10.3 The Land Charges Register

10.3.3 Difficult Cases
- 10.3.3.1 Estate Contracts
- 10.3.3.2 Equitable Easements
- 10.3.3.3 Family Right of Occupation

10.3.4 Registering and Searching for a Charge

10.3.5 The Effect of Registering a Charge

10.3.6 The Effects of Failing to Register a Charge

10 Unregistered land

10.4 Overreaching

10.5 The Doctrine of Notice
- Actual
- Constructive
- Imputed

10.6 Comment

10.1 Introduction to Part III

Part II of this book considered the main types of estate and interest that can exist in land, their characteristics and the rules for creating them. Chapters 10 and 11 are concerned with a different issue: what are the rules for resolving disputes between people claiming conflicting interests over the same legal estate in land? In many cases such disputes will arise when the estate changes hands and there is a conflict between the new owner of the land and a person who owns another, pre-existing interest in the land, such as an easement. Not all disputes are triggered by a sale: they can also arise because of a breakdown in the relationship between neighbours or when a mortgagee enforces its security. One of the tasks of lawyers handling the sale and purchase of land is to identify any potential conflicts and resolve them prior to the transfer of the land to the new owner.

The law of England and Wales has two distinct sets of rules for resolving land disputes: those that apply to *unregistered land* (considered in this chapter) and the rules of *registered title* (considered in Chapter 11). It is important to recognise that the systems of unregistered and registered title are fundamentally separate and different (see Section 11.1 for a comparison between the two systems). The rules of registered title are by far the more important of the two sets today. An estimated 80% of the potential number of titles in England and Wales have already been registered, and the remainder of these titles must be registered the next time that they are transferred, or made subject to a first legal mortgage. Landowners can also register their title voluntarily. The rules relating to adverse possession of registered land introduced by the LRA 2002 (see Section 3.3.2) make voluntary registration attractive to owners of large areas of land, and intense work is being done by the Land Registry to encourage local authorities, charities and fund managers to register title to their land. However, it is still important to have some understanding of the rules about unregistered land. A significant minority of titles remain unregistered and the title to these must be investigated using the unregistered land rules as part of the process of first registration.

As in other areas of land law, the rules are easier to grasp if they are seen as answers to real questions. For example, suppose that Dan and Sam are about to complete their purchase of a house and have just found out about Jean who lives in the attic and has paid the mortgage instalments for the past five years. Further, their prospective new neighbour, Lloyd, tells them that they cannot alter the outside of their house. They want to know whether they can get rid of Jean, and whether they can install a bay window at the front of the house. Their question is, 'Do Jean and Lloyd own interests which will affect us?' At the same time, Jean and Lloyd (who claims to own the benefit of the restrictive covenant) would each ask: 'Will Dan and Sam be able to defeat my interest?' (The same questions arise in relation to a buyer of any interest in land, such as a mortgagee or a lessee: see Section 2.1.)

In order to answer such questions, it is necessary to be able to:

1   identify all the interests which can exist in land, and
2   decide whether they are capable of binding the present (or future) owner of the land.

If the title is registered, the answer to the second question will depend upon the requirements set out in the LRA 2002 for this type of interest. In unregistered land it will usually depend upon whether the interest is legal or equitable. In both cases, therefore, a glance at the summaries of the preceding chapters is likely to be useful.

10.2 Unregistered Land: the General Framework

The basic rules that apply to unregistered land today are those set out in the box.

Basic Rules of Unregistered Land

A buyer in good faith and for money or money's worth of a legal interest is bound by:

◆ any pre-existing legal interest, except an unregistered *puisne* mortgage (see Section 10.3.2), and
◆ any interest which must be registered under the Land Charges Act 1972, and is properly registered, and
◆ any other interest:
  – which could not have been registered under the Land Charges Act 1972, and
  – which has not been overreached within the statutory limits imposed in 1925, and
  – of which the buyer has actual, imputed or constructive notice.

A buyer of an equitable interest is bound by almost all pre-existing legal and equitable interests (see Section 10.3.6).

Legal interests are normally discovered during the enquiries made before purchase, but if, for example, a buyer later found a legal mortgage she would be bound by it. Of course, the seller would be liable in damages if she has failed to deliver the unburdened land she had promised.

When the land is unregistered there are, therefore, four sets of rules to be applied in turn:

▷ All prior *legal* interests, except for *puisne* mortgages (which fall within the scope of the Land Charges Act 1972) will automatically bind the owner of the land.
▷ The Land Charges Act 1972 contains a list of burdens on unregistered land requiring protection by entry in the *Land Charges Register* (see Section 10.3).
▷ *Overreaching* (Sections 10.4 and 11.4.2) simplifies the buying of land which is subject to a trust, so that a buyer need not worry about beneficiaries: if the buyer pays the purchase price to two trustees (or a trust corporation), any beneficial interests under the trust are automatically detached from the land and attached to the money.
▷ *The doctrine of notice* was explained in Section 1.5 (and see Section 10.5).

10.3 The Land Charges Register

10.3.1 Introduction

The introduction by the 1925 legislation of the need to register certain interests in land was intended to protect both the buyer of the land and the holder of the interest by releasing them from the uncertainties of the doctrine of notice. Thus, registering an interest in the appropriate register is deemed to be 'actual notice' of the charge, so that it binds the buyer, while failure to register usually means that the charge is void, and so does not bind her. Of the five separate registers kept by the Land Charges Department under the Land Charges Act

(LCA) 1972 (which replaced the Land Charges Act 1925), the most important is the Land Charges Register (see below). Land charges are burdens on land; there are 11 altogether, divided into 'classes' A to F. The interests which can be registered there are, in theory, those which are otherwise difficult for the buyer of land to discover; equally, it would be hard to protect them by notice. These registerable interests are mostly equitable and are often described as 'commercial' rather than 'family' interests (trusts). Since 1925, family interests are dealt with by overreaching.

Many students find the presence of a register within a system called 'unregistered land' confusing and counter-intuitive. It is important to remember, however, that the question of whether land is registered or unregistered refers to the status of the title to the land (that is, how ownership is proved), rather than how particular interests in the land are protected (see Section 1.4.2 and Chapter 11). The Land Charges Register must not be confused with the registers of title to registered land (see Chapter 11). Neither should it be confused with the register of local land charges held by each local authority under the Local Land Charges Act 1975. The register of local land charges records those burdens on land, either financial, perhaps resulting from non-payment of council tax, or restricting the use or development of the land, such as tree preservation orders.

10.3.2 The Registerable Charges

Under s.2 LCA 1972, the following interests are registerable in the Land Charges Register held by the Chief Land Registrar:

Class	Interest
A	charges created by a person applying under a statute.
B	charges created by a statute, not by a person's application: for example a charge on land created under the Legal Aid Act 1988.
C(i)	a *puisne* mortgage: this is a legal mortgage where the borrower did not deposit the title deeds with the lender; it is therefore frequently not a first mortgage.
C(ii)	a limited owner's charge: this arises where an owner's interest is limited by a trust: if she pays a tax bill herself instead of mortgaging the land to pay it, she owns this equitable interest.
C(iii)	a general equitable charge: this seems to cover, for example, an equitable mortgage of a legal estate without deposit of title deeds, and certain annuities.
C(iv)	an estate contract: a contract to transfer a legal interest in land (see below).
D(i)	an Inland Revenue Charge: a charge on land arises automatically if the tax due on an estate at death is not paid.
D(ii)	a restrictive covenant *created since 1925*, excluding leasehold covenants.
D(iii)	an equitable easement *created since 1925* (see below).
E	annuities: now obsolete.
F	a spouse's right of occupation in the matrimonial home (see below).

The most important classes of Land Charge are C(i), C(iii), C(iv), D(ii), D(iii) and F (note that classes C(i) applies to a legal interest – the other classes of land charge in this list are equitable rights).

10.3.3 Further Details of Difficult Classes

10.3.3.1 Estate Contracts

> [An] estate contract is a contract by an estate owner ... to convey or create a legal estate, including a contract conferring ... a valid option of purchase, a right of pre-emption or any other like right. (s.2(4)(iv) LCA)

As shown in Section 2.3, a buyer of land (whether of a fee simple or a lease or some other interest) is normally recognised as having some equitable interest in the land as soon as there is a contract: this right is an estate contract. Most solicitors do not bother to register estate contracts because the contracts are nearly always successfully completed. If, however, completion is likely to be delayed, or if the buyer is suspicious of the seller, then the charge should be registered. Some types of contract should always be registered, including:

- *Options to purchase.* An option to purchase arises, for example, where Maria agrees that Jason can buy her land at a certain price, if he decides he wants to. An option to purchase will bind a purchaser only if protected by registration in the Land Charges Register. However, the same seems not to be the case for a right of pre-emption (or a right of first refusal – where, for example, Maria agrees with Jason that if she decides to sell her land she will offer it first to him) even though such a right is also an estate contract. In the case of *Pritchard* v. *Briggs* [1980] Ch 338 it was held that no interest can arise until the decision to sell is made. This means that the right of pre-emption can only be registered when it is capable of being exercised (that is, when Maria decides to sell). The decision in *Pritchard* has been heavily criticised and was distinguished in *Dear* v. *Reeves* [2002] Ch 1 (although that case was not about the LCA 1972).
- *Equitable leases* that are also estate contracts must be registered. In *Hollington Bros Ltd* v. *Rhodes* [1951] 2 All ER 578n the owner of the equitable lease failed to protect it by registration and it was therefore held void against the buyer of the freehold reversion – even though the buyer of the freehold had known about the equitable lease from the start and had paid less in consequence.
- *A tenant's option to renew a lease, or to buy the freehold.* These options are registerable interests within this class; this is so even if the option is contained within a legal lease and was known about by all parties (*Phillips* v. *Mobil Oil Co Ltd* [1989] 1 WLR 888).

10.3.3.2 Equitable Easements

This is:

> an easement, right or privilege over or affecting land created on or after 1st January 1926 being merely an equitable interest. (s.2(5)(iii) LCA)

Unfortunately, this definition is not as simple as it appears. An equitable easement often arises out of an informal arrangement which no one would think of seeing a solicitor about, in which case it is unlikely to be protected by registration. In *ER Ives Investment Ltd* v. *High* [1967] 2 QB 379, a block of flats was being built on a bomb-site and it was discovered that the foundations trespassed on the neighbouring plot. Mr High, the owner of that plot, agreed (unfortunately not by deed) that he would allow the foundations to remain there if he could use a drive over the developer's land. He then built a garage on his own land at the end of the drive. This arrangement was clearly an equitable easement but it was never protected by registration as a Class D(iii) land charge. Both plots of land changed hands and the new owners of the flats decided they wanted to stop their neighbour's use of their drive. They argued that the equitable easement was void for non-registration. The Court of Appeal decided that the LCA 1925 (the case preceded the 1972 Act) 'was not the end of the matter' since there were rights arising from the mutuality principle and from estoppel (see Section 13.4) which were not affected by the failure to register. Mutuality is an ancient principle: a person cannot reject a burden, the neighbour using the drive, so long as she wants to enjoy a related benefit, the trespass of the foundations (see also Section 9.5). The estoppel arose because the landowner had allowed Mr High to spend a considerable amount on building the garage, knowing that Mr High believed himself to have a legal right to use the drive. Mr High was, therefore, allowed to continue to use the drive so long as the foundations of the flats remained on his land (see also Section 13.4.)

Ives v. *High* represents one of the very few examples of courts finding a way around the LCA in order to arrive at a just result. In most cases, the principle may be expressed as 'Register or be damned!'

10.3.3.3 Rights of Occupation for Spouses and Civil Partners

Section 30 of the Family Law Act 1996 (as amended by the Civil Partnership Act 2004) gives a spouse or civil partner who is not already a co-owner a statutory right to occupy the dwelling-house owned by the other spouse. This right of occupation, available to either party to the marriage or civil partnership, was originally created under the Matrimonial Homes Act 1967 in an attempt to solve some of the problems which can arise when one party to the relationship (historically, usually the husband) is the sole legal owner of the home. Under the pre-1967 law he could sell it and run off whenever he liked, and the deserted partner could not protect herself and their children in advance – see *National Provincial Bank Ltd* v. *Ainsworth* [1965] AC 1175. In theory, the Class F charge is a simple, cheap and efficient solution. In *Wroth* v. *Tyler* [1974] Ch 30, the contracts were exchanged for the sale of the family home, which was in Mr Tyler's sole name. A day later Mrs Tyler registered a Class F land charge. This prevented Mr Tyler from being able to transfer the house to the buyers with vacant possession. In the circumstances, however, the court refused to grant the claimants the equitable remedy of specific performance because this would force Mr Tyler to begin proceedings against his wife. Instead, the court awarded the claimants damages calculated to place them in the same financial position that they would have been had the sale been completed.

Wroth v. *Tyler* is, however, somewhat unusual. Many non-owning partners do not discover the possibility of registering a Class F charge until it is too late, and it is of no use to people living together who are not married or in a Civil Partnership. Although the right of occupation is binding on a purchaser if it has been protected by registration, the court has a discretion to terminate the rights against a purchaser where it is just and reasonable to do so (see s.34(2) FLA 1996), placing on a statutory footing the decision in *Kaur* v. *Gill* [1988] Fam 110).

10.3.4 Registering and Searching for a Charge

Registering an interest is a simple matter. Its owner fills in a short form giving her own details, the nature of the charge and the name of the owner of the land which is subject to the charge (the estate owner). All charges are registered against the name of the landowner and not against the land itself. Such a name-based register causes all kinds of problems, not least because people who fill in forms make typing errors. Apparently the register contains charges registered against people with first names like Nacny, Brain and Farnk. If the wrong name is given on the charge registration form, and the purchaser searches against the correct name, the purchaser will normally take free from the charge. In an extraordinary case where both the registration and the search were against (different) incorrect names, the attempt at registration was held to be valid against a mortgagee, who had taken two years from his discovery of the mistake to take action (*Oak Cooperative Building Society* v. *Blackburn* [1968] Ch 730).

Registration protects an interest that is valid, but cannot perfect an invalid interest. Although it is, of course, possible to register ineffective charges on the register, registration alone does not make the charge valid. For example, a prospective purchaser may need to ensure that the benefit and burden of a registered restrictive covenant have run with the land. The Registrar has the power to remove invalid charges (to 'vacate the register'). In fact, many charges in the register are a waste of space (including the many estate contracts which have been completed and the *puisne* mortgages which have been redeemed). The Register thus tends to increase rather than reduce the apparent burdens on title.

To search for a charge is also a simple matter requiring a form giving the names of the people who have owned the land, and the appropriate fee. Legal professionals can also make searches electronically and by telephone. Anyone can search the Register, but it is usual – and safer – to have an official search. The staff at the Registry search against the estate owners' names as requested and send back a form giving details of any charges they discover. In practice, these are often already known to the buyer from the investigations before exchange of contracts (see Section 2.2).

The official certificate of search is conclusive (s.10 LCA 1972); if it fails to give details of a charge, the charge will be void, despite the fact that the charge is appears on the register (the owner of the charge will receive compensation for the negligence of the Registry). The official certificate also gives the person who required the search 15 working days' protection from having any further charges registered (s.11 LCA 1972). Thus, once the official search has been made, the buyer is safe provided the sale is completed within the 15 days.

One of the problems with using the Land Charges Register is that it is possible that a charge was registered, say in 1930, against the name of the then estate owner, but that today's buyer of the land is unable to discover her name because it is hidden 'behind the root of the title' (the document establishing the seller's title over a minimum of the last 15 years: see Section 3.2). The buyer is deemed to have notice of the registered charge and to be bound by it although no amount of prudence could have uncovered it. In these circumstances, the buyer can claim compensation (s.25 LPA 1969). As time passes, more and more charges lie behind the root of title. Wade described this problem as a 'Frankenstein's monster' which grows more dangerous and harder to kill as the years pass (Wade [1956] CLJ 216), although his fears have yet to be realised.

10.3.5 The Effect of Registering a Charge

Section 198 LPA 1925 (as amended) states that:

> The registration of any instrument or matter in any register kept under the Land Charges Act 1972 ... shall be deemed to constitute actual notice ... to all persons and for all purposes connected with the land affected ...

The Land Charges system is, therefore, a statutory way of giving notice of an interest to a buyer of land. Registration of a charge binds everyone because registration is 'actual notice'. The pre-1926 rules of actual, constructive and imputed notice (see Section 10.5) are, therefore, not relevant to interests that are caught by the LCA 1972. A prudent buyer cannot now protect herself through diligent enquiries, because she has actual notice of any properly registered charge, whether or not she could ever have found it in the Register. The only exception to the rule that registration is actual notice is where the official search certificate fails to mention a charge that has been properly registered (see Section 10.3.4). It is therefore effectively the official certificate of search which counts as notice, not the Register.

10.3.6 The Effect of Failing to Register a Charge

As shown in *Hollington Brothers Ltd* v. *Rhodes* [1951] 2 All ER 578n, an unregistered estate contract does not bind the buyer: it was void. However, the rules of voidness are in fact more detailed:

Unregistered Land Charges: s.4 LCA
- Classes A, B, C(i), C(ii), C(iii), F are void against anyone who gives *'value'* for *any* interest (s.4(2),(5) and (8)).
- Classes C(iv), D(i), D(ii), D(iii) are void against anyone who gives *'money or money's worth'* for a *legal* estate (s.4(6)).

Charges in the first group are therefore void for non-registration against anyone who buys an interest in the land, whether legal or equitable. 'Value' means money, money's worth or an agreement to convey land in consideration of marriage. It is interesting to note that in *registered* land, marriage has ceased to be valuable consideration. The Law Commission ((1998) Law Com No 254) was of the view that:

> ... marriage consideration is an anachronism and should cease to be regarded as valuable consideration in relation to dealings with registered land. A transfer of land in consideration of marriage is in substance in most cases a wedding gift (para. 3.43).

The second group of charges is only void for non-registration against a person who buys a *legal* estate and who has paid *money or money's worth for it*; 'money's worth' means exactly what it says, that is anything which is worth money, such as other land or company shares. Where someone is buying only an equitable interest, or is getting married as consideration (that is, not paying money or money's worth), an unregistered charge in this group is not void as far as she is concerned. Whether or not she is bound depends not on the LCA 1972 but on the doctrine of notice (Section 10.5).

It is only when the burdened land changes hands that a charge becomes void for non-registration. Between the original parties, the charge is, of course, enforceable and damages for breach of contract may still be available even if a charge is void against a later buyer of the land. Anyone who gains land through adverse possession or as a gift will also be bound by all interests in the land, whether or not protected by registration, because she is not a buyer.

Section 4 LCA 1972 is given even more force by s.199 LPA 1925 which provides that an unregistered charge is void even if the buyer actually knew about it:

> A purchaser shall not be prejudicially affected by notice of ... any instrument or matter capable of registration under the provisions of the [LCA 172] ... which is void or not enforceable against him under that Act ... by reason of the non-registration thereof.

This section has been ruthlessly interpreted by some judges, as in the *Hollington Bros* case [1951] 2 All ER 578, where express notice in writing of an unregistered estate contract (an option to renew a lease) was held to be irrelevant. This was taken even further in *Midland*

Bank Trust Co Ltd v. *Green (No. 1)* [1981] AC 513. A father granted his son a 10-year option to purchase his farm, which the son was managing and occupying with his family. This was an estate contract, registerable as a Class C(iv) land charge, but which the son never registered. Later the father changed his mind about the option and discovered that, if he sold the legal estate in the land to 'a purchaser for money or money's worth', the son's estate contract would be void. He did just that; the purchaser being his wife, mother of the owner of the unregistered charge. She knew about the father's scheme and paid far less than the market value of the land. One after another, those concerned in the conflict died and the executors had to sort out who had owned what, and who was now entitled to it. The House of Lords (reversing the Court of Appeal) held that the unregistered charge was void against the mother. She was the purchaser of the legal estate for money and that was all that was needed:

> The case is plain: the Act is clear and definite. Intended as it was to provide a simple and understandable system for the protection of title to land, it should not be read down or glossed; to do so would destroy the usefulness of the Act (Lord Wilberforce at p. 528).

Unlike the position in registered land (see Section 11.7.2), the LCA 1972 makes no special allowance for a person in occupation of the land. It seems that the 1925 legislation was intended to give occupies some degree of protection. Section 14 of the LPA 1925 expressly provides that:

> This part of this Act shall not prejudicially affect the interest of any person in possession or in actual occupation of land to which he may be entitled in right of such possession or occupation.

Section 14 is in Part I of the LPA 1925, but unfortunately it was wrongly placed there; it should have been moved to the LCA when that Act was carved out of the original 1922 Act (see Section 1.2). This means that s.14 cannot affect either s.199 LPA 1925 or the LCA 1972 (neither of which are in Part 1 of the LPA 1925).

In *Lloyds Bank Plc* v. *Carrick* [1996] 4 All ER 630, an estate contract to buy a long lease of a maisonette was void for non-registration against a later mortgagee. Although the terms of the contract were not recorded in writing, Mrs Carrick had paid the full price to the seller, her brother-in-law, and had moved in. As the contract, made in 1982, pre-dated the Law of Property (Miscellaneous Provisions) Act 1989 (see Section 2.4) these acts were sufficient to make the contract enforceable. However, the title to the lease was never actually transferred to Mrs Carrick. The brother-in-law subsequently secretly mortgaged the property to Lloyds Bank which, when he defaulted on the repayments, sought possession. Mrs Carrick argued that her brother-in-law either held the property on a bare trust for her (as any seller does between exchange of contracts and completion) or under a constructive trust (see Section 13.3) or through estoppel (see Section 13.4). If the trust arguments had found favour with the Court of Appeal, then Mrs Carrick's rights against the bank would have depended on the doctrine of notice – since she was in occupation, the bank would have had constructive notice of her interest. However, the Court held that her rights arose as a consequence of the contract, and her failure to protect it by registration as a land charge meant that it was void against the bank.

The harsh simplicity of these cases, where the buyer either knew or could easily have discovered the interest of the occupier of land, is the sort of thing that makes people cynical about lawyers and their justice. Just as in *Midland Bank Trust* v. *Green*, the opposite result would have been reached in *Carrick*, as Morritt LJ pointed out, if the rules of registered land (which offer protection to occupiers who have rights in the land – see Section 11.7.2) had applied: the farmer's son would have been able to exercise his option and Mrs Carrick would have kept her home.

10.4 Overreaching

In order to simplify the process of buying and selling land subject to a trust, it was intended by the framers of the 1925 scheme that trust interests should all be capable of being over-reached (s.2 and s.27 LPA 1925).

Providing the buyer of any interest in land pays the purchase price to at least two trustees or a trust corporation, beneficial interests under a trust are kept behind the 'curtain' of over-reaching, a curtain which the buyer need not lift. The rights of the beneficiaries are automatically detached from the land and attached to the purchase price in the hands of the trustees (see Chapter 12 for the roles of trustees and beneficiaries in 'trusts of land').

None of the LCA 1972 interests, such as equitable charges, restrictive covenants and estate contracts, can be overreached. As Robert Walker LJ pointed out in *Birmingham Midshires Mortgage Services Ltd* v. *Sabherwal* (2000) 80 P & CR 256:

> The essential distinction is ... between commercial and family interests. [A commercial interest] cannot sensibly shift from the land affected by it to the proceeds of sale. [A family interest] can do so ... since the proceeds of sale can be used to acquire another home (at p. 263).

The doctrine of overreaching is considered in more detail in Section 11.4.2.

10.5 The Doctrine of Notice

If an interest cannot be registered because it does not fit into the categories set out in the LCA 1972, the next step is to decide whether the interest can be overreached. If it cannot be over-reached (or if it has not been, because, for example, there was only one trustee), then any conflict between the interests of buyers and owners of pre-existing interests must be resolved by the pre-1925 rules. The same is true for a buyer of land who is not the kind of buyer against whom an unregistered charge is void under the LCA (see Section 10.3.6).

In these situations, the conflict between the owner of a *legal* interest in land and the owner of some pre-existing *equitable* interest in it must be resolved by the doctrine of notice. A buyer in good faith of a legal estate for value ('equity's darling') is only bound by equitable interests of which she had notice (see Section 1.5). Notice can be actual, imputed or constructive (see the box, opposite).

In *Kingsnorth Finance Co Ltd* v. *Tizard* [1986] 1 WLR 783, a husband was the sole legal owner of the family home, but his wife shared the equitable interest in it. The marriage deteriorated and Mrs Tizard spent most of her nights away from home, unless her husband was away on business. Despite this, she looked after the house, cooked the children's meals and kept most of her belongings there. Mr Tizard mortgaged the house without telling his wife and went to America with the money. Mrs Tizard's equitable interest in the house had not been over-reached because the mortgage advance had only been paid to one trustee (her husband): see s.2 LPA 1925. Judge Finlay QC held that the mortgagee finance company had constructive or imputed notice of Mrs Tizard's equitable rights because she was, on the facts, 'in occupation'. The bank's agent should have made more enquiries about the wife because the agent knew

Notice

Actual:	has the mind of the purchaser 'been brought to an intelligent apprehension of the nature of the incumbrance which has come upon the property so that a reasonable man, or an ordinary man of business, would act upon the information and would regulate his conduct by it...' (*Lloyd* v. *Banks* (1867-8) LR 3 Ch App 488, per Lord Cairnes LC at 490).
Constructive:	'Constructive notice is the knowledge which the courts impute to a person... either from his knowing something which ought to have put him to further inquiry or from his wilfully abstaining from inquiry, to avoid notice,' (*Hunt* v. *Luck* [1901] 1 Ch. 45, per Farwell J at p. 52). Constructive notice will only extend to the facts which would have been discovered had the necessary further enquiries been made.
Imputed:	a purchaser is deemed to have the same actual or constructive notice as that of her professional advisors (s.199(1)(ii)(b) LPA 1925).

that the Mr Tizard was married, even though he had described himself as single on the mortgage application form:

> the plaintiffs had, or are to be taken to have had [through their agent], information which should have alerted them to the fact that the full facts were not in their possession and that they should make further inspections or inquiries; they did not do so and in these circumstances I find that they are fixed with notice of the equitable interest of Mrs Tizard (at p. 794)

What a prudent buyer ought to do depends on the facts of each case. There is no need to open drawers and wardrobes to see what clothes are there, but in suspicious circumstances an unannounced visit should probably be made. In this case, there should have been further enquiries and Mrs Tizard should have been interviewed.

The generous view taken of occupation in this case applies to all cases of constructive notice. In the *Tizard* case it was probably the right decision, although the wife's occupation there was borderline. Of course, if the finance company had paid two trustees, Mrs Tizard's interest would have been overreached and she would have had to leave the house.

Table 10.1 shows some of the interests which have been held to be binding upon a purchaser of land as a result of the doctrine of notice. It must be stressed, however, that, since

Table 10.1 The Doctrine of Notice in Unregistered Land.

Case	Type of Interest
ER Ives Investments Ltd v. *High* [1967] 2 QB 379	Equitable easement, mutual rights, estoppel
Binions v. *Evans* [1972] Ch 359	Contractual licence
Shiloh Spinners Ltd v. *Harding* [1973] AC 691	Equitable lessor's right of re-entry
Kingsnorth Finance Co Ltd v. *Tizard* [1986] 1 WLR 783	Equitable interest behind a trust

any interest in unregistered land which is not governed by the rules of the LCA 1972 and which has not been overreached is subject to the doctrine of notice, this is a residual open-ended category. Note also, that all pre-1926 restrictive covenants and equitable easements are subject to the doctrine of notice, as well as Class C(iv) and Class D charges against a purchaser for marriage.

10.6 Comment

Interests in unregistered land are governed by an assortment of rules. The Land Charges Act 1972 represents a small part of the system, but its complexity usually absorbs more time than its importance deserves. The major problem must be the way in which, contrary to the aim of the 1925 draftsmen, buyers can destroy the unregistered interests of occupiers even though they knew, or ought to have known, about them before buying the land. It is also unjust and unjustifiable, since it is relatively easy for a buyer to inspect land and discover an occupant: to enforce a rule protecting occupiers would not necessarily lead to injustice through uncertainty – indeed, this is what happens in registered land.

Other problems with the LCA are the narrow definitions of the registerable interests, the illogical difference between the provisions for voidness, the nature of the name-based register and the way in which the system tends to clog titles rather than to clear them. These have led to much criticism. Various reforms have been suggested; but the final answer seems to be that of the 1956 Report on Land Charges (Cmnd 9825). The Committee confessed that 'to rectify the machinery is a task beyond the wit of man' (Wade [1956] CLJ 216). However, the importance of the actual custom and practice of conveyancers is shown by the fact that, 'fortunately, none of these deficiencies seem to matter in real life' (Wade, p. 234).

The difficulties are such that lawyers have given up, in the expectation that, if all the land in the country ever becomes registered, the Land Charges Register can be given a quick and efficient burial, preferably in an unmarked pauper's grave. However, it would be over-optimistic to expect that the move towards universal registration of title will solve all the problems encountered by buyers and sellers of land. The story of the tensions between the rights of people with interests in land and those of the buyers of that land (often a bank or building society lending money on the security of a mortgage) continues in the next chapter.

Summary

10.1 The rules for determining whether the owner of a legal estate in land is bound by another person's interest in that land depend upon whether title to the land is already registered.

10.2 A buyer of any interest in unregistered land is automatically bound by (nearly) all existing legal interests in the land.

10.2 Eleven 'commercial' interests must be registered in the Land Charges Registry if they are to bind a buyer of unregistered land.

10.3 If interests which are registerable under the Land Charges Act have not been properly registered against the correct name of the estate owner, or do not appear on the official search certificate, they do not bind the buyer even if she actually knew about them.

10.4 Much of land charges registration law is complex, illogical and unfair, but probably impossible to reform.

10.5 'Family' (trust) interests are not registerable but can be overreached by a buyer who pays two trustees.

10.6 If an equitable interest is not registerable and has not been overreached, the rights of a buyer of a legal interest in unregistered land depend on the doctrine of notice; the buyer of an equitable interest is probably bound by any existing equitable interests.

Exercises

10.1 When does equity's darling appear on the scene in unregistered land?

10.2 Against whom is an unregistered land charge void?

10.3 Did the House of Lords come to the right decision in *Midland Bank Trust Co* v. *Green*?

@ **10.4** Hilary is the sole legal owner of a four-storey house, title to which is unregistered, and which is subject to a restrictive covenant that it should be used as a private dwelling house only. She lives on the first floor and her aged mother, Lucy (who contributed a quarter of the cost of the house when it was bought), occupies the ground floor.

Hilary is a compulsive gambler on the Stock Exchange and recently lost a good deal of money. She met Emma at the hairdresser's and in the course of a chat they agreed that Emma should rent the basement of Hilary's house for three years. Emma moved in and has paid rent regularly. Hilary then accepted £2,000 from Clive, a colleague, as a deposit on a ten-year lease of the top floor of her house. Nothing was put in writing for tax reasons.

Six weeks later Hilary decided to emigrate. Clive has discovered that she has made an agreement in writing to sell the whole house to Dee.

Clive, Lucy and Emma seek your advice.

@ **10.5** An online quiz on the topics covered in this chapter is available on the companion website.

Further Reading

Harpum, 'Purchasers with Notice of Unregistered Land Charges' [1981] CLJ 213
Thompson, 'The Purchaser As Private Detective' [1986] Conv 283
Wade, 'Land Charge Registration Reviewed' [1956] CLJ 216
Yates, 'The Protection of Equitable Interests under the 1925 legislation' (1974) 37 MLR 87

Chapter 11

Registered Title

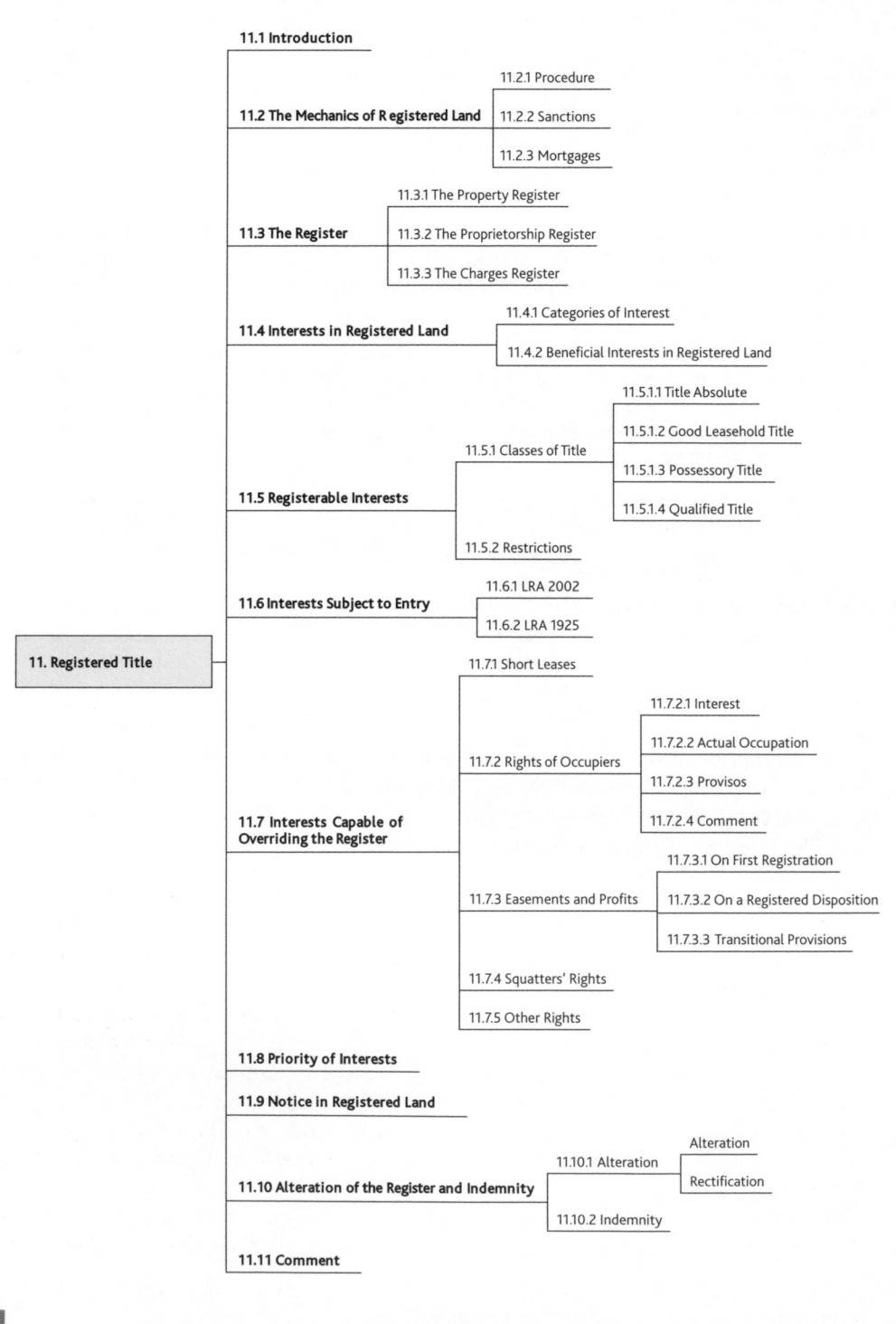

- **11.1 Introduction**
- **11.2 The Mechanics of Registered Land**
  - 11.2.1 Procedure
  - 11.2.2 Sanctions
  - 11.2.3 Mortgages
- **11.3 The Register**
  - 11.3.1 The Property Register
  - 11.3.2 The Proprietorship Register
  - 11.3.3 The Charges Register
- **11.4 Interests in Registered Land**
  - 11.4.1 Categories of Interest
  - 11.4.2 Beneficial Interests in Registered Land
- **11.5 Registerable Interests**
  - 11.5.1 Classes of Title
    - 11.5.1.1 Title Absolute
    - 11.5.1.2 Good Leasehold Title
    - 11.5.1.3 Possessory Title
    - 11.5.1.4 Qualified Title
  - 11.5.2 Restrictions
- **11.6 Interests Subject to Entry**
  - 11.6.1 LRA 2002
  - 11.6.2 LRA 1925
- **11. Registered Title**
- **11.7 Interests Capable of Overriding the Register**
  - 11.7.1 Short Leases
  - 11.7.2 Rights of Occupiers
    - 11.7.2.1 Interest
    - 11.7.2.2 Actual Occupation
    - 11.7.2.3 Provisos
    - 11.7.2.4 Comment
  - 11.7.3 Easements and Profits
    - 11.7.3.1 On First Registration
    - 11.7.3.2 On a Registered Disposition
    - 11.7.3.3 Transitional Provisions
  - 11.7.4 Squatters' Rights
  - 11.7.5 Other Rights
- **11.8 Priority of Interests**
- **11.9 Notice in Registered Land**
- **11.10 Alteration of the Register and Indemnity**
  - 11.10.1 Alteration
    - Alteration
    - Rectification
  - 11.10.2 Indemnity
- **11.11 Comment**

11.1 Introduction

The idea of a register of landownership was promoted in the nineteenth century by a non-lawyer, Robert Torrens, who worked in a deeds registry in South Australia. He was dismayed by the complexity of traditional unregistered conveyancing and devised a system in which the titles to individual estates in land are recorded and ownership depends not upon deeds but upon the entries in the centrally held register. His scheme, which worked efficiently in Australia, gradually spread through the common law world, although title registration was never widely accepted in the USA.

After two earlier attempts in the nineteenth century to introduce a system of voluntary land registration in England, some success was achieved when the Land Transfer Act 1897 made registration compulsory in London. A more effective scheme (although not the Torrens system) was introduced by the Land Registration Act 1925, eventually extending the system of registration across England and Wales, district by district. The move towards complete registration of all land has accelerated in recent years. In 1990, all districts of England and Wales became areas of compulsory land registration, in which freehold land and leases over 21 years were required to be registered on sale (and, in the case of such leases, on creation). In 1998, previously unregistered freehold land and legal leases over 21 years were required to be registered, not just on sale, but whenever transferred or subject to a first legal mortgage. The Land Registration Act 2002 has now extended compulsory registration to leases with more than seven years to run in order to include the increasing number of shorter commercial leases.

A strategic objective of the Land Registry is to complete the Land Register by 2012. There are currently more than 21 million titles on the Register, accounting for between 80 and 90 per cent of the estimated potential titles and 60 per cent of the total land area. The Land Registry is taking positive steps to persuade owners of unregistered titles, predominantly the Crown Estate, public bodies and the owners of large private estates, of the advantages of land registration.

The historical complexity and lack of clarity in the registered land system had long been recognised, and over the years a number of amendments to the 1925 Act were introduced. In 1998, the Law Commission and Land Registry together published their consultative document 'Land Registration for the Twenty-First Century', Law Com No 254, which contained a summary and criticism of the existing law along with initial proposals for a radical reform of the registered title system. Major changes to how registered title worked in practice were required to facilitate a move from paper based land transactions to electronic conveyancing. A draft Bill was published in Law Com No 271 in 2001, which was enacted as the Land Registration Act 2002. Most of the LRA 2002 came into force on 13 October 2003, replacing the LRA 1925. The operation of the 2002 Act is supported by the regulatory framework contained in the Land Registration Rules 2003.

The 2002 Act has brought about major changes to the system of title registration. Perhaps the most important will be a progressive introduction of voluntary electronic conveyancing from spring 2009 which allows the instantaneous creation and transfer of estates and interests in land. The Electronic Communications Act 2000 has implemented the legal changes necessary for the future reforms to take place, and the move towards electronic conveyancing has already started with a trial of registering the discharge of mortgages by electronic means.

Traditionally, there are three essential elements or principles of title registration, known as 'Mirror', 'Curtain' and 'Guarantee'. The Register is supposed to *mirror* the actual structure of title and third-party rights in the land, so that, in theory at any rate, a potential buyer (or anyone else, for that matter) simply has to read the entry in order to discover who owns the land and who else has an interest in it – the uncertainties of the doctrine of notice should have no place in a system of registered title. The *curtain* principle refers to overreaching, the mechanism by which land subject to beneficial trust interests can safely be bought (see Section 11.4.2). Finally, since it is fundamental that there should be confidence in the system, the state *guarantees* the accuracy of the titles on the Register and will indemnify anyone who suffers loss as a result of any mistake on it.

The main differences between registered and unregistered title are summarised in Section 1.4.2 and Table 1.2). Fundamentally, in unregistered land, title is based on possession, established by producing the title deeds, whereas in registered land it is the registration of ownership at the Land Registry which counts.

Although the distinction between legal and equitable estates is preserved in registered land, the LRA 2002 contains its own rules for determining the impact of land interests upon third parties. A deed alone is not normally sufficient to create a legal interest in registered land – the interest must be completed by entry on the register if it is to have effect at law. Most equitable interests will also only bind a purchaser if they have been protected by registration. The main exception to these rules is the limited number of interests which enjoy what is known as 'overriding' status (see Sections 11.4.1 and 11.7).

It is very important to remember that:

1   land registration is based on the registration of title to (*ownership* of) an estate in land: lesser rights are registered against the relevant registered estate and not in their own right or against the name of one the original parties (as in the Land Charges Register); and

2   the Land Charges Register has no connection with registered title: it is a register of some types of rights held over unregistered land.

11.2   The Mechanics of Registered Land

Before we examine some of the technicalities of the system of registered title in England and Wales, it may be helpful to consider how the scheme operates in practice.

11.2.1   Procedure at the Land Registry

Title is first registered, and later dealings are recorded, by filling in the appropriate form and sending it with the fee to the District Land Registry. On first registration, the Registrar checks the title as if he were buying it and decides whether the title is good enough for 'absolute title' (see Section 11.5.1.1), or only something less. Any benefits he discovers will be entered on the Register, as will any burdens, such as restrictive covenants found in the Land Charges Register. Once the land has been registered, however, anything in the Land Charges Register becomes irrelevant. Any other details, such as the title number of the freehold reversion of a lease, will also be noted in order to ensure that the Register really does mirror the title to the land. If Registry staff make a mistake, there are provisions for compensation: the State indemnity (see Section 11.10).

It used to be the case under the 1925 scheme that, on registration, a land certificate containing a copy of the Register would be issued to a new proprietor by the Registry, and would have to be produced when registering a notice or a restriction, or disposing of the land. The Law Commission and the Land Registry considered them unnecessary, and incompatible with electronic conveyancing. However, after consultation, and in order to reassure those who are not convinced by this policy, the Registry now issues 'title information documents' to the registered proprietor whenever the Register is changed.

11.2.2 Sanctions for Failure to Register

Interests which are capable of substantive registration (legal freeholds and legal leases over seven years) are each given their own unique title numbers. Such interests must be registered when there is a transaction which affects the legal title: whether a transfer of all or part of the legal estate, a grant of a new lease of over seven years or a first legal mortgage (s.4 LRA 2002). Where this first registration is a consequence of the *transfer* of the legal freehold or legal lease over seven years and no application has been made to the Registrar to register the title within two months of the conveyance, the legal title, which has already been vested in the new owner under the traditional unregistered procedure, will revert to the former owner who will hold it on a bare trust for the new owner (s.6, 7 LRA 2002). If the first registration concerns the *creation* of a new lease, such failure to register will merely take effect as a contract for valuable consideration (s.7 LRA 2002). In other words, if the first registration rules are not complied with, only equitable titles ultimately pass. If title to the land is already registered, the legal title will only pass to the new owner if the disposition goes through the Register (s.27 LRA 2002). Until that time, all the purchaser will own is the equitable title. The period between completion of the transaction and its registration is referred to as the 'registration gap.' One of the aims of electronic conveyancing is for completion of the transaction and registration to be completed simultaneously via a computer link with the Land Registry, thus abolishing the 'registration gap'.

11.2.3 Mortgages in Registered Land

Section 23(1)(a) LRA 2002 has abolished the creation of mortgages by lease and sublease in registered land (see Section 7.2.1). The view of the Law Commission is that, when compared to the charge by way of legal mortgage, they are long-winded and complex and do not lend themselves easily to electronic conveyancing.

Mortgages are entered as registered charges against the title number of the legal estate or estates to which they relate. Where there is more than one registered charge, priority between them is determined according to the date of registration, unless the chargees agree otherwise (which they may do without the chargor's consent).

11.3 The Register

The Register, the mirror of the title to the land, is held on computerised record at one of 24 District Land Registries. It is now an open record and, for the payment of a small fee, anyone can easily get a copy of an individual Register, either by completing a form and sending it to the appropriate District Land Registry, or instantaneously online through the Land Registry website.

Each individual Register is divided into three sections:

Divisions of the Register
- Property Register
- Proprietorship Register
- Charges Register

11.3.1   The Property Register

This part of the Register describes the title to the land (freehold or leasehold) and any benefits attached to it (such as the benefit of an easement). One plot of land may have several registered titles – for example the freehold and one or more long leases; each has its own title number and entry in the Register. The address is given and reference is made to a plan on which the plot of land is outlined in red. Thus, unlike the Land Charges Register, the Land Register is a 'title-based', not a 'name-based' register.

11.3.2   The Proprietorship Register

This gives the nature of the title under the registration system; there are several kinds (see Section 11.5.1). The Proprietorship Register states the name and address of the owner, who is called 'the registered proprietor'. (In problem questions therefore, any reference to 'fee simple owner' suggests that the land is not yet registered. However, any reference to a 'registered proprietor' means that the land is registered.) The Proprietorship Register also contains any restrictions to which the land is subject, protecting some third-party interests by limiting the power of the registered proprietor to deal with the land (see Section 11.5.2).

11.3.3   The Charges Register

This part of the Register contains details of burdens on the land, including the interests which, in unregistered land, would appear in the Land Charges Register.

11.4   Interests in Registered Land

The basic rule in a conflict between a registered proprietor and the owner of a third-party interest in the land is that a registered proprietor is bound by:

1   any valid interest which is shown on the Register, and
2   by any interests which override either the first registration of the title or subsequent dispositions by the registered proprietor.

11.4.1   Categories of Interests in Registered Land

The normal range of interests – freeholds, leases, easements etc. – still exists in registered land. However, the LRA 2002 superimposes a new set of categories onto the traditional structure:

- **Registerable estates** These are the most important interests and must be substantively registered (Section 11.5).
- **Interests which are subject to an entry on the Register**. Almost all property interests in land can be protected by entering them on the Register (Section 11.6). Unless an interest is capable of overriding the register, it will normally only be binding upon a transferee for value of the registered estate if it is noted on the Register (s.29 LRA 2002). Some legal interests must be completed by registration see s. 27(1) LRA 2002. The most important of these are expressly created legal easements (s.27(2)(d)) and legal charges (s.27(2)(f)). At present, failure to register such interests means that they are unprotected equitable interests. Once comprehensive electronic conveyancing dispenses with the distinction between transaction and registration it will be impossible to create equitable interests in this way.

▶ **Interests which are capable of overriding the first registration or subsequent dispositions by the registered proprietor** This category of interests, although binding on everyone who gains a later interest in the land, is not protected by entry on the Register and can only be discovered by means of inspection and enquiry. These interests are listed in LRA 2002, Schedules 1 and 3 (Section 11.7).

11.4.2 Beneficial Interests in Registered Land

One of the three principles which underlie registered land is the drawing of a 'curtain' over any beneficial interests held under a trust of land. This, in turn, reflects the wider policy objective of trying to ensure that dealings with title can be completed as simply and conveniently as possible. Consequently, beneficial interests under a trust are one of the few classes of interest that cannot be protected by entering a notice of that interest in the register of title (s.33(a) LRA 2002; see Section 11.6.1). The only way to 'protect' a beneficial interest is by entering a restriction that prevents any disposition of the title being registered unless the proceeds of sale are paid to two or more trustees (Land Registration Rules 2003, r. 94; see Section 11.5.2). However, this form of restriction will not result in the new registered proprietor being bound by the beneficial interest. Instead, it ensures that the beneficial interest is overreached by any disposition of the land; the rights of the beneficiaries are automatically detached from the land and attached to the purchase price, which is now in the hands of the trustees (see Chapter 12 for the roles of trustees and beneficiaries in 'trusts of land').

The conditions that need to be satisfied for overreaching to occur are set out in s.2 and in s.27 LPA 1925. Providing the buyer of any interest in land pays the purchase price to at least two trustees or a trust corporation, beneficial interests under a trust are kept behind the 'curtain' of overreaching. If, however, the buyer pays the purchase price to a single trustee only, any beneficial interests will not be overreached. If the beneficiary is in actual occupation of the land concerned, his 'non-overreached' interest may be capable of overriding the disposition of the land, and, therefore, binding on the purchaser (see Section 11.7.2).

Overreaching beneficiaries' interests simply by paying two trustees is very convenient for buyers. In theory, the beneficiaries are happy too because they are entitled to their share of the proceeds in the safe hands of their trustees. Two trustees are less likely to run off with the cash than a single trustee, but this is not unknown: see, for example, the case of *City of London Building Society* v. *Flegg* [1988] AC 54 (see Section 11.7.2.1). In reality, overreaching is only convenient for beneficiaries if they agree that the money is as good as the land. The Law Commission has recommended (Law Com No 188) that the consent of beneficiaries in occupation should be obtained before overreaching can take place (as is common practice where there is only one trustee), but this recommendation has not been taken up.

The decision in the case of *State Bank of India* v. *Sood* [1997] Ch 276, whilst making sound commercial sense, further prejudices the position of beneficiaries. In breach of trust, two trustees mortgaged a house which they held on trust for themselves and five other beneficiaries. The mortgage secured past indebtedness and future borrowing, and no capital money was paid to the trustees. In a somewhat strained interpretation of s.2 LPA, the Court of Appeal held that this was a transaction which enabled the bank to overreach the equitable rights of the beneficiaries despite the fact that no money was paid to the two trustees: the overreaching took effect on the execution of the charge and at that time the interests of the beneficiaries became attached to the equity of redemption. This decision is consistent with the policy of encouraging free alienability of land and conforms with lending practice, but removes the protection for beneficiaries which is normally in the capital money paid to the trustees. Peter Gibson LJ stated:

> Much though I value the principle of overreaching as having aided the simplification of conveyancing, I cannot pretend that I regard the resulting position in the present case as entirely satisfactory. The safeguard for beneficiaries under the existing legislation is largely limited to having two trustees or a trust corporation where capital money falls to be received. But that is no safeguard at all, as this case has shown, when no capital money is received on and contemporaneously with the conveyance (at p. 290).

11.5 Registerable Estates

These are the interests which, on sale, transfer or first legal mortgage (and also, in the case of leases, on creation), must be substantively registered with independent title and their own title number. Essentially, this means freeholds, and leases granted for more than seven years (although, by s.118 LRA 2002, this period of seven years can be, and probably will be, reduced in the future by the Lord Chancellor). In addition, certain other short leases must be registered, the most important of which are reversionary leases (see Section 5.3.2.1) granted for less than seven years which take effect in possession after three months from the date of the grant (an example might be student tenancies granted in May or June but not taking effect until the new academic year in September or October).

11.5.1   Classes of Title

In unregistered land, some titles, such as a title obtained by adverse possession, are in practice not as secure as others, since there are no title deeds to prove it. In registered land the Register reflects the actual state of the title to the land, so it is necessary to classify the titles to show how strong they are. The classes of title available differ slightly between leasehold and freehold (ss.9,10 LRA 2002) and there is provision for weaker titles to be upgraded (s.62 LRA 2002).

11.5.1.1 Title Absolute

'Absolute' freehold or leasehold title is the strongest class of title available: the registered proprietor with absolute title has a better right than anyone else to the land (although there are still circumstances where the title might be open to alteration by courts or the Registrar (see Section 11.9)). Absolute title is subject only to third-party interests protected on the Register and by interests which have overriding status (Section 11.7); if the registered proprietor is a trustee, his rights are also subject to the trust or, if a lessee, to the covenants in the lease.

11.5.1.2 Good Leasehold Title

Good leasehold title is given to a leasehold estate when the Registrar is satisfied that the registered proprietor is entitled to the lease; because the freehold has not yet been registered, the Registrar is unable to guarantee that the freeholder had the right to grant the lease.

11.5.1.3 Possessory Title

'Possessory' titles are rare; they are granted by the Registrar when the alleged owner's title is based only on possession, not on title deeds. The Registrar guarantees the title only as far as dealings after first registration are concerned; no promises are made concerning the right of the first registered proprietor to the land.

11.5.1.4 Qualified Title

'Qualified' titles are almost unheard of; they are granted only if the Registrar has some specific reservation about the title.

11.5.2 Restrictions

A restriction may be entered in the Proprietorship Register by the registered proprietor or the Registrar preventing the registered proprietor dealing with the title unless certain conditions are met (s.40 LRA 2002). The most commonly encountered restriction is that used to protect beneficiaries under a trust by requiring payment to two trustees before a sale or other disposition will be registered (Land Registration Rules 2003, r. 94). This restriction, combined with the prohibition on references to beneficial interests on the register (see Section 11.6), gives effect to the 'curtain' principle in registered land.

11.6 Interests Subject to an Entry on the Register

11.6.1 The LRA 2002

It is possible to protect almost all types of interest in land by entering a notice in the Charges Register to the relevant title number (s.32 LRA 2002). Only five types of interest cannot be protected in this way. These are listed in s.33 LRA 2002, and the most important are:

- trusts of land; and
- leasehold estates for a tem of three years or less (unless they are required to be registered by another section of the LRA; and
- restrictive covenants between a lessor and lessee that relate to the premises demised by the lease.

Several of the excluded interests are capable of overriding the Register, at least in certain circumstances (see Section 11.7). Other interests capable of overriding (a lease with a term of between three and seven years, for example) may override the register or may be protected by a notice. Indeed, the Land Registration Rules 2003 impose a duty on anyone applying for registration to disclose any unregistered interests which they are aware of that override registered dispositions (see rules 28 and 57). Once an interest capable of overriding has been entered on the register it will cease to be overriding, even if the notice is subsequently deleted from the Charges Register – (see ss.29(3) LRA 2002). Interests that are not capable of overriding the Register must be entered on the Register if they are to be binding on purchasers of the registered title. In the 1925 scheme this group of interests was named 'minor interests'. This term is not found in the LRA 2002, but is still used in textbooks and judgments.

11.6.2 The LRA 1925

The LRA 2002 provides two main ways to protect interests on the register: directly by use of a notice (see Section 11.6.1) and indirectly by use of a restriction (see Section 11.5.2). In the 1925 scheme there were four such methods. Students will need to be aware of them as they will still be encountered in cases decided under the 1925 provisions.

▷ **Restriction**

Like their namesakes in the LRA 2002, restrictions imposed conditions that needed to be satisfied if a disposition of the land was to be registered. Prior to 13 October 2003 restrictions were only entered with the consent of the registered proprietor.

▷ **Notice**

A notice registered before 13 October 2003 required the agreement of the registered proprietor (except for the registration of a spouse's right of occupation).

▷ **Inhibition**

An inhibition could be placed on the Proprietorship Register by order of the court or the Registrar forbidding any dealing with the land. Although quite rare, they were used in cases of bankruptcy or suspected fraud. Since 13 October 2003 the same effect is achieved using a special form of restriction.

▷ **Caution**

There were two kinds of caution under the 1925 Act.

1   A *caution against first registration*, which, on first registration, allowed the cautioner an opportunity to argue his claim to a third-party interest in the land. This is the only type of caution used by the LRA 2002.

2   A *caution against dealing*, preventing any disposition of the land unless the cautioner had been informed and had been given the opportunity to object and, again, argue his case for an interest in the land. There can be no new cautions against dealing from 13 October 2003: the same affect is achieved by a unilateral form of notice (which does not require the consent of the registered proprietor – ss.34(2)(b) and 35 LRA 2002).

11.7   Interests Capable of Overriding the Register

There are certain third-party interests which are not required to be protected by entry on the Register but which override the buyer's interests, whether or not he knew, ought to have known, or even could have known, about them. Since they do not appear on the Register, the greater the number of interests which are given overriding status, the less the Register acts as an accurate reflection of the title. Overriding interests are, therefore, potentially a considerable crack in the 'mirror'. The traditional explanation given for the existence of overriding interests is that people who have the benefit of these particular rights cannot reasonably be expected to protect them through registration. By their very nature, some interests do not lend themselves to protection by entry on the Register. Easements created through prescription or by implication and the rights of people in actual occupation of the land are examples of interests that fall into this category. The 1925 scheme also gave overriding status to a number of other types of interests that could be expected to be reasonably apparent to any purchaser, including, for example expressly created legal easements and legal leases for 21 years or less. This helped to reduce the amount of information held at the Land Registry to practicable proportions in a pre-computer age. By the end of the twentieth century the Law Commission and the Land Registry were agreed that the list of potential overriding interests should be rationalized ((2001) Law Com No 271, para. 2.25), and the 2002 Act has reduced the number and scope of these interests.

Since a buyer of unregistered land will already be bound by third-party interests under the rules of unregistered conveyancing, the 2002 Act makes certain distinctions between those interests which will override first registration (listed in Schedule 1) and those which will override subsequent, registered dispositions of the land (listed in Schedule 3). The main overriding interests will now be examined in turn.

11.7.1 Short Leases (Schedule 1, para. 1; Schedule 3, para. 1)

Leases granted for more than seven years are substantively registerable (Section 11.5). Legal leases granted for seven years or less override on first and subsequent registration and a purchaser will be bound by them. Note that certain special types of lease must be substantively registered (and will not have overriding status) even if they do not exceed seven years (s.4(1)(d)(e) and (f)). The most important example is a reversionary lease taking effect more than three months after the date of the grant.

11.7.2 Rights of Occupiers (Schedule 1, para. 2; Schedule 3, para. 2)

The LRA 2002 recognises the need to protect the third-party interests of people who are in actual occupation of land but who have not protected their rights in the land by registration, perhaps because the right had arisen informally or because they thought that the mere fact of their occupation was enough protection against a purchaser (see (2001) Law Com No 254, para. 5.61). The provisions in the LRA 2002 replace s.70(1)(g) LRA 1925, which was, perhaps, the most contentious and certainly the most litigated of the overriding interests under the 1925 Act. Much of the case law concerning s.70(1)(g) remains relevant. However, care must be taken when using this case law as the provisions of the 2002 Act modify the old law in several important ways. A brief comparison of the provisions is set out in Table 11.1 at the end of Section 11.7.2.4.

In order to override, both Schedules provide that the interest must be '[a]n interest belonging to a person in actual occupation, so far as relating to the land of which he is in actual occupation'. Schedule 3 contains certain exceptions which prevent the interest of an occupier from overriding *subsequent registered dispositions* of the land. These are considered below, but it is first necessary to examine the meanings of 'interest' and 'actual occupation'.

11.7.2.1 Interest

The interest must be a proprietary interest in the land, for example possessory rights arising out of a period of adverse possession, or an estate contract (a contract to buy land). A beneficial interest under a trust of land is sufficient (see *Williams & Glyn's Bank Ltd* v. *Boland* [1981] AC 487) as is a right arising out of an estoppel (s.116 LRA 2002). Most licences to occupy land are not seen as property interests: in *Ashburn Anstalt* v. *Arnold* [1989] Ch 1 a 'mere contractual licence would not be binding on a purchaser of land even though he had notice of the licence'. However, if such a licence affected the conscience of the buyer, then a constructive trust might be imposed (see Sections 13.3 and 14.4). The beneficial interest under such a trust would almost certainly be sufficient to potentially override. Some rights are expressly excluded by statute: rights of occupation under the Family Law Act 1996; rights under the Access to Neighbouring Land Act 1992; an original tenant's right to an overriding lease under the Landlord and Tenant (Covenants) Act 1995.

It must be stressed that occupation, of itself, is insufficient to override the interests of a purchaser. Contrasting examples (both relating s.70(1)(g) LRA 1925) will show the necessity of being able to establish an interest in the land. In *Williams & Glyn's Bank Ltd* v. *Boland* [1981] AC 487, Mrs Boland had a beneficial interest in the family home, but had failed to protect it on the Register. Her husband, the sole registered proprietor, subsequently mortgaged the house to the bank. He was unable to repay the loan and the bank wanted to sell the house. The House of Lords decided that Mrs Boland's beneficial interest included the right to occupy and was sufficient to amount to an interest in the land. Coupled with her actual occupation (and the fact that the bank had made no enquiry of whether she had an interest in the land), this amounted to an overriding interest which would take priority over the mortgage.

At first sight the facts of *City of London Building Society* v. *Flegg* [1988] AC 54 seem similar to that of *Boland*. Like Mrs Boland, Mr and Mrs Flegg had an unprotected beneficial interest under a trust in a house. However, in their case the property was vested in two registered proprietors (Mr and Mrs Flegg's daughter and son-in-law), who were both parties to the mortgage. Despite the fact that the Fleggs were in actual occupation and no enquiry had been made of them, the building society was able to defeat their interest. The parents had argued (successfully in the Court of Appeal, following *Boland*) that they had a right to occupy the land under a trust when the mortgage was registered, and that they therefore had an overriding interest which should defeat the building society. The House of Lords held that, from the moment that the lender overreached the beneficial interests by paying the mortgage money to two trustees, the beneficiaries no longer had a right to occupy the land but merely a right (under the rules of the old trust for sale) to share in the proceeds of sale (for the rules of overreaching, see Section 11.4.2). Lord Templeman said:

> The right of the [beneficiaries] to be and remain in actual occupation of Bleak House ceased when [their] interests were overreached by the legal charge ... There must be a combination of an interest which justifies continuing occupation plus actual occupation to constitute an overriding interest. Actual occupation is not an interest in itself (at pp. 73, 74).

Flegg was applied in *State Bank of India* v. *Sood* [1997] Ch 276 where the interests of the five beneficiaries were overreached on execution of the charge to the bank, even though no capital money was payable (see Section 11.4.2).

The moral for beneficiaries is that they must protect themselves by applying for a restriction to be entered on the Register: a beneficial interest cannot be protected by a notice (see s.33 LRA 2002). However, if there is only one legal owner (as in *Boland*), the beneficiary is safe for as long as he remains in actual occupation (unless, of course, a second trustee is appointed). Conversely, a buyer of registered land paying two trustees is safe from any beneficial owners provided that the moneys are paid to both trustees (as in *Flegg*). Buyers of land from a single registered proprietor remain subject to what Lord Templeman referred to in *Flegg* as 'the waywardness of actual occupation', although for a prudent buyer this is significantly mitigated by the provisos in Schedule 3, para. 2.

11.7.2.2 Actual Occupation

Since *Williams & Glyn's Bank Ltd* v. *Boland* [1981] AC 487, whether or not a person is 'in actual occupation' is a question of fact, not of law. One of the arguments used by the bank in that case was that Mrs Boland could not occupy the house in her own right: despite her beneficial interest her occupation was 'nothing but a shadow of her husband's'. Lord Wilberforce declared this doctrine, based on the perceived unity of husband and wife, obsolete. What constitutes 'actual occupation' in any given case will depend on the nature of the land concerned. The courts have been understandably reluctant to try to suggest a single test: as Lord Oliver of Aylmerton said in *Abbey National Building Society* v. *Cann* [1991] 1 AC 56 'occupation' is a concept which may have different connotations according to the nature and purpose of the property which is claimed to be occupied. It does not necessarily, I think, involve the personal presence of the person claiming to occupy. A caretaker or the representative of a company can occupy, I should have thought, on behalf of his employer. On the other hand, it does, in my judgment, involve some degree of permanence and continuity which would rule out mere fleeting presence. A prospective tenant or purchaser who is allowed, as a matter of indulgence, to go into property in order to plan decorations or measure for furnishings would not, in ordinary parlance, be said to be occupying it, even though he might be there for hours at a time (at p. 93).

In *Abbey National Building Society* v. *Cann* the House of Lords held that a mother whose belongings were moved into her new house some 35 minutes before completion of the purchase was not sufficiently in occupation at the time as her occupation lacked the necessary degree of 'permanence and continuity'.

A person may be deemed to be in actual occupation even though he is elsewhere. It is essential, however, that there is sufficient physical presence 'to put the purchaser on notice that there is someone in occupation' (*Malory Enterprises Ltd* v. *Cheshire* [2002] Ch 216, Arden LJ at para. 81). Schedule 3, para 2(c) LRA 2002 provides that if such physical presence is lacking, the interest will not be overriding unless the purchaser had actual knowledge of it (see Section 11.7.2.3).

A related question is the stage at which the person must be in actual occupation. It was established in *Abbey National Building Society* v. *Cann* [1991] 1 AC 56 that, for s.70(1)(g), both the right and the occupation must have existed at the moment the transfer was executed, rather than at the time of registration, as the statute seemed to indicate. This would appear to remain the relevant time and date for cases falling within paragraph 2 of Schedule 1 of the 2002 Act. Schedule 3, para. 2, however, expressly states that the interest and the occupation must exist 'at the time of the disposition'. The editor of Wolstenholme & Cherry's Annotated Land Registration Act 2002 suggests that this may alter the relevant date to the date of registration (since under s.27(1) LRA 2002 the disposition will not operate *at law* until registration has been completed – see Wolstenholme & Cherry, 2004, para. 3.173A). Even if this is the case, the discrepancy will be eliminated by the introduction of simultaneous completion and registration as part of electronic conveyancing.

Where a person has a right over land, but is only occupying part of that land concerned, only the land actually occupied will be subject to the overriding interest. The express provisions to this effect in Schedule 1, para. 2 and Schedule 3, para. 2 reverse the decision in *Ferrishurst* v. *Wallcite* [1999] Ch 355.

A tenant who has sublet all or part of his land is not in actual occupation of the land for the purposes of Schedules 1 and 3 LRA 2002. Intermediate lessors must, therefore, protect their leasehold interest by registration against the freehold title, unless the lease has overriding status in its own right as a legal lease for seven years or less (Section 11.7.1). This is a change from the situation under the 1925 scheme which also gave overriding status to the interests of a landowner who was 'in receipt of rents and profits'. The 2002 Act removed this protection except where the landowner's interest existed and was protected under s.70(1)(g) before 13 October 2003.

11.7.2.3 *When the Interest of a Person in Actual Occupation will not Be Overriding*

11.7.2.3.1 On a Registered Disposition   Under Schedule 3, the interest of a person in actual occupation does not override a disposition of registered land when:

1   the occupier does not disclose his right when asked about it, when he could reasonably have been expected to do so (para. 2(b)); or

2   the person's occupation is not obvious on a reasonably careful inspection of the land and where the purchaser does not have actual knowledge of the interest (para. 2(c)); or

3   the interest being claimed is a reversionary leasehold estate which takes effect in possession after three months from the date of the grant and which had not taken affect at the date of the disposition (para. 2(d)). Such leases must be registered in their own right. It is unlikely that this third exception will occur very often.

11.7.2.3.2 On First Registration   The three exceptions only apply when there has been a disposition of land that is already registered; Schedule 1, para. 2 does not impose the same conditions upon a person in actual occupation who is claiming that their interest overrides the first registration of the title concerned. However, the interest will only be capable of overriding if it survived the transfer (or other disposition) giving rise to first registration. This will usually depend upon whether the purchaser has notice of the interest (see Section 10.5).

11.7.2.4 Comment

Paragraph 2 protects those occupiers who have an otherwise unprotected interest in the land. When electronic conveyancing becomes compulsory many such interests (including, for example, estate contracts) will need to be registered to come into existence at all. As a result, there will no longer be an interest on which Paragraph 2 can bite. The paragraph will be restricted to protecting those occupiers' interests which have arisen informally, through resulting or constructive trusts or through estoppel. Given the policy behind the 2002 Act, this makes sense but, as has been seen, certain anomalies and injustices remain – *Boland* represented the high point of protection for beneficial owner-occupiers in registered land, but decisions since 1981 such as *Flegg* and *Cann* have shown a gradual withdrawal from it.

The effect of *Boland* was that institutional lenders began, properly, to ensure that there were no resident beneficiaries with rights. Anyone who was going to live in the house was required to agree that the mortgage would take priority over his or her interest, if any. As a result, occupying beneficiaries were less likely to be caught out by a secret mortgage or sale by their trustee. Beneficiaries who were aware of their rights in the land also began to insist on their names being placed on the legal title, so that their co-owners could not mortgage the land without their agreement and, as in the case of *Flegg*, destroy their property rights. This, in turn, has almost certainly contributed to the considerable increase in the number of cases of undue influence in recent years, which itself has led the courts to develop principles which must be followed by mortgage lenders in order to prevent their commercial interests being defeated (see *Royal Bank of Scotland Plc* v. *Etridge* [2002] 2 AC 773 and Section 7.4.4).

11.7.3   Easements and Profits (Schedule 1, para. 3; Schedule 3, para. 3)

In line with the policy of reducing the number of interests which are binding despite not appearing on the Register, only legal easements and profits are now capable of overriding the register. The 2002 Act effectively reverses the controversial case of *Celsteel Ltd* v. *Alton House Holdings Ltd (No. 1)* [1986] 1 WLR 512 which held that both legal and equitable easements were overriding interests within the 1925 scheme.

Table 11.1 Comparison of s70(1)(g) LRA 1925 with Schedule 1, para. 2 and Schedule 3, para 2 LRA 2002.

	LRA 1925	LRA 2002	
	s.70(1)(g)	Schedule 1, para. 2	Schedule 3, para 2
Who is protected?	A person: (i) in actual occupation or (ii) in receipt of rents and profits	Only a person in actual occupation	
What land is affected?	All land over which the interest is claimed, provided the claimant is in occupation of part of that land	Only the land actually occupied by the claimant	
Main exceptions	Enquiry was made of the person in occupation and the rights were not disclosed	*Rights which are not binding on the purchaser because of the rules of Unregistered Land (for example, failure to register a land contract as a Land Charge). In such cases there is no interest in the land for the occupation to protect*	(i) Enquiry was made of the person in occupation and he failed to disclose the right when he could reasonably have been expected to disclose it. (ii) The purchaser did not actually know about the interest and the interest would not have been obvious on a reasonably careful inspection of the land.

11.7.3.1 On First Registration

All *legal* easements and profits valid at the date of the disposition triggering first registration override first registration (Schedule 1, para. 3).

11.7.3.2 On a Registered Disposition

Section 27(2)(d) and Schedule 3, para. 3 substantially limit the types of legal easement and profit which can override subsequent dispositions of the registered estate. Those expressly created after the date of registration (or 13 October 2003, if later) *must* be registered and cannot override a registered disposition. However, an easement or profit which has arisen informally, either impliedly or through prescription (see Section 8.5) is capable of overriding, unless (para. 3(1)):

- the new proprietor did not actually know about it, *and*
- its existence was not apparent on a reasonably careful inspection of the land.

Even if these conditions are not satisfied an informally created easement or profit can still override the disposition if the person entitled to it can prove that it had been exercised in the year before the disposition was made (para. 3(2)). The proviso in para. 3(2) protects what Law Com No 271 terms an 'invisible' easement (para. 8.70), such as a right of drainage, which could otherwise be easily defeated. This provision encourages owners of easements which are used only intermittently to protect them by registration rather than rely on them being disclosed to the prospective purchaser during pre-contract enquiries (which provides actual knowledge of the interest). This reform is an attempt to find a balance between the two competing objectives of protecting important third-party rights in land and the need not to burden land with rights which a new owner could not have discovered.

11.7.3.3 Transitional Provisions

Clearly, many easements and profits which would have had overriding status under the 1925 Act are excluded from protection under Schedule 3. In order that the benefit of these pre-existing rights is not lost, Schedule 12, para. 9 provides that easements and profits which existed as overriding interests under s.70(1)(a) before 13 October 2003 will continue to have overriding status. In addition, an easement or profit created impliedly or by prescription within a period of three years from that date will have overriding status, even if the new registered proprietor did not have actual knowledge of it, it was not obvious on a reasonable inspection and it had not been used for a year before the disposition.

11.7.4 Squatters' Rights

The law on adverse possession of registered land has been covered in Chapter 3. These reforms, along with the new regime of adverse possession in registered land, are an enticement to land owners with unregistered title to apply voluntarily for first registration. This is an important part of the strategy of the Land Registry in moving towards complete registration of titles.

However, a further question arises as to whether a new registered proprietor will be bound by the existing rights of an adverse possessor of the land. Under the 2002 Act, the rights of a squatter that will override first registration are any rights under the Limitation Act 1980 of which the first registered proprietor has notice (s.11(4)(c) LRA 2002). In other words a squatter who has successfully adversely possessed the (unregistered) land for 12 years, even though no longer in possession, will be able to have the Register altered in his favour, provided that the new owner had notice of the adverse possession.

11.7.5 Other Rights Which Override Registration

For the sake of completeness it is necessary to consider other rights which override. Perhaps the most important of these is the local land charge. Although not appearing on the Register, anyone contemplating the purchase of land will automatically check at the local authority's Local Land Charges Registry for any local land charges affecting the property. Other rights which will bind a purchaser on first registration and subsequent transfers of the land are: customary rights; public rights; an interest in coal or a coal mine; and certain rights to mines and minerals.

There is a further category of old s.70(1) overriding interests which had their origin in feudal tenure and currently retain overriding status. These interests, such as manorial rights, have been described as 'relics from past times' ((2001) Law Com 271, para. 8.88) and will be phased out ten years from the introduction of the Act, on 13 October 2013. They will not necessarily disappear altogether (since if they had, the state would perhaps be in breach of ECHR Article 1, Protocol 1), because their owners have until October 2013 to protect them by registration or, if the land is not yet registered, by a caution against first registration.

In exceptional circumstances an otherwise unprotected interest may give rise to a constructive trust that will override the register. This occurred in the case of *Lyus* v. *Prowsa Developments Ltd* [1982] 1 WLR 1044. Mr and Mrs Lyus had acquired an option to purchase a plot of land in a housing development. The developer went bankrupt and the mortgagee sold the land to Prowsa. This first sale was expressly subject to the option, although it did not have to be as the option was not an overriding interest (Mr and Mr Lyus were not 'in actual occupation') and it had not been protected by entry on the Register. When Prowsa sold the land on, the question arose as to whether the option was enforceable. Dillon J imposed a constructive trust on the buyer because it would be a fraud if Prowsa were allowed to renege on its express undertaking to the mortgagee in favour of Mr and Mrs Lyus. It is important to note that the constructive trust that arises in these circumstances is not based upon the doctrine of notice (see Section 11.9), but upon whether 'the conscience of the estate owner is affected so that it would be inequitable to allow him to deny the claimant an interest in the property' (per Sir Christopher Slade, *Lloyd* v. *Dugdale* [2002] 2 P & CR 13, at para. 52).

It is interesting to compare Lyus with decisions in unregistered land such as *Midland Bank Trust Co Ltd (No 1)* v. *Green* [1981] AC 513 (see Section 10.3.6). Although many people would say that justice was done in Lyus, the case creates another blank spot on the magic mirror of the Register. In the recent case of *Halifax Plc* v. *Curry Popeck* [2008] EWHC 1692 Ch, Norris J concluded, albeit obiter, that the reasoning in *Midland Bank Trust Co Ltd (No 1)* v. *Green* was more consistent with the wording and intention of s.29 LRA 2002 than the approach taken in Lyus.

11.8 The Priority of Interests in Registered Land

If a registered estate is sold or mortgaged for valuable consideration (which, by s.132(1) LRA 2002, does not include marriage or merely nominal money consideration), the new owner is bound only by those third-party interests protected by entry on the Register and by those which override registration, even if he has notice of any unprotected interest (ss.29, 30 LRA 2002). As a corollary to this, therefore, someone who receives land as a gift, either *inter vivos* or by will, takes it subject to any unprotected third-party interests.

In all other circumstances, third party interests are ranked in order of their creation, not in order of registration (s.28 LRA 2002). Therefore, an unprotected third-party interest will have priority over one which, even though created later, has been protected on the Register.

11.9 Notice in Registered Land

A main objective of the scheme of registration is to do away with the difficulties caused by the doctrine of notice. Law Com No 271 stated that the doctrine 'as a general principle ... has no application whatever in determining the priority of interests in registered land' (para. 5.16). The report recognised, however, that on first registration, the new proprietor would take the land subject to any rights under the Limitation Act 1980 of which he had notice (see Section 11.7.4). It also recognised that something similar to notice is relevant in two further categories of interests that have overriding status: the interests of those in actual occupation (Section 11.7.2) and certain legal easements (Section 11.7.3). However, the report was at pains to point out that 'notice' in these circumstances is not the same as the old doctrine of notice in unregistered land, but comes from a conveyancing rule which requires a seller to disclose to the buyer any burdens on the land which would not be obvious on a reasonable inspection and which the buyer does not know about.

11.10 Alteration of the Register and Indemnity

The Land Registry is concerned to ensure that the Register accurately reflects the title interests and third-party interests in the land, since prospective new owners have no choice but to rely on it. Even so, however careful the Registrar may have been at first registration, and however carefully a buyer may have checked the Register, a registered proprietor might find he has in fact bought nothing since, under certain circumstances, the Register can be altered.

11.10.1 Alteration

The provisions on alteration of the Register are found in Schedule 4 of the 2002 Act. This Schedule provides that the court may order alteration (para. 2) and the Registrar may alter the Register (para. 5) in order to correct a mistake on the Register, bring it up to date or to give effect to any estate, right or interest excepted from the effect of registration. The Registrar is also able to remove superfluous entries.

There is a certain kind of alteration known as a 'rectification' (which should not be confused with the same term used in the 1925 Act and which had a much wider meaning). Rectification is defined in Schedule 4, para. 1 as the correction of a mistake in circumstances where the correction prejudicially affects the title of the registered proprietor. No rectification may take place against the title of a registered proprietor in possession without his consent unless he substantially contributed to the mistake through fraud or carelessness, or unless it would be unjust for any other reason (paras. 3(2) and 6).

The distinction between an alteration which amounts to rectification and one which does not can be seen in the recent case of *Barclays Bank Plc* v. *Guy* [2008] EWCA Civ 452. Ten Acre Limited purportedly acquired a 48 acre site from Mr Guy by virtue of a transfer document dated June 2004 and was subsequently registered as proprietor of the land. In March the following year the company granted a legal charge to Barclays Bank. The company subsequently became insolvent. Mr Guy claimed that the original transfer document was void, and sought to set aside both the original transfer and Barclay's legal charge. Section 58 of the LRA 2002 provides that proprietorship register is conclusive, even when the registered proprietor was not actually entitled to be registered as such (as would be the case her, if the transfer was void). Consequently, it was not enough for Mr Guy to establish that the transfer of the land to the company was void, he must also obtain rectification of the register. Had Mr Guy taken action earlier to substantiate his allegations against Ten Acre Limited, there seems little doubt that the court could have ordered rectification. Unfortunately, however, no action was taken until after the bank's legal charge had been entered on the register. Lloyd LJ held that Mr Guy was not entitled to rectification against the bank (the removal of the legal charge from the register) because:

> I simply cannot see how it could be argued that if the purchaser or chargee knows nothing of the problem underlying the intermediate owner's title, that the registration of the charge or sale to the ultimate purchaser or chargee can be said to be a mistake. That seems to me inconsistent with the structure and terms of the 2002 Act (at para. 23).

11.10.2 Indemnity

Schedule 8 provides for state compensation to be paid for loss caused by rectification or failure to rectify. Anyone hoping for an indemnity must take care, since para. 5 provides that there will be no compensation if the loser caused the loss by fraud or lack of proper care, and his compensation will be reduced if his negligence contributed to his loss.

11.11 Comment

The 2002 Act has fundamental consequences for the way lawyers think about and deal with land. It facilitates the inevitable introduction of compulsory electronic conveyancing which, providing concerns over the security of the process are overcome, will require conveyancers to communicate directly with the Register by means of a secure computer network. Except for interests arising informally, the creation or transfer of interests will only be achievable through the act of registration, thus eliminating the problems of the 'registration gap' which currently exists between disposition and registration, and removing the need for a formal written documentation (including contracts and deeds). The distinction, as we currently understand it, between equitable and legal interests in land will disappear, since many interests will not exist at all until they are registered. This may well mean that the role of estoppel (see Sections 13.4 and 13.5) will continue to grow in importance.

The Land Registry's aim of completing the Register within the next decade or so means that it must continue to find ways of encouraging landowners to register unregistered titles. Progress is being made (some 700,000 hectares were added to the total area of registered freehold land in England and Wales in 2006/7), but many landowners are reluctant to have their titles open to public inspection, whilst others will not wish to pay the fees associated with registration. There is provision within the 2002 Act for voluntary registration of freeholds and leases over seven years (s.3) with reduced Registry fees payable. The Registry is currently developing 'strategic programmes of registration' in order to carry out their aim, and will reassess its progress after five years. The Act itself encourages landowners to register their titles. We have already seen how the new rules on adverse possession may stimulate voluntary registration. In addition, s.79 makes specific provision for the Queen to grant herself freehold title out of her demesne land, which she must then register. Demesne land is land which the Crown holds for itself as the 'ultimate feudal overlord' and which is not therefore held on a fee simple or term of years – the only estates which can be registered. The Law Commission believes that this could lead to the disappearance of feudal tenure in England and Wales – see (2001) Law Com No 271, para. 2.37).

One major shift in legal thinking, reflected in the 2002 Act, is that it has now been accepted by the Law Commission and the judiciary that registered and unregistered title are two distinct systems and that it is permissible for them to produce different results on similar facts:

> it is now highly desirable that land registration in England and Wales should develop according to principles that reflect both the nature and the potential of land registration ... there seems little point in inhibiting the rational development of the principles of property law by reference to a system that is rapidly disappearing, and in relationship to which there is a diminishing expertise amongst the legal profession ... both the computerisation of the register and the move to electronic conveyancing make possible many improvements in the law that cannot be achieved with an unregistered system ((1998) Law Com No 254, para. 1.6).

Although some may regret the passing of unregistered conveyancing, registration of title to land is generally considered 'A Good Thing'. Nonetheless, it is valuable to consider its failings and limitations. Only then is it possible to decide whether, as is usually assumed, registration of title really is of benefit to all buyers and sellers of land. For example, it is clear that title registration does not, of itself, solve the conflicts of interests seen in this and the preceding chapter, especially the extent to which occupiers should be protected. Land can be enjoyed in different ways, and people have different needs in relation to it.

At least some of the difficulties are caused by the fact that the Land Register was originally introduced simply to replace repetitive examinations of the title deeds, but this limited aim has now been overshadowed by the need to make the Register as far as possible a perfect mirror of title in preparation for the electronic revolution to come. The danger is that simplification of the conveyancing process becomes the rationale of all land law, at the expense of another, equally important, land law principle, security of occupation.

Summary

11.1 Registration of title to land is designed to provide a simple and efficient form of conveyancing, by providing a guaranteed mirror of most rights in the land and promising state compensation for loss.

11.2 The LRA 2002 abolished the LRA 1925 in order to simplify the law on registered title and to prepare the way for electronic conveyancing.

11.3 The Register is divided into three sections: property, proprietorship and charges. Each part of the Register contains specific information about the land, the title and the burdens on the land.

11.4 Interests in registered land are also divided into three groups: registerable estates, interests which are subject to registration and interests which override registration.

11.5 Legal freeholds and leases over seven years are substantively registerable; title to them may be absolute, possessory or qualified, or good leasehold.

11.6 Interests which override registration are listed in Schedules 1 and 3 (depending on whether it is a first registration or a subsequent registered deposition), and include interests such as easements, leases and the interests of people in actual occupation of land. Overriding interests override any buyer of an interest in registered land. Certain transitional provisions apply.

11.7 Other registerable interests are 'everything else'; they are (normally) only binding on a purchaser for valuable consideration if they are entered on the Register by the appropriate method – notice or restriction.

11.8 The Register may be altered, even against a registered proprietor in possession (rectification). The state may provide compensation where anyone suffers loss by reason of rectification, but this does not include a proprietor who has effectively bought nothing because of a pre-existing interest which overrides registration.

Exercises

11.1 What goes where on the Land Register?

11.2 Which interests can be substantively registered with their own title number?

11.3 Which interests which override registration, and what is their importance?

11.4 When are registerable interests, other than title interests, binding?

11.5 Why do the provisions for alteration and indemnity detract from the basic principles of title registration?

11.6 Jake was the registered proprietor with absolute title of Albatross Cottage. He agreed by deed to sell it to Agnes, aged 80, for £140,000. Agnes paid Jake the price and moved in, but failed to register the transaction at the Land Registry because she did not believe in lawyers. Soon afterwards, Jake brought Maria to see the cottage. Maria met Agnes briefly in the kitchen, and asked her what she was doing there. Agnes replied that she was just having a cup of tea. Maria liked the cottage so much that she offered Jake £160,000 for it. Jake agreed to sell it to her.

Maria paid Jake the price and registered the transfer. Jake gave her the keys and she moved in when Agnes was in Majorca for a month. Agnes has now returned and seeks alteration of the Register against Maria.

Who will win?

Would your answer be different if Jake and his sister Josephine were joint registered proprietors?

11.7 An online quiz on the topics covered in this chapter is available on the companion website.

Further Reading

Battersby, 'More Thoughts on Easements under the Land Registration Act 2002' [2005] Conv 195

Clarke, ed, *Wolstenholme & Cherry's Annotated Land Registration Act 2002* (London: Sweet & Maxwell, 2004)

Dixon, 'The Reform of Property Law and the Land Registration Act 2002: A Risk Assessment' [2003] Conv 136

Dixon, 'Proprietary Rights and Rectifying the Effect of Non-registration' [2005] Conv 447

Law Commission Consultative Document: *Land Registration for the Twenty-First Century*, (1998) Law Com No 254

Law Commission Report: *Land Registration for the Twenty-First Century: A Conveyancing Revolution*, (2001) Law Com No 271

Part IV

Trusts of Land

Proprietary Estoppel

Chapter 12

Trusts of Land

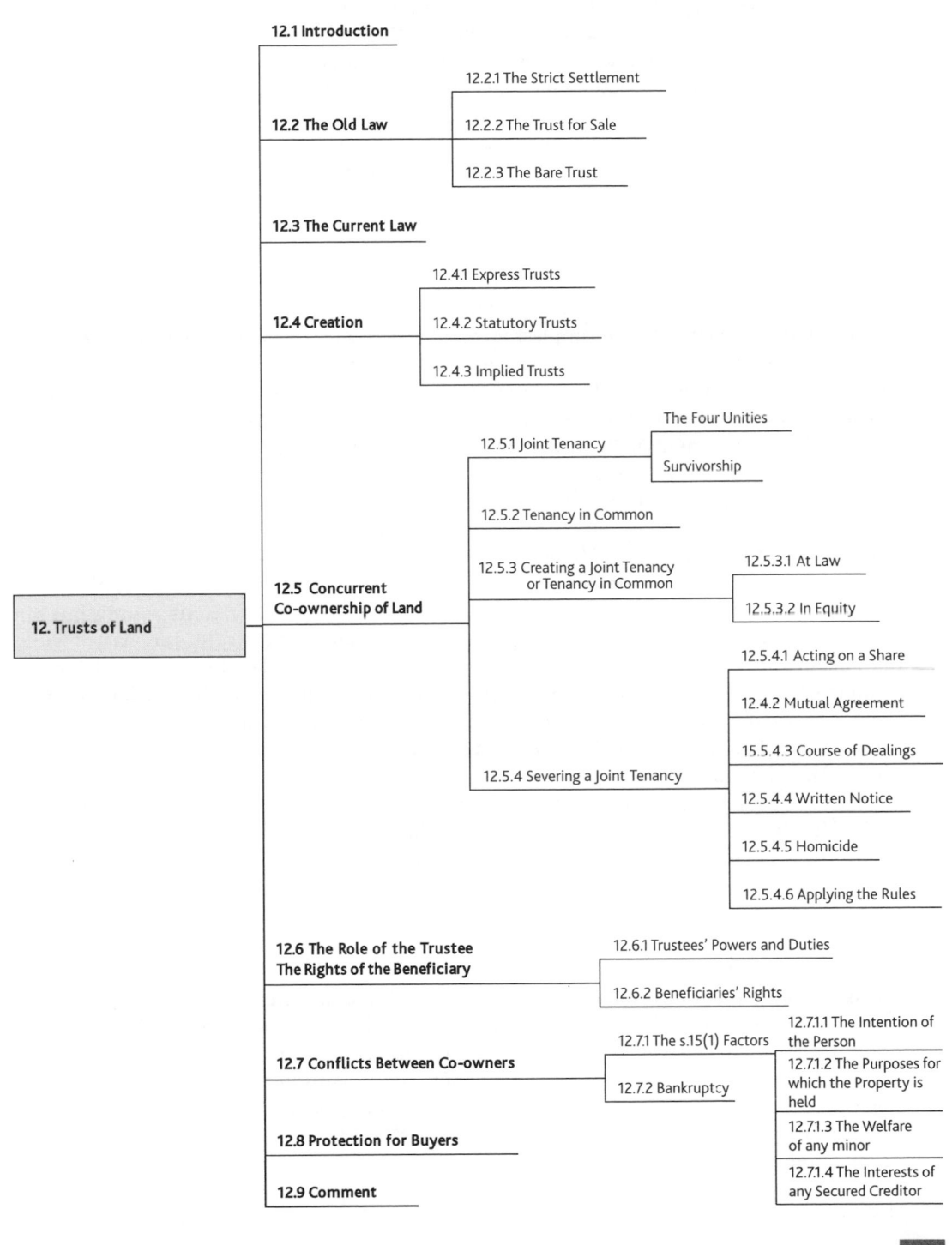

12.1 Introduction

Much of this book has been concerned with dividing up or sharing the enjoyment of land: for example between a tenant (entitled to possession) and a lessor (entitled to the rent), or between an owner of land and her neighbour who is allowed to use a path over it. This chapter and the next examine how the *ownership* of land can be shared.

The general policy of the law, as has been discussed in previous chapters, is to ensure as far as possible that land should be easily alienable: that is to say, capable of being bought and sold without undue delay or expense. At the same time it is important that land can be shared by more than one owner (either successively or concurrently) with some measure of security, in order to satisfy the needs and ambitions of landowners. The mechanism by which the law attempts to balance these apparently competing objectives is the *trust*. Some aspects of trusts may already be familiar (see, for example, the doctrine of overreaching and cases such as *Boland* and *Flegg* in Sections 11.4.2 and 11.7.2.1).

The basic principle of the trust is a division between the legal and equitable (or 'beneficial') ownership of the land. In the simplest form of a trust, a trustee holds the legal title for the benefit of the beneficiary. However, in trusts of land, trustees are often also beneficiaries at the same time. This is particularly common where a couple are the legal owners of family property, holding it on trust for themselves as beneficial co-owners.

Modern developments in this area of law are largely the result of the growth in landowner-ship by ordinary families. If a family breaks up, those involved will need to resolve the ownership of the family property. The effects of this can be far-reaching, since, as well as providing the family home, which is perhaps the real and symbolic focus of family life, the land may be the most valuable financial asset owned by any family member.

The courts often have to analyse open-textured and informal family arrangements within the formal structure of trust law; as a result, some of the case law is interesting but not straightforward. The topic is made more challenging because the basic rules are part of wider equitable principles. Further, because many cases lie on the boundary between land law and family law, there can be unseen conflicts of values. To put it rather crudely, land law is gener-ally concerned with 'justice through certainty', while family law is more interested in 'justice in the individual case'. Where the demands of certainty and individual justice diverge, there is bound to be some confusion.

There used to be two main kinds of trusts of land: the strict settlement and the trust for sale. The strict settlement was used by the great landowning families to hold on to the land they owned over successive generations, while the trust for sale developed as a means of holding land as a temporary investment. A third type of trust, the bare trust of land, was the subject of considerable academic opinion, but little case law. The Trusts of Land and Appointment of Trustees Act 1996 (TLATA) replaced all three kinds of trust with the simple 'trust of land'. Since 1 January 1997 all trusts of property which consist of or include land are 'trusts of land' (including all of the trusts for sale of land in existence on that date). TLATA prohibits the creation of any new strict settlements (those created before 1997 continue to be subject to special rules). While this new law provides a radical and simple conceptual basis for trusts of land, much of the old law of trusts remains in place – including the rules on the creation of trusts, co-ownership and overreaching. Some knowledge of the pre-1997 rules is required, as they will almost certainly be encountered when reading cases that remain relevant today.

12.2 The Old Law

12.2.1 The Strict Settlement

The traditional family arrangements of the aristocracy were aimed at preventing the fragmentation of their great estates. Settlements involving complicated inheritance rules were created within the family, which sometimes restricted improvements of the land and prevented sale over many generations. Successive reforms were made over centuries to prevent long-lasting settlements (the 'rules against perpetuities') and to free the land from too many restrictions. In 1925, the Settled Land Act provided an elaborate and expensive legal mechanism to govern these trusts; under this Act the 'tenant for life' (the current beneficial owner of the land) became a trustee of the settlement and could deal fairly freely with the land.

Section 2 TLATA states that (with very limited exceptions) strict settlements may no longer be created. Such trusts were already virtually obsolete because of punitive tax laws. However, a strict settlement could still be created by accident, for example in a home-made will, or when a child inherited land, so that the regime had become an expensive trap for the uninformed (and for careless solicitors). For further details of the old cumbersome and technical rules of strict settlements see Cheshire, 2006, pp. 400–26 and the Appendix to Megarry and Wade, 2008, Chapter 9.

12.2.2 The Trust for Sale

Until 1997, a trust was a strict settlement if there were *consecutive* beneficial interests, unless it expressly called itself a trust for sale. Any trust with *concurrent* beneficial interests had to be a trust for sale, so this kind of trust included not only family land (for example, where cohabitees were the co-owners) but also land which was held commercially (for example, by a partnership of solicitors).

The trust for sale was imposed on many family arrangements by the LPA 1925. However, this kind of trust was never really appropriate for these circumstances, which is why the TLATA replaced it with the 'trust of land'. The essence of the problem was that, under a trust for sale, the land was deemed to have been bought mainly as an investment (which, a century ago, was often true), so there was an 'immediate and binding duty' to sell the land, with a power to postpone sale in order to receive the rental income. The changing pattern of landownership during the twentieth century meant that land was, with increasing frequency, bought for owner-occupation rather than income generation. In the minds of most home-owners, sale was merely a possibility at some time in the future, not the main purpose of acquiring the land. Despite this, the trustees' duty of sale meant that even if only one of the trustees wanted a sale, the land had to be sold. Section 30 LPA 1925 gave the courts a discretion about ordering sale, and a long line of case law resulted from the tension between the duty to sell – when one family member wanted to turn the land into money – and the need of the rest of the family to stay in their home. Such conflicts will, of course, still arise and the provisions of the TLATA now provide a statutory replacement for the old law (see Section 12.7).

A further problem with the duty to sell arose as a result of the equitable principle that 'equity looks on that as done which ought to be done'. Without the land being sold the courts treated it as though it had already been: the 'doctrine of conversion'. Consequently, the beneficiaries behind a trust for sale did not have an interest in land, but merely in the 'proceeds of sale'. However, a number of cases showed that, although the beneficiaries in theory were only interested in the proceeds of sale, in practice they might still be recognised as having some interest in the land itself. In the well-known case of *Bull* v. *Bull* [1955] 1 QB 234 a son, the sole trustee of the trust for sale and a joint beneficiary under it, wanted to evict his mother (the other beneficiary), but the court held that her interest in the land included a right to occupy it. In *Williams & Glyn's Bank* v. *Boland* [1981] AC 487 (see Section 11.7.2.1) the House of Lords held that a beneficial interest in land held on a trust for sale could be a sufficient interest to be protected by occupation of the trust land under s.70(1)(g) LRA 1925 (now Sched. 1, para. 2 and Sched. 3 para. 2 LRA 2002).

In the end, because the machinery of the trust for sale and its accompanying doctrine of conversion were simply inappropriate to the reality of family landowning, there could be no solution to the problem. Now the TLATA has replaced the old trust for sale with the new 'trust of land', and s.3 has abolished the doctrine of conversion for all trusts, except for a trust for sale created by a will where the testator died before the Act came into effect.

12.2.3 The Bare Trust

A bare trust arises when the land is held for the sole benefit of a beneficiary of full age. The wording of the 1925 legislation led to considerable uncertainty about the powers of the trustee of such a trust, with an apparent discrepancy between registered and unregistered land (see Megarry and Wade, 2008, sections 12-008 to 12-010). All bare trusts of land now fall within the provisions of the TLATA.

12.3 The Current Law on Trusts of Land

The TLATA 1996 was the result of the Law Commission's proposals ((1989) Law Com No 181):

> We consider that the present dual system of trusts for sale and strict settlements is unnecessarily complex, ill-suited to the conditions of modern property ownership, and liable to give rise to unforeseen conveyancing complications (at p. iv).

Part I of the Act imposed a new, simpler system on almost all trusts of land – see the box, opposite.

12.4 Creation of Trusts of Land

A trust of land may be created expressly, by statute, or impliedly.

12.4.1 Express Trusts

An express trust must be evidenced in writing, signed by the person creating it, in order to be enforceable by the beneficiaries (s.53(1)(b) LPA 1925). It must declare the nature of the beneficial ownership and the terms of the trust.

12.4.2 Statutory Trusts

When land is conveyed or transferred to two or more people a statutory trust of land will be imposed under ss.34–36 LPA 1925 in the absence of any express declaration of trust. All co-owned land is, therefore, held on trust, even if the trustees and beneficiaries are the same people.

Summary of Part I of the TLATA

◆ A trust of land is 'any trust of property which consists of or includes land' (s.1(1)) subject only to the very limited exceptions in s.1(2).

◆ Section 2 prevents the creation of any new strict settlements, or the addition of land to an existing strict settlement.

◆ New trusts for sale can be created expressly, but since the trustees can now postpone sale indefinitely, there is little point in doing so unless the purpose of the trust is that the land should be sold, as in *Barclay* v. *Barclay* [1970] 2 QB 677.

◆ Section 5 (with Schedule 2) amended the rules in ss 34–6 LPA 1925 which imposed the trust for sale onto concurrently shared trust land.

◆ The Act sets out the powers and duties of trustees of land (including duties to consult the beneficiaries, replacing s.26 LPA 1925). Trustees are no longer under a duty to sell the land, but have the power either to sell or to retain it.

◆ Sections 12 and 13 give some beneficiaries a statutory right of occupation (see Section 12.6.2) in place of the common law right recognised in *Bull* v. *Bull* [1955] 1 QB 234.

◆ Sections 14 and 15 introduced a new scheme for dealing with disputes between people with an interest in trust land, in place of s.30 LPA 1925.

◆ The Act made transitional provisions for trusts existing on 1 January 1997: most former trusts for sale became subject to most aspects of the new regime.

◆ Under s.16, buyers of trust land that is not yet registered continue to be given special protection (see Section 12.8).

12.4.3 Implied Trusts

It is also possible for a person to gain a beneficial share in land in circumstances in which there is no express or statutory trust. In certain circumstances equity will find that the land is co-owned because of the conduct of the relevant parties. These trusts are known as resulting and constructive trusts, and are dealt with (alongside proprietary estoppel) in the next chapter.

12.5 Concurrent Co-ownership of Land

Before 1925, there were four methods of co-owning land, and any of them could exist either at law or in equity. Only two methods now survive: 'joint tenancy' and 'tenancy in common'. A joint tenancy can be legal or equitable but, since 1925, a tenancy in common can only exist in equity (ss.1(6), 34(1), 36(2) LPA 1925).

12.5.1 Joint Tenancy

Blackstone describes the joint tenancy as a 'thorough and intimate union' (Blackstone's Commentaries, ii, 182). The basic principle is that, as far as outsiders are concerned, the owners are regarded as one person. They are united in every way possible, through the four 'unities' (see box, overleaf).

The Four Unities

◆ Possession:
  all the joint tenants are entitled to possess the whole of the land.
◆ Interest:
  they each hold an identical interest (freehold, leasehold, etc).
◆ Title:
  their interest was obtained by the same document.
◆ Time:
  their interest vested in them at the same time.

(easily remembered by the acronym: PITT)

In *A. G. Securities* v. *Vaughan* [1990] 1 AC 417 (see Section 5.3.3), for example, a claim that there was a joint tenancy of a lease failed because the claimants had arrived at different times. Indeed, on the facts of the case Lord Oliver found that none of the four unities was present, not even that of possession.

The basis of joint tenancy is that the joint tenants do not have shares in the land: together they own the whole of it. As a consequence, and very importantly, joint tenants enjoy the 'right of survivorship' (*ius accrescendi*). The joint tenants are 'all one person', and if one dies it is as if she had never existed. The survivors still own the whole of the land and there is nothing for the heirs of the dead joint tenant to inherit. It follows, therefore, that the last survivor of joint tenants will own the whole land absolutely.

The risk involved in the right of survivorship may seem unfair, but in fact it is quite convenient that legal ownership of trust land should not be affected if one co-owner at law dies. In equity, on the other hand, although joint tenancy is possible, the risks can be inconvenient; for this reason, equity 'leans against' this form of co-ownership (see Section 12.5.3).

Since a tenancy in common can only exist in equity, the legal title to any co-owned land must be held by the co-owners as joint tenants (ss.1(6), 34(1), 36(2) LPA 1925). In addition, there can be no more than four legal joint tenants (s.34(2) Trustee Act 1925). If title to land is conveyed to more than four people, the first four named on the deed who are willing and at least 18 years old and mentally competent will be the legal joint tenants (the trustees): the remainder will be beneficial owners only. There is no restriction on the number of joint tenants in equity.

12.5.2 Tenancy in Common

Tenancy in common is often referred to as an 'undivided share': although the land is held in separate shares, it has not been physically partitioned. Tenancy in common requires only the unity of possession (although all three of the other unities may also be present) – and there is no right of survivorship. When a tenant in common dies, she can leave her undivided share to anyone she pleases. This is the reason why tenancy in common is no longer possible at law (ss.1(6), 34(1), 36(2) LPA 1925). If legal tenancies in common were permitted, rather than merely investigating one title, a purchaser would have to investigate the individual titles of each tenant in common, adding considerably to the time and expense of conveyancing.

Any attempt to create a legal tenancy in common will vest the legal title in the purchasers (or the first four of them named in the conveyance if more than four) as joint tenants, holding the land on trust for all of the purchasers as tenants in common (s.34(2) LPA 1925). However, as far as a buyer of land is concerned, the interests shared in equity are 'behind a curtain': she can overreach all the beneficial interests (whether joint tenancy or tenancy in common) by paying the trustees (who will, of course, be legal joint tenants) providing there is more than one of them (see Section 11.4.2).

12.5.3 Creation of a Joint Tenancy or Tenancy in Common

12.5.3.1 At Law

At law there are no problems. As discussed above, a joint tenancy at law arises whenever a legal interest in land is shared concurrently, that is, whenever land is conveyed into the names of two or more people (s.34(2) LPA 1925).

12.5.3.2 In Equity

In equity, there may be either a joint tenancy or a tenancy in common; or a combination of the two.

The starting-point in determining whether a person is a beneficial joint tenant or a beneficial tenant in common is the maxim that 'equity follows the law' (see *Stack* v. *Dowden* [2007] 2 AC 432 at paras. 33, 54 and 109. Despite this principle, however, equity tends to incline against the unpredictability of the right of survivorship. As a result, a beneficial tenancy in common will exist, not only where one of the unities is missing, but also if there is a particular reason for inferring that there was no intention to create a joint tenancy. In addition, there are three circumstances in which equity *presumes* a tenancy in common.

No intention to create a beneficial joint tenancy can be shown by:

- creating a tenancy in common expressly in the deed; or
- using words which show an intention that the owners should have shares ('words of severance') in the conveyance. Examples include 'equally', 'in equal shares', 'amongst' and 'share and share alike'. An example is *Barclay* v. *Barclay* [1970] 2 QB 677 (Section 12.3) where land was left 'equally' under an express trust in a will to the testator's five children.

Equity *presumes* a tenancy in common where:

- there are unequal contributions to the purchase price;
- the co-owners are business partners or are acquiring the land for businesses purposes; or
- they are lending money on a mortgage.

In each case the presumption can be rebutted if there has been an express agreement to create a joint tenancy (see *Malayan Credit Ltd* v. *Jack Chia-MPH Ltd* [1986] AC 549).

12.5.4 Severing a Joint Tenancy

'Severance' is the conversion of an equitable joint tenancy into a tenancy in common. Severance may arise out of the wishes of one or more of the joint tenants, but will also occur by operation of law in certain circumstances. When a joint tenant severs her beneficial interest she becomes a tenant in common in equity with an equal share of the value of the property, whenever it comes to be sold. From the moment of severance the right of survivorship will cease to apply to her: her interest will pass to her heirs on her death (and, conversely, her interest in the property will not increase automatically on the death of any of the other tenants).

In what follows, it must always be remembered that, because there cannot be a legal tenancy in common, a legal joint tenancy cannot be severed (s.36(2) LPA 1925). This means that any severance of the beneficial interests will not automatically affect the legal title. When analysing problems concerning co-ownership it can be helpful to show the various interests diagrammatically, using a single box to show a joint tenancy (see Figure 12.1) and a series of joined boxes for a tenancy in common (see Figure 12.2).

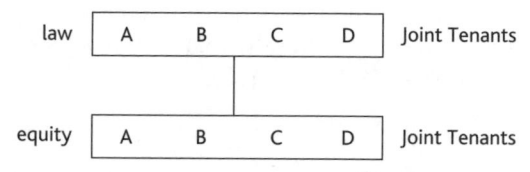

Figure 12.1 Legal joint tenants holding for themselves as beneficial joint tenants.

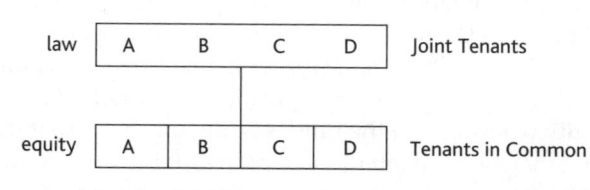

Figure 12.2 Legal joint tenants holding for themselves as beneficial tenants in common.

Anything which creates a distinction between equitable joint tenants amounts to a severance. Equity has recognised three methods of severing a joint tenancy of personal property (listed by Page Wood V-C in *Williams* v. *Hensman* (1861) 1 John & H 546, and these are now accepted as applying also to real property (s36(2) LPA 1925):

1   By 'an act of one of the parties interested operating on her own share'.
2   By mutual agreement.
3   By a 'course of dealing' ('mutual conduct') which shows a common intention to sever.

There are, in addition, other methods of severance:

4   By notice in writing of immediate severance (created by s.36(2) LPA 1925).
5   Where a joint tenant kills another joint tenant: if the right of survivorship operated in such circumstances, the killer might be 'profiting from her own wrong'.
6   Where a joint tenant has become bankrupt. When a person is adjudged bankrupt all her property is vested in the trustee in bankruptcy (see also Section 12.7). The vesting of the land in the trustee in bankruptcy is an operation on the bankrupt's share (see method 1, above) by act of law.

These methods are examined in more detail below. It should be remembered that whether severance has taken place always depends on the evidence; each case 'depends on its own facts'. Frequently, the trigger for any dispute will be the death of one co-owner, and the question may arise as to whether there has been a severance of the equitable joint tenancy some time before the death.

12.5.4.1 Acting on a Share

If a joint tenant assigns her share during her lifetime the assignee will take it as a tenant in common with any remaining joint tenants. Granting a mortgage or charge over her interest will sever it. However, leaving the interest to a third party by will does not sever the joint tenancy: the right of survivorship means that a joint tenant has no interest to leave by will provided that at least one other joint tenant survives her (see *Gould* v. *Kemp* (1834) 2 My & K 304). The rules are explained in more detail in Megarry and Wade, 2008, sections 13-038 to 13-040.

12.5.4.2 Mutual Agreement

Severance by mutual agreement requires the agreement of *all* of the joint tenants. However, the agreement does not have to be capable of specific performance (see Chapter 2). In the words of Sir John Pennycuick in the case of *Burgess* v. *Rawnsley* [1975] Ch 429:

> The significance of an agreement is not that it binds the parties; but that it serves as an indication of a common intention to sever ... (at p. 446).

12.5.4.3 Course of Dealings

Severance by course of dealings differs from that by mutual agreement in that severance will be inferred from the conduct of the parties: there is no need for a meeting of minds between the joint tenants. In *Burgess* v. *Rawnsley* [1975] Ch 429, the Court of Appeal considered the possibility of a course of dealings as well as mutual agreement (see Section 12.5.4.2). Mr Honick and Mrs Rawnsley met at a Scripture rally. After a few months of friendship, they bought the house in which Mr Honick lived, as joint tenants at law and in equity. He thought they were going to get married; she merely intended to live in the upper flat. After a year or so, they discovered each other's error and agreed orally that he should buy her share. However, they did not finally agree a price and nothing more was done before Mr Honick died three years later. Mrs Rawnsley claimed the whole house by right of survivorship. As to a course of dealing between Mr Honick and Mrs Rawnsley, Lord Denning MR said:

> It is sufficient if there is a course of dealing in which one party makes clear to the other that he desires that their shares should no longer be held jointly but be held in common ... it is sufficient if both parties enter on a course of dealing which evinces an intention by both of them that their shares shall henceforth be held in common and not jointly (at p.439)

The 'course of dealing' argument failed in *Greenfield* v. *Greenfield* (1979) 38 P & CR 570. Two brothers owned a house as joint tenants in law and equity; each married, and converted the house into two maisonettes, sharing the garden and some bills. When the elder brother died his widow claimed that the division of the house showed an intention to sever the beneficial joint tenancy and that she had inherited her husband's tenancy in common. Fox J held:

> The onus of establishing severance must be on the plaintiff ... It seems to me that on the facts, the plaintiff comes nowhere near discharging that onus. Neither side made clear any intention of ending

the joint tenancy. The defendant had no intention of ending it and never thought that he or [his brother] Ernest had ended it (at p. 578).

12.5.4.4 Written Notice

Neither a unilateral, unstated intention to sever nor verbal notice by one party to another has ever been sufficient to sever a joint tenancy. By s.36(2) LPA 1925, however, a written notice by one joint tenant to another will suffice.

No agreement from the other joint tenant is required for a valid s.36(2) notice. Nor is it necessary to give the notice in any particular form, provided that it is worded in such a way as to make it clear that an immediate severance is being sought. Expressing a wish to sever the joint tenancy in the future will not be sufficient (see *Re Draper's Conveyance* [1969] 1 Ch 486 and *Harris v. Goddard* [1983] 1 WLR 1203.

It is not even necessary for the notice to be physically received by the other joint tenants for it to be effective. In *Kinch v. Bullard* [1999] 1 WLR 423, a wife, suffering from a terminal illness, was intending to divorce her husband. They were both the beneficial joint tenants of the matrimonial home and, since she no longer wanted the right of survivorship to operate, she instructed her solicitors to send him a notice severing the joint tenancy. The solicitors sent the letter by first-class post but, before it was delivered, the husband suffered a serious heart attack. The wife, realising she would lose half the house if her husband died with the joint tenancy having been severed, destroyed the letter as soon as it arrived. Her husband died a week or so later and never learned about the letter. After the wife died the following year an action was brought by the husband's executors, who claimed that the joint tenancy had been severed by the written notice and they were therefore entitled to the husband's half-share in the property. The case turned upon whether the notice of severance had been properly served. By s.196 LPA 1925, a notice is properly served 'if it is left at the last known place of abode or business in the United Kingdom of the ... person to be served'. In this case, the court held that service occurred (and the notice became effective) when the letter fell through the letter box onto the mat. The wife's destruction of the letter failed, therefore, to prevent her severance of the joint tenancy through which otherwise she would have gained the whole of the property by the right of survivorship.

12.5.4.5 Homicide

The principle that a person should not benefit from her own crime (the forfeiture rule) means that in most cases a joint tenant will not be allowed to enjoy the benefits of survivorship if she criminally causes the death of another joint-tenant. It is not clear, however, whether this principle works through severance or by imposing a constructive trust (see Megarry and Wade, 2008, section 13-049 for the reasons why this may be important).

Section 2 of the Forfeiture Act 1982 gives the court the power to modify the effect of this rule in cases other than murder 'where the justice of the case required it'. The Court of Appeal exercised this power (albeit by a majority) in the tragic case of *Dunbar v. Plant* [1998] Ch 412. Miss Plant and Mr Dunbar attempted to kill themselves following a suicide pact; Miss Plant failed, but Mr Dunbar succeeded. Although the forfeiture rule applies in cases of aiding and abetting a suicide such as this, it was held that, under the particular circumstances of the case, the couple's joint tenancy of their house had not been severed. Consequently, Miss Plant was entitled to the whole of the beneficial interest in the proceeds of sale (the house had already been sold).

12.5.4.6 Applying the Rules

Problem questions on co-ownership require a step-by-step analysis of what happens to the legal and equitable ownership. This is, perhaps, most easily done initially with the help of a diagram.

Imagine that a group of five people – **Annie, Belinda, Charlie, Dee** and **Ellen** – buy a house as joint tenants in equity, each contributing equally to the purchase price. As they are all over 18 years old, the first four become the legal owners as joint tenants holding on trust for all five. Certain events now take place, each of which may affect the legal ownership or sever the equitable joint tenancy. A description of each event and an analysis of its effect are set out in Figures 12.3–12.6.

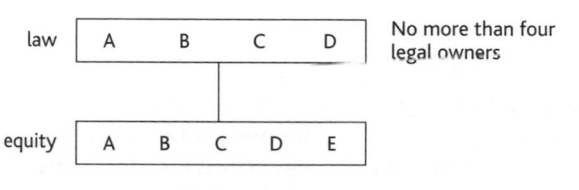

Figure 12.3 At the start.

Figure 12.4 Annie dies.

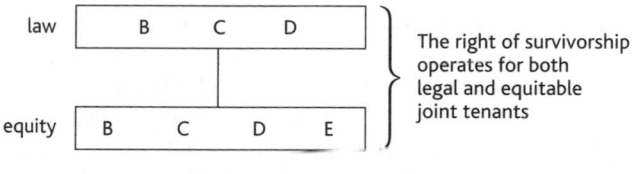

Figure 12.5 Belinda sells her share to Xena.

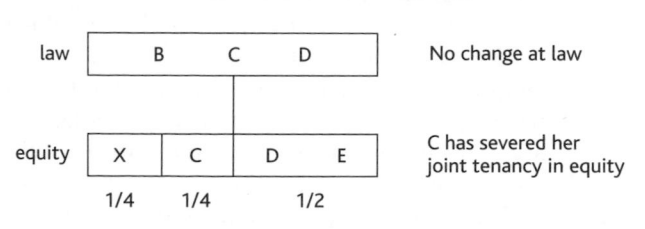

Figure 12.6 Charlie gives written notice of severance to Dee and Ellen.

This kind of problem question often ends by stating that some of the surviving co-owners now want to sell and others want to remain in the property, inevitably requiring a discussion of the case law under ss.14, 15 TLATA (see Section 12.7).

12.6 The Role of the Trustees and the Rights of the Beneficiaries

The trustees of a trust of land hold the legal title to the land. Their rights and duties are subject to the general law of trusts, the rules contained in the TLATA and to the particular provisions (if any) of the trust in question (s.8 TLATA). The powers of trustees of charitable, ecclesiastical and public trusts continue to be limited in special ways that lie outside the scope of this book.

Normally, trustees are appointed in the trust deed, or, in the case of implied trusts, the trustees will be the persons who hold the legal title. If there is no trustee (for example if land is conveyed to a child who by s.1(6) LPA 1925 cannot own land) the court can appoint trustees. Sections 19–21 of TLATA give beneficiaries a measure of control over their trustees, in that they can require the appointment of a new trustee or the retirement of a current trustee, unless the settlor has expressly specified that the beneficiaries should not have this power.

12.6.1 Trustees' Powers and Duties

Section 6(1) TLATA provides that the trustees 'have all the powers of an absolute owner': thus, they may sell, mortgage, lease or otherwise deal with the land. It is possible for these powers to be restricted by the terms of the trust (s.8(1)), although it is not possible to exclude the trustees' statutory power to postpone sale (s.4). Section 6(3) TLATA expressly gives trustees the power (subject to the terms of the trust) to buy land with trust money as an investment, or for occupation by a beneficiary or 'for any other reason'. In exercising these powers, the trustees must 'have regard to the rights of the beneficiaries' (s.6(5)). Section 13 gives the trustees the power to 'exclude or restrict' the entitlement of any of the beneficiaries to occupy the land. This section is considered alongside the statutory right to occupy in Section 12.6.2.

The TLATA extends to all trustees of trusts of land the duty to consult beneficiaries. Section 11(1) provides that, subject to a contrary intention being expressed in the trust:

The trustees of land shall in the exercise of any function relating to land subject to the trust –
(a) so far as practicable, consult the beneficiaries of full age and beneficially entitled to an interest in possession in the land, and
(b) shall so far as consistent with the general interest of the trust, give effect to the wishes of those beneficiaries, or (in case of dispute) of the majority (according to the value of their combined interests).

This section will not normally apply to an express trust created before 1997 (s.11(2)(b)).

Where the beneficiaries are of full age and capacity, the role of trustees may be limited or unnecessary. Thus, s.6(2) restates the old rule that if such beneficiaries 'are absolutely entitled to the land', the trustees can convey the land to them. Subject to the terms of the trust, the trustees may also have the power to divide up ('partition') the land for any purpose, but only if the beneficiaries are adult tenants in common, absolutely entitled, and they all consent (s.7). The trustees may also (again, subject to the terms of the trust) delegate their powers to these beneficiaries (s.9), thus allowing beneficiaries in occupation to carry on the routine management of the land themselves.

However, despite these apparently unlimited powers, it is still possible – as under the old law – to make dealings with the trust land subject to the consent of a particular person or persons (s.8(2)). For example if a spouse dies and leaves her property to her children, it could be a term of the trust that the property could only be sold with the consent of the surviving spouse who might well also have the right to live there, thus ensuring that the property remains unsold, at least for a time.

12.6.2 Beneficiaries' Rights

The beneficiaries of a trust of land are generally entitled to whatever the trust provides for them. Their rights under the old trust for sale depended on the original purposes of the trust, which posed a conceptual problem for land lawyers, since the purpose of a trust for sale was, in theory, for the land to be sold straight away. Equity, therefore, saw the interests of the beneficiaries as being in the proceeds of sale rather than in the land and was slow to recognise that the beneficiaries might have a right to live there (see Section 12.2.2). The TLATA, having abolished the doctrine of conversion, also provides a statutory right for beneficiaries to occupy the trust land.

Section 12 states that a beneficiary is entitled to live in the house 'if the purposes of the trust include making the land available for his occupation'. This right to occupy is subject to it being available and suitable for occupation by the beneficiary. In *Chan* v. *Leung* [2003] 1 FLR 23, the Court of Appeal had to decide whether a large house in Surrey was suitable for occupation solely by Miss Leung, a university student. Jonathan Parker LJ stated that:

> 'suitability' for this purpose must involve a consideration not only of the general nature and physical characteristics of the particular property but also a consideration of the personal characteristics, circumstances and requirements of the particular beneficiary (at para. 101).

Despite its size and the expense of its maintenance, the judge did not consider the house unsuitable for Miss Leung, especially as she would only wish to occupy it until the end of her studies. Even if this had not been the case, she had previously been living there with her partner, and the judge 'would have taken some persuading' that it was unsuitable for her now he had left.

Section 13 TLATA gives the trustees certain responsibilities in cases where beneficiaries are entitled to occupy the land, as is common in trusts of the family home where adults share beneficial interests. It provides that where there is more than one beneficiary, the trustees have the power to exclude one or more, but not all, of the beneficiaries from the land (s.13(1)). They must not act 'unreasonably' (s.13(2), and may impose on an occupying beneficiary 'reasonable conditions' (s.13(3)). Examples of such conditions might include paying expenses relating to the land or paying compensation to a beneficiary who has been reasonably excluded from occupation (ss.13(5),(6)). In making such decisions, the trustees must take into account the intentions of the creator of the trust, the purposes of the trust and the circumstances and wishes of the beneficiaries (s.13(4)). However, the powers contained in s.13 cannot be used to prevent anyone already in occupation (whether or not they have a beneficial interest in the land) from continuing in occupation, or in an attempt to induce them to leave (s.13(7)).

An example of the difficulties which may arise in these situations can be illustrated by the case of *Rodway* v. *Landy* [2001] Ch 703. Two doctors in partnership bought a property together from which to run their practices. They fell out, and one of them sought an order for the property to be sold to her (under s.14 TLATA; see Section 12.7). The other asked the court to order that, since they were both trustees as well as beneficiaries, they could use their powers under s.13 to divide the property in two, allowing one partner exclusive occupation of one part of the property, and the other partner exclusive occupation of the other part. The Court of Appeal was of the opinion that if the building lent itself to division in this way, the trustees were entitled under s.13 to exclude the beneficiaries' entitlement to occupy all of the building. The Court also held that, under s.13(3) the trustees could require the beneficiaries to contribute to the cost of adapting the building. Here, of course, the trustees and the beneficiaries were the same people, and the case also serves as an example of the separation of the roles and functions of trustees and beneficiaries.

In the recent case of *Re Barcham* [2008] EWHC 1505 Ch (on appeal from the County Court), Blackburne J considered whether a person falling outside the scheme in ss.12,13 TLATA was entitled to compensation if excluded from the property. Mr and Mrs Barcham were the registered proprietors of their bungalow when Mr Barcham was declared bankrupt in 1994. The couple continued to live in the bungalow until Mr Barcham's trustee in bankruptcy sought an order for its sale in 2006 (see Section 12.7.2). The question arose as to whether the trustee in bankruptcy was entitled to any payment from Mrs Barcham for her occupation of the premises for the previous twelve years. Mrs Barcham argued that the Court had no power to award the trustee in bankruptcy compensation because he was not a beneficiary entitled to possession, and, therefore, was not eligible for compensation under s.13 TLATA. Blackburne J held that TLATA did not prevent the Court exercising its wider generable equitable jurisdiction in such cases.

> Where the [TLATA] scheme applies, it must be applied. But where it plainly does not I do not see why the party who is not in occupation of the land in question should be denied any compensation at all if recourse to the court's equitable jurisdiction would justly compensate him (at para. 20).

12.7 Conflict between Owners of Trust Land

If the provisions for consultation and the gaining of consents are not observed and the land is sold or mortgaged in breach of trust, aggrieved beneficiaries can, in theory, sue their trustees. However, it is, where possible, far better to prevent misdealing by asking the court to settle any disputes.

The relevant statutory provisions are ss.14, 15 TLATA and s.335A of the Insolvency Act 1986. Section 14 gives anyone with an interest in the trust property the right to apply to the court. As well as the beneficiaries and the trustees, therefore, secured lenders and purchasers of the land who find themselves subject to the interests of a beneficiary whose rights were not overreached can turn to s.14, as can the trustee in bankruptcy of one of the co-owners.

Section 14(1) TLATA allows any trustee or beneficiary of a trust of land, or anybody with an interest in the trust property, to apply to the court which, under s.14(2), may make any order it thinks fit:

(a) relating to the exercise by the trustees of any of their functions (including an order relieving them of any obligation to obtain the consent of, or to consult, any person in connection with the exercise of any of the functions), or

(b) declaring the nature or extent of a person's interest in property subject to the trust.

Section 15(1) lists several matters to which the court is to have regard when determining an application under s.14. If one of the parties has been made bankrupt and her trustee in bankruptcy (who represents the interests of the creditors) applies for an order for sale, the relevant factors will be those contained in s.335A Insolvency Act 1986 (s.15(4) TLATA). When the application concerns the exclusion of occupation rights under s.13, the court also must have regard to 'the circumstances and wishes' of each of the beneficiaries who might have a right to occupy (s.15(2), see *Rodway* v. *Landy* (Section 12.6.2)). In other applications, the court must normally take into account the wishes of the majority of adult beneficiaries currently entitled to the equitable ownership, according to the value of their beneficial interest (s.15(3)).

Where a civil partnership or marriage breaks down, any co-owned land is normally dealt with by way of a property adjustment order under the Civil Partnership Act 2004 or the Matrimonial Causes Act 1973, rather than under s.14.

12.7.1   The s.15(1) Factors TLATA

The list of factors in s.15 is not exhaustive, nor does s.15 give any indication of how the factors are to be weighted should they conflict in a particular case: that is a matter for the court to determine. Many of the cases likely to inform the court's deliberations predate the TLATA, and reflect the principles developed under s.30 LPA 1925, the forerunner to s.15 TLATA. It should be remembered, however, that the court's discretion under s.30 was more limited than under TLATA. The presumption in favour of a sale (see Section 12.2.2) meant the court had to begin by determining the underlying purpose of the trust for sale; only if this purpose was still achievable could the court block the trustees' duty of sale.

12.7.1.1 The Intention of the Person or Persons (if any) Who Created the Trust
This factor is most likely to be referred to where the trust was created expressly and the intention of the settlor is discernable from the document creating the trust. For example, in *Barclay* v. *Barclay* [1970] 2 QB 677 the trust was created by a will in which the testator directed that '...my bungalow "Rosecot" and everything else I possess to be sold by my executor and the proceeds divided' between certain persons. In that case, decided under the old law applicable to trusts for sale, the declared intention that the bungalow be sold was enough to preclude any possibility of the claimant beneficiary having a right to occupy it. However, if a similar case were to be decided under s.15(1), the express intention of the executor would have to be balanced with the other three factors considered below.

12.7.1.2 The Purposes for Which the Property Subject to the Trust is Held
In *Jones* v. *Challenger* [1961] 1 QB 176 the house had been bought by a husband and wife as a matrimonial home, but the marriage had broken down and the wife had left. There were no children and the Court of Appeal held that the house should be sold because, 'with an end of the marriage, [the] purpose [of the trust] was dissolved and the primacy of the duty to sell was restored' (Devlin LJ, p. 183). In *Bank of Ireland Home Mortgages Ltd* v. *Bell* [2001] FLR 809 the Court of Appeal agreed with the trial judge who had concluded that the purpose of using the house as a family home ceased, if not as soon as the husband left (never to return), then certainly by the time the bank began possession proceedings a year and a half later.

There seems to be a considerable overlap between the first two factors listed in s.15(1), and the courts often consider the two factors together (see, for example, *Holman* v. *Howes* [2005] EWHC 2824 Ch, at para. 64 (this aspect of the judgment was not criticised on appeal). The latter factor is probably a little wider, especially where the purpose of the trust may have evolved over time. In *First National Bank Plc* v. *Achampong* [2003] EWCA Civ 487, for example, Blackburne J tentatively distinguished the original intention that the house provide a a *matrimonial* home for original purposes from its later purpose as a *family* home for them and their children (see para. 65).

12.7.1.3 The Welfare of any Minor Who Occupies or Might Reasonably Be Expected to Occupy any Land Subject to the Trust as Her Home

In the cases decided under s.30 LPA 1925, the courts distinguished between homes purchased merely to provide accommodation for the owners (as in *Jones* v. *Challenger* [1961] 1 QB 176, above) and those intended to provide a home for the co-owners and their children. In *Re Evers' Trust* [1980] 1 WLR 1327, a house had been bought by an unmarried couple who had three children. The man left and applied for an order for sale in order to take out the money he had contributed towards the purchase price. Ormrod LJ found that the underlying purpose of the trust was to provide a family home and, since that purpose still subsisted, albeit without the man, declined at that time to make the order.

Section 15(1)(c) now requires the interests of any children who (or who might be expected to) occupy the trust land as their home to be considered separately from the purpose of the trust. Although there has been relatively little judicial consideration of s.15(1)(c), it does seem clear that the mere presence of children (or grandchildren) living on the land will not be sufficient to make the factor relevant. The court will need to be provided with specific evidence as to how the children's welfare will be affected should an order for sale be granted. As Blackburne J explained in the Court of Appeal case of *First National Bank Plc* v. *Achampong* [2003] EWCA Civ 487:

> While it is relevant to consider the interests of the infant grandchildren in occupation of the property, it is difficult to attach much if any weight to their position in the absence of any evidence as to how their welfare may be adversely affected if an order for sale is now made. It is for the person who resists an order for sale in reliance on section 15(1)(c) to adduce the relevant evidence (at para. 65).

12.7.1.4 The Interests of any Secured Creditor of any Beneficiary

Under the s.30 jurisprudence, where the party seeking an order for sale was a creditor, the courts applied the principles based on bankruptcy cases (see below), with the result that, unless there were exceptional circumstances, the interests of a secured creditor would take precedence over the wishes of the beneficiaries (*Lloyds Bank Plc* v. *Byrne* [1993] 1 FLR 369). Now, however, the purpose of the trust is only one consideration among several in s.15 to be taken into account by the court.

In *Mortgage Corp Ltd* v. *Shaire* [2001] Ch 743, a case in which a secured creditor brought an action under s.14 for possession of the trust property following mortgage arrears, Neuberger J held that there was nothing to indicate that the interests of a secured creditor should take precedence over the other factors listed in s.15. The court was clear that s.15 was intended to enable the courts to exercise a wider discretion than formerly in favour of families as against secured creditors. With regard to previous authorities, he stated:

> ... there are obvious dangers in relying on authorities which proceeded on the basis that the court's discretion was more fettered than it now is. I think it would be wrong to throw over all the earlier cases without paying them any regard. However, they are to be treated with caution, in the light of the change in the law, and in many cases they are unlikely to be of great, let alone decisive, assistance (at p. 761).

Despite *Shaire*, the Court of Appeal returned to the previous orthodoxy of *Byrne* in *Bank of Ireland Home Mortgages Ltd* v. *Bell* [2001] FLR 809. Although s.15 had increased the scope of the discretion available to the court:

...a powerful consideration is and ought to be whether the creditor is receiving proper recompense for being kept out of his money, repayment of which is overdue (Peter Gibson LJ, at para. 31).

In this case, there was no equity in Mrs Bell's property, the debt was continuing to increase, and her son was almost 18 (minimising the relevance of s.15(1)(c)). The court found little difficulty in ordering sale. In *First National Bank Plc* v. *Achampong* [2003] EWCA Civ 487 the Court of Appeal adopted the reasoning in *Bell*, despite the presence of infant grandchildren.

Prominent among the considerations which lead to that conclusion is that, unless an order for sale is made, the bank will be kept waiting indefinitely for any payment out of what is, for all practical purposes, its own share of the property (Blackburne J at para. 65).

Despite the unfortunate consequences for the occupiers, there is a certain logic behind the decisions in *Bell* and *Achampong*, since it is open to a creditor to initiate bankruptcy proceedings, then have the case heard under s.335A Insolvency Act 1986 and thus avoid s.15 (see *Alliance and Leicester Plc* v. *Slayford* (2001) 33 HLR 743; see Section 7.3.1.5).

12.7.2   Bankruptcy: s.335A Insolvency Act 1986

Section 15(4) TLATA provides that where the s.14 application is made by the trustee in bankruptcy of one of the parties the case must be considered not under s.15 but under s.335A Insolvency Act 1986. The court must make such an order 'as it thinks just and reasonable', having regard to the interests of the bankrupt's creditors and all the circumstances of the case except for the needs of the bankrupt. Where the trustee in bankruptcy's application relates to a dwelling house which has been the home of the bankrupt or the bankrupt's spouse or civil partner or former spouse or former civil partner, the court will also have to take into account the extent to which the spouse or partner contributed towards the bankruptcy, the spouse or partner's needs and resources and the needs of any children. However, by s.335A(3), once a year has passed since the bankruptcy was declared, the court:

shall assume, unless the circumstances of the case are exceptional, that the interests of the bankrupt's creditors outweigh all other considerations.

This reference to exceptional circumstances in s.335A(3) has given statutory effect to a principle developed in recent years by the courts. In *Re Citro (Domenico) (a bankrupt)* [1991] Ch 142, a case heard under the s.30 common law jurisprudence, the Court of Appeal considered the nature of exceptional circumstances. The disruption of losing a home and changing schools is 'not uncommon', and therefore not exceptional; Nourse LJ described this as 'the melancholy consequences of debt and improvidence with which every civilised society has been familiar' (at p. 157). As Brown concluded ((1992) 55 MLR 284 at p. 291):

In the necessary balancing exercise between creditors as against bankrupts and their families, the former will always win in the end, and that end comes sooner rather than later.

Before *Re Citro*, only in *Re Holliday* [1981] Ch 405 had the court postponed sale in a bankruptcy case: here the spouse had made himself bankrupt, the creditors were not pressing for repayment, there were young children, and the wife would have been unable to find accommodation elsewhere in the area with her share of the proceeds of sale. As if that were not enough, the bankrupt had left his wife for another woman. Asking the question 'in all the circumstances of the case, whose voice in equity ought to prevail?', a different Court of Appeal from that in *Re Citro* had felt able to postpone sale for five years.

Under the Insolvency Act, if the court finds that there are exceptional circumstances it may postpone sale or refuse it entirely. At first instance in *Judd* v. *Brown* [1998] 2 FLR 360, Harman J refused sale where the bankrupt's wife was suffering from cancer and undergoing chemotherapy; in *Re Raval* [1998] 2 FLR 718 an order for sale against a paranoid schizophrenic, for whom a move to a smaller house away from the support of her family and friends could have caused a relapse, was postponed for a year in order to allow suitable accommodation to be found for her. In *Claughton* v. *Charalambous* [1999] 1 FLR 740 the bankrupt's spouse, who was aged sixty and suffered from renal failure and osteoarthritis, lived in a house adapted for her with a chair lift. Finding these circumstances to be exceptional, Jonathan Parker J confirmed the decision of the County Court suspending the order for sale indefinitely. The decision seems to have been influenced by the fact that the creditors were unlikely to receive anything from the sale of the property, as its value was more than taken up in costs.

It appears, then, that the courts are prepared to offer a measure of protection to the family home in cases where a member of the family is suffering from a serious or terminal illness and whose health would be further prejudiced by a forced removal from her home. In *Barca* v. *Mears* [2004] EWHC 2170 Ch the defendant raised the question of whether the narrow approach to 'exceptional circumstances' was consistent with the right to respect of the home and family life under Article 8 of the European Convention on Human Rights. Mr Nicholas Strauss QC (sitting as a Deputy Judge of the High Court) had no difficulty in deciding that there were no exceptional circumstances in this case. However, he also noted:

> ... it may be incompatible with Convention rights to follow the approach taken by the majority in *[Re] Citro*, in drawing a distinction between what is exceptional, in the sense of being unusual, and what Nourse L.J. refers to as the 'usual melancholy consequences' of a bankruptcy. This approach leads to the conclusion that, however disastrous the consequences may be to family life, if they are of the *usual kind* then they cannot be relied on under section 335A; they will qualify as 'exceptional' only if they are of an unusual kind, for example where a terminal illness is involved (at para. 40).

12.8 Protection for Buyers of Trust Land

A buyer of land (including a mortgagee) subject to a trust can overreach the beneficial interests. Providing payment is made to two or more trustees or a trust corporation the buyer 'shall not be concerned with the trusts' (s.27 LPA 1925, and see Section 10.4). However, there are still potential traps for a buyer, no matter how careful she may be.

One such problem is where land formerly owned by joint tenants is vested in a single serving tenant. How is the buyer to know whether the beneficial joint tenancy remained intact until the last death? If the beneficial joint tenancy was severed (see Section 11.4.2) there could be a number of beneficial interests in the land that will not be overreached unless a second trustee is appointed. Section 1 Law of Property (Joint Tenants) Act 1964 allows the buyer of unregistered to presume that the joint tenancy remained unsevered provided that:

1   the conveyance states that the seller is solely and beneficially entitled to the land;
2   no note or memorandum signed by the joint tenants or one of them has been made on the title deeds recording that the joint tenancy was severed; and
3   none of the joint tenants has been adjudged bankrupt (this can easily be discovered by a bankruptcy search in the Land Charges Register).

Where the terms of the trust makes any sale subject to the consent of more than two people, s.10 TLATA provides that the purchaser only has to be sure that two have actually consented. In unregistered land, a purchaser is further protected since she is not concerned whether the trustees are acting in the interests of the beneficiaries or whether they have been consulted (s.16(1)). Section 16(2) provides that a purchaser will still get good title, even if the disposition is in breach of trust, so long as she does not have actual notice of it. Like the 1964 Act, the protection in s.16 is not extended to purchasers of registered land. This has prompted some academic discussion as to whether a breach of trust will affect the overreaching ability disposition of registered land (see Ferris and Battersby ([1998] Conv 168)).

12.9 Comment

The Trusts of Land and Appointment of Trustees Act 1996 provides a coherent conceptual foundation for trusts of land. Although not without its own difficulties, it extends and clarifies the roles of trustees and beneficiaries in relation especially to partition, consultation, rights of occupation and delegation, and gives beneficiaries limited powers in respect of the appointment of trustees. Recent cases indicate, however, that the interests of secured creditors remain paramount when the courts are asked to decide whether trust land should be sold or retained.

The doctrines of joint tenancy and tenancy in common on the whole work quite well. However, the rules about severance of an equitable joint tenancy – on which so much may depend – are sometimes uncertain and often unjust. It has even been suggested that the equitable joint tenancy should be abolished, in order to avoid 'much troublesome and expensive litigation' (Thompson [1987] Conv 29, p. 35).

Some problems remain, not least for family members when a co-owner faces s.14 proceedings from a secured creditor or a trustee in bankruptcy. Although s.15 TLATA and the Insolvency Act 1986 was designed to provide a compromise between the needs of the family and the wishes of the creditors to get at their money, in most cases the court will order the home to be sold. This can be contrasted with the introduction of 'homestead legislation' in New Zealand and in North America, an approach which reflects the different priorities in those jurisdictions. Under the New Zealand Joint Family Homes Act 1964, for example, a home registered by spouses as a 'joint family home' will, in most cases, be secure in cases of bankruptcy or attack by creditors (see Omar [2006] Conv 157). It is unlikely, however, that such an approach will be adopted here.

Summary

12.1 The trust divides the legal title to land (held by the trustees) from the equitable (or 'beneficial') ownership of the land. In England and Wales all co-owned land is held on trust.

12.2 An interest under a trust of land may arise expressly, or by statute, or by a resulting or constructive trust.

12.3 Prior to 1997 there were two main types of trust. Strict settlements developed as a way in which families could hold land through several generations; trusts for sale were created to hold land as a temporary investment. The TLATA prohibits new strict settlements. Apart from existing strict settlements, any trust relating to land is now 'trust of land' with power to sell or retain the land.

12.4　Under the old trust for sale, equity regarded the beneficial interest as an interest in money, not in land, although this was sometimes ignored in order to protect occupiers of land. The TLATA abolished the doctrine of conversion and also gives some beneficial owners a statutory right to occupy the trust land.

12.5　Legal title to land may only be shared under a joint tenancy, and the maximum number of legal joint tenants is four. Joint tenants share the unities of possession, interest, title and time, and take the risk of the right of survivorship.

12.6　Equitable co-owners may be joint tenants or tenants in common, depending on whether there have been words of severance or on the general circumstances of the creation of the trust; tenants in common share the unity of possession.

12.7　Equitable joint tenants can sever their tenancy and become tenants in common.

12.8　Trustees of a trust of land have, subject to the terms of the trust, the powers of an absolute owner of land; this may include powers to transfer the land to adult beneficiaries absolutely entitled; to partition the land; to delegate their powers to beneficiaries. They have duties to consult the beneficiaries and to make reasonable decisions in relation to beneficiaries occupying the land.

12.9　Beneficiaries have the right to be consulted, and may have the right to occupy or receive compensation.

12.10　Under a trust of land, any trustee or beneficiary can go to court for an order of sale or otherwise. The court may make such order as it thinks fit, but where a party is bankrupt, the land will probably be sold after a year, unless the circumstances are 'exceptional'.

Exercises

12.1 Why was the doctrine of conversion abolished?

12.2 How do you know if co-owners are joint tenants or tenants in common when a trust of land is created? Why is it important?

12.3 When is a joint tenancy severed?

12.4 When do beneficiaries have the right to occupy trust land?

12.5 When does land subject to a trust have to be sold?

@ **12.6** Five friends, Denise, Michael, Florence, Jacob and Ben, who had just graduated and found jobs, bought a house, intending to share it while they established themselves in their new careers. They each contributed £10,000 to the deposit and were equally liable for the mortgage repayments.

Denise decided to leave her job and sail round the world, so she sold her share of the house to her friend Amanda who has now taken over her mortgage liability.

Florence and Michael became lovers and had a baby. Since the house is large, they want to divide it into two maisonettes, keeping the smaller one for themselves. The others want to keep it as it is.

Ben's business investments have failed and he thinks he might be made bankrupt.

Discuss the rights of all the parties and explain what might now happen to the land.

@ **12.7** Read A Matter of Trust on the companion website. What further steps would you recommend that Alexia and her co-purchasers take?

@ **12.8** An online quiz on the topics covered in this chapter is available on the companion website.

Further Reading

Dixon, 'Trusts of Land, Bankruptcy and Human Rights' [2005] Conv 161

Ferris and Battersby, 'The Impact of the Trusts of Land and Appointment of Trustees Act 1996 on Purchasers of Registered Land' [1998] Conv 168

Omar, 'Security Over co-owned Property and the Creditor's Paramount Status in Recovery Proceedings' [2006] Conv 157

Pascoe, 'Section 15 of the Trusts of Land and Appointment of Trustees Act 1996 – A Change in the Law?' [2000] Conv 315

Pascoe, 'Right to Occupy Under a Trust of Land: Muddled Legislative Logic?' [2006] Conv 54

Tee, 'Severance Revisited' [1995] Conv 104

Chapter 13

Implied Trusts and Proprietary Estoppel

13.1 Introduction

13.2 Resulting Trusts

13.3.1 Constructive Trusts

13.3 What Share of the Beneficial Interest?

13.3.2 Establishing a Beneficial Interest

13.3.2.1 Express Common Intention

13.3.2.2 Inferred Common Intention

13.3.3 Distributing the Beneficial Interest?

Express agreement

No express agreement

13. Implied Trusts Proprietary Estoppel

13.4.1.1 The Expectation

13.4.1 Establishing an Estoppel

13.4.1.2 Detrimental Reliance

13.4 Proprietary Estoppel

13.4.2 The Remedy

13.5 Constructive Trusts and Proprietary Estoppel Compared

13.6 Comment

13.1 Introduction

> In an ideal world, those who intend to own property or a share in it would do three things: they would agree what they intended to do; they would then record their intentions; and they would take legal advice to ensure that what they wanted had been achieved in a manner which the law recognises. However ... life is not like that (Clarke, P. [1992] Fam Law 72).

The previous chapter explained how trusts of land can be created by an express declaration of trust, or by statute in cases where land is transferred to more than one person without such an express declaration. The opening sections of this chapter consider the circumstances in which the courts will impose an implied trust – either a resulting or a common intention constructive trust. It also considers how the courts quantify the shares of the beneficial owners. Section 13.4 explores the operation of proprietary estoppel, a doctrine also discussed in Chapters 2 and 14.

It is relatively rare for commercial cases concerning implied trusts in land to come before the courts, at least when compared to the number of cases concerning family homes. However sensible it might be for two people to sort out their property and financial arrangements before they buy a house, or before a person moves in to live with someone who already owns a house, this does not always happen. In the latter case, in particular, to open these kinds of negotiations at such a time might be thought to be somewhat calculating and risk undermining the relationship between the parties. Equally, such thoughts might never have crossed the parties' minds at such an emotional stage in their relationship. Alternatively, there may have been some informal understanding that the person who does not own the legal title will contribute towards the mortgage repayments, or financially in some other way to their shared lives.

Problems almost inevitably arise when the relationship between the parties breaks down or when a mortgage lender tries to gain possession of the land because of mortgage arrears. When a marriage or civil partnership comes to an end, the courts have considerable powers to make the best provision in the circumstances under the Matrimonial Causes Act 1973 and the Civil Partnership Act 2004. However, these powers are not available in other circumstances, including, for example, disputes between partners who are neither married nor civil partners, between siblings or friends living together, and cases where a mortgagee is seeking possession. In these situations, the general principles of property law apply, although the courts seem increasingly willing to apply them in a nuanced way when the family home is involved.

In 2007 the Law Commission, after a wide consultation, proposed a new statutory scheme to apply to cohabitants living in a joint household who are neither married nor in a civil partnership ((2007) Law Com No. 307, *Cohabitation: The Financial Consequences of Relationship Breakdown*). However, as Baroness Hale observed in *Stack* v. *Dowden* [2007] 2 AC 432, a few months before the report was published:

> but, unlike most Law Commission reports, this one will not contain a draft Bill. Implementation will therefore depend, not only upon whether its proposals find favour with Government, but also on whether the resources can be found to translate them into workable legislative form (at para. 47).

It seems that Baroness Hale's concerns are justified. Despite the broadly positive reception of the report, the Government has no proposals, at present, to introduce the proposed scheme, or any alternative provision for family property.

In considering resulting trusts and intention-based constructive trusts, this chapter focuses upon two sets of circumstances. The first, and most common, is where the legal title is vested in A, and B is trying to show that she has a beneficial interest in the land. If she can do so, she must also establish exactly what that interest was. Less common is where A and B hold the legal title as beneficial joint tenants without any express declaration as to their respective beneficial entitlement.

The simplest form of solution in such circumstances is the doctrine of resulting trusts (Section 13.2). However, this doctrine is now almost redundant in cases concerning the family ownership of land. In most domestic cases the court will seek to discern from the wider circumstances of the case what the parties intended (hence the term 'common intention' constructive trust). If a claimant is unable to establish either a resulting or a common intention constructive trust, she may still be able to establish some right to the land through estoppel. The doctrine of proprietary estoppel and its relationship with resulting and constructive trusts is considered in Sections 13.4 and 13.5.

13.2 Resulting Trusts

A resulting trust can arise when a person contributes towards the purchase price of land, but the legal title is transferred into the name of someone else. In such circumstances, the *presumption* is that the parties intended that the legal owner hold the land on trust for the benefit of the contributor. Thus, when Mrs Boland (see *Williams & Glyn's Bank Ltd* v. *Boland* [1981] AC 487, see Section 11.7.2.1) contributed to the purchase price of the house, Mr Boland, as the sole registered proprietor, was deemed to be holding the land on trust for himself and his wife through a resulting trust.

When the land that is subject to a resulting trust is sold, the proceeds of sale are divided between the co-owners in direct proportion to their contributions to the purchase price. If the contribution is by way of a gift or a loan to the legal owner, the presumption of a resulting trust will be rebutted, and the contributor will not gain a beneficial interest (see, for example, *Fowkes* v. *Pascoe* (1874-75) 10 Ch App 343). There is also an old doctrine called the 'presumption of advancement'. The courts used to presume that money given by a husband to his wife, or by a parent to her child, for the purchase of land was a gift, and that it was not intended that the parent should acquire any interest in the land. In *McGrath* v. *Wallis* [1995] 2 FLR 114 the Court of Appeal followed the modern line that this presumption is now a 'judicial instrument of the last resort' and is rebuttable by even the slightest evidence. Here, where a father had provided money to help his son buy a house for them to live in together, there was evidence (from an incomplete deed) of an intention that the land was to be held on trust for them both as tenants in common. Therefore, the presumption of advancement did not operate and, when the father died intestate, the son's sister was entitled on the intestacy to a share in her father's interest in the land.

Since nowadays people tend to depend on mortgage loans to finance the purchase of their homes, it is common for people who do not hold legal title to attempt to establish a beneficial interest in the land through their contributions to the mortgage repayments. Accepting liability for a mortgage at the time the property is purchased may be sufficient to give rise to a resulting trust, as in the case of *Cowcher* v. *Cowcher* [1972] 1 WLR 425. However, merely contributing to the repayments of a mortgage granted by the legal owner is not sufficient (see *Curley* v. *Parkes* [2004] EWCA Civ 1515).

In the recent case of *Stack* v. *Dowden* [2007] 2 AC 432, the House of Lords indicated that cases involving family land in joint names should normally be approached as cases of common intention constructive trusts rather than resulting trusts (see Section 13.3). The reason for this is that it allows the court much more flexibility in determining the terms of the trust and the extent of the various beneficial shares. '...a resulting trust "crystallises" on the date that the property is acquired' (Peter Gibson LJ, *Curley* v. *Parkes* [2004] EWCA Civ 1515 at para. 18, whereas the doctrine of common intention allows the court to take a wide variety of factors into account in order to determine the terms of the trust (see, for example, the list given by Baroness Hale in *Stack* at para. 69).

However, the court must look to the true natures of the transaction to determine which type of trust is the appropriate one to use. The fact that all of the parties to a transaction are related does not necessarily mean that the arrangement is not a business enterprise. In *Laskar* v. *Laskar* [2008] 1 WLR 2695 a mother and daughter joined together to purchase the mother's council house, with the purpose of renting it out to tenants. Neuberger LJ (who dissented from the *ratio* in *Stack* v. *Dowden*, but not its outcome) held that despite the familial appearance of the case, it gave rise to a resulting trust because:

> the primary purpose of the purchase of the property was as an investment, not as a home ... To my mind it would not be right to apply the reasoning in *Stack* v. *Dowden* to such a case as this, where the parties primarily purchased the property as an investment for rental income and capital appreciation, even where their relationship is a familial one (at para. 17).

13.3 Common Intention Constructive Trusts

13.3.1 Constructive Trusts

Constructive trusts are potentially much wider than resulting trusts. They arise in a number of circumstances, of which *common intention*, considered below, is only one. For a detailed explanation, see 2008, Oakley, *Parker & Mellows The Modern Law of Trusts*, Chapter 10.

During the late 1960s and 1970s, Lord Denning MR used the constructive trust as a means of achieving a fair solution to family disputes over land. Such remedial constructive trusts could be imposed by the courts whenever people found themselves in a situation where one would naturally trust the other because of the underlying social consensus on what was 'fair'. A remedial constructive trust might therefore be imposed whenever a person would otherwise get 'a manifest and unfair advantage' and where it would be unconscionable for the legal owner to deny a claimant's beneficial interest. The remedial constructive trust is used in other common law jurisdictions. For example, the Australian case of *Rasmanis* v. *Jurewitsch* (1969) 70 SR (NSW) 407 concerned three legal and beneficial joint tenants (A, B and C). A killed B, and the question arose as to how the beneficial entitlement was now shared. If the beneficial joint tenancy was automatically severed by the homicide (see Section 12.5.4.5), then A and C would hold the legal title on trust for themselves and B's estate in equal shares as tenants in common. The Court of Appeal of New South Wales felt that this would mean that A profited by his crime, and instead imposed a constructive trust with the beneficial interest being divided one third to C and the remaining two-thirds to A and C as joint tenants.

There has been some significant judicial support for the remedial constructive trust over the years since it was championed by Lord Denning MR, including, for example, the speech of Browne-Wilkinson in *Westdeutsche Landesbank Girozentrale* v. *Islington LBC* [1996] AC 669. However, the courts of England and Wales have continued largely to reject the remedial constructive trust in favour of a doctrine based more firmly on the principles of property law as set out by the House of Lords in the two seminal cases of *Pettitt* v. *Pettitt* [1970] AC 777 and *Gissing* v. *Gissing* [1971] AC 886.

13.3.2 Establishing a Beneficial Interest

Where there is no express or statutory trust (because, for example, the legal title is vested in only one, rather than both, people sharing the house), the court must first determine whether the claimant is entitled to a beneficial interest in the land, before establishing the extent of that interest. An important leading case is *Lloyds Bank Plc* v. *Rosset* [1991] 1 AC 107. Mr and Mrs Rosset wished to buy a semi-derelict farmhouse using money from a Swiss trust fund. The trustees of the fund insisted that legal title was transferred to Mr Rosset alone, and he was subsequently entered as the sole registered proprietor. For six months, Mrs Rosset supervised the renovation and decorated the house. In subsequent possession proceedings brought by a mortgagee, she claimed an equitable interest under an informal trust. This, she argued, would enable her to claim an overriding interest under s.70(1)(g) LRA 1925 (see Section 11.7.2) and thus defeat the mortgage that had been taken out by Mr Rosset without her knowledge. The House of Lords held that she had not shown that she had gained an interest, and therefore the bank was able to defeat her claim.

Since the land was held in the sole name of Mr Rosset, and since there had been no express declaration of trust, Lord Bridge said that an equitable interest would only arise if Mrs Rosset could demonstrate that there had been a *common intention* that she should own a share in the land. This could be shown by either:

1   An *express agreement* that the land should be co-owned, together with some act by the claimant to her detriment or some significant alteration of her position in reliance on the agreement. This would give rise to rights, according to Lord Bridge, under a constructive trust or proprietary estoppel (see Section 13.4);
2   or, in the absence of an express agreement, *an act by the claimant from which the court may infer a common intention*, giving rise to an interest under a constructive trust. Lord Bridge thought that the only act which would be sufficient would be the direct contribution of money (such as the repayment of a mortgage) towards the purchase of the property.

Mrs Rosset failed under the first category because there had been no express agreement that she should have a beneficial interest, and under the second category because her work on the house did not amount to a sufficient act from which to infer such an agreement.

13.3.2.1 Express Common Intention

In *Rosset*, Lord Bridge approved the earlier Court of Appeal decision in *Grant* v. *Edwards* [1986] Ch 638 in which a man and a woman lived together for about ten years and had two children. He had told her that her name should not go on the legal title of the house that they shared because this might prejudice her divorce proceedings. Although clearly he never intended that she should have a beneficial share in the house, nevertheless the Court of Appeal was prepared to find that his excuse for not putting her name on the title amounted to evidence of a common intention, since otherwise no excuse would have been needed. In addition, the couple had shared equally some money left over from an insurance claim when the house had partly burnt down. The woman had acted to her detriment in reliance on the common intention by paying all the household bills:

> In a case such as the present, where there has been no written declaration or agreement, nor any direct provision by the plaintiff of part of the purchase price so as to give rise to a resulting trust in her favour, she must establish a common intention between her and the defendant, acted on by her, that she should have a beneficial interest in the property ... In my judgment [she must prove] conduct on

which [she] could not reasonably be expected to embark unless she was to have an interest in the house (Nourse LJ at p. 646).

As the claimant had established that there had been a common intention that the house should be co-owned and that she had relied on this to her detriment, the Court imposed a constructive trust on the man and awarded her a share of the beneficial interest.

In *Hammond* v. *Mitchell* [1991] 1 WLR 1127 a man and woman lived together for 12 years in a bungalow registered in his name. He had promised her that she was equally the owner of the property but said that he could not put her name on the Register for tax reasons. There were also several businesses and a house in Spain, and she claimed a half share in all of these. Waite J, in some despair at the detailed and conflicting evidence and the 19 days of the trial, finally awarded her a half-share in the bungalow. The full flavour of the dispute can only be gained from reading the report: there was evidence of a promise that the land was half hers, of her involvement in the businesses and their sharing of whatever money they had, and of her agreement to risk any interest she might have in the bungalow as security for a bank loan for business purposes. All these taken together showed a common agreement plus an act to her detriment. She therefore satisfied the first *Rosset* category. However, the judge commented:

> The primary emphasis accorded by the law in cases of this kind to express discussions between the parties ... means that the tenderest exchanges of a common law courtship may assume an unforeseen significance many years later when they are brought under equity's microscope and subjected to an analysis under which many thousands of pounds of value may be liable to turn on fine questions as to whether the relevant words were spoken in earnest or in dalliance (at p. 1139).

In *Chan* v. *Leung* [2003] 1 FLR 23 (referred to in Section 12.6.2), Mr Chan formed a relationship with Miss Leung, who, in return for a share in the business helped him in his business affairs while he was in prison in Hong Kong. He also promised her that he would divorce his wife, marry her and provide her with a house. They bought a house in England in the name of a company in which they were the sole shareholders, and lived there together until the relationship broke down three years later. Miss Leung successfully claimed a beneficial share in the property, arguing that there was an express agreement that she should have half of the house, which she had relied on by helping Mr Chan with his business interests and uprooting herself from Hong Kong. Just as in *Hammond* v. *Mitchell*, the whole course of the parties' relationship was examined. At the trial there had been a lengthy rehearsal of the evidence and much had turned on whose version of the events was believed by the judge:

> The judge having heard the witnesses over a considerable time, inevitably had a feel for the case which this court cannot have (Jonathan Parker LJ at para. 89).

13.3.2.2 Inferred Common Intention

Under this second category, the claimant must establish that there are sufficient grounds for the court to infer the presence of an agreement to share ownership of the land. This is not the same as saying that the court can impose a trust or impute an agreement wherever it would be fair to do so. Lord Neuberger explained the difference between inference and imputation in *Stack* v. *Dowden* [2007] 2 AC 432:

> An inferred intention is one which is objectively deduced to be the subjective actual intention of the parties, in the light of their actions and statements. An imputed intention is one which is attributed to the parties, even though no such actual intention can be deduced from their actions and statements, and even though they had no such intention. Imputation involves concluding what the parties would have intended, whereas inference involves concluding what they did intend (at para. 126).

In *Rosset*, Lord Bridge indicated that he considered nothing short of a monetary contribution to the purchase would be sufficient to justify such an inference. There is support for this view from the earlier case of *Burns* v. *Burns* [1984] Ch 317, where an unmarried couple lived together for 19 years in a house, legal title to which was held by the man. The woman brought up their children, kept house and, when the children were older, she took a job which allowed her to contribute to the housekeeping and buy various household items such as a washing machine. She also decorated inside the house. When their relationship ended, her claim to a beneficial interest failed:

> What is needed, I think, is evidence of a payment or payments by the plaintiff which it can be inferred was referable to the acquisition of the house ... the mere fact that the parties live together and do the ordinary domestic tasks is, in my view, no indication at all that they thereby intended to alter the existing property rights of either of them (Fox LJ at pp. 328, 331).

Although high, it should be noted that the level of the hurdle for establishing inferred intention is lower than what is required for a resulting trust. The payments of mortgage instalments and a discount given to a sitting tenant by the landlord selling a flat are sufficient to found an inferred common intention, but not a resulting trust (see *Curley* v. *Parkes* [2004] EWCA Civ 1515 at para. 16).

However, there is some indication that the strict approach taken by Lord Bridge in *Rosset* is being relaxed. Indeed, in the earlier case of *Gissing* v. *Gissing* [1971] AC 886 the House of Lords had pointed towards a more liberal approach. Lord Diplock was of the opinion that indirect financial contributions to the household expenses might be sufficient to enable a claimant to gain a beneficial interest, but only if they enabled the legal owner to make the mortgage repayments. Nicholas Mostyn QC, sitting a deputy judge in the Family Division observed in *Le Foe* v. *Le Foe* [2001] 2 FLR 970 (a case in which a mortgagee was seeking possession):

> I have no doubt that the family economy depended for its function on [the wife's] earnings. It was an arbitrary allocation of responsibility that [the husband] paid the mortgage ... whereas [the wife] paid for day-to-day domestic expenditure (at para. 10).

The question of what is sufficient to justify inferred common intention was recently considered (albeit *obiter*) in *Stack* v. *Dowden* [2007] 2 AC 432.

> There is undoubtedly an argument for saying, as did the Law Commission in *Sharing Homes, A Discussion Paper* [(2002) Law Com No 278], para 4.23 that the observations, which were strictly obiter dicta, of Lord Bridge of Harwich in *Lloyds Bank Plc* v. *Rosset* [1991] 1 AC 107 have set that hurdle rather too high in certain respects (Baroness Hale, at para 62).

These remarks suggest a lowering of the level of the hurdle that must jumped be for common intention to be inferred, to include less direct contributions.

13.3.3   What Share of the Beneficial Interest?

Once a court has found that an informal arrangement has resulted in the creation of a beneficial interest behind an informal trust, it must then go on to quantify the share of the equity to which the successful claimant is entitled. This is unlikely to be a problem where the parties have expressly agreed the size of their respective shares.

> In the olden days, before registration of title ... conveyances of unregistered land into joint names would in practice declare the purchasers' beneficial as well as their legal interests. No one now doubts that such an express declaration of trust is conclusive unless varied by subsequent agreement or affected by proprietary estoppel: see *Goodman* v. *Gallant* [1986] Fam 106. That case also establishes

that severance of a beneficial joint tenancy results in a beneficial tenancy in common in equal shares (per Baroness Hale, *Stack* v. *Dowden* [2007] 2 AC 432 at para. 49).

The law has been much less clear, however, about how to quantify the beneficial interest where there is no express agreement. Two approaches can be identified. In the first, based on resulting trust principles, the parties are entitled to a share of the beneficial interest in proportion to their contribution to the purchase price. This approach, however, now seems to have been superseded by the second approach described by the Law Commission in *Sharing Homes, A Discussion Paper* (2002, Law Com No. 278) as:

> a 'holistic approach' to quantification, undertaking a survey of the whole course of dealing between the parties and taking account of all conduct which throws light on the question what shares were intended (at para. 4.27).

In *Oxley* v. *Hiscock* [2005] Fam 211, Mrs Oxley and Mr Hiscock had both contributed to the purchase of the house that they shared. Despite being advised to the contrary by her solicitor, Mrs Oxley agreed that the house be registered in the sole name of Mr Hiscock. Since the purchase of the house in 1991 both parties contributed towards the maintenance and improvement of the property from pooled resources. When the relationship between the parties broke down, the court was asked to determine their beneficial shares in the proceeds of sale. The trial judge divided the proceeds of sale in equal shares. After a monumental review of the law, Chadwick LJ reached the following conclusion:

> in a case where there is no evidence of any discussion between them as to the amount of the share which each was to have – and even in a case where the evidence is that there was no discussion on that point ... [it] must now be accepted that (at least in this court and below) the answer is that each is entitled to that share which the court considers fair having regard to the whole course of dealing between them in relation to the property. And, in that context, 'the whole course of dealing between them in relation to the property' includes the arrangements which they make from time to time in order to meet the outgoings ... (at para. 69).

After considering the history of the parties' relationship – and their respective contributions – the Court of Appeal concluded that a fair division of the proceeds of sale of the property would be 60 per cent to Mr Hiscock and 40 per cent to Mrs Oxley.

In the earlier case of *Midland Bank Plc* v. *Cooke* [1995] 4 All ER 562 the wife contributed £550 to the original purchase (her share of a wedding present) of the matrimonial home. The trial judge held that this entitled her under a resulting trust to about 7 per cent of the value of the house. However, the Court of Appeal held that once there was evidence of the common intention to share the property, then the judge has to:

> undertake a survey of the whole course of dealing between the parties relevant to their ownership and occupation of the property and their sharing of its burdens and advantages ... [The court] will take into consideration all conduct which throws light on the question what shares were intended. Only if that search proves inconclusive does the court fall back on the maxim that 'equality is equity' (per Waite LJ at p. 574).

Here, the court felt that it was very clear from the wife's involvement in their complex financial arrangements that the parties had intended to share the property equally. The wife was therefore awarded a half share in the equitable ownership.

Although the 'holistic approach' gives the court considerable scope to discern a solution when there has been no agreement between the parties, '... it does not enable the court to abandon that search [for the parties' intention] in favour of the result which the court itself considers fair' (per Baroness Hale, *Stack* v. *Dowden* [2007] 2 AC 432 at para. 61). The situation before the House of Lords in *Stack* v. *Dowden* was different from those discussed above because in that case both Mr Stack and Ms Dowden were registered proprietors of the land concerned (and, therefore, joint tenants at law). Unfortunately when they completed the Land Registry form when purchasing the land, they failed to indicate (by ticking the relevant box on the form) whether they held the beneficial interest as joint tenants or tenants in common. Normally in these circumstances it is presumed that the parties hold the beneficial interest as joint tenants, since 'equity follows the law.' In *Stack* v. *Dowden*, however, a majority of the House of Lords accepted that there were *exceptional* cases where the unexpressed intentions of the parties could displace this assumption. The court should use the same approach as that taken in the cases concerning a single legal owner cases (see *Oxley* and *Cooke* above). Baroness Hale provided a substantial list of factors that might be relevant (at para. 69): unfortunately she gave no guidance as to what circumstances were sufficiently exceptional to allow the holistic approach to rebut any presumption of joint tenancy.

13.4 Proprietary Estoppel

Chapter 2 considered whether proprietary estoppel can come to the aid of a person who has suffered detriment because an agreement to buy land does not comply with s.2 Law of Property (Miscellaneous Provisions) Act 1989 contract (see Section 2.5). The application of the doctrine is, however, much wider than this, and has an important role to play when a person is attempting to establish a right in another person's land. In some ways, the proprietary estoppel is similar to the constructive trust (see Section 13.3). For example, in *Lloyds Bank* v. *Rosset* [1991] 1 AC 107, Lord Bridge discussed rights acquired 'under a constructive trust or proprietary estoppel'. However, it is probably best to treat implied trusts and proprietary estoppel as two separate, although not unrelated, doctrines. Resulting and constructive trusts provide a successful claimant with a beneficial interest in the land as equitable co-owner. Proprietary estoppel is a much more flexible creature and the courts have considerable discretion as to the nature of the remedy that they can award. The distinctions between the two doctrines are considered in more detail in Section 13.5.

13.4.1 Establishing an Estoppel

A successful argument of estoppel can prevent a person enforcing her strict legal rights if to do so would be unfair on a claimant who has acted to her detriment as a result of that person's actions or representations. In contract law the doctrine is known as promissory estoppel and is thought to provide a defence only. In land law, the doctrine of proprietary estoppel has a greater scope and can found an action – in other words, it can be a 'sword' as well as a 'shield'. Lord Scott summarised the underlying principles of proprietary estoppel in the case of *Yeoman's Row Management Limited* v. *Cobbe* [2008] 1 WLR 1752:

> An 'estoppel' bars the object of it from asserting some fact or facts, or, sometimes, something that is a mixture of fact and law, that stands in the way of some right claimed by the person entitled to the benefit of the estoppel. The estoppel becomes a 'proprietary' estoppel – a sub-species of a 'promissory' estoppel – if the right claimed is a proprietary right, usually a right to or over land but, in principle, equally available in relation to chattels or choses in action (at para. 14).

Over the years, the doctrine has developed from a fairly strict set of requirements – the so called 'five *probanda*' (criteria) of *Willmott* v. *Barber* (1880) LR 15 Ch D 96 – to the more flexible modern approach of Oliver J in *Taylor Fashions Ltd* v. *Liverpool Victoria Trustees Co Ltd* [1982] 1 QB 133:

> I am not at all convinced that it is desirable or possible to lay down hard and fast rules ... [T]he more recent cases indicate, in my judgment, that the application of the ... principle ... requires a very much broader approach which is directed rather at ascertaining whether, in particular individual circumstances, it would be unconscionable for a party to be permitted to deny that which, knowingly or unknowingly, he has allowed or encouraged another to assume to his detriment than to inquiring whether the circumstances can be fitted within the confines of some preconceived formula serving as a universal yardstick for every form of unconscionable behaviour (at pp. 149, 151–2; approved by the Privy Council in *Lim Teng Huan* v. *Ang Swee Chuan* [1992] 1 WLR 113).

The question therefore is whether it would be unconscionable if someone were to go back on her assertion or encouragement. In *Re Basham (decd)* [1986] 1 WLR 1498 a man had promised his stepdaughter that if she looked after him he would leave his house, formerly her mother's, to her in his will. In reliance on his promise, over many years she had cooked for him, maintained the house and taken legal action in relation to a boundary dispute, and her husband had refused a better job elsewhere. It would therefore have been unconscionable for him to deny his promise. He died intestate, however, but as a result of the stepdaughter's successful claim of proprietary estoppel, the man's heirs were prevented from relying on their legal right to inherit. The trial judge, Edward Nugee QC, explained estoppel as:

> where one person, A, has acted to his detriment on the faith of a belief, which was known or encouraged by another person, B, that he either has or is going to be given a right over B's property, B cannot insist on his strict legal rights if to do so would be inconsistent with A's belief (at p. 1503).

The effect of decisions such as *Taylor Fashions* and *Re Basham* is that, if as a result of the defendant's conduct the claimant has an expectation that she has, or will have, rights in the defendant's land and she acts to her detriment in reliance on that expectation, then she will have raised an 'equity' in the land in her favour which can be satisfied either by the defendant or, failing that, by the award of a remedy by the court. Although arguments centre on an examination of whether the claimant has such an expectation, and then on whether she has relied to her detriment on this:

> it is important to note at the outset that the doctrine of proprietary estoppel cannot be treated as subdivided into three or four watertight compartments ... [It is] apparent that the quality of the relevant assurances may influence the issue of reliance, that reliance and detriment are often intertwined ... Moreover the fundamental principle that equity is concerned to prevent unconscionable conduct permeates all the elements of the doctrine. In the end the court must look at the matter in the round (per Robert Walker LJ in *Gillett* v. *Holt* [2001] Ch 210 at p. 255).

13.4.1.1 The Expectation

The expectation in the claimant can be raised either by an express representation as to her present or future rights in the land, or by 'wilful silence'. In the latter case, an estoppel may be established if a landowner, knowing the true position, stands by while the claimant does something on the landowner's land in the mistaken belief that the land belongs to her. As Lord Wensleydale stated in *Ramsden* v. *Dyson* (1866) LR 1 HL 129:

> If a stranger build upon my land, supposing it to be his own, and I knowing it to be mine, do not interfere but leave him to go on, equity considers it to be dishonest in me to remain passive and afterwards to interfere and take profit (at p. 168).

To establish an estoppel the claimant must normally establish that she believed the assurance given to her to be irrevocable: it is not enough to hope, or even confidently expect, that the person who has given the assurances will keep her promise. For example, an agreement labelled 'subject to contract' will not normally be sufficient to give rise to an estoppel since:

> the would-be purchaser's expectation of acquiring an interest in the property in question is subject to a contingency that is entirely under the control of the other party to the negotiations (per Lord Scott, *Yeoman's Row Management Limited* v. *Cobbe* [2008] 1 WLR 1752 at para. 22).

It seems, however, that a valid estoppel can arise where the circumstances being relied on also give rise to a constructive trust (see the discussion of *Yaxley* v. *Gotts* [2000] Ch 162 in Section 2.5).

Exceptionally, however, it now seems to be accepted that a promise that a person will inherit under another's will can be sufficient a representation on which to base an estoppel claim, even though a will can be revoked at any time up to the death of the person who made it. In *Gillett* v. *Holt* [2001] Ch 210, the Court of Appeal was asked to consider the claim of Mr Gillett who, as a boy, had been befriended by a wealthy farmer. At the farmer's suggestion, Mr Gillett had left school early without any formal qualifications, had gone to work for the farmer and had continued to do so for some 40 years, giving up opportunities to develop his career. During this time the farmer gave him and his family repeated assurances that he would inherit the farm and the farm business, and he executed a will to that effect. Eventually, however, the farmer transferred his attentions to someone else, dismissed Mr Gillett from his employment and excluded him from his will. Mr Gillett argued that the farmer was estopped from doing this, since he had relied on the farmer's repeated representations that he would one day inherit the farm, rather than pursuing his own career as a farmer. The Court of Appeal agreed with him, finding that it was the detrimental reliance on the promise of inheriting under the will which made the promise binding, even though the will itself could later be revoked.

13.4.1.2 Detrimental Reliance

Once the claimant has shown that she was encouraged to act in a certain way, the courts will presume that her actions were in reliance on that encouragement, unless the legal owner is able to rebut this presumption (see *Greasley* v. *Cooke* [1980] 1 WLR 1306, below). The question is one of whether the acts would have been undertaken in any case as part of the relationship between the parties, or whether they were undertaken in reliance on the promise. The expenditure of money is usually sufficiently clear an act to show reliance on a promise. For example, in *Pascoe* v. *Turner* [1979] 1 WLR 431, a woman who had been promised that the house in which she was living 'was hers' spent 'a quarter of her modest capital' – a few hundred pounds – on maintaining and improving the property. The true owner, her former partner, was estopped from denying her interest in the house.

Acts in reliance, though, may be something other than the expenditure of money. For example, Mr Gillett would hardly have acted as he did had it not been for the farmer's assurances. In *Greasley* v. *Cooke* [1980] 1 WLR 1306, a young woman went to work as a maid in a household. After some time, she formed a relationship with one of the sons and lived with him as if she were his wife. Although she was no longer paid for her work, she continued to look after the family, including a daughter who was ill, and was assured that she could live in the house for the rest of her life. Her partner, who had inherited the house, died, and the heirs attempted to evict her. Lord Denning MR held that her unpaid work in caring for the family, especially the daughter, amounted to acts in reliance on the assurances that had been made to her.

13.4.2 The Remedy – Satisfying the Equity

A successful estoppel claim has the effect of raising an equity in the property. The courts must then find a means of 'satisfying the equity', and they have considerable discretion, within equitable principles, as to what remedy (often referred to as *relief* in estoppel cases) to award to the claimant.

It might be thought that the obvious relief would be to require the defendant to fulfil the promise. However, an 'expectation-based' approach potentially impinges on the law of contract and the doctrine of consideration, as well as on the rules of formality in land law. There are also practical problems with such an approach. Not only does it assume that the claimant's expectations are clearly focused upon a specific interest in the land, but it could lead to injustice where the consequences of honouring the expectation are disproportionate to the detriment the claimant will suffer if the promise is not kept. As Robert Walker LJ observed in *Jennings* v. *Rice* [2003] 1 P & CR 8:

> The essence of the doctrine of proprietary estoppel is to do what is necessary to avoid an unconscionable result, and a disproportionate remedy cannot be the right way of going about that (at para. 56).

The approach generally now taken by the courts is summarized by Mason CJ in the Australian case of *Commonwealth of Australia* v. *Verwayen* (1990) 170 CLR 394:

> A central element of that doctrine is that there must be a proportionality between the remedy and the detriment which [it] is its purpose to avoid (at p. 414).

However,

> that does not mean that the court should ... abandon expectations completely, and look to the detriment suffered by the claimant as defining the appropriate measure of relief (per Robert Walker LJ, *Jennings* v. *Rice* [2003] 1 P & CR 8 at para. 51).

Instead,

> The court's aim is ... to form a view as to what is the minimum required to satisfy [the equity] and do justice between the parties. The court must look at all the circumstances, including the need to achieve a 'clean break' so far as possible and avoid or minimise future friction (Robert Walker LJ in *Gillett* v. *Holt* [2001] Ch. 210 at p. 237).

The minimum necessary to satisfy the equity of estoppel will vary according to the circumstances of each individual case. In *Pascoe* v. *Turner* [1979] 1 WLR 431 (see Section 3.4.1.2), the court ordered the legal owner of a house to convey the fee simple to the claimant. Without more, this appears to be a windfall for the claimant and unjust on her former partner. In fact, the man was prosperous and, according to Cumming-Bruce LJ:

> determined to pursue his purpose of evicting her from the house by any legal means at his disposal with a ruthless disregard of the obligations binding on conscience (at p. 438).

The court felt that the woman could only be protected from the man's harrassing behaviour by requiring him to perfect his gift and convey the land to her. The award of some lesser right in the land, such as a licence to remain there during her lifetime, would not have been enough to achieve this. Similarly, in *Re Basham (decd)* [1986] 1 WLR 1498, the stepdaughter was awarded the house that had been promised to her. In *Yaxley* v. *Gotts* [2000] Ch 162 (see Section 2.5), Mr Yaxley received a long lease of one of the flats in the building he had been renovating.

In *Campbell* v. *Griffin* [2001] EWCA Civ 990, Mr Campbell had initially been a lodger in the house owned by a retired couple. He gradually took on responsibilities as their carer and they came to rely on him completely and treated him as their son. They assured him that he had a home for life and the husband changed his will in order to leave Mr Campbell a life interest in the house. The husband died before the wife, who took the property by right of survivorship as the sole surviving joint tenant. She, however, was unable to make a will in the man's favour because she was suffering from senile dementia. Mr Campbell established that he had an equity in the property through estoppel. However, the Court of Appeal felt unable to give effect to the promise of a life interest, since this would have been disproportionate to the detriment Mr Campbell had suffered, and unfair on others who were to benefit from the estate. Mr Campbell was awarded £35,000, charged on the property.

Similarly, in *Gillett* v. *Holt* [2001] Ch 210, the court did not require the farmer to fulfil all his promises to Mr Gillett, who instead was awarded the freehold of the farmhouse and some land, along with £100,000 to compensate him for his exclusion from the farm business. In *Jennings* v. *Rice* [2003] 1 P & CR 8, an old woman's part-time gardener became, over the course of a number of years, her unpaid full-time carer, even sleeping on the sofa in her sitting room during the last three years of her life. Despite promising him that the house would be his one day, the woman never made a will. After her death, the man made a claim on her estate for the house. Although his argument of estoppel was successful, the Court again emphasised the need for proportionality between the expectation and the detriment. Instead of fulfilling his expectation by ordering the transfer of the house, the Court awarded him £200,000, less than half its value.

On occasion, this approach, being essentially based on restitution, may result in no award at all being made, even though the claimant is successful in her estoppel claim. In *Sledmore* v. *Dalby* (1996) 72 P & CR 196, Mrs Sledmore sought possession of a house she owned against Mr Dalby, her son-in-law, who had lived there for many years. Mr Dalby had undertaken some work on the property initially in reliance on an assurance that his wife would be left the property after her parents' death and subsequently (his wife having died) on the assumption that he would be able to live there for the rest of his life. However, Mrs Sledmore had little money, was in danger of losing her home and had a greater need for the house than her son-in law. He could afford to pay for his own accommodation and, was actually only spending a few nights each week at the house. The Court of Appeal granted possession to Mrs Sledmore, and nothing to Mr Dalby on the basis that this was the 'the minimum equity to do justice to the respondent on the facts of this case' (per Roch LJ at p. 205):

> The effect of any equity ... has long since been exhausted and no injustice has been done to the defendant (per Hobhouse LJ at p. 209).

13.5 Constructive Trusts and Proprietary Estoppel Compared

It is probably clear from the discussion above that there is a degree of overlap between constructive trusts and proprietary estoppel. In *Yaxley* v. *Gotts* [2001] Ch 210, Robert Walker LJ stated:

> At a high level of generality, there is much common ground between the doctrines of proprietary estoppel and the constructive trust ... [a]ll are concerned with equity's intervention to provide relief

against unconscionable conduct, whether as between neighbouring landowners, or vendor and purchaser, or relatives who make informal arrangements for sharing a home, or a fiduciary and the beneficiary or client to whom he owes a fiduciary obligation (at p. 176).

In *Jennings* v. *Rice* [2003] 1 P & CR 8, he was of the view that:

> Sometimes the assurances, and the claimant's reliance on them, have a consensual character falling not far short of an enforceable contract ... [and] the proprietary estoppel may become indistinguishable from a constructive trust (per Robert Walker LJ, at para. 45).

In both constructive trusts and proprietary estoppel there is detrimental reliance on an understanding that the claimant will gain an interest in the land. However, whereas a constructive trust is based on an agreement between the parties, an estoppel does not require there to be a meeting of minds. An estoppel arises because the courts will not permit a legal owner to stand back while the claimant acts in reliance on a mistaken belief as to her rights.

A further difference arises when considering the nature of the remedy a successful claimant might obtain. Under a constructive trust, she will have a beneficial interest in the land which is deemed to have arisen at the time of the acts of detrimental reliance. The only question will be the extent of the share to be awarded by the court. In proprietary estoppel, however, the nature of the right is not known until the court gives its decision. As discussed above, the relief granted to give effect to an estoppel can range from the award of the fee simple (as in *Pascoe* v. *Turner*) to nothing at all (as in *Sledmore* v. *Dalby*).

It is also necessary to consider whether rights arising under a constructive trust or a proprietary estoppel are binding on third parties, such as later mortgage lenders or purchasers of the land. The rules on the circumstances in which a beneficial interest under a trust is binding are now well established (see Sections 10.4, 10.5, 11.4.2 and 11.7.2). Case law also indicated that an equity arising from proprietary estoppel could bind a purchaser of registered land under s.70(1)(g) LRA 1925 (see *Lloyd* v. *Dugdale* [2002] 2 P & CR 13), and this is now confirmed by s.116 LRA 2002. It seems, therefore, that such an equity can now be protected by the entry of a notice on the Register, although this is unlikely to happen, since the person in whose favour the equity has arisen will probably not know that it should be formally protected. However, when coupled with actual occupation, the equity will be an interest overriding subsequent dispositions (see Section 11.7.2). A major difficulty remains, however: the precise nature of the right will not be known until the court has granted relief.

13.6 Comment

The present law on the acquisition of interests under implied trusts is unsatisfactory, particularly in so far as it relates to family property. The law is based on finding that the parties had a common intention to share the beneficial ownership of the land. There are real evidential difficulties in establishing that an express agreement existed sufficient for Lord Bridge's first category in *Rosset* – see, for example, the comments of the judge in *Hammond* v. *Mitchell* (Section 13.3.2.1). Lord Bridge's second category of a common intention inferred from the conduct of the parties is based on a fiction (despite attempts to distinguish between imputed intention and implied intention). In reality, since there may well have been no such common intention, the non-legal owner claiming an interest in the land only when her possession is threatened, either by a mortgagee or when the end of her relationship with the legal owner.

The law operates to discriminate against claimants – most commonly female cohabitees – for two reasons. First, while the traditional role of a man is seen to be to earn money which would go towards the purchase of the house, that of a woman is not generally considered to be exclusively financial. As well as less well-paid employment outside the home, a woman is more likely to be responsible for the day-to-day care of children and of the home itself. In taking only money into account as an 'act referable to land', the judges have adopted a commercial definition of the contribution necessary to gain an equitable interest which denies the realities of family life.

Second, the reliance on agreement and common intention is based on a contractual and property-based analysis which is often inappropriate when exploring family relationships based on trust. For judicial decisions in this area to rest on a contract (a private law voluntarily created by two equally placed individuals), rather than on the wider communal under-standing of the nature of a trust relationship, is as inappropriate as was the old trust for sale applied to modern family land (see Section 12.2.2). The same criticism can be levelled at proprietary estoppel, which, whilst in some ways a much more flexible doctrine, still gener-ally requires an assertion from the legal owner that the claimant has or will obtain an interest in the land.

It can be argued therefore that this contractual and commercial basis does not go far enough, and that domestic law should adopt the wider understanding of constructive trusts, based on unconscionablity, found in other common law jurisdictions.

> Although the resulting trust is an unsuitable basis for developing proprietary restitutionary reme-dies, the remedial constructive trust, if introduced into English law, may provide a more satisfac-tory road forward. The court by way of remedy might impose a constructive trust on a defendant who knowingly retains property of which the plaintiff has been unjustly deprived. Since the remedy can be tailored to the circumstances of the particular case, innocent third parties would not be prejudiced and restitutionary defences, such as change of position, are capable of being given effect (per Lord Browne-Wilkinson, *Westdeutsche Landesbank Girozentrale* v. *Islington LBC* [1996] AC 669 at p. 716).

In Canada, for example, the constructive trust is based on the doctrine of unjust enrich-ment rather than intention. A 'remedial' constructive trust there will arise in circum-stances where the legal owner has been enriched by some benefit, not necessarily financial, conferred on him by the claimant, providing there is no 'juristic' reason for this, such as a contractual obligation or a gift (see, for example *Sorochan* v. *Sorochan* (1986) 29 DLR (4th) 1).

In its 2002 discussion paper, *Sharing Homes* (Law Com No 278), the Law Commission reviewed what it described as the 'unfair, uncertain and illogical' law on the property rights of unmarried couples. Recognising the need for reform, it considered the proposal that, where a home is shared and the non-legal owner makes a direct or indirect financial contribu-tion, or contributes in terms of domestic work on the home or towards the relationship, that person might gain a share of the home under a statutory trust proportionate to her contribu-tion (unless, of course, the non-legal owner is a tenant or a lodger, or unless the contribution is intended as a gift or a loan). In the end, however, the Law Commission concluded that such property-based reform would be too difficult to achieve because:

> the infinitely variable circumstances affecting those who share homes have rendered it impossible to propose the scheme as a viable and practicable reform of the law (para. 1.27).

Summary

13.1 Resulting and constructive trusts are trusts which are created informally.

13.2 A resulting trust requires a direct contribution to the initial purchase price of the property or to the mortgage.

13.3 Under resulting trust principles, the beneficiary will gain a share in the property proportionate to her contribution to the purchase price.

13.4 A common intention constructive trust will be imposed on the legal owner when there has been an agreement that the claimant should have a beneficial share in the property, and the claimant has detrimentally altered her position in reliance upon that agreement.

13.5 The agreement necessary for a common intention constructive trust can be demonstrated by evidence of an express agreement between the parties, or it may be inferred where there are sufficient grounds for the Court to do so.

13.6 Under a constructive trust, the courts now tend to adopt a 'broad brush' approach to the quantification of the beneficiary's interest, seeking, through an examination of their whole relationship, to establish how the parties intended the property to be shared.

13.7 Proprietary estoppel has many similarities to a constructive trust. A successful claimant will establish an equity in the property through detrimental reliance on an expectation, encouraged by the legal owner, that she will get an interest in the land.

13.8 In order to satisfy the equity raised by a successful estoppel claim, the courts aim to achieve proportionality between the remedy and the detriment suffered and will award the minimum remedy necessary.

Exercises

13.1 What do you have to do to get a beneficial share in land under an informal trust?

13.2 How do you know what share you will get?

13.3 What is proprietary estoppel, and how does it differ from a constructive trust?

13.4 Is the law in this area satisfactory?

@ **13.5** Jerome, who used to be a prosperous businessman, was the sole registered proprietor of a house which he bought in 1993 for £200,000, paying for it with £20,000 from his savings and the rest by means of a mortgage. Two years later, he asked his student girlfriend, Lena, to move in with him, telling her that she would always have a home there. Lena looked after the house and garden, and carried out any maintenance on the property. In 1996, Jerome's business failed and he took paid employment, but did not earn enough to cover all the outgoings. Lena, therefore, gave up her studies and took a job, and her contributions to the household budget enabled Jerome to pay the mortgage. Two months ago, Jerome was killed in a road accident. In his will he left everything to his mother, who has told Lena to leave the house, now worth £400,000, since she wants to sell it. Advise Lena.

@ **13.6** An online quiz on the topics covered in this chapter is available on the companion website.

Further Reading

Bridge, 'Sharing Homes: Property or Status' in Cooke (ed), *Modern Studies in Property Law, Volume 2* (Oxford: Hart, 2003)

Clarke, 'The Family Home: Intention and Agreement' [1992] Fam Law 72

Gardner, 'The Remedial Discretion in Proprietary Estoppel' (1999) 115 LQR 438

Pawlowski, 'Beneficial Entitlement – Do Indirect Contributions Suffice?' [2002] Fam Law 190

Pawlowski, 'Beneficial Entitlement – No Longer Doing Justice' [2007] Conv 354

Robertson, 'The reliance basis of proprietary estoppel' [2008] Conv 295

Siddle, 'Cohabitation' [2002] Fam Law 727

Thompson, 'Constructive Trusts, Estoppel and the Family Home' [2004] Conv 496

Part V

Licences in Land

Chapter 14

Licences

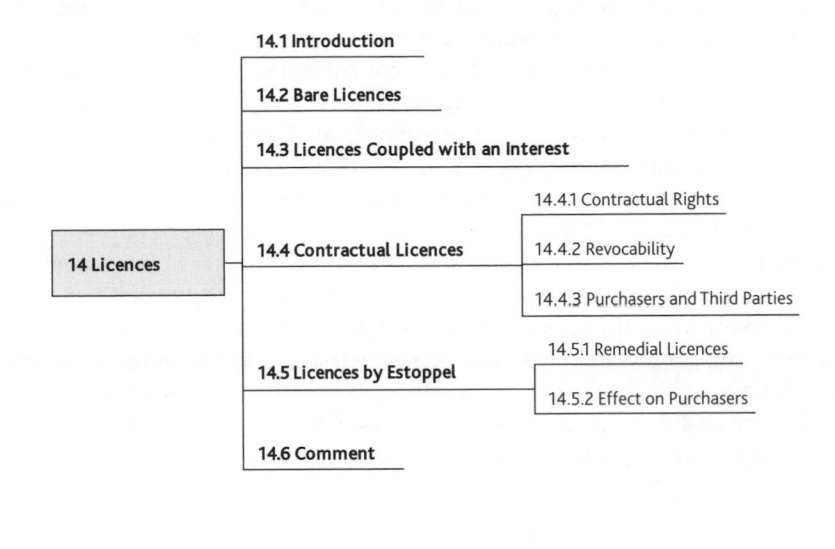

14.1 Introduction

14.2 Bare Licences

14.3 Licences Coupled with an Interest

14 Licences

14.4 Contractual Licences

14.4.1 Contractual Rights

14.4.2 Revocability

14.4.3 Purchasers and Third Parties

14.5 Licences by Estoppel

14.5.1 Remedial Licences

14.5.2 Effect on Purchasers

14.6 Comment

14.1 Introduction

A person who has a licence to be on another's land has that person's permission to be there – in other words, a licence prevents someone from being a trespasser. In a different context, Chapter 5, on leases, examines those situations in which a person who was unable to establish that she had a lease, perhaps because there was no exclusive possession, may instead have had a licence to be on the land. Similarly, someone who fails for lack of formality in a claim to have an easement may well hold a licence to go on to her neighbour's land.

This chapter aims to examine the nature of licences and, in particular, the extent to which they might be interests in land – property rights – or whether they are merely personal rights. The distinction is important, since property rights attach irrevocably to the land, are sold along with the land and, if protected in the appropriate way (see Chapters 10 and 11), will bind a purchaser of the burdened land and benefit the purchaser of any dominant land.

Licences cover a huge variety of activities. A fan at a football match is a licensee, as is a secretary working in an office, a customer in a shop, a paying guest in an hotel, and perhaps a cohabitee sharing her lover's house. Licences may last for a few minutes or for life, and can be created within a family or a commercial setting. It is hardly surprising that there are several types of licence and that the rights and remedies of licensees differ widely.

Licences can be divided into the following categories:

1   Bare licences
2   Licences coupled with an interest in land
3   Contractual licences
4   Licences by estoppel

14.2 Bare Licences

A bare licence arises when the landowner gives permission for another person to be on her land. This may be express, such as an invitation to a friend to come in and have a cup of coffee, or implied, such as for a postal worker delivering letters. Such licences are gratuitous – given without consideration – and can lawfully be revoked whenever the landowner wishes.The licensee must then leave within a reasonable time or she becomes a trespasser and may be physically removed. This kind of licence cannot be transferred by the licensee to another person and neither can it bind someone who buys the land from the licensor.

14.3 Licences Coupled with an Interest in Land

When a person owns a *profit à prendre* (a legal interest giving her the right to take something from another person's land; see Chapter 8), she will be unable to exercise the right without a licence to go on to the land. So, for example, the owner of a profit of piscary (the right to take fish) automatically has a licence to cross the servient tenement to get to the river. The licence cannot be revoked and will continue for as long as the interest exists, binding third parties in the same way as the profit.

14.4 Contractual Licences

A contractual licence is created wherever a person has permission to be on another's land as part of a contract between them, such as the fan at the football match and the paying guest in the hotel, who are both contractual licensees. Contractual licences are common and will generally arise expressly.

In the 1970s, however, the Court of Appeal used the device of the implied contractual licence as a solution in cases of disputes in certain kinds of family relationships, such as the one which arose in *Tanner* v. *Tanner (No 1)* [1975] 1 WLR 1346. In this case, a woman moved from her Rent Act protected tenancy into a house bought by her married lover for her to live in with their twin children. When he later formed a relationship with another woman and tried to evict her, the Court of Appeal held that she had a contractual licence which could not be revoked until the children reached the age of majority (18). However, since she had already been rehoused following the first instance decision which went against her, she was awarded £2,000 to compensate her for her loss. This contractual analysis is problematic when applied to family and domestic arrangements, especially when taking into account the traditional contractual requirements of consideration and the intention to create a legal relationship, and nowadays it is likely that such cases would be argued on the basis of estoppel (Section 14.5).

14.4.1 Contractual Rights

The rights of a contractual licensee depend upon the terms of the contract. Lord Greene MR stated that:

> A licence created by a contract ... creates a contractual right to do certain things which otherwise would be a trespass. It seems to me that, in considering the nature of such a licence and the mutual rights and obligations which arise under it, the first thing to do is to construe the contract according to ordinary principles (*Winter Garden Theatre (London) Ltd* v. *Millennium Productions Ltd* [1946] 1 All ER 678 at p. 680).

It is often assumed that a contractual licence is worth less than a lease, and this may be true in regard to the licensee's security if the land is sold and, in general, licences do not attract the statutory protection afforded to leases. However, there are occasions when it is more beneficial to be a licensee than a tenant under a lease. For example, in *Wettern Electric Ltd* v. *Welsh Development Agency* [1983] 1 QB 796, a company held the licence of factory premises which were so badly constructed and became so unsafe that the licensee company had to leave. It successfully sued for breach of an implied term that the premises would be fit for their purpose; this term could not be implied into a contract for a lease, not being one of the 'usual' covenants (Section 6.3), but in a licence the ordinary rules of contract law applied. Judge Newey QC explained that:

> The sole purpose of the licence was to enable the plaintiffs to have accommodation in which to carry on and expand their business ... If anyone had said to the plaintiffs and the defendants' directors and executives at the time when the licence was being granted: 'Will the premises be sound and suitable for the plaintiff's purposes?' they would assuredly have replied: 'Of course; there would be no point in the licence if that were not so.' The term was required to make the contract workable (at p. 809).

14.4.2 Revocability

There has been a continuing debate on whether a contractual licence can be revoked by the licensor. In *Hurst* v. *Picture Theatres Ltd* [1915] 1 KB 1, for example, a cinema customer was physically removed because the owner (wrongly) believed he had not paid for his ticket. The Court of Appeal decided that the licensor should not have turned the licensee out and he was entitled to damages for false imprisonment and breach of contract. The decision was based on the argument that the equitable remedies of specific performance of the contract and an injunction to prevent the breach would, in theory, have been available to the customer, who therefore was seen by equity as having a right to remain in the cinema and thus could not be a trespasser.

In the *Winter Garden Theatre* case [1946] 1 All ER 678, the theatre owner attempted to revoke a licence allowing a theatre company to produce plays and concerts in its theatre, although there was no provision in the contract for him to do this. The House of Lords stated that whether a contractual licence could be revoked depended entirely on the construction of the contract. In this case, the licence was not intended to last forever and could therefore be determined by the theatre owner on reasonable notice.

Verrall v. *Great Yarmouth BC* [1981] 1 QB 202 is a clear example of a case in which a contractual licence could not be revoked. Following a change in its political control, a local council tried to revoke a licence to use a hall for a two-day conference which it had previously granted to an extreme right-wing political organisation. It was held that the council could not do so. Damages for breach of contract would not be sufficient remedy since no alternative venue was available, so the Court of Appeal unanimously held that the contract should be specifically enforced. Lord Denning MR said:

> An injunction can be obtained against the licensor to prevent [the licensee] being turned out. On principle it is the same if it happens before he enters. If he had a contractual right to enter, and the licensor refuses to let him come in, then he can come to the court and in a proper case get an order for specific performance to allow him to come in (at p. 216).

Where a person is occupying premises as her residence under a contractual licence she will enjoy additional rights by virtue of the Protection from Eviction Act 1977 (see also Section 6.2.1.3). In most cases, the licensor will not be entitled to recover possession of the premises without either a court order or the licensee's consent, even if the licence has expired (s.3(2B)). If the licence is a periodic one then licensee will be normally be entitled to four weeks' written notice before the licence can be determined (s.5(1A)).

14.4.3 Effect on Buyers of Land and Other Third Parties

If it is correct that in some circumstances a licence cannot be revoked, then a relevant question is the effect of such a licence on a purchaser of the land from the licensor. Has an irrevocable licence now become an interest in the land to which it relates, thus binding third parties, or does the traditional view prevail, that a licence is merely a personal right?

King v. *David Allen & Sons Billposting Ltd* [1916] 2 AC 54 is an example of the traditional approach. The licence in this case was to fix advertising posters to the licensor's wall. The licensor then granted a long lease of the building, a cinema, and the leaseholder prevented the licensee from fixing the posters. The House of Lords held that the licensor was liable to pay damages for breach of contract. Although the cinema leaseholder was not a party to the case, Lord Buckmaster LC several times referred to the licence as a purely personal right and not an interest in land. Consequently the licence did not bind the cinema leaseholder.

However, in *Errington* v. *Errington & Woods* [1952] 1 KB 290, a father paid the deposit on a house and told his son and daughter-in-law that, if they continued in occupation and paid the mortgage instalments, the house would be theirs. When the father died, the son moved in with his mother, who had inherited the house, and she sought possession against her daughter-in-law. The Court of Appeal held that the arrangement was a contractual licence: if the licensees had paid the whole of the mortgage, the father, had he lived, would have been ordered to transfer the house to them. This contractual licence could not be revoked so long as one of the licensees kept to their side of the bargain, and it would bind a purchaser with notice:

> The couple were licensees, having a permissive occupation short of a tenancy, but with a contractual right, or at any rate, an equitable right to remain as long as they paid the instalments, which would grow into a good equitable title to the house itself as soon as the mortgage was paid ... contractual licences now have a force and validity of their own and cannot be revoked in breach of contract. Neither the licensor nor anyone who claims through him can disregard the contract except a purchaser without notice (per Denning LJ, at pp. 296, 298).

In later years it was Lord Denning's view that equity would enforce a contractual licence against anyone who ought fairly to be bound by it. In *Binions* v. *Evans* [1972] Ch 359, for example, a contractual licence permitting a widow to remain in a cottage for the rest of her life bound, under a constructive trust, buyers of unregistered land who had agreed to take the land subject to her rights:

> Wherever the owner sells the land to a purchaser, and at the same time stipulates that he shall take it 'subject to' a contractual licence, I think it plain that a court of equity will impose on the purchaser a constructive trust ... It would be utterly inequitable that the purchaser should be able to turn out the beneficiary (per Lord Denning MR, at p. 368).

The view of Denning LJ in *Errington*, that contractual licences can bind third parties, was discredited in *Ashburn Anstalt* v. *WJ Arnold & Co* [1989] Ch 1. However, the Court of Appeal in *Ashburn Anstalt* approved Lord Denning's imposition of a constructive trust in the later case of *Binions* v. *Evans*. In that case the constructive trust was necessary to protect the licensee against unconscionable dealing by the new legal owners who had expressly agreed to uphold her rights. Nevertheless, the court took a restrictive view on the use of constructive trusts in such situations, since:

> [t]he court will not impose a constructive trust unless it is satisfied that the conscience of the estate owner is affected. The mere fact that that land is expressed to be conveyed 'subject to' a contract does not necessarily imply that the grantee is to be under an obligation, not otherwise existing, to give effect to the provisions of the contract (per Fox LJ, at p. 25).

14.5 Licences by Estoppel

14.5.1 Remedial Licences

Chapter 13 considered how detrimental reliance on an expectation encouraged by the legal owner gives rise to an equity which may be satisfied by a remedy designed to do justice between the parties and compensate the claimant for the detriment she has suffered. This remedy may sometimes be the award of an estate in the land, as in *Pascoe* v. *Turner* [1979] 1 WLR 431 (Section 13.4). It is frequently something less, and the award of a licence for the claimant to remain on the land is not uncommon.

In *Inwards* v. *Baker* [1965] 2 QB 29, a son was encouraged to build a bungalow on his father's land by the father's promise that the son could remain on the land. The son built the bungalow, but when the father died his heirs claimed the land. The Court of Appeal held that, since the father would have been estopped from going back on his promise and the heirs were in the same position as the father, the son's equity should be satisfied by the award of a licence to stay on the land.

In *Greasley* v. *Cooke* [1980] 1 WLR 1306 (Section 13.4.1.2), the former maid who had lived in the house for many years was awarded an irrevocable licence to continue to occupy it for as long as she wished.

Effect on Buyers of Land

It is evident that Lord Denning felt that estoppel rights were capable of binding a buyer of the land. In *Inwards* v. *Baker*, for example, he said, 'any purchaser who took with notice would clearly be bound by the equity'. He followed this in *ER Ives Investment Ltd* v. *High* [1967] 2 QB 379 (for the facts, see Section 10.3.3.2): since the earlier owner of the flats would have been estopped from denying the garage owner a right to use the drive belonging to the flats, successors in title to that earlier owner were also bound.

In *Re Sharpe (a bankrupt)* [1980] 1 WLR 219, a woman lent £12,000 to her nephew to buy a maisonette on the basis that they would live there together. He became bankrupt, and the trustee in bankruptcy, having contracted to sell the maisonette, sought a possession order against her. Although the case was decided on the basis that the woman had a contractual licence to remain in the property until the loan was repaid, Browne-Wilkinson J said:

> If the parties have proceeded on a common assumption that the plaintiff is to enjoy a right to reside in a particular property and in reliance on that assumption the plaintiff has expended money or otherwise acted to his detriment, the defendant will not be allowed to go back on that common assumption and the court will imply an irrevocable licence or trust which will give effect to that common assumption (at p. 223).

This licence was binding on the trustee in bankruptcy. Although the judge was not required to express a view on the position of the purchaser from the trustee, he thought that it was possible that the rights of a purchaser without express notice of the contract would have prevailed over those of the licensee.

In unregistered land, whether a licence by estoppel will bind a purchaser will usually depend upon whether the purchaser had notice of the equity (as in *Ives* v. *High*). In registered land, s.116 LRA 2002 provides that an equity by estoppel is capable of binding purchasers, provided, of course, that it is combined with actual occupation (Schedule 1 para 2 and Schedule 3, Para. 2 LRA 2002: see Section 13.5).

14.6 Comment

If one thing is clear about licences, it is that there is not one answer to the questions, 'Are licences interests in land?', 'Are they property?'. The probable conclusion to be drawn from the brief summary in this chapter is that most licences are not. However, licences combined with a recognised interest in land, usually an estoppel, will benefit from the proprietary character of that interest.

Not that long ago these issues were the subject of frequent investigation by academics, some embracing the idea that twentieth-century land lawyers had produced a new interest in land, perhaps equivalent to the development of the restrictive covenant in the nineteenth century.

> The courts seem to be well on their way to creating a new and highly versatile interest in land which will rescue many informal and unbusinesslike transactions, particularly within families, from the penalties of disregarding legal forms. Old restraints are giving way to the demands of justice (Megarry and Wade, 1984, p. 808).

From this viewpoint, some licences were symbols of a new form of property, a right to share, which would take its place beside the traditional private and exclusive property rights.

After *Ashburn Anstalt* (Section 14.4), however, this seems no longer to be the case (compare section 34-019 of Megarry and Wade, 2008 which replaces the paragraph from 1984 edition quoted above). The 'old restraints', such as the need for certainty of conveyancing and its formal processes, appear to have reassumed their importance, although in registered land the equity raised by a proprietary estoppel retains its proprietary character, a character that is now expressly recognized by the LRA 2002.

Summary

14.1 A licence is a permission to be on land: it may be a bare licence or one coupled with an interest in the land such as a *profit à prendre*, or may arise through contract or estoppel.

14.2 A bare licence can be revoked at any time.

14.3 A licence coupled with an interest in land will last as long as the interest in question.

14.4 Whether a contractual licence can be revoked depends on the terms of the contract.

14.5 An estoppel licence may be awarded by the court when a person acts to her detriment in reliance on a promise that she will gain an interest in land.

14.6 Licences by estoppel and licences that give rise to a constructive trust may bind a buyer of land.

Exercises

14.1 What is an 'interest in land'?

14.2 Can contractual licences be revoked on reasonable notice?

14.3 Are licences property?

@ **14.4** John and Linda are the registered proprietors of a large house. When they bought it 15 years ago, it was very run-down and they did not have the time or money to renovate it by themselves. They therefore agreed with Hannah and Joshua (Linda's sister and brother-in-law) that they would move in and help with the work; they said Hannah and Joshua would be able to make their home there. Hannah won £15,000 in the lottery and lent it to John and Linda so they could pay for a new roof. Joshua gave up his job to work on the house and look after John and Linda's children. He has been in hospital since falling off a ladder when mending one of the chimneys last year.

John and Linda are now going to separate. They have transferred the land to Damien who has been registered as proprietor. Advise Hannah and Joshua.

@ **14.5** An online quiz on the topics covered in this chapter is available on the companion website.

Further Reading

Anderson, 'Of Licences and Similar Mysteries' (1979) 42 MLR 203
Dewar, 'Licences and Land Law: An Alternative View' (1986) 49 MLR 741
McFarlane, 'Identifying Property Rights: A Reply to Mr Watt' [2003] Conv 473

Index